POINT
WILDERNESS WAR IN VIETNAM AND CAMBODIA
A MEMOIR

JAMIE C. THOMPSON

Copyright © 2019 by Jamie Campbell Thompson, III

All rights reserved. No part of this book may be reproduced or reused in any manner without the written authorization of the copyright owner except quotations used in book reviews.

Author website: https://jamiethompson.us

Cover design by Carlo Neira

Dedication

This book is dedicated to everyone who served his or her country honorably in Vietnam, Cambodia, and Laos, regardless of what country that might have been. War is not an easy thing. Those who survive it must strive to live usefully beyond it. It isn't helpful to harbor hatred or hold grudges.

Photo credits:

Photos are at the ends of chapters to which they relate. The first number identifying each photo in the following list is the chapter number.

Only Photo 6-1 originally belonged to the author.

Photos taken by or originally belonging to Steve Warner, a friend of the author, and used with the authorization of the Stephen H. Warner Collection, in Special Collections and Archives, Musselman Library, at Gettysburg College, Gettysburg, Pennsylvania, are indicated by (SW) at the end of photo designations. (https://www.gettysburg.edu/)

Photos taken by or originally belonging to Jerry Pickering, also a friend of the author, were given to the author by Jerry in the early 1970s. These are indicated by (JP) at the end of photo designations.

6-1   The author, newly minted Sgt E-5 graduate of NCO School
15-1 Saddled up and ready to hump (SW)
15-2 Setting up a two-man hooch in an NDP (SW)
19-1 Resupply Day – Hot meal in the field (SW)
21-1 Sgt Jerry Pickering, S2/S3 NCO 5/7 Field HQ at FSB Neal Cambodia May 1970 (JP)
21-2 Spc Steve Warner, USARV Army Reporter, in the field with grunts (SW)
21-3 Family in the Montagnard Village (JP)
21-4 Montagnard woman at work in her hooch (SW)
21-5 Firebase Neal, Cambodia, May 1970. LFT-155mm Howitzer (JP)
21-6 Firebase Neal, Cambodia, May 1970. RT – 8" Gun (JP)
23-1 Jerry Pickering peeking through the window of Jamie's Hooch, FSB Neal May 1970 (JP)
24-1 Montagnard Village Elephant arriving at FSB Neal for rice, May 1970 (SW)
24-2 Elephant waits while villagers prepare to load it with rice (JP)
24-3 Captured NVA rice is loaded for transport to Montagnard village(SW)
24-4 Montagnards watch as elephant takes rice to their village (JP)
26-1 Medic beside slick demonstrating a Jungle Penetrator – How author was medevacked (SW)
27-1 Leaving Cambodia, Firebase Neal evacuates, late June 1970 (SW)
30-1 Half-culvert guard position on a berm; similar to those atop bunkers on Nui Ba Ra (SW)
44-1 Chaplain in the field (SW)
48-1 Crashed slick we blew up with two cases of C-4 to deny technology to the enemy (JP)
49-1 Grunts take lunch break in the boonies during Monsoons (SW)
49-2 Monsoon mud NDP (SW)

Appreciations

I owe immeasurable thanks to my late wife Nancy and our daughter Sarah. Both urged me for years to share my Vietnam experiences with them and with others if I could muster the will to do it. In the early years after my return from Vietnam, I was adrift. When I met Nancy seven years after my discharge, I could have gone either up or down. Because of her patience, kindness, understanding, and love I went up. For that I owe her much more than I could ever tell her in words. Nancy died in the summer of 2015 following a twelve-year battle with metastatic breast cancer. It was a terrible ordeal, which like so many other things in her life she endured with quiet strength and dignity. Sarah has always been the joy of our lives and the person of whom I am prouder than anyone else. I love them both beyond measure and I know that love is reciprocated. Without them, my life would mean little and this book would never have been written. I'm also writing this book for my two beautiful and precious granddaughters. I hope this will help them realize that their "Bah" was once a younger, more active person than the one they know today.

    Kurt Raymond Stephan shared NCO school, OJT, and service in Vietnam with me. His memory helped me avoid factual errors and fill in blanks. Our half-century of friendship continues to be a treasure.

    Janette Knutson Stone provided invaluable help as I was trying to remember the details of my R&R in Sydney, Australia. A native Australian, she worked in Sydney during the time I was there, and as a fellow author made constructive suggestions that improved that part of my narrative.

    Gettysburg College, Gettysburg, Pennsylvania, kindly gave me permission to include several photos from its Stephen H. Warner Collection in this memoir. I especially want to thank Robin Wagner, dean of the library and Amy Lucadamo, archivist, for their kind and invaluable assistance.

My sister Julia King Balko helped me remember details of family life and provided badly needed encouragement when writing this just seemed too much. Her support was essential and valued.

My good friend and fellow veteran Allan J. Johnson graciously read the manuscript looking for mistakes that writers can't see in their own work; extra, repeated and missing words they don't notice because they see what they meant to say. This was very important because spell check doesn't find them all either!

I also want to thank Allan and my other good friends and relatives who encouraged me to continue this project to completion. A word here and a hug there can make the difference between failure and success when one feels stress to complete a project. Thank you one and all.

Table of Contents

Dedication	i
Photo Credits	ii
Appreciations	iii
Table of Contents	v
Preface	ix

Chapters

1 –	The Setting	1
2 –	Training Begins	8
3 –	Basic Heats Up	17
4 –	The Fog of Infantry AIT	27
5 –	A Taste of Freedom	38
6 –	Rattler on the Flank, NCO School	46
7 –	A Short Visit Home	59
8 –	OJT; Les and Dora's Place	65
9 –	Butt Sergeant; Plane Planner	80
10 –	CQ and Leave	90
11 –	Leaving the World	99
12 –	Tay Ninh	110
13 –	Outpost on The Edge; First Patrol	120
14 –	What It Means to Be a Grunt	132
15 –	Into the Boonies	138
16 –	Humping Begins; Bees	151
17 –	Claymores and Arc Lights	160
18 –	Wood; Bu Dop; The Dunes	167
19 –	The Parrot; Into Cambodia	179
20 –	Ambush; Tickets to the World	188
21 –	Neal; A New Friend; Montagnards	199
22 –	Trumpets; Wilderness AO	212
23 –	Jamie's Hooch	220
24 –	The Flood; The Body Bag	227
25 –	Footfalls in the Jungle; Magic Forest	245
26 –	Ho Chi Minh Trail; Rice and Blood	254

27 – Respite	267
28 – Danger Is a Relative Thing	276
29 – A Mountain Climb	285
30 – Nui Ba Ra	296
31 – Rats	305
32 – Kinship across Time; Section Eights	313
33 – Numba One	322
34 – Awful News	333
35 – Doc's Place	338
36 – Spit Shined	349
37 – Another Month; The Leech	356
38 – Back to the Bush	365
39 – Fear	371
40 – Trust	379
41 – Night Visitor; Wait a Minute	385
42 – The Ears; The Vase; Dehydration	392
43 – FSB Snuffy; The Fifty	397
44 – River Crossing; Kit Carson Scout	403
45 – The Waiting Room	410
46 – Down Under	420
47 – The RSL	433
48 – Up Over and Back Out	447
49 – Monsoon; On the Same Wavelength	459
50 – Trial by Bunker	468
51 – Brothers in Arms	475
52 – Christmas in the Nam	481
53 – The Freedom Bird	487
54 – Back in the World	496
Epilogue	507
Afterword	512

Appendices

Appendix 1 – Terms and Definitions	514
Appendix 2 – NCO School Statistics	529
Appendix 3 – Men Killed in 5/7 Bn 4/1970-1/1971	530
Appendix 4 – U.S. Casualties 4/1970-1/1971	532
Appendix 5 – Place Names	533

Map – Areas of Operation   536-37

About the Author   538

Preface

It took five decades to write about my experience in Vietnam because I wasn't sure my tour of duty was worthy of a memoir or would be of interest to anyone. There were other reasons, like not wanting to bring my own feelings to the surface or to hurt anyone else's, and simply being so busy living my life that I didn't have the time or energy to do it. But a few years ago I decided to write it because I realized that the ordinary daily life—the nuts and bolts existence of American infantrymen in the Vietnam War—was slipping away into the fog of history.

I've done my best to recall and reconstruct my experiences. All major incidents actually occurred and are described as accurately as I can recall them. Most characters in the book have been fictionalized either because I can't remember their real names and personal details or because some incidents might hurt or embarrass them or their relatives. The few real characters whose actual names or nicknames are used are identified in the Epilogue.

Researching and writing was a major ordeal for several reasons. One was the sheer effort and time involved, and the other was the emotional toll it took on me. Without realizing I'd done so, I had avoided thinking in depth about Vietnam from the moment I left the place. As I wrote, I had to remember and describe details I'd buried safely away. It was as emotional as living the events in the first place, and in some cases more so since I can now fully feel what I couldn't allow myself to feel then because of the immediate needs of the circumstances.

The memoir is entitled Point because I walked point whenever my squad had the assignment. Doing research for the book has made me even more aware of the danger of my situation now than I was at the time, and I certainly knew it was dangerous then. But it seemed the right decision. I can only explain it as being due to a kind of temporary insanity.

There will always be debate about America's involvement in Vietnam's civil war and what was gained and lost by it. It's not the purpose of this book to engage in that debate. I've simply described what it was like for me as an infantry sergeant. The book's Afterword does include my present-day thoughts about the Vietnam War, but that is separate from the body of the book.

A list of relevant place names and a map showing the areas where my unit operated are included, as are a list of terms and definitions and a few tables of statistics.

I hope this work is interesting and informative and may be of use to those wanting to know more about the Vietnam War from the perspective of the point of the American spear.

POINT

Chapter 1 – The Setting

In 1969, in the 4086th year since ancient Vietnam coalesced under the Hung Kings and the 1031st year since Vietnam re-won its independence from imperial China, Richard Milhous Nixon, the fifth U.S. President to send American military personnel to Vietnam, sent me a letter. "The President of the United States, To Jamie Campbell Thompson, III… Greeting: You are hereby ordered for induction into the Armed Forces of the United States, and to report at Selective Service System local board 101, Des Plaines, Illinois, on April 7, 1969 at 7:30 a.m."

So I entered the U.S. Army in the fiftieth year since Ho Chi Minh first called for international support for and recognition of an independent Vietnam free from French colonial rule, the twenty-ninth year since Ho and his supporters began fighting against a succession of foreign overlords of Vietnam, and the nineteenth year of U.S. Military involvement in French Indo-China/Vietnam.

My situation was hardly unique. Over 9,000,000 Americans or more than four percent of all Americans served on active duty in the U.S. military during the peak years of the Vietnam War (1964-1975) and between September 1950 when the first U.S. military advisors were sent to Vietnam and the end of ground combat operations in March 1973 approximately 2,650,000 U.S. military personnel (about 1.2% of the U.S. population at the time) served inside the borders of Vietnam.

I spent the week after getting my draft notice partying with my five roommates in a house we rented two blocks west of the main gate of the University of Arizona. When the week of debauchery ended, I packed up all my belongings and made the 1,700-mile drive from Arizona to Illinois. Arriving at my parents' house, I felt like a visitor there for the first time in my life.

Of course, I was welcomed and loved, but there was little serious discussion, because there really wasn't anything anyone could say that had more importance than the reality I was facing. At the time, over 180 American servicemen were being killed in combat every week. Now, I was to be part of it, at the age of twenty-four.

Raised in an affluent suburb of Chicago, in an area not yet completely developed, I grew up both used to and spoiled by the comforts provided by modern America. I was also comfortable in the natural world and proficient in the use of small arms. Rifles, pistols, hunting, fishing, and trapping were as familiar to me as color television, stereo sound systems, and air-conditioning. It was well that my life experiences included more than just the civilized amenities.

But I guess I should start at the beginning. I was born at the height of World War II on June 2, 1944, in Winston-Salem, North Carolina. My father was attending the Bowman Gray School of Medicine there. My mother worked in a factory, assembling anti-aircraft proximity fuses until shortly before my birth. She used to tell me she remembered my birthday because it was four days before D-Day and "the Allies had to be sure you were all right before they invaded." Since I was a "third," named after my father and grandfather, through adolescence I was known only as "Cam" from my middle name of Campbell. I never liked that nickname, so the minute I left home I dropped it in favor of my true first name.

Until I was thirteen, my family moved frequently because of my father's medical education requirements, military service during World War II and the Korean War, and establishing his practice. But from eighth grade until I left for college, we lived in the first and only house my parents ever owned, the house I was now visiting as I awaited my induction into the U.S. Armed Forces.

The old farmhouse sat on six acres on a lake in the exclusive Chicago suburb of Barrington Hills. It was beautiful rolling country, sprinkled with woods and dotted with lakes and streams—legacies of the last glaciers as they melted back to the north 10,000 years ago. Orchard Lake, surrounded by apple orchards well past their prime, had only two other houses on it when we moved there in 1957. I trapped muskrats, hunted ducks, and spent most at-home time fishing, shooting, hiking, and exploring. It was a wonderful adolescence that made me feel a strong kinship with our early pioneers.

After graduating from high school in 1962, I attended the University of Arizona in Tucson—mostly because *Playboy* magazine rated it the number two "play" school in the country. Number one, the University of Wisconsin at Madison, was out because it was less than 100 miles from home. I didn't make it through the first semester at the U of A because of too many trips to Mexico, where I could drink at eighteen. I spent the next five years alternately attending Morningside College in Sioux City, Iowa, and Northwestern University in Evanston, Illinois; or working part-time jobs. I was a rudderless young man with little self-discipline. The concept of being a real adult like my father seemed an impossible task. I didn't know how to do it or even if I could pull it off at all. I was a dreamer, scared and confused about what to do with my life.

In the fall of 1967, I briefly considered volunteering for the military. My father felt it would be good for me in terms of building and shaping my character. Whenever he was particularly frustrated with my lack of direction, he'd say, "Son, what you need is to go into the Army." So I visited an Army recruiter and took a battery of aptitude tests. The results presented me with two choices of military occupational specialty: translator (after Army language school) or helicopter pilot.

The translator job would likely post me on an Aleutian Island listening to Russian military communications. The pilot job would likely land me in Vietnam, where the life expectancy of helicopter pilots at the time was less than ninety days. I had second thoughts. Because of my uncertainty about what I wanted to do with my life, I didn't get around to applying for a student draft deferment until after this flirtation with enlistment.

I ended up back at the U of A in Tucson in January of 1968. And the next week, my first draft notice arrived, ordering me to report to my "local" draft board in Illinois. I called and explained that, as the law required, I had notified the board in writing and received its okay before I made the move to Tucson. They checked, found I was right, and since I'd already paid my tuition, they cancelled the draft notice.

After nearly a year in Tucson, I spent my Christmas vacation back at my parents' house in Illinois. On Christmas morning, I called my girlfriend Kara in Tucson, a girl I loved deeply. I told her I'd gotten a bathrobe and a couple of books for Christmas and asked what she'd gotten.

"Engaged," she said.

I was stupefied. I'd been planning to ask her to marry me when I returned to Arizona. After a long pause, I said, "Well, I wish you the best of luck," and hung up.

To say I was emotionally devastated is an understatement. Kara was bright and good, kind and gentle, with a fragility about her that made her all the more appealing. In the first weeks after meeting, we'd spent many hours talking, usually in booths in the Student Union cafeteria. We had a deep emotional connection and I thought she felt about me as I did about her.

Kara was in two of my classes, which I never attended again. Final exams were given in late January 1969. I failed all my courses but one, in which I got an A. But the damage was done. I was placed on academic probation and within a month received my new draft notice.

So it was that in the early morning hours of April 7, 1969, my parents drove me from their home to the train station in Barrington. After a brief stop at my local draft board office, which was located near the train station in Des Plaines, I arrived at the induction center in Chicago by 9:00 a.m. with about a dozen others.

I'd been there before. It was where I'd taken the aptitude tests eighteen months earlier. I wondered whether an Aleutian

Island might not have been preferable to where I was likely headed now. I sighed and followed the directions I was given.

By the time we had our physical exam, our little group had merged into a group of many hundreds. There were questions, measurements, and blood tests. The guy in front of me dropped to the floor in a dead faint at the sight of the needle or the blood; I'm not sure which. Then there was the anal exam, which involved standing in line in my jockey shorts with twenty other guys. On command we faced away from the doctor, dropped our shorts, bent over, and used our hands to spread our butt cheeks. The doctor walked the line with a flashlight, peering into the gaping butt cracks, checking boxes, and making notes on a clipboard. This was, I later decided, the military's first step in its continual effort to eliminate all traces of embarrassment and shame in its members ... and all traces of individuality. It worked!

Back in our clothes, we took aptitude tests, which I recognized from before. We were handed packets of papers, seemingly randomly, and were told to go into a room and grab a seat. We stared at the walls for maybe two minutes, when in walked a Marine NCO wearing a lot of ribbons.

"Hello, gentlemen," he said loudly. "I'd like you to look through the papers you have in front of you. Those of you with pink sheets, welcome to the United States Marine Corps!"

There was a collective gasp, the noise of rapidly shuffled paper, and murmurings of "Whew," "Shit," "Oh my God," "Jesus," and more than a few groans. With relief, I realized I didn't have a pink sheet in my stack of papers.

"All right," the marine bellowed, "You gentlemen with the pink sheets, follow me!" He turned sharply and was followed out by seventeen men with slumped shoulders and bent heads.

In the early afternoon, I received word that I'd be flown to Fort Bliss, Texas, for Basic Training. It was ironic that I would end up only 320 miles from Tucson, where I received my draft notice in the first place.

At the Fort Bliss Reception Center that evening, we lined up, answered as our names were called, and were walked directly to the base barbershop. Inside, I sat briefly as electric shears cut off all my hair. There was no fanfare, no discussion, and no finesse on the part of the barbers. One or two recruits protested and tried to escape the process, apparently in the forlorn hope that somehow they were still going to get out of this, meaning the Army. I accepted my fate as stoically as I could.

When the last man was shorn, we were assigned barracks and told to grab a quick meal at the mess hall. After we returned, fifteen names were called, mine among them. The sergeant who led us to a classroom snapped to attention and saluted as a first lieutenant entered the room.

"Hello, men," the lieutenant said. "First, let me welcome you to the United States Army and to Fort Bliss, Texas. We've gathered you here because you are eligible to attend Officer Candidate School at Fort Benning upon satisfactory completion of your Basic Training."

I was surprised, since I'd only completed three years of college and thought only college grads could become officers. Then I realized that the casualty rate in Vietnam had probably created a shortage. The lieutenant spoke at some length about the honor being bestowed on us and the benefits of being an officer: better pay, greater respect both in and out of the Army, and the chance to learn leadership skills that would benefit us for the rest of our lives. All of this was certainly true.

After a few more minutes he said, "All right, men. I'll try to answer any questions you might have."

I raised my hand.

"Yes?" he said.

"Sir, this is entirely voluntary, isn't it?"

"Yes, it is."

"If we accept the offer, how long would we have to serve in the Army, sir?" When I had considered enlisting in 1967, I had learned a few things about the Army that my companions might not know.

"Those who choose to go to OCS would be converted from draftee status to volunteer enlistee and would have a term of service of three years and ten months."

"Sir, during that time, how many tours would we serve in Vietnam?" I already knew the answer to this, but I wanted him to say it in front of the others.

After a slight hesitation, he answered. "Two, most likely."

"Thank you, sir," I replied.

When the lieutenant was satisfied there were no further questions, he asked who would like to sign up for OCS. No one in our group did, and we were walked back across the street to our barracks.

I slept that night, but not particularly well.

Chapter 2 – Training Begins

Somewhere around 5:00 a.m. we were rousted from sleep by the yelling of a drill sergeant as he beat the bottom of a metal bucket. In a haze, I heard something about having ten minutes to shit, shower, shave, and get into formation on the street outside. I was new at this, so I didn't complete all my bathroom functions in the allotted time, but I did make it outside with everyone else.

We had trouble forming into a coherent rectangle but managed it and were walked to the mess hall. Except for a few drill sergeants, we were the first troops there. I was impressed with the amount of food: scrambled eggs, hash browns, toast, fruit, bacon, milk, oatmeal. Nothing fancy, but it was pretty good and very filling.

By 5:40, we were ushered out the door and to the supply warehouse, where we were issued our first uniforms. Everything was olive drab in color: T-shirts, boxer shorts, socks, shirts, pants, baseball cap, and garrison cap. We were also issued a cloth belt, brass buckle, boots, two pairs of bootlaces, black shoe polish, shoeshine cloth, can of Brasso (brass polish), toothbrush, toothpaste, comb, two towels, a bar of soap, and a duffel bag into which we threw all the other stuff.

We slung the duffels over our shoulders and formed up for the walk back to the barracks, where we were to change into our new uniforms and form up on the street in fifteen minutes. This gave me just enough time to complete the bathroom functions I'd skipped earlier, thank heaven.

Once in formation, we were walked to a large paved area and merged into a group of about 400. A wiry drill sergeant with many decorations on his starched uniform stepped up on a platform and introduced himself.

"Men, I'm Senior Drill Sergeant Colfax. Welcome to Basic Training at Fort Bliss, Texas! You men are now part of the Third Training Battalion, Second Training Brigade. We're going to assign you to your companies and introduce you to your company drill sergeants. As I call your name, move behind the formation and form up facing your drill sergeant. We'll be filling you with a lot of information and even more rules and regulations in the next eight weeks, but when you finish your training, you *will* understand why the United States Army is *the* best trained and best disciplined army in the history of the world."

Despite my natural inclination toward skepticism, I felt a deep, hot sense of pride well up within me.

Sergeant Colfax introduced Drill Sergeant Longoria and read out about 100 names to form up as Company A. I was called and found myself in a group of men who were different almost to a man from those I'd started with in Chicago.

Drill Sergeant José Longoria stood before us, looking squared away in his starched uniform, immaculate "Smokey Bear" hat, ribbons and braid. His boots brightly reflected the sun. Though no taller than I, he was built like a bridge abutment.

We marched into the barracks and up the stairs to the fourth floor. Large jars on shelves throughout the barracks were marked SALT TABLETS. The thought that this was probably not a good omen flitted through my mind, but I had no time to dwell on it.

Folded neatly at the foot of each bed were sheets, pillowcase, and an olive drab blanket. In the center of each bed was a footlocker. We put our duffel bags on our beds and gathered in groups along the center aisle to watch as Drill Sergeant Longoria and three others, who had appeared from somewhere, showed us the proper way to make our beds and place our gear and belongings in our footlockers. It took over an hour before all of us had seen a demonstration. It was another hour before our drill sergeant was satisfied with our first efforts at making our beds and stowing our gear.

After that, he blew a whistle and told us to gather near the stairs. There were several doors beyond the staircase. One was to our communal bathroom, or latrine as it was called in the military. It had eight toilet stalls with sides but no doors, a row of sinks—each with its own mirror—and the shower, which had eight or ten shower heads spaced around the walls.

"As you will remember, my name is Drill Sergeant José Longoria. You may not call me José. You may not call me Sergeant Longoria. You *will* call me Drill Sergeant Longoria, or just Drill Sergeant. Are we clear?"

"Yes, Drill Sergeant," we answered in unison.

"I can't *hear* you," he barked at us.

"Yes, Drill Sergeant!" we shouted.

He had his clenched fists on his hips and swayed a bit from side to side in the exact manner and with the exact facial expression I remembered seeing Mussolini use while strutting before a cheering throng in a World War II TV documentary. I was uneasy about my immediate future, to say the least.

"This is not going to be easy for any of you," Longoria said. "It is not my job to make it easy for you. It is my job to make you into good soldiers. And I will do that. You will find that I am every bit as tough as I look. But as long as you do as you're trained and ordered to do, we'll get along fine. If you don't, you are going to get a bad case of the Lon-Go-Ria." He pronounced it to rhyme with diarrhea. "And you do not want a bad case of the Lon-Go-Ria. Are we clear?"

"Yes, Drill Sergeant!" we yelled, with real feeling.

"Better," he said. "Now follow me to chow."

We followed silently as he led us to the mess hall on the ground floor of our building. The chow hall was a large open area with a small table to the right of the entrance, where a sergeant sat and checked off our names as we announced ourselves and entered. Part of this seemingly meaningless exercise in officiousness was to burn our service numbers into our brains by requiring us to recite our names and serial numbers every time we entered the mess hall.

It was far from a quiet matter of rote. Quite often the recorder would yell, "What? I can't *hear* you," after which we would yell our names and numbers at the top of our lungs. This was sometimes repeated three or four times before a man was allowed to enter and eat.

Serial numbers always began with either the letters R A or U S. The R A stood for regular army and signified that the trainee had enlisted, while U S meant those who had been drafted. I got the distinct impression as time went by that many of the recorders seemed to think that forcing draftees to reveal their status in the crowded mess hall would somehow embarrass or demean them. They were wrong about that, but we continued to play the game throughout the training cycle. And it did succeed in burning my serial number permanently into my brain.

The food was plentiful and loaded with protein and carbohydrates: lots of beef and potatoes and similar fare. I liked the food and was always ravenous. The simple fact was that I'd never worked so hard in my life and eating was almost my only creature comfort, despite the daily yells at the entrance.

Our lives were constant drudgery without any breaks for the first five weeks. We spent hours learning how to form up into sharp-edged formations, march in step, and make crisp turns and coordinated starts and stops. We got good at it.

We learned in the second week that if a trainee was above the weight specified for his height at the end of his training cycle, he would immediately be run through another cycle. If he was still overweight after a second cycle, he'd be medically discharged. Enduring a second Basic was unthinkable for most of us, so this was a huge incentive to get into shape. We did pull-ups and lots of push-ups. In fact, most of us did many more push-ups as punishment for indiscretions—imagined and real—than we did as part of our organized PT (physical training). We got good at that, too.

I realized one day in the third or fourth week that we were all beginning to look physically alike except for height. We looked like we'd been remade into clones by the Army, which of course we had. One of the exceptions was a fellow from East Texas. He was a gentle giant of barely eighteen, about six-foot-four who'd never been away from home before. He'd been caught with one marijuana cigarette (a.k.a. "joint" or "number") and brought before a judge who gave him a choice of five years in State prison or enlisting in the Army. All of us liked him, felt protective of him and knew he was ill-suited for the Army. He was quite overweight when we started, and he remained overweight throughout the eight weeks. This was remarkable given that the drill sergeants took turns running him back and forth through the low-crawl pit for two hours every evening. And he was never given PX (Post Exchange) privileges, so he couldn't buy candy, chips, or other fattening snack foods. Maybe his weight retention had something to do with the fact that the other hundred of us made darn sure he got all the candy and snacks he could eat.

We all spent a good deal of time in the low-crawl pit, but just a fraction of what our overweight friend did. The training function of the pit was to teach us how to crawl as low to the ground as possible to protect us from enemy fire. This meant crawling forward using only our elbows, knees, and inside edges of our boots. This is not as easy as it sounds but is essential, since it's the only way to move under fire without exposing your head, back, or butt.

We learned how to clean and carry our M14 rifles. These were kept under lock and key in a separate building and only issued when we went to classes to learn how to break them down, clean, oil, and put them back together; when we were trained to stand in formation, salute, and march with them; and when we fired them on the range.

One aspect of our training that made an impression on me was bayonet training. There were two main parts to it. One was jousting with pugil sticks, where we faced off one-on-one with poles with padded ends and tried to get our opponent on the ground by pushing, tripping or knocking him down. The other was thrusting, where we used rifles with bayonets to jab, parry, thrust, and impale tires and man-shaped dummies stuffed with straw.

"All right, men!" Drill Sergeant Longoria would scream, leading us through the mantra that accompanied this training. "What's the motto of the bayonet fighter?"

"Kill. Kill. Kill," we shouted.

Longoria would cup a hand to his ear. "What? I can't *hear* you!"

"Kill! Kill! Kill!" we'd yell, even louder.

At nearly twenty-five years old, I was seven years older than most of my fellow trainees and chuckled inwardly when we went through the drill. While it was humorous to me, because it was not going to make me one iota less human, I had no doubt it was having a far greater effect on many of my younger companions.

In our third week, we were bused to our field training area for the first time. The trip took about two hours to travel 100 miles north of the main fort to the White Sands Missile Range (WSMR) in New Mexico. Technically, the WSMR was a different Army base from Fort Bliss, but they were geographically attached and seamlessly integrated in the training of recruits. It was an adventure just getting there, more so if the air conditioning on the bus wasn't working.

A large billboard in the middle of nowhere displayed a beer bottle pouring golden beer into a frosty glass and proudly stated PEARL BEER, THE BEST-SELLING BEER IN TEXAS. I had tasted it once and found that hard to believe. I enjoyed the long drives to White Sands. They were breaks in the routine and also trips into the wild country that I loved so much. There was little evidence of civilization along the entire route, other than the road and the beer signs. Even when we reached the training area the "improvements" were few and far between. This part of the desert consisted of deep, loose sand caught up here and there in hummocks by tough desert brush. Most of the hummocks were low, but a few were as much as twenty feet high. The country was cut up by washes as we called them in Arizona (arroyos as they're called in New Mexico and West Texas and draws as they're called in the High Plains). I had seen similar terrain in Arizona, but with more and larger vegetation than that found in White Sands. It's the kind of place that looks like it would be impossible to get lost in, but which I knew from personal experience in the desert could completely disorient the uninitiated.

Our training area was about fifty miles south of the Trinity Site (also on the WSMR) where the first atomic bomb had been detonated less than twenty-four years earlier. Occasionally we would see contrails from rockets twisting their way straight up into the clear blue sky, not something you usually see. It was a bit surreal.

On one of our trips to White Sands, we trained in the use of the Army's standard issue sidearm, the M1911A1, a .45 caliber semi-automatic pistol. It packs a heavy punch and if you hit someone with it, they *will* go down. But it's not easy to do. The slug is heavy, which causes two things to happen: the pistol moves when it fires, and the slug drops precipitously in flight. Both make hitting a target more a matter of luck than skill. The exercise was just to familiarize us and wasn't scored in any formal way that went into our records, a fortunate circumstance. We also spent considerable time that day breaking down and reassembling the M1911. Thank heaven I never had to fire one again.

The next time we travelled to the WSMR we threw live hand grenades from specially constructed concrete trench bunkers. These were designed so that if a trainee dropped or failed to throw one very far, the grenade would roll into a concrete slot that deflected the blast straight up and away. Drill sergeants were ready to toss out any live grenades that happened to miss the slot.

I was not comfortable with grenades. I never fully trusted them not to detonate early, and I didn't like the fact that once the pin was pulled and the handle released there was no way to stop it from exploding. There is a four-second delay, and they were as safe as human ingenuity could make such a destructive device, but still they weren't my cup of tea. It bothered me that it was possible for a grenade to have both its pin and its safety clip pulled free by vegetation—a situation that seemed likely enough in jungle combat to be a valid concern.

During Basic Training, the PT Test (Physical Training Test) was the most important method the Army used to measure success in training recruits. We had to pass it to graduate. And graduating—leaving—was very important to me. The PT Test consisted of five events: the low-crawl for forty yards, an obstacle course, a man-carry for 150 yards, a one-mile run, and the horizontal ladder—which was twenty-five feet long and entailed a down-and-back traverse hanging below it, using only hands and a swinging body to make the trip. All events had to be performed within prescribed times in order to achieve a passing score. Minimum scores of sixty points on each event (300 points on the entire test) were required to graduate.

This was a difficult challenge for nearly all of us, but especially for some of us, and I was among the latter. We took the test four or five times during our eight weeks. In the beginning, we were required to score 200, but as we progressed through our training cycle, the required scores were increased to reflect our improved physical fitness and skill levels. I was always just above the required scores—good enough, but no great shakes. This did not go unnoticed by Drill Sergeant Longoria or his superiors.

In mid-May, we were trucked out to the PT area. As always, cattle trucks were used to transport us—tractor trailers with air vents and a single door on the right side with a ramp that folded outward to the ground. Inside, narrow shelves on both sides served as benches. There was never enough room for all of us to sit, so most of us stood. This was an early indication to me of the place ordinary soldiers occupied on the Army's totem pole.

When it was our platoon's turn, we marched to the designated start. I don't remember the sequence of the events, but I know it ended with the mile run. A few of my fellow trainees really enjoyed the PT test; I always dreaded it, especially the run. I was never a good distance runner, getting so winded I would struggle mightily to finish, often getting cramps in my side that would not go away for a long time.

Running the mile was something that caused me as much apprehension as anything I've ever experienced in my life—before, during, or since. The other PT events were merely hard.

On that May morning, I was a little off my feed. It was just one of those days. I did well on the first four events and was determined to do my best on the run. It was painful, but I finished and was nowhere near the last to cross the finish line. I was utterly exhausted and terribly relieved that it was over. Drill Sergeant Longoria told us our scores. Mine was 284—not terrific, but all right.

I had survived.

Chapter 3 – Basic Heats Up

The following Wednesday, we went on bivouac—a two-night, three-day campout on the White Sands Missile Range. I enjoyed the bus ride as always but had no idea what the next few days would bring.

First was tear gas training that included removing our gas masks inside a small building filled with CS "tear" gas and remaining calm. This was the only time I ever saw CS gas. Next was the Quick-Kill Course, where we used BB guns and fired at targets and other trainees along a sinuous trail in a particularly hummocky area. The idea was to fire quickly at genuine threats, holding our fire when friendlies or nonthreatening things appeared. We wore clear plastic visors to protect our eyes, but the BBs were damned painful when they hit you, even through clothing. We also went through a Live-Fire Course, moving through low-crawl pits as machine-gun bullets streaked just above the wire. This was capped off with classroom training sessions given by combat veterans who talked about commonsense things related to everyday life in the field.

Early Friday morning—May 23, our last day in the field—we donned web belts, harnesses, and canvas packs of the type used in World War II and Korea. This was fitting, since our chow was C-rations, mostly dated 1954 to 1957. We formed up on the sandy track and were led out on our twelve-mile march. At 7:30 a.m. the temperature was about ninety.

The march was hard. The heat was oppressive. The sun glared down from a cloudless sky and more heat and light reflected upward from the sand. Thick clouds of dust rose and lingered in the shimmering air. As we plodded onward, our progress was made slower and our exertion harder by the depth and looseness of the sand. At the eight-mile mark, some of us began to fall back through the ever-loosening formation toward the rear ranks. Drill Sergeant Longoria wasn't there, but the two drill sergeants with us were on the lookout for this. They cajoled, threatened, and intimidated with shouts. When this didn't work, they assigned two of the fitter trainees to fall back and pull the stragglers to a front rank. This worked temporarily, but I again fell back, which really upset the drill sergeants. They assigned two more men to fall back and grab my arms. But this time they told the two men to double-time me completely around the formation. This meant running me around the formation as it kept moving forward in the loose sand.

Apparently, I'd been chosen as the example to other potential stragglers, because this double-timing around the moving formation continued until we completed the march. This means I marched at least fifteen miles in all. I went through five sets of "escorts," most of whom became exhausted stragglers themselves as a result. The drill sergeants wouldn't relieve them from pulling me around at double-time until they began to stumble and fall.

I knew I was going to die. My mouth was so dry I couldn't swallow, so I stopped trying. I was dehydrated and stopped sweating somewhere between miles ten and eleven. My mind was vacant beyond the need to continue putting one foot in front of the other and making it around the front of the formation so I could slow down a little as the formation moved ahead while we moved back along it. My heart was beating like one of those huge hammer presses used to forge steel, but at machine-gun speed. My breathing sounded like a punctured CO_2 cylinder. The pain in my sides and legs was a sharp gnawing. I would have been delirious, only I couldn't think or talk.

Somehow I survived this. I remember entering the tent and savoring the bright hot shade it provided. Someone brought me a full canteen. After wetting my lips, which hurt at the touch of wetness, I slowly drank it dry over the next few minutes. Word spread that it was over 110 degrees. We were given time to eat, but I couldn't do it.

When we arrived back at our barracks, Senior Drill Sergeant Colfax addressed us. "Men, congratulations on successfully completing your bivouac. You're nearing the end of your training cycle, and it's time to get in shape."

I didn't like the direction his talk was taking.

"For that reason, those who scored below two hundred eighty on your last PT test will form up in one hour and take the PT test again. The rest of you have the weekend off, on-base only, starting as soon as you are dismissed."

The mere thought of taking the PT test in my condition of total exhaustion and in 110-degree heat caused me extreme anxiety. I still wasn't thinking well, so it took a few seconds for his words to register. Thank God, I'd scored 284 on my last PT test. I felt like a man on death row who had just received a last-second pardon.

"Remain in formation, while the names of those who need to take the PT test this afternoon are read out."

I was so debilitated standing still in the afternoon heat that I had trouble thinking at all. I couldn't wait for the last name to be called, so I could get inside and lie down on my bunk. *"It won't be long now,"* I thought, as William Smith was called out and then Filiberto Teran ... and then Jamie Thompson. I jerked to alertness. *"No, that's wrong! I scored higher than 280,"* my broken brain screamed out in silence. My next thoughts were scrambled and desperate. I knew I could not take a PT test and survive. I was sure of it; as sure as I'd ever been of anything.

The drill sergeant concluded, "Those of you whose names I called, form up here at 1600 for transport to the PT area."

I have never been a person who panics, not before or since this incident, but I was panicked then. *"Oh my God,"* I thought. *"What am I going to do? I cannot and will not take a PT test this afternoon. I really can't. It'll kill me."* I wandered aimlessly into the barracks, not knowing what to do. A few of my fellow trainees were sitting in lounge chairs, but most had made a beeline upstairs to take showers. I walked here and there and back and forth in utter confusion. Then I vaguely remembered having seen "Help" numbers on the barracks wall phones, so I went to the nearest one and read the sticker. It said something to the effect that trainees who were in a crisis should call this number for immediate assistance. There would be no negative repercussions. I didn't know what else to do, so I dialed.

I was in a bad way, and the person who answered the call had no doubt of that. When I realized the helpline was linked to a chaplain, my heart sank. I wasn't a religious person. But I was desperate, so I followed the directions and arrived at the chaplain's office. At first the chaplain, an Army captain, tried to minimize my concerns and assure me I could take a PT test and be just fine.

"You don't understand," I said. "I *cannot* do it! I nearly died on the bivouac this morning. I can't take a PT test today." I blathered on for a good five minutes.

Finally, the chaplain said, "All right, wait outside and I'll be with you in a few minutes."

I had a glimmer of hope, but was still a basket case, lost and adrift in a dark and unfamiliar sea.

About ten minutes later the chaplain came out. "Come with me. We're going to see the battalion CO."

This panicked me, but I meekly followed the chaplain to the office of Major Tomlinson, whom I'd only seen at a distance up until that moment. I came to attention and saluted. Even in my state of mind, I realized that the helpline was bullshit, designed to give trainees false hope, that the CO was the decision-maker in the room, and that their lives were in his hands.

Major Tomlinson looked me squarely in the eye. "Explain the problem to me, Trainee."

I did so in a voice I hardly recognized, one that varied in pitch and trembled more often than not. I did my best to be objective. I explained the last four miles of the bivouac march and told them I was sure I was going to die. I told these two strangers things I never intended to say out loud to anyone, not even to my family or closest friends. Tears poured uncontrollably down my face.

"You've *got* to understand. Everyone has a breaking point, a point beyond which they can't go. Everyone! And right now, I've reached mine." I stood there, a husk of the man I'd been before that morning's march. "And when we formed up outside the barracks, Drill Sergeant Colfax said only trainees who scored below two hundred eighty on their last PT test would have to take the test this afternoon. I scored two hundred eighty-four. My name should not have been called." I was trembling. "This isn't right. It isn't fair! I cannot do anything more. You've taken everything I have. I don't have ANYTHING left!"

After a few seconds the officers glanced at one another and seemed to confirm a previous consensus. On some level I thought I should feel humiliated, but I didn't. Broken, yes, but humiliated, no.

The chaplain said, "Major Tomlinson and I think you will still make a good soldier, so we're not going to put this in your record."

At hearing this, I was appalled by this strange and inappropriate—to my ears—response to my utter desperation. But the upshot was that I would not take that afternoon's PT test. I would, however, be required to take the final PT test of the training cycle the following Tuesday. My relief was offset considerably by the thought of taking the test in a few days, but I didn't show it.

I never forgot my breakdown but hadn't focused on it in much detail until writing about it here. It was one of the most important experiences of my life. A personal breakdown teaches that there are absolute limits on what we are able to do and helps protect us from repeating the experience by letting us recognize the warning signs. This is humbling, but humility is a plus that makes us stronger. It makes us more tolerant, more empathetic, and more accepting of human frailty than we would otherwise be. This provides a broader, more complete, and honest understanding of ourselves and of human nature. And finally, knowing one's breaking point means never crying wolf before it's truly reached. Knowledge of one's true breaking point pushes a person's endurance far beyond where it was thought to be before, or at least that's how it's affected me.

No one ever mentioned a word about this incident after my meeting with the chaplain and the CO. For my fellow trainees, the reason was obvious; they saw what I went through and knew they could not have endured it without serious consequences either. For the Army chain of command, it's less clear. But I believe the chaplain and CO knew that what was done to me was wrong and exceeded permissible training rules. And they knew that the temperature on that bivouac march—officially 114 degrees—exceeded the upper limit for physical training allowed by the Army Training Manual by about ten degrees. In short, they didn't want the matter to see the light of day.

By Tuesday, I'd recuperated and was probably stronger and fitter than I'd ever been. I heard a lot of tips about how to make the test easier, and two seemed reasonable to me, so I tried them. I took an aspirin tablet before leaving the barracks and ate a Hershey bar on the way to the PT field. I don't know how much to credit those tricks of the trade and how much to credit my total focus and determination that I would not go through a second cycle, but I scored 328 and never had to take another PT test as long as I lived.

The day following the test, twenty names were called out for training with the M16 rifle, mine among them. I figured, given my average physical prowess, that I and the others were likely going to be made clerks or drivers, so the Army was making sure we learned the rudiments of the M16 before we left Basic because we'd never see one again.

All our previous training had been with the M14, the standard rifle since 1959. Where the M14 could fire as fast as you could pull the trigger, the M16 fired an entire clip with one trigger pull. It had a selector switch that could be flipped while in use. This switch allowed it to be set on Safe, Fire (for semi-automatic) and Auto (for full automatic). It wasn't as accurate as the M14, but accuracy wasn't the point; firepower was. The philosophy was that if you put out enough lead you'd likely hit someone, but even if you didn't it would keep the enemy down and unable to fire back effectively. It was the proper philosophy.

The last Friday of my eight-week Basic Training was Memorial Day weekend. I was a few days short of turning twenty-five, the only trainee old enough to rent a car. We were allowed off-post that night with a curfew time of midnight. Four of us took a cab to the car rental agency at the airport. From there we drove across the international bridge into Juarez. I didn't ask whether this was okay, because I suspected it wasn't and didn't want to know the answer.

Anyway, we eventually found our way to the red-light district, which was just a block off the main drag. We wandered from one cantina/house of ill repute to another for several hours, but I kept returning to one where there was a girl whose looks fascinated me. She looked pure Indian (Native American), had flawless bronze skin, shiny black hair and beautiful bone structure and was, to my eye, strikingly alluring. She barely spoke English, which was good because as the evening wore on my language and demeanor deteriorated considerably. After a number of cervezas, I realized I was starving and should eat to keep from getting too inebriated. The cantina served no food other than chips and salsa, so I wandered back toward the main street. The place was full of street vendors and ordinary people walking about, laughing and talking in both English and Spanish. It was colorful, vibrant and happy. I walked by a street vendor selling tacos and asked what kinds he had. I eventually settled on mushroom and beef. I knew I might be taking a chance, but they were hot and smelled delicious. To my great relief they were wonderful, so I ate four of them! After that, I went back to the cantina with the striking girl.

Being a smidgen Indian myself probably fueled my imagination and erotic fascination with the girl in question. At any rate, after another cerveza, I asked her if she wanted to make love with me. She didn't seem to understand what I said, so in my pitiful Spanish I said, "Vamos a la cama... cuánto?" Awareness dawned in her expression and she said, "Cinco dólares." I said, "Okay," and stood up. She led me down a hallway in the back where we proceeded to enjoy each other's company in relative privacy in a dingy unlocked room on a bed that may not have had the cleanest linens. The relief was fantastic and total. It was literally the first and only time during my eight weeks of Basic when I truly relaxed. Too bad it was only for twenty minutes or so.

At 11:15 I rounded up my three friends and we headed back. It would be close by the time we returned the car at the airport and made it back to the barracks. So, to be sure at least they wouldn't get in any trouble, I decided to drop my friends off on the fort before returning the car. That turned out to be a mistake.

At the gate, I had to explain that we were trainees and that I was dropping my friends off at our barracks. They passed us through, but two minutes later, an MP vehicle pulled up behind us and flashed its lights as I was creeping along the fort's streets. Right from the start, the MP was nasty and arrogant. I asked him why he stopped me, since I was not speeding and had broken no traffic laws. He accused me of questioning his authority.

The situation deteriorated. He let my friends go and dragged me before the CQ (charge of quarters—a temporary company commander when the actual commander wasn't available at times like holidays, the middle of the night, and weekends). The CQ was a little less of an ass, but still wrote me up and told me to report to the Company CO's office at 1300 hours the next day.

The next morning the rental agency picked up the car, which cost me an extra twenty dollars. I reported to the CO and told him what had transpired, including my belief that I had been stopped solely because the MP didn't like the fact that trainees could have any fun. The CO was sympathetic, but gave me an Article 15 that docked my pay that month by forty-five dollars (about a quarter of my total monthly pay).

An Article 15 is an administrative punishment that can be meted out on the authority of unit commanders, without the need to go through higher authorities or military courts. It's applied only to minor infractions. I was not happy with this outcome because it was unjust, but at least it was over and done with.

Sunday afternoon we practiced marching drills and went on parade (marched in a large formation past a reviewing stand of officers and interested onlookers). We were treated to speeches from the commanders and finally, in a smaller formation, from Senior Drill Sergeant Colfax. He reminded us of what he'd said when we arrived, about the United States Army being the best trained and best disciplined army in the world.

"Do you believe that now?" he shouted.

"Yes, Drill Sergeant!" we bellowed in unison. Warmth spread through my chest, because I really did believe that.

"All right. When I dismiss you, you will find your orders posted on the bulletin boards inside your barracks. You will all be leaving in the morning. I wish you success in your Army careers. Dis-missed!"

We milled around, shouting to each other as we made our way to our respective barracks. When I could get to the bulletin board, I found my name and beside it, "Advanced Individual Training: Infantry, Fort Ord, California." I was shocked—partly because I expected to be a truck driver or clerk typist, but mostly because the prospect of nine more weeks of drudgery depressed me.

This was not the last time I would be reminded that there is logic ... and then there's Army logic. Gradually and somewhat grudgingly, I came to understand that Army logic made sense when viewed from an Army perspective.

I had expected the worst to be over. Now I felt there was no end in sight. I used a pay phone to call my parents and tell them where I was going next and to say I wasn't sure I could take much more of this. I even said that going over the hill (Absent Without Leave or AWOL) seemed more and more appealing. By the end of the conversation, my reason had returned. My mood improved even more when I found out that our fat fellow trainee had somehow failed to lose any weight and had orders for another cycle of Basic. *"You're halfway home,"* I thought.

That evening, when things had quieted down, Drill Sergeant Longoria came into our bunk area.

Our company trainee commander yelled, "Ten-shun!"

We sprang to attention at the ends of our bunks, facing the center aisle.

Sergeant Longoria quickly said, "At ease." He used a normal tone of voice, which we had never heard from him before. "Before you leave, I want you to know that I'm proud of you, all of you. It's not easy making the transition from the comfort of civilian life to the hardships and discipline of the military. But you've been one of the best trainee companies I've ever led. There will be many challenges ahead, but based on your performance here, there's no doubt in my mind you'll handle all of them just fine."

After chow that evening I knocked on Sergeant Longoria's door.

"Do you need something, Trainee?" he asked.

"No, Drill Sergeant. I just wanted to thank you. You were hard on us, but you had to be. Above all, you were fair, and I appreciate that. I don't know what's gonna happen from here on, but I know I'm a better and stronger man than I was when I got here. You had a lot to do with that, and I just want to say thanks. I'll never forget it."

I stuck out my hand and he shook it.

Chapter 4 – The Fog of Infantry AIT

A dozen of us were bused to the airport where we boarded a commercial jet for San Francisco. About forty-five minutes after takeoff I looked down from 30,000 feet and over the tops of the Catalina Mountains could make out most of Tucson, Arizona. I felt a pang of longing for what I feared was my forever-lost youth.

Everything I now possessed fit with room to spare into the olive drab duffel with my name and service number stenciled on its side. We hand-carried our files, so I looked through mine during the flight. There was no mention of my interaction with the chaplain and the CO, but the Article 15 was there. Granted it was an insignificant thing, but it offended my sense of justice, so I removed the form and disposed of it in the bathroom. Of course, the pay deduction was a matter of record, so my action was only symbolic, but it made me feel better anyway. The only things I left Basic with were my meager belongings, a sharpshooter badge with rifle bar for proficiency with the M14, a marksman badge with automatic rifle bar for proficiency with the M16, and a self-confidence that was new to me.

A change of planes in San Francisco put us on a small propeller plane bound for a little Army airfield on Fort Ord, about 100 miles to the south. From there we were bused a short distance to the Fort Ord barracks: World War II rectangular wooden two-story structures large enough to house about 100 men—fifty upstairs and fifty at ground level. The beds, or racks as they're called in the military, were two-tier bunks. Their steel frames were quite sturdy, considering how many troops had used them over the preceding thirty years.

After a brief welcome and orientation, we gathered in a hall with an elevated stage, where the CO of our training battalion introduced us to First Sergeant Robert Harper, our battalion's head drill sergeant. Harper was a huge hulk of a man, a black veteran of three tours in Vietnam, whom I immediately liked and trusted. There was something in his face that said he knew what we were in for, wasn't happy about it, and was determined to do everything in his power to give us the best chance to survive it. He told us that, because Fort Ord was a relatively small fort, we would be speed marching to almost all our training sites for the entire nine-week AIT cycle.

"Don't worry. You'll learn what speed marching is soon enough, and by the end of the cycle you'll be in top-notch physical condition."

These were prophetic words.

The next morning, we were rousted at 0515 hours, given fifteen minutes for the three S's, and formed up in a neat formation at precisely 0530. A trainee volunteered or was assigned the duty of carrying our Company Guidon (pronounced guide-on). The guidon was a small, swallow-tailed flag atop a six-foot wooden staff with our battalion number on top and company letter designation below. Both the flag and the person carrying it were called the guidon.

Our barracks were less than a mile from the Pacific Ocean, so the fog was as thick as soup. I was to discover it usually was in the mornings. The command was given to left face, which we did with professional crispness. This positioned the guidon at the front left corner of our formation.

"Forward ... HARCH!"

After ten steps, a new command was given. "Quick time ... HARCH!"

Like a well-oiled machine, we stepped up our pace. Quick-timing is a moderate shuffling jog. At first it seems deceptively easy, but as the minutes pass it gets more difficult, partly because of the effort involved in adjusting the shuffle to stay in step with everyone else and to maintain a formation. However, quick-time was not a speed we marched at for long. It was merely a transitional step, so to speak. At some point between a few seconds and a few minutes, the dreaded command reverberated through our ranks.

"Double time ... HARCH!"

Double-time is a run in synch with everyone in the unit. Granted it was like the first few laps of a long-distance Olympic race, but it dragged on ... and on ... and on ... and could sometimes be a pretty fair test of endurance—especially before sunrise and even more especially, if the runner hadn't completed all three of his S's before starting.

This was our dawn routine for the next nine weeks. I never knew how many trainees were at Fort Ord, but it was the summer of 1969, the height of U.S. involvement in Vietnam. Many companies ran in the early morning mist at Fort Ord that year, each following its own twirling guidon, possibly toward oblivion. Most of us lost ourselves in private thoughts during our morning runs. We were tiny pieces in a huge unstoppable human enterprise that was invisible to most Americans but part of history that would forever change our lives.

As we reached cruising speed, the drill sergeant began to chant a marching cadence. It was designed to help us stay in step with one another, but it did much more than that. This was it:

Drill Sergeant: "Your Momma was home when you LEFT." All: "You're RIGHT!"
Drill Sergeant: "Your Daddy was home when you LEFT." All: "You're RIGHT!"
Drill Sergeant: "Your girl was home when you LEFT." All: "You're RIGHT!"
Drill Sergeant: "Sound off." All: "ONE, TWO."
Drill Sergeant: "Sound off." All: "THREE, FOUR."
All: "ONE, TWO, THREE, FOUR... ONE-TWO, THREE-FOUR!"

"Your Momma was home when you LEFT." "You're RIGHT!"
"Your Daddy was home when you LEFT." "You're RIGHT!"
"Your girl was home when you LEFT." "You're RIGHT!"

"Jody was home when you LEFT." "You're RIGHT!"
"Jody got your girl when you LEFT." "You're RIGHT!"
"Jody's got your girl now, so ONE, TWO, THREE, FOUR… ONE-TWO, THREE-FOUR!" "You're RIGHT!"

"You had a good home, but you LEFT." "You're RIGHT!"
"You had a good home, but you LEFT." "You're RIGHT!"
"Jody was there when you LEFT." "You're RIGHT!"
"Your baby was there when you LEFT." "You're RIGHT!"
"Sound off!" "ONE, TWO."
"Sound off!" "THREE, FOUR."
"ONE, TWO, THREE, FOUR… ONE-TWO, THREE-FOUR!"

"Your baby was lonely, as lonely could be,
Till Jody provided the com-pa-ny.
Ain't it great to have a pal,
Who works so hard just to keep up morale"?
"Sound off!" "ONE, TWO."
"Sound off!" "THREE, FOUR."
"ONE, TWO, THREE, FOUR… ONE-TWO, THREE-FOUR!"

"You ain't got nothin' to worry about,
He'll keep her happy 'til you get out.
An' you won't get home 'til the end of the war,
In nineteen hundred and seventy-four!"
"Sound off!" "ONE, TWO."
"Sound off!" "THREE, FOUR."
"ONE, TWO, THREE, FOUR… ONE-TWO, THREE-FOUR!"

Double-timing through the fog of Ford Ord, singing these marching cadences, following a half-seen twirling guidon was a nearly mystical experience. Sound was muted by the fog, so we felt as though we were enclosed in our own moving cocoon... a sort of secret world only we lived in. Sometimes we'd think we were hearing sounds other than our own chants... and sometimes we were. We would begin to hear a different cadence getting closer and closer, being chanted by another company of infantry trainees following a different guidon. As the two invisible companies of men approached one another we could make out their words as we continued to sing out our own cadence ever louder. Sometimes we might catch a glimpse of a different twirling guidon and its following group of men passing by us mere feet away. Then they and their cadence were again enveloped by the mist.

A cadence that I especially remember went something like this. Each line was first spoken by the Drill Sergeant and then repeated loudly and somberly by all of us.

"The warning order's given; the Captain's had his say.
You pray to God you'll see another da-a-a-ay.
Vi-et-na-a-a-am, Vi-i-et-na-a-a-am."

"We see the napalm burning and hear the cries of pain.
We pray to God that we don't get the sa-a-a-ame.
Vi-et-na-a-a-am, Vi-i-et-na-a-a-am."

Somehow these morning marches were the catalyst that began to transform us into soldiers who took real pride in withstanding adversity. I think almost all of us began to feel deep within us that as a group working together, we were formidable. Even though I knew I was in a kind of artificial reality, I also knew this was the only reality I needed to adapt to for the next two years. Much to my surprise, I was proud to do it.

In Basic there had been a chance that the Army, in its wisdom, might not send me to Vietnam, but now I knew that—barring a miracle—I would be going there as a combat infantryman. This really didn't surprise me; I'd expected it to happen sooner. For five years, I'd been more certain that I'd someday be fighting in Vietnam than I'd ever been about anything else my future might hold.

Between 1940 and 1973, all young men understood from early boyhood that they could be called upon to serve in the military. Most of us accepted this as an obligation of citizenship, as the way we earned the right to live in our wonderful country. It's not that we lacked moral qualms, frustrations, and even anger about having our lives disrupted for years while facing injury and death; it was just accepted as our duty—a duty our fathers, uncles, and older brothers accepted in their time. The Vietnam War was just my time to serve.

I knew that if an ancestor of mine was of military age during war, he served. In World War II my father, two uncles, and one grandmother served. A third uncle was a merchant seaman on the Murmansk runs. I knew all these people—loved and respected them. My father's three best friends were killed in World War II. Serving honorably in the military was a big step toward becoming a man. For most young men today, in their heart of hearts, I suspect it still is. The difference is that extraordinary efforts are no longer required to avoid it and doing so doesn't carry the stigma it did then.

After a few days of classroom training, we headed out to our first field location three miles from our barracks. True to his word, Drill Sergeant Harper took us out in formation. When we reached the edge of the developed part of the fort, he had us stretch out to single file along a dirt trail. Then he started us speed marching.

It wasn't quick time or double-time; it was exactly what he called it, a speed march. It was still essentially a walk, but a fast one, in which we stretched our legs much farther forward than ever before. For a person with my body type—long torso and short legs—it was hell.

We arrived at the training site and seated ourselves on the ground facing a low stage with a backdrop with two doors. Two sergeants stepped out, introduced themselves, and proceeded to tell us some of the history of Vietnam and how that history affected the Vietnamese people in the present. It was interesting, if much too brief. We learned that historically China had been a conquering enemy and that Vietnamese people had a phobia about being touched on the head. "So don't go around patting any young kids on the head, even if you mean well. And certainly, never do that to a Vietnamese adult."

I was already familiar with the basics of recent Vietnamese history. I knew Ho Chi Minh was Vietnam's equivalent of George Washington; that he fought the Japanese occupiers during World War II and the French when they tried to reassert colonial dominion. I knew he was still the nominal leader of North Vietnam. What I didn't know was that he started out expecting the U.S. to embrace and support his efforts to achieve independence from France. This was logical since the U.S. had fought for its own independence from British colonial rule. Over time, he became disillusioned and then embittered toward the U.S.

We ate hot lunches trucked out to us and speed marched back to the barracks late in the afternoon. This was our routine for the next nine weeks. We rose before dawn, did our double-time run, speed marched to training sites all over Fort Ord, and then speed marched back.

The countryside was beautiful at Fort Ord. The fort straddled the Coast Range, which at this point, just east of the southern curve of Monterey Bay is a narrow area of hills and foothills resembling the terrain found near the Ohio River in Indiana and Kentucky but with more meadows and fewer trees. The highest elevation was just over 600 feet, but considering that this was sandwiched between sea level at the Pacific Ocean on the west and the twenty to fifty-foot elevations of the Central Valley on the east, these "hills" looked and felt like the small mountains they are. The higher part of the area is a hilly plateau consisting of grassy meadows interspersed with rock outcrops, intermittent small streams, a surprising number of ponds and marshes, numerous lone oak trees and occasional patches of deciduous woods. Because of the mild moist air, but low precipitation, colonies of several varieties of ice plants were also located throughout the area. I loved the natural environment there and found it fascinating. Once, when standing on a rock outcrop at the highest point around, I felt a mild earthquake through the soles of my boots.

My body was being re-formed by Army training once again. At this point, the old me had been destroyed, and the new me had not yet developed the required muscle tone to excel at speed marching. I would invariably slip farther and farther toward the rear after a mile or two, but interestingly—perhaps because of my experience on bivouac—I never fell all the way to the rear of the line, let alone straggled behind it.

Drill Sergeant Harper saw that I was struggling over a particularly steep and uneven stretch of trail and dropped back alongside me.

"I know this is hard for you right now," he said, "but it *will* get better, and you *can* adjust to it. You can do much more than you think you can, and this training will convince you of that. For now, just keep putting one foot in front of the other, do the best you can, and you *will* make it. Every day from now on it will get better."

"Thank … you … Drill Sergeant," I puffed out between labored breaths. I knew he told the truth, I believed him, and I appreciated his humanity more than I could say. True to his words, it did get easier. It was never a cakewalk, but my body made the transition to a machine that could move much faster than ever before, faster than I even thought possible.

In my fourth week, I was selected for a special assignment as a participant in the Survival, Evasion, and Escape Training exercise for a different AIT infantry company. The training involved being dropped off "behind enemy lines" in total darkness with few directions. When trainees were dropped off, they had only a rough idea where they were and an even rougher one of where "friendly" lines and units were located. Their task was to navigate through enemy positions to reach the friendly positions without being seen. If caught, they were to provide no information—beyond what the Geneva Convention required, which was name, rank, and serial number—and do everything in their power to escape. All trainees had to complete the training in their sixth or seventh week.

My job was to play the role of an enemy guard at a camp where "prisoners" were held and interrogated. I got an hour of instruction and a weapon with blank ammo. I was placed under the overall command of a major and the immediate command of Sergeant First Class Smith. The major, Smith, and most of my fellow guards were combat veterans, some of them from multiple tours. There were only a few of us newbies.

At first, there was little to do beyond touring our camp to become familiar with its various "facilities" and taking smoke breaks on the perimeter. However, by 2230 hours, captured soldiers began arriving. They were brought before the major, who would interrogate them with the help of Sergeant Smith. The POWs were blindfolded with their wrists tied behind them. They were pushed around a bit and screamed at repeatedly, but to their credit none of them gave up anything beyond name, rank, and serial number. Then they were turned over to the exclusive control of Sergeant Smith for incarceration.

Most prisoners were shoved into bamboo cells, with guards standing watch nearby. Two were selected for a different fate. Smith ordered another guard and me to handle these two. He had us tie their elbows tightly together behind them. I was uncomfortable with this, but did as I was ordered. He then demanded the name and strength of their unit. They refused to answer with more than name, rank, and serial number. Smith had us force them to their knees in front of a bench. He pushed them backwards over the bench into unnatural and excruciatingly painful positions. They screamed in pain, but neither gave up any information. I knew this had gone too far ... but did nothing.

Smith ordered us to move the POWs to a pit on the far west side of the camp. It was a chilly night, and the pit was muddy at the bottom. None of us could see the bottom in the pitch blackness, but Smith told us there were Punji stakes and snakes down there.

Punji stakes are pointed bamboo stakes pushed into the ground, sharp ends upward. In Vietnam, the enemy dug pits on trails, pushed sharpened bamboo stakes points-up in the bottom, smeared feces on the bamboo points, and covered the pits with woven mats of elephant grass or palm fronds covered with leaf litter. They could kill or maim anyone falling on them, either through initial contact or later though infection.

Smith ordered us to force the two POWs into the pit. Despite their vehement protests, we did this. One was frantic with fear, pleading and yelling that he was terrified of snakes. The pit was so deep that the tops of their heads were just level with the ground. They were still blindfolded, and Sergeant Smith ordered us to push them to their knees with our rifle butts. Eventually, he left.

When he was out of earshot, I said to the still screaming POW, "Try to calm down, and don't move around too much. If there are Punji stakes, you don't want to injure yourself."

I was unsettled, disturbed that I had found it so easy to inflict pain on anyone, let alone a fellow trainee. I found it hard to believe that the U.S. Army condoned the kind of treatment we had meted out to these two men. About half an hour later, the major came by our guard position and asked what we were doing there.

I told him we were guarding two POWs in the pit.

"Who ordered you to put those men in the pit?"

"Sergeant Smith, sir," we answered in unison.

"Get those men out of that pit right now and untie them," he said.

When the major saw that their arms were tied at the elbow as well as the wrist, he asked, "Did Sergeant Smith order them to be tied that way, too?"

"Yes, sir," we answered.

"All right. Take these two soldiers to the HQ and wait for me there."

"Yes, sir," I answered with as much relief as concern about my own fate.

Within an hour, the two were trucked back to their barracks. My fellow guard and I submitted written statements describing the entire incident. I later learned that Smith was reduced two grades in rank to sergeant E-5, a significant punishment. Based on what I know now, it's clear to me that Smith was suffering from PTSD and was clueless about it. The Army didn't punish me, but I learned a lesson that stayed with me.

When given a seemingly "permissible" reason, I'm capable of despicable, uncharacteristic behavior … as I suspect many of us are. Knowing this, I've successfully guarded against allowing it to happen again. Ironically, a completely unacceptable event made me a better person for the rest of my life, including during my service in Vietnam.

Chapter 5 – A Taste of Freedom

That year the Fourth of July fell on a Friday. Amazingly, we would be off duty from Thursday noon until Monday morning. If we got a pass to leave Fort Ord we had to report back to base by midnight on Sunday. I was lonely for female companionship, missed Kara, and still had a hole in my heart where she'd once been. I hadn't spoken to her since late winter, but called anyway; her brother answered and gave me her new number. When I reached her, she told me she'd broken her engagement and moved out of her parents' house. I thought this was a good move for her since they'd coerced her into the engagement. She'd be happy to see me if I could make it to Tucson, so I determined to find a way.

No flights out of Northern California worked within my time and money constraints, so I rented a car to drive the 325 miles to LA, where I could catch an affordable flight to Tucson.

It felt strange to be free for the first time in over three months. It's more than a little ironic that American military service, which exists primarily to defend freedom, is the best lesson in how it feels not to be free, to have freedom taken away from you. It certainly makes freedom taste sweeter. When my military service ended, I never took freedom for granted again.

I made it to LAX two and a half hours before my flight. While I waited, I talked to a Marine recruit from Camp Pendleton. He was a nice kid, though a bit more shell-shocked than I was. Army recruits ran one mile before breakfast, but Marines ran three. In fact, it sounded like everything was harder. He may have been in Basic, whereas I was in AIT, but I realized how lucky I'd been not to get that pink slip.

I arrived in Tucson around 11:00 at night, rented a car, and got a room at the Motel Six on the west side of town. The next morning, I called Kara and we agreed to have dinner. When I went to her apartment to pick her up, it quickly became clear that neither of us really wanted to go to dinner.

We talked for hours. One thing led to another and we ended up in bed together for the first time.

Suffice it to say that we did not consummate the deal. I rolled off and chuckled.

Kara naturally asked, "What's funny?"

"Nothing is funny," I answered. "I was just thinking we were so serious that I was on the verge of asking you to marry me. And to find out that we're not sexually compatible after all that is almost unbelievable. It's no one's fault; it's just the way it is."

We put ourselves back together and talked for many more hours, promising to keep in touch. We parted friends. The next morning, I drove back to the airport and flew back to LA. I was okay, which surprised me.

The following weekend, I called my parents and told them I still thought about going over the hill, but guessed I probably wouldn't. They said they thought that was the right decision and that it was important to think about long term consequences before making important decisions. I also told them I'd been thinking of taking the Infantry NCO Candidate Course.

"There's a slight chance that I might not be sent to Vietnam if I don't go to NCO School, and if I sign up for it I'm guaranteed to go. But in the end," I explained, "I think I'm going over one way or the other and it makes more sense to go as a sergeant, 'cause I'll have a little more control over my destiny, and without extending my time in the Army the way OCS would have."

They both told me they were proud of me and loved me, and that was the most important thing of all.

The following week, it was my turn to go through Survival, Evasion, and Escape Training. I was captured within three hours. You'd think I'd be fearful of receiving treatment like what I'd inflicted, but I really wasn't. For one thing, I was pretty sure it would be quite a while before anything like that happened again. And then there was the fact that I'd already seen the POW camp. I was brought before a major and a staff sergeant along with another POW. Our wrists were tied behind our backs, and we were interrogated using the same verbal intimidation technique that was used when I was a guard. Both of us stuck to name, rank, and serial number despite some shoving and manhandling. Then we were blindfolded and walked to the east side of the camp. The guards tied our ankles and dropped us into a wet, muddy pit, telling us it had snakes in it.

When the guards moved off to have a smoke, I whispered to my pretty badly shaken comrade that we needed to get ourselves untied. We succeeded in getting back-to-back and were able to untie each other's wrists. Once that was accomplished we removed the blindfolds and untied our ankles. We could see nothing in the pit, but I started feeling around the sides until I found some planks. I pulled on these until I'd removed four or five of them.

"Come on," I said. "There's a tunnel here."

"Where does it go?"

"I have no idea, but anyplace is better than this damn pit. I knew there was a steep downslope on the east side of camp and hoped the tunnel might break through to open air.

We felt our way along for what seemed like fifty feet. The tunnel was small and we constantly bumped our heads, shoulders, or hips against the top and sides. I was worried it might be a dead end—or worse that it might collapse. When we finally emerged into open air through a tangle of brush, we were well outside the POW camp perimeter. It was a moonless night, but we made our way across the slope and up to higher ground. We were picked up by friendlies about an hour after sunrise and returned to our barracks for much needed showers and rest.

The following Sunday I had a free afternoon, so I walked over Highway 1, and then about a hundred yards beyond Stilwell Hall, the Fort Ord Soldiers Club, to the cliff at the edge of the Pacific Ocean. I stared out over the immense grayness, trying to grasp its vastness and imagine what the future would hold for me ... and how long or short that future might be. The sea was frothy, with waves continually marching from beyond the horizon to the shoreline below. The crashing waves roared in my ears, the wind whipped my face, and the grayness absorbed me. Occasionally I wiped grains of sand from my eyelashes, but mostly I just stared at the horizon and wondered what I'd find on the other side.

Being immersed in nature is an experience we should allow ourselves from time to time. It grounds us in ways nothing else can, because we're part of it. All the things that were about to change my life forever, or even end it, were nothing to the ocean. It would continue to pound the shore whether I was there or not. The clarity with which I understood my insignificance in the grand scheme of things provided a perspective that helped me. After about an hour, I walked back. *Let the chips fall where they may. I'm signing up for NCO school. I'll be doing what I can to gain control over my future.*

That evening, July 20, 1969, at 1956 PDT, U.S. Astronaut Neil Armstrong stepped off the ladder of NASA's lunar module Eagle to become the first human to set foot on the surface of the moon. This was a big deal, arguably one of the biggest in human history. Most people watched or listened as he did it. I wasn't one of them, because I was in the Army and was guarding the finance building at Fort Ord. A few of us in the AIT training companies were assigned to walk guard duty that night, probably because the regular MP guards wanted to watch the moon landing.

I wasn't happy about it, but I reported to the MP office as ordered. It was a small room, located near the center of the developed part of the fort, with three or four desks, an equal number of landline phones, and a radio set up on a counter against one wall. I was issued an M1911, semi-automatic .45 caliber pistol with belt, holster and three rounds of ammunition.

I then received a few minutes of instruction from an MP captain, which included these pertinent points: "You are not to place any of the live rounds in the weapon's chamber or magazine unless you, or the facility you are charged with guarding, are under imminent threat. And you are not, under any circumstances, to relinquish control of your sidearm to anyone until your guard shift has been completed."

When the captain finished, an MP corporal drove me to the finance building and told me to walk completely around the building, staying alert to any unusual activity and altering my speed and direction occasionally until I was relieved four hours later. I circled the building time and again. For about an hour and a half nothing happened. I saw no one, not even a passing vehicle.

"Geez," I thought, *"everybody and his cousin are watching the moon landing on TV. Everybody, but me, that is. But one thing's certain; I'll remember where I am and what I'm doing at this instant of time, for as long as I live."*

I searched the sky for the moon, but it was nowhere to be seen. The night was cool, with a slight breeze wafting from the hills to the ocean. The air was fresh and wonderful, with a tingle of tall grass and ice plants. I knew the breeze would reverse direction by morning, mixing moist air from the ocean with the cooler air over the land. There would be fog the next day for sure.

My thoughts were pushed to the back of my mind as an MP car approached slowly and stopped in front of me. An MP sergeant got out and walked over to me.

"Hello, Trainee," he said, "What are you doing here?"

"I'm guarding the finance building, Sergeant."

"Really, and how are you going to do that, Trainee?"

I was beginning to sense a problem with this guy. "If I or the building are seriously threatened, I'll shoot the perpetrators, Sergeant."

"And how will you do that, Trainee?"

"With the .45 caliber M1911 sidearm I'm carrying, Sergeant."

"Well then, I hope that gun's loaded, Trainee."

"It might be ... or it might not, Sergeant." I answered.

"Well, we'd better make certain, Trainee. Hand it over for inspection."

"I can't do that, Sergeant."

"What do you mean, you can't do that? I'm ordering you to do it right now!"

"No, Sergeant."

"Why the fuck not?" he bellowed, less than eighteen inches from my face.

"Because an MP captain ordered me not to relinquish possession of my weapon to anyone under any circumstances while on guard tonight."

"That's nonsense. How can we be sure whether or not your weapon is loaded?"

"WE can't, Sergeant, but I can."

"Let me get this straight, Trainee. You're refusing my direct order to hand over your weapon for inspection?"

"That's correct, Sergeant."

"This could get you in serious trouble," he shouted.

"Maybe, but I'm choosing to obey a direct order from a higher authority, Sergeant."

At that, he seemed flustered, but it was probably just an act. "So that's it?"

"That's it, Sergeant." I said more calmly than I felt.

"Well, we'll see about this," he said, turning away. He drove away and I never saw or heard anything more about this incident. I didn't like the fact that his intrusion had interrupted my walk around the building. Whether he meant it to or not, his challenge had created an effective diversion for anyone who might have wanted to rob the building. I didn't know for sure, but since issuing live rounds to trainees was highly unusual, I suspected that guarding the finance building was a bit more important than most guard assignments. For all I knew, there could be millions of dollars inside. Within a few minutes, I was back in my routine, again thinking of fog and oceans and astronauts on the moon.

At a little past 2200 another MP car pulled up. I was relieved and a new trainee dropped off to replace me. We returned to the MP office, where I turned in my weapon, belt and holster, and the three live rounds. The items were signed in and I signed out. For about fifteen minutes I was allowed to stand around watching the aftermath of the moon landing on a little black and white TV set up in a corner for the occasion, and then I was dismissed and told to return to my barracks. A sliver of New Moon peaked above the eastern horizon just as I approached the entrance to my barracks building. I turned to stare at it for a few seconds, sighed, opened the door and went inside. I crawled into my bunk at around 2300 and got less than six hours sleep before beginning yet another day of Infantry Training the next morning. And, yes, there was fog, lots of thick, heavy, cloaking fog.

Ten days later we graduated from AIT. There was a formal ceremony, and all the graduating companies marched past a reviewing stand in perfect military order, company guidons flying proudly in the California sun. What I remember most, though, was the indoor ceremony held for our company. The battalion commander and our company commander were there, as were all our drill sergeants. But the one man we all wanted to hear from was Sergeant Harper. After everyone else said their piece, he moved to the center of the stage. The gentle giant who had helped us through a rite of passage unlike any we had experienced spoke softly and clearly.

"Men, I want you to know I'm proud of you. What you've been through here was not easy, but all of you did it and did it well. You are soldiers now and will serve each other and our country with honor, courage, and integrity. Most of you will go to Vietnam and serve in the infantry. That will be hard, and not all of you will survive. But you have a much better chance now than you had before you came here."

At this point, you could have heard a pin drop. All of us were swimming in deep personal thoughts. Strangely, perhaps, I felt pangs of loss, as I realized this time and place and the people I knew here were about to enter my past, never to be seen again.

Harper concluded his remarks. "There's one more thing you need to know about Vietnam."

Everyone bent forward imperceptibly waiting for any last pearl of wisdom Drill Sergeant Harper could share with us.

"You will never do any speed marching in Vietnam!"

When the laughter died down, Harper's smile receded. "You will walk more softly, more quietly, and more alertly than you have ever done. All the time! Everywhere! Is that clear?"

"Yes, Drill Sergeant," we shouted in unison.

"I can't *hear* you!" Harper shouted back, with a smile from ear to ear.

"Yes, Drill Sergeant!" we screamed at the top of our lungs.

"Good! Now, Dis-missed! Get out of here and on your way."

Chapter 6 – Rattler on the Flank; NCO School

The day following Drill Sergeant Harper's farewell, I flew to Chicago to see my family for the first time in over four months. I was a changed man. For one thing, I was in top physical condition. Just a few years earlier I'd been a chubby little guy. My first transformation occurred when I got interested in girls. My sisters laughed when they saw me running laps around the house or rowing our twelve-foot rowboat many miles around the lake for hours. It worked, but there was no comparison to the shape I was in now.

I enjoyed the time with my family but wasn't very talkative. The surroundings and the people were the same, but I wasn't. I didn't understand it—or even try—but I knew I'd never again relate to this place or to my family in quite the same way I had in the past. I was a restless spirit, needing to get on with it.

The Noncommissioned Officer Candidate School would be a twenty-four-week course: twelve weeks of training at Fort Benning, Georgia, followed by twelve weeks of on-the-job training (OJT) at military bases scattered across the country. My training was to be in the military occupational specialty (MOS) 11-Foxtrot-40. 11-F-40 signified infantry operations and intelligence sergeant. We would immediately be promoted from the rank of private to the rank of corporal. This meant an increase in pay, paltry as it was in those days. We would now be called "Candidate" or "Corporal," depending on the circumstances. If we were taking instruction, it would be "Candidate," but if we were exercising anything resembling the actual duties of an NCO, it would be "Corporal." When we graduated we'd be sergeants (or "shake 'n bakes" or "instant NCOs" as some people would refer to us, often in a less than complimentary way).

It was after dark and pouring rain when I arrived at Fort Benning a few days later. Bob Dylan's latest hit, "Lay, Lady, Lay," was playing on the radio as I struggled to see through the misty rain. I reported to the HQ and was assigned to an 11-

F-40 NCO training company. At the company barracks, I met the two staff sergeants in charge. I handed one my orders, and he introduced himself as Staff Sergeant Josh Allen. His companion was Staff Sergeant Matt Knecht.

After making my bunk, I hit the sack and slept until I was roused by the familiar shouts and bangs of sergeants starting yet another training day. This was my eighteenth week of it, and it was beginning to wear thin. By now the rushed morning ablutions were automatic. We formed up outside the barracks, waiting for our run to begin. Instead we were marched to the mess hall for a hearty meal that included some kind of granular mush.

"Hey, Castro," I said to Gordon Castro, the platoon mate to my right, "any idea what this grainy stuff is?"

Castro was a thin, nervous looking fellow from Miami, who was much more together than he let on. "No idea man," he said between mouthfuls of egg.

I later found out it was grits, apparently made by grinding corn. I'd heard of grits, but never seen or eaten any.

NCO school turned out to be a cakewalk in terms of the physical training—compared to Basic and AIT. I'm not sure if it really was easier or just seemed easier because I was in the best physical condition of my life. We only ran our mile a few times a week, usually in mid-morning, not before dawn. There were plenty of physical challenges though, like the jump tower, rappelling, and the obstacle course. But mostly NCO school was classroom work and hands-on training. We learned more about Vietnamese culture and traditions of the Army—most particularly the Infantry, Queen of Battle. We learned the rudiments of parachuting, map reading, and infantry tactics as well as how to call in artillery and air strikes, and operate numerous weapons.

After our fifth week, most of us got passes to leave base on Saturday night. I'd heard it was homecoming week at Auburn University, forty-five minutes away. I asked around and found a fellow candidate, Kurt Stephan from Minnesota, who was willing to split car rental costs to go and check the place out. We didn't know anyone there, weren't familiar with the place, and the game was long over when we arrived, but we enjoyed strolling under huge oak trees near the center of town. We had dinner and drove back, arriving at our barracks by midnight, as sober as church mice.

In our eighth week, which fell in mid-October, we went on a two-day bivouac. This did not involve a twelve-mile forced march, thank God. Instead, each company moved out into the wilds of the heavily forested hills in the remote parts of Fort Benning. We were to move as though we were in the hostile jungles of Vietnam. A first lieutenant and two sergeants first class, all of whom were Army Rangers, accompanied us. Their job was to mentor and train, but mostly observe and evaluate our abilities as future NCO leaders.

One of us would be selected by the Rangers to be acting company commander for four to six hours and then switch off with someone else. I was chosen first, receiving a set of topo maps and a briefing.

Reading topographical maps is an art. Many people are terrible at it and even the best can sometimes make mistakes. It takes experience using them to get good at it. We'd been through an orienteering course some weeks earlier, which frankly was a cluster-fuck waste of time. But I had field knowledge from hiking and hunting in Arizona and canoeing in the Boundary Waters of Northern Minnesota. Besides, from an early age I'd loved maps of all kinds and spent hours studying them. I studied the terrain and planned a route to our destination.

Our mission was to recon a position where intelligence indicated the "enemy" had established a strong point, and then return undetected to an extraction point. I had little to go on beyond a general location atop a hill where it was thought the enemy was set up.

I got the company strung out in single file and placed two flankers 100 feet to the sides and slightly ahead of the front of the formation, two more to the sides of the center, and two more off the sides of the rear. All was silence except for the muted crunch of leaves under our boots.

About two miles in, the flanker on our right center uttered an involuntary "Holy shit!"

I was not happy. His exclamation was too loud for stealth.

I halted the company and loudly whispered, "What is it?"

"A snake!" was the immediate response.

"So what?" I said.

"It's the biggest damn snake I've ever seen," he replied. "I'm gonna shoot it!" Shooting it was possible because at point blank range even blanks can be deadly to small critters.

"No!" I snapped. "I'm coming. Don't shoot; you'll give away our position."

I made my way up the slope. Outside of zoos and jungle movies, it was also the largest snake I'd ever seen: an Eastern Diamondback Rattlesnake about six feet long and as big around as my biceps. It was slithering slowly in the same direction our company was moving, half under and half on top of the leaf litter and well camouflaged. Eastern Diamondbacks can be deadly, but it was a cool day in deep shade. This had slowed the snake's metabolism.

"Stay here and keep an eye on it, while I move the company ahead. I'll send a new man out to replace you. Make sure the flanker behind you sees the snake and avoids it, then rejoin the company."

"Are you sure you don't want to kill it? I mean look at the thing!"

"I'm sure," I answered. "He's no danger to us, unless we make a commotion and give our position away."

"I guess," he replied somewhat doubtfully.

"Don't kill it!" I emphasized as strongly as I could in a whisper.

I explained the situation to the new flanker, Jerry Pickering—a tall solid guy from Oklahoma—and sent him out to the right. Then I motioned to the company to start moving again. Ol' Man Rattler lived to see another day.

Several hours later we reached an open hilltop with a two-track dirt road crossing it. I halted the company, sent flankers down the road to both sides, and gave the order for the company to cross the road.

Suddenly the Ranger lieutenant said, "Halt!" It was the first time any of our evaluators had done anything to question or alter my decisions.

"Sir?" I asked in surprise.

"Why are you crossing the road, Corporal?"

"Because we haven't reached our objective, sir."

"Yes, we have, Corporal," he said—rather pompously, I thought.

"Sir," I replied in a respectful manner, "our objective is the next major hilltop, which is approximately a thousand meters north-northeast of here."

"You're wrong, Corporal. This hilltop is our objective and we've already reached it. Tell the men to break in place, and eat some chow. We can move out in half an hour."

I felt my face warming and turning red. "Yes, sir," I answered through clenched teeth.

I sent lookouts fifty meters out to each compass point and 100 meters each direction down the road. Everyone found spots to sit and open their C-rations. I nibbled a few bites of canned spaghetti and meatballs, packaged in July 1956 according to the stamp on the can. I was still fuming.

The two Ranger sergeants were sitting together off to the edge of our main body. After fifteen minutes, I couldn't stand it any longer and walked over.

"Can we do something for you, Corporal Thompson?" one asked.

"I don't know, Sergeant. Can I talk to you about where our objective is?"

"Sure."

"I know for certain our objective is not this hill, but the next one. The lieutenant is wrong. Is there anything we can do about it?"

They glanced at one another with small smiles. I couldn't tell whether it was a knowing smirk, as if to say, "Here's another green troop who thinks he knows more than we do," or a knowing acknowledgement that, "Here's another green troop who hasn't learned Army ways yet." Heck, I'm still not sure.

One of them said, "No. There's nothing you can do without being insubordinate to a superior officer."

"But it's wrong!" I said.

"Maybe, but that doesn't matter."

I wandered back to my pack and fumed even more. I managed to finish the spaghetti. Strings of expletives ran through my angry brain.

About twenty-five minutes into our half-hour lunch break, the lieutenant got a radio call from HQ asking him why his company hadn't reached its objective yet. He immediately became flustered and shaky, which was not usual for officers. He uttered a few "yes, sirs," "no, sirs," and "I understand, sirs," before ending with, "Right away, sir!"

He turned to me. "Corporal, get the men moving toward that next hill to the northeast."

"Yes, Sir," I said. Within thirty minutes I'd spread the company out at the southern base of the correct hill and moved slowly up to scout the top with a few men. We found an enemy position that was too well defended for a force our size. I relayed this assessment to the lieutenant, who called it in to HQ and then I received, quite literally, new marching orders.

The bivouac was uneventful from then on, except that I was left in command all the first day and half of the next. Almost as an afterthought, they gave the job to another guy around ten the next morning and then switched it every two hours until we returned to our starting point.

The following Monday evening we had another of the endless snap inspections conducted by our platoon sergeants. These were designed to instill in us a strict adherence to the smallest details of military protocol and SOP. Our bunks were checked to make sure the sheets and blankets were tight and had proper tucked-in corners. Our foot lockers were inspected to make certain we had every item we were supposed to have—and no unauthorized items—and that everything was exactly where it was supposed to be and in exactly the correct form.

I've never been an orderly person when it comes to my stuff. When I have what I need and know where to find it, that's enough. Keeping a shoeshine brush on top of a shoeshine cloth no more than one inch to the left of a single can of black shoe polish, which had to be no more than one inch to the left of a can of Brasso, which had to be on top of a folded cotton polishing cloth, et cetera ad infinitum, was not something that came easily to me.

As he looked through my locker, an exasperated Sergeant Allen said, "Candidate Thompson, report to the platoon office at 1930 hours."

"Yes, Sergeant," I replied crisply.

At the appointed time, I knocked lightly on the door to the offices where Allen and Knecht administered the day-to-day operations of our platoon.

"Come in, Candidate," called a voice.

"Candidate Thompson, reporting as ordered, Sergeant!" I came to attention in front of their desks.

"At ease, Candidate. Do you know why you're here?" asked Sergeant Knecht.

"I imagine it has something to do with the snap inspection earlier, Sergeant." I replied.

"Yes, it does. You'd make staff sergeant E-6 out of this course if you kept a neater locker, Candidate. Did you know that?"

"No, Sergeant. I didn't."

"Do you think you can do that over the next four weeks, Candidate?"

"I honestly don't know, Sergeant," I replied with complete sincerity. "I know it seems like a simple thing, but for some reason I find adhering to rules that I find arbitrary and nonsensical to be nearly impossible. I will do my best, but whether that's going to be good enough, I just don't know."

Allen and Knecht exchanged glances and Allen said, "Well, it would be a shame to miss such an opportunity, but all you can do is your best. And we expect your best. Is that understood?"

"Yes, Sergeant. I appreciate you talking to me about this."

"You're dismissed, Candidate," said Sergeant Knecht.

The next day was Veterans Day, so we had the day off, but were restricted to base. I noticed that James, one of my platoon mates, had a black band around an upper arm and finally asked him about it.

"It's a sign to show solidarity with all the people who're marching in Washington this Saturday."

"What's happening Saturday?" I asked.

"National Moratorium to End the War in Vietnam," he explained.

"Oh, yeah. I heard something about that. I'm surprised the Army is letting you wear the armband on duty."

"Yeah, me, too!" he said. "Allen and Knecht, talked to me about it and said they understood my feelings about the war, but since I wasn't doing anything disruptive, they were going to ignore it unless someone higher up made an issue of it."

I greatly admired James's conviction and wasn't sure I would have done the same if I felt as strongly in opposition to the war as he did. The way I did feel about it was uncertain. It's difficult to imagine now, but in 1969 I was like most Americans in that I trusted my government to act responsibly in the best interests of the people. Even though I harbored great doubts about the war, I wasn't willing to break the law to protest it or break with family tradition and avoid military service. I hoped the government understood the situation better than I did and was right to be sending young Americans to the far side of the planet to fight.

The following weekend those of us who hadn't screwed up in some way were given weekend passes. My bunkmate Jared asked if I'd like to go with him and Kent Shepard to

Kent's home in Tampa, Florida, for an overnight. Having never been to Tampa, I jumped at the chance.

About halfway there, Jared said, "Hey, Jamie. Wanna try one of these?"

"What is it?" I asked.

"Pickled pigs' knuckles," said Jared.

"Geez, I don't know. I've never had one."

"They're good!" said Jared.

"Okay, I'll give it a shot." Jared reached back with the jar and said, "Just grab one outta there."

It was a slimy piece of bone with almost no meat on it, or at least none that any creature other than a saber-tooth tiger could have accessed and torn free. It didn't taste good to me and was kind of like nibbling on a golf ball that had been submerged in a dill pickle jar for a couple years. I struggled with it for a minute or so and then, since it was natural and biodegradable, threw it out the window.

"What did you do that for?" asked a genuinely hurt Jared.

What followed was one of those things that is seared deep into my memory and that I regret saying. "Well, it tastes like shit—or what I imagine shit tastes like, and it's really not edible."

"You're just not used to it. It's real good when you get onto it," said Kent.

"Guys, where I come from, it's garbage. I mean, really garbage. We throw it away and eat the rest of the pig. The thing is, the South is the only part of the country that's ever lost a war, and after the Civil War food was so scarce people had to learn how to eat a whole bunch of stuff they never would have eaten before. Over the years, they convinced themselves it really wasn't garbage."

As soon as the words were out of my mouth, I regretted them. But the damage was done. No response came from the front seat. In fact, no words were spoken at all for the next thirty miles.

That night we went to a college party hosted by one of Kent's sisters. There was music, beer, laughing, and conversation. Unlike my old self, I just observed from the periphery. I had become a more serious person and had little to party about.

I realized for the first time that I was totally focused on surviving the next few years. I had little interest in anything less consequential. It's not that I was a stick in the mud exactly—I laughed and joked around with my Army buddies—but I just couldn't completely unwind.

The next morning we woke early (from routine) and started the drive back. We took our time, stopping here and there for something to eat or just to look at the scenery. It was a good break, as much because it wasn't too long to break our routines as for the diversion.

Thanksgiving was the following week, and we had the day off, restricted to base. I called my family. My mother surprised me by announcing she'd be flying down for the graduation ceremony, and we could fly back to Illinois together the next day.

We received orders on Saturday for our three months of OJT, essentially learning to be NCOs in the real Army world. I was assigned to the 4/30 Infantry at Fort Sill, Oklahoma. Kurt Stephan was also assigned there. I looked forward to it because it was closer to Arizona, the place I'd considered home for most of the previous seven years.

Early Monday afternoon we finished packing—it's not hard when everything you own fits into a single duffel—and our platoon sergeants made their farewell speeches. It was a poignant event, at the end of which we received our official promotion orders, effective 2 December 1969. Our new lapel pins were attached immediately, and most of us headed to the cleaners to get the chevrons sewn on our dress uniforms. A few, including Kurt Stephan, received staff sergeant E-6 rank, but most received sergeant E-5... including me.

Tuesday finally arrived. In late morning, we marched in review past bleachers filled with Army brass and a few family members. I didn't spot my mother at that time, even though I knew she was there somewhere. We were quite the martial sight!

That evening all 175 of us in Class 3-70 F, 105th Company filed into the auditorium and into our designated seats in efficient military order. My mother was supposed to be there, but I hadn't yet seen her, so I kept looking around for her. Finally, I saw her walking in the main door side-by-side and in animated conversation with Colonel Piper. I was surprised, but not overly much. Colonel Piper was the Commander of the NCO School at Fort Benning, the top dog. My mother had a knack for such encounters that began in her high school years and ended only with her death in her nineties. Somehow people of wealth, power, position, and influence were drawn to her, and she to them. It wasn't anything overt that she did, it was just her appearance and presence that seemed to act like a bright light or a magnet. They were comfortable in one another's company. My mother Didi was quite a remarkable and interesting character, and I loved her dearly!

This graduation was a much more formal affair than the one at AIT. There was a large stage in the front with a podium in the center and tables run out at both sides with eight Platoon Staff Sergeants (two for each platoon in our company), and six officers, including Colonel Piper. Several of the officers spoke of the importance of training NCOs for leadership in the new Army, a bit about the training we had received, both generically and in terms specific to the jungle warfare in Southeast Asia. A few short laughs erupted from us from time to time when comments were made about how we thrived in mud and enjoyed our runs to dry off. Then Colonel Piper spoke about how well our class had done and said he was proud to command such a fine group of young leaders.

At the end, each of our names was called out in alphabetical order by platoon. We climbed the steps at one end of the stage, walked to the center and stood at attention in front of our platoon staff sergeants. As we did, one SFC affixed the robin's egg blue fourragère (pronounced foor-a-zhair), a braided rope also known simply as the Infantry Blue Cord, over our right shoulder signifying that we were in the infantry – something I was very proud of then and now.

I try to "stay above" rituals and personal recognition and remain unaffected by them, but often fail. Just as happened when I graduated from Basic and AIT, I was moved. I don't think I showed it outwardly, but I sure felt it inside. I had come to realize that commonsense, reason and morality aside, serving honorably in the armed forces of the United States, doing my duty for my country, was very important to me as it is for many young men; it always had been and always would be. Some argue that it was naïve or immoral or both to serve in the military during the Vietnam War—and some other wars—but it is possible to serve with honor even in questionable and unjust wars, and in fact it's even more important that our soldiers, sailors and airmen do so in such wars. When I walked off that stage, I was proud to be a sergeant in the U.S. Army Infantry … and my family and ancestors were or would have been proud, too.

Less than a minute after the last new shake 'n bake NCO returned to his seat, at a nod from Colonel Piper, his Adjutant said, "Congratulations, NCOs! DIS-MISSED!"

At that point, I made my way to my mother and gave her a big hug. She had a calm, "told you so" look on her face. We never spoke about it, but I took it to mean that she'd known all along that I'd never go over the hill and wasn't at all surprised that I'd done just fine in the Army. She'd rented a car, so we drove to my barracks to pick up my duffel bag. I showed her around and introduced her to SFCs Allen and Knecht, newly minted SSG Kurt Stephan, and the few other platoon mates who hadn't already flown the coop. Then we made a brief stop at the NCO School HQ where I signed out for my one-week leave before reporting to Fort Sill and drove to Atlanta's Municipal Airport (now Hartsfield-Jackson Atlanta International Airport).

It was December 2, 1969.

The author, newly minted Sgt E-5 graduate of 11-F-40 NCO School
December 1969.
(photo 6-1)

Chapter 7 – A Short Visit Home

When we got to the airport, we picked up our tickets, found our flight information and walked toward our gate. I was walking along, making small talk over my shoulder, when I realized my mother wasn't answering. I turned fully around and saw her about a hundred feet behind me, practically sprinting to catch up.

When she got close enough to hear me, I said, "I apologize. I guess all that speed marching in AIT permanently changed my physiology. I didn't realize I was walking fast."

"Walking fast doesn't begin to describe it," she said, trying to catch her breath, "You were in a track meet!"

Actually, I felt like I'd been walking in slow motion and imagined that passersby wondered what the heck was wrong with me.

When we made it home, my sister Mimi, a high school senior, came downstairs and gave me a huge hug; my sister Julie wasn't home because she was a junior at the University of Kentucky in Lexington. After a few words with my father, I was off to bed.

I slept like a log, though I felt strange sleeping in the same place I'd slept in from eighth grade through high school and beyond. I was—and yet somehow wasn't—the same person. I had more self-confidence and knew that the limits of what I could do were light-years beyond what I'd believed them to be before entering the Army.

At the same time, I appreciated the warm, safe, and secure world my parents had built for me. The stable nurturing environment I'd found so boring was valuable beyond measure and had enabled me to gel, in my own good time, into whatever it was that I was becoming as an adult.

I poured myself a cup of coffee and looked out the kitchen window at a new off-white convertible. I could hear my mother typing her weekly newspaper column in her office, so I walked in and asked about it.

"Oh," she said, "your father got it for you."

I went outside. It was a pretty car—a 1970 Mercury Cougar XR-7 convertible. I looked inside and it was sleek, with leather bucket seats and modern instrument panel. It was a sharp car, but it wasn't my 1965 Ford Galaxie 500XL convertible, which I'd dearly loved. I wished my father had talked to me before he'd traded it in.

Next, I walked slowly around the property, noted how much the willows my father and I had planted eleven years before had grown, and admired the barn we'd built together. Among other things, my father was a frustrated architect, I think. He was fantastic at drawing up plans to build things, but practicality, functionality and ease of maintenance down the road never seemed to be considerations. A case in point was the barn. He designed it to have its entire south wall, fifty feet in length, lean farther south at its top than at its bottom. It was a fascinating modern look, but he'd insisted that one of the two swinging doors at each end of the barn be hinged directly to the leaning end posts/studs. This, of course, meant that whenever those doors were opened they wanted to swing hard and fast all the way to the south with an almost irresistible force. Cool looking, but utterly impractical, bless his heart. But I learned a lot from him... maybe as much from his mistakes as from anything else.

He had also insisted on using white asbestos composite shingles for the entire siding which was an immense area. His reasoning was that they were fireproof, true enough, and would never need painting, also true. However, they were very expensive and extremely brittle. We had to buy a special tool to press the nail holes through each and every shingle as we worked, because nailing directly through them would shatter them. Their brittleness, of course, also meant that they were very prone to cracking, breaking and falling off because of freeze-thaw, hail, or strong winds... all things Northern Illinois experiences in abundance. And replacing the broken shingles – a never ending job in the first place – was made far more difficult because the shingles needed to be slid under the edges of the shingles above. This meant that replacing one broken shingle often resulted in breaking and having to replace several more in the process! In short, those asbestos shingles were a nightmare. But in the brief intervals when they were all in place, they looked great... as they did on that December day in 1969! Oh, and in the mid-1960s when we put them up, there was beginning to be some talk that maybe asbestos might be a health risk. Of course, my father being an M.D. thought the risk was overblown. Yep, I loved my father dearly!

Lest I give a very false impression of my father, I must add that in almost every way other than building projects, he was the smartest person I've ever known. He and I looked so much alike that a girl in my high school once asked me if my father's office was on North Michigan Avenue in Chicago. I told her it was and asked how she'd known that. "Because when I was there the other day, I saw a man entering a building near Saks Fifth Avenue who looked exactly like an older version of you." "Yep," I answered, "That was him, all right."

My father was a psychiatrist in private practice in Chicago. He paid for his college education as leader of his own jazz band. He was an accomplished piano player, music writer and arranger. Through his college years at the University of Kentucky, he hosted a radio program focused on American music, most particularly on jazz. It was produced in Lexington but broadcast nationwide; it developed a large and very loyal following which generated many letters of appreciation from across the country. After college, he worked in Chicago and on tour for Tex Benecke in 1939-41 arranging music and playing piano in Benecke's band on stage and on radio. But by 1941, he'd decided to go into medicine mainly because it would allow him to have a stable family life, rather than staying with music, which I think was his true love. His father and mother were both M.D.s and raised him in a comfortable middle-class lifestyle in Berea and Lexington, Kentucky.

A valuable life lesson he learned and passed on to his children through the telling of it was his experience with polio. We forget now, but until the 1950s polio was a common illness, mostly among children, that paralyzed thousands of people for life and killed many of them. When my father was seven or eight years old, polio paralyzed his left leg. He couldn't move that leg at all and had to use a crutch to get around. The prognosis was that there would never be any improvement. But his father (Jamie Sr.) refused to accept that. Every evening when he came home from work he would take my father outside and have him stand beside a child's pull-along wagon, help him bend his left leg and place his knee in the wagon bed, have him hold the pull handle with both hands, and push himself and the wagon forward on the driveway with his right leg, the good leg. After about ten feet, he'd help him turn the wagon around and change legs. My father said this drove him crazy because he couldn't move the wagon at all trying to use his left leg, the paralyzed leg; tears often streamed down his face from hopeless frustration. But his father would not let him stop trying to do it and would stay with him for a solid hour urging him on. After three or four months, my father could make tiny movements with that paralyzed leg. After six months, he could move the wagon a few inches at a time. This went on for a whole year, until he had trained entirely different muscles to do the job his paralyzed ones could never do again. In adulthood, there was no discernible difference in his two legs. From the wagon experience onward, when my father set his mind to something, he accomplished it. I think it's fair to say, the same is true of his three children, too.

    He was a highly intelligent and thoughtful man who understood the injustice and evil nature of living in a society that overtly discriminated against Black people, as was the case in the American South (which included Kentucky) in the first two-thirds of the twentieth century. He once explained to me that in Lexington most Whites never gave Blacks or racism any thought because they never saw Blacks. The town and every aspect of its society were completely segregated/separated from one another. He wanted to leave this baggage behind him and not burden his children with it. So he left the South as soon as he could... even though he loved Kentucky deeply and always thought of it as his true home.

I cherished every minute I spent alone with him. One summer night, when I was about fourteen, he and I took a walk out to the middle of our three-acre lawn. It was a rare, crystal clear night, with no wind, and a moonless sky. The stars were dazzling in their clarity.

We were both quietly looking up at the night sky, when I said, "Jamie (I was raised to call my parents by their first names), I can't understand infinity. How can anything have no end?"

With no hesitation, he said, "Well, son, if space did have an end or an edge, what would be on the other side?" Since that moment, I've had no problem with the concept of infinity. He had that way about him. His mind was like a surgeon's scalpel; it cut right through to the heart of an issue. He was wrong about things occasionally, but it was so rare that usually no one else in the family – other than my mother – could see that he was wrong until some time had passed. We tended to assume he was always right.

He had such a strong personality and such a powerful mind and intellect that I felt like an amoeba in comparison. My goal in life was to be as smart, as learned, and as successful as my father. But he'd set the bar so high that I didn't believe that was possible, so I didn't try very hard to grow up. I'm not blaming him at all for my being a "late bloomer" because he was simply being himself, a very exceptional human being.

When I returned to the house from my walk, I spent some time with my mother. Having a one-on-one talk with Didi was the most natural feeling in the world. One thing was different about this talk, though. There was an unspoken distance between us. I visualized a thick horizontal line with a thin line gradually splitting away from it starting when I went to college. For a long time the distance between the two lines was slight, but when I got drafted, it widened. Now that my immediate future would take me into a war, the line was veering away at a steeper angle. I was sad that the distance was increasing, but knew it was natural and right.

The week passed in a blur, but did allow me to unwind from eight straight months of military training. I needed the break. It helped to transition me from absorbing mode to acting mode. I looked forward to Fort Sill, but I was a bit apprehensive, too.

Learning is one thing; doing is something else entirely.

Chapter 8 – OJT; Les and Dora's Place

Two days was plenty of time to drive to Fort Sill, so I packed my duffel and a few changes of civvies, threw them into the trunk of my new Cougar XR-7 and headed southwest. I spent that night in a motel in southwest Missouri and reached Fort Sill after dark on Sunday evening. I checked in with the CQ and was assigned a bunk in a nearby brick barracks building.

I didn't like the arrangement. It was a large open room with metal bunk beds for a hundred men arranged in rows. It was chilly, spartan, dull, and tended to echo every little sound, including the snores of my barracks mates. Eventually, I fell asleep, but was aroused at 0545 by the yelling of the platoon sergeant.

At 0600 on the dot, I was standing in formation in front of the barracks. A bugler played reveille as the American flag was slowly raised to the top of the pole. Roll was called, and we walked informally to the mess hall. There was no yelling of service numbers, just a leisurely queuing up in the chow line and watching as the mess hall staff scooped the morning's fare onto plates. As always, the food was good: nothing fancy, but filling and very American.

After breakfast, I put things away in the footlocker at the foot of my bed and glanced out the window. *"Well that can't be,"* I thought. I'd driven through Oklahoma before and considered myself an expert on U.S. geography, but I didn't know of any mountains here.

As I looked long and hard toward the north, my platoon sergeant said, "Meet me downstairs in a few minutes, Sergeant Thompson. I'll escort you to your duty station and introduce you."

Crossing the street, we passed groups of soldiers wandering the areas around the buildings with small bags, policing the area for litter, debris, and cigarette butts—one of the menial tasks required daily by the military. We entered the headquarters of the 4th Battalion, 30th Infantry Regiment, and went up a flight of stairs.

I was ushered through a door to the front of a cluttered desk, and my guide said, "Sergeant Samuels, this is Sergeant Thompson, who's newly graduated from NCO Academy." He handed Samuels my orders. "He's all yours."

Master Sergeant Len Samuels was middle-aged and a bit thick in the waist, with a full head of gray hair. He had a somewhat harried but capable look, and an expression of long-suffering mixed with even-tempered kindliness. I was unsure what my job would be, but felt it would be all right.

Samuels looked up. "Welcome to Operations and Training, Sergeant. You can call me Len when we're here in the S-3 office. It's not practical to constantly use rank identifiers in a work environment."

"All right, Sergeant—I mean, Len," I said. I'd had military protocol drilled into my head and would have to modify it somewhat to operate in a non-training, everyday Army environment. "My name is Jamie."

"Jamie, I'm sure you know that Fort Sill is the Army's primary Artillery fort. The 4/30 is the only infantry unit here and exists to train the Artillery in the rudiments of infantry tactics."

"Thanks Len, I was wondering about that."

"As you saw on the door, this is the staff office for Operations and Training. We make sure day-to-day operations run smoothly, that all the battalion's operational needs—like vehicles, transportation, and every other thing imaginable—are met, and make certain that the unit's internal infantry training and external training for the Artillery are current."

I nodded.

"There's a plaque in the hall that gives our history. I suggest you read it. But for now, let me assign you a desk." Samuels rose and led me to a desk against the wall. "This will be your home for the next three months. Take some time to get oriented and read that plaque. I'll bring you your first assignment in a few minutes."

"Thanks ... Len." I settled into my desk chair and glanced around. Surrounding the desk were various and sundry books of Department of Defense and Army procurement and training regulations. A typewriter and plenty of pens and paper were on the desk. I got up and looked out the window. There, again, I could make out the rugged outline of what sure looked like a mountain range, poking above the distant horizon. I wandered down the hall and read the plaque. The 4/30 was a unit that had served with distinction since the time of the Philippine Insurrection in 1901, for which it received a Presidential Unit Citation. Through no fault of its own, the battalion had missed most combat actions since then, while the rest of the 30th Infantry Regiment had seen more than its share in both world wars. I returned to my desk just in time for Len to drop a handful of forms on my desk.

"Look through these and put together a list of all the items being requested," he said. "Bring it to me when you're done."

I did as he asked, but wondered why he'd need a list of requests when the forms *were* lists of requests. *Oh well, ours not to reason why...*

I began poring through the forms, which were requisitions from various subordinate units and offices for everything from boxes of chalk to tires to fuel. Just before lunch, I walked my list over to Samuels and asked him where he wanted them.

"In there is fine," he said, gesturing to the inbox on his desk. "Go get some chow. I'll see you back here at 1300 sharp."

"Yes, s—, I mean ... Len. See you then."

Near quitting time, which was 1630, I handed the next batch of files to Len.

"Thanks, Jamie. I'll look these over and get with you in the morning."

Kurt Stephan was just leaving his S-2 (Intelligence and Security) office, so we met up in the hallway and walked back to the barracks together.

"Kurt, what do you say we take a drive this weekend," I said. "We can explore the mountains north of the fort."

"Mountains? That could be fun. Okay," he replied.

The next morning, Len skimmed through the list I'd put together and tossed it in the wastebasket. "Now that you know what kinds of things we requisition, purchase, transport, and distribute," he said, grinning, "I'll teach you how we do those things."

I had already concluded that the list was Len's clever way of familiarizing me with the stuff we handled. And for the next two weeks, Len worked closely with me as I learned the ropes. Some items were in Army stockpiles scattered here, there, and everywhere around the country; others had to be purchased directly. The types of items and their costs determined whether we bought them from specific sources that had Army contracts or directly from the closest and least expensive source. It was complicated, but like most other things in the government, there were rules and SOPs for almost every situation.

I found out that the range to the north was called the Wichita Mountains and that a wildlife refuge of the same name bordered Fort Sill along most of its northern edge. On our first weekend, Kurt and I drove out the main gate, stopped for gas and got a map. We decided to drive north on the Interstate for a few miles and then take the Medicine Park exit to the wildlife refuge and the mountains.

While it certainly wasn't Arizona, I felt better just seeing mountains and better yet being in them. As we headed west from I-44 on Highway 49, the country quickly changed from sweeping grassland prairie to low, rocky hills, with short grass. Within a few miles, the mountains came fully into view. For several reasons they were strange and interesting to my eye. They were very rocky, but all the rock appeared to be the same pinkish color. Normally that would mean limestone or sandstone tinted with oxidized iron (rust). But these rocks were hard, jagged granite, not smooth and relatively soft like limestone or sandstone. Also, even though the mountains clearly weren't very high in altitude, in many places they had what looked like a tree line. As this was registering on my mind, we entered the tiny town of Medicine Park, Oklahoma.

It was ramshackle in appearance, so we decided to investigate the mountains first and come back later to look over the town. Just beyond the western edge of Medicine Park we passed the sign marking the boundary of the Wichita Mountains National Wildlife Refuge. A half-mile further and we saw our first buffalo. From there on we were typical tourists enjoying new discoveries. We turned north onto the Mount Scott Road and discovered that it made its way all the way to the top by spiraling completely around the mountain, something I'd never seen before… and haven't since. The view from the top, at an elevation of 2,464', is well worth the three-mile-drive. Stretching away to the northeast are the predominantly grass-covered Great Plains, with the large Lake Lawtonka Reservoir hugging the mountain's base on the east and north more than 1100 feet below. But the view from southwest to northwest is of the boulder strewn landscape of the ancient Wichita Mountains clothed in gnarled oak trees and peaks largely devoid of vegetation. A bit farther into the Refuge we saw several magnificent elk; today elk are thought of as forest animals, but their original range was mostly on the plains.

From close down below, the mountains looked a little less impressive than they had as we approached from the east partly because we were at a higher elevation, but mostly because we were looking up their relatively gradual southwestern slopes toward the tops, which gave the illusion that the mountains were lower than they were. There were several small reservoirs near the road, which we thought might be worth investigating further, but then again might not. After an hour or so we turned around and headed back to Medicine Park.

We were hungry by now and looked for a place to grab some food. Not finding any place in the town of Medicine Park proper, we stopped at a beer and burger joint just outside it called Les & Dora's Place. Inside, Kurt wandered over to the jukebox and I went to the bar and asked if we could get something to eat.

"Sure, how about burgers and fries?" the woman asked in a throaty Oklahoma twang.

"That would be great. Can we get a couple of beers, too?"

She looked at me and patiently said, as I'm sure she had many times before, "Under the law, I can't serve you anything alcoholic other than three-two beer unless you're a member of our club and have placed your own alcohol with us. If you do that, we keep your alcohol behind the bar and serve it to you for the price of service and whatever mixers we use. Is three-two beer okay?"

"That will be fine." I'd heard of similar laws, but hadn't been victimized by them before. "Say, how much does it cost to become a member of your club?"

"Ten bucks for a calendar year," she responded.

As the electric rotisserie oven warmed up our frozen burgers and fries, Kurt and I decided we'd join. I had a feeling we might spend quite a bit of time at Les & Dora's.

The next day we drove back to the mountains and checked out a couple of the reservoirs, ponds really, that we'd spotted the day before. Around three in the afternoon we stopped at Les & Dora's, bought memberships, and received cards good for one year from date of purchase.

During my first six weeks at Fort Sill, the office work was routine and rather monotonous. Fortunately, I did have some field duties. One involved acting as a vehicle commander for an armored personnel carrier, APC. This required me to wear a special helmet with earphones and microphone, and stand with my head and shoulders through the open hatch as the APC tore cross-country through woods, fields, and half-frozen streams. It was one of the exercises we put on for visiting brass and for civilians during open-house days. When the APC hit major bumps or dips—or otherwise left the ground—I thought I might be thrown out of the thing, but it was fun.

Many of the vehicles we managed were non-functional, either in part or in total. The Vietnam War had been raging for four years and vital components were in extremely short supply. In my APC, all the internal communications were down. Normally, the vehicle commander relayed information to the driver concerning obstacles, traffic, potential threats, and targets. But without any way to communicate, my sole function was to take up space and be seen looking like an APC commander. I performed that function to the letter.

Often, parts were scrounged from our vehicles and sent directly to the war. That was understandable, as far as it went. But it was unacceptable that we could never seem to get replacement parts. Despite that, we had to meet operational standards—at least on paper—even if it was impossible. It was a stupid game in which everyone understood what was going on, but no one would admit it for various reasons.

We were notified on Monday that a major motor pool inspection would be conducted by higher headquarters on Saturday. To pass, ninety percent of our vehicles had to be in working order. The reality was that only forty percent were marginally operational, and many couldn't even start because so many vital components had been cannibalized.

We spent the week planning how to pass the inspection with the stationary husks parked in our motor pool. We called in the mechanics and devised a plan we hoped would work. For every type of vehicle we had, we would make sure at least one was fully functional or at least appear to function. Then we would delay and maneuver the inspectors so we could take parts from the already inspected "functional" vehicles and install them in non-functional ones to at least get them to start before the inspectors examined them. Of course, the whole scheme would fail if the inspectors happened to ask for a test drive of the wrong vehicle. It was a nightmarish version of musical chairs.

All the sergeants from our staff offices were present, as were all the motor pool mechanics. We worked feverishly, out of view of the inspectors, to coordinate parts removals and installations in an unforgiving and tightly coordinated manner which also had to be flexible enough to adjust to unforeseen actions by the inspectors. In some ways it was the most complex military operation in which I ever participated.

The first tank started and was driven around for a bit and then parked back in its proper place. Next, a deuce-and-a-half (two-and-a-half-ton truck) was inspected. It was also started and driven. Then an APC was started, driven, and returned to its spot. Next, a jeep received the same treatment. When it was time for the second tank, the carburetor and fuel pump from the first tank were already installed, and it started and passed muster. Then another deuce-and-a-half passed, with its newly installed starter borrowed from the first, and so on. Luckily, the inspectors didn't ask to have any of our inoperable vehicles do more than start. By noon the inspection was over, we were exhausted, and most amazing of all, we passed. We felt good that the 4/30's reputation was intact, but bad about the crappy condition of our motor pool.

After the inspection, Kurt and I stopped at a liquor store to buy a quart of generic Vodka, a quart of J&B Scotch and a quart of Wild Turkey bourbon. Wild Turkey has the distinction of being 101 proof, as opposed to the eighty-six proof of 'normal' bourbon. We were determined to get our money's worth at Les & Dora's! That night we drove out to Medicine Park, handed our liquor over to Dora, who duly recorded the deposit, and drank much more than we should have. I found it interesting that so many Indian jokes made the rounds in a state heavily populated with Indians. At one point, I cautiously asked Dora about it. She said, "Hell, we're all at least part Indian, that's why it's okay for us to tell 'em." That made complete sense in an Oklahoma way.

Les came in around 7:00 and joined Dora behind the bar. After a bit, Dora said to the assembled customers, all six or eight of us, that she had news for us. "We want you guys to know that we're movin'."

"No!" blurted a local at the corner table.

"Oh, hell," said Dora, "it's not THAT kind of move! We bought that vacant building down the road a quarter-mile or so to the west and we're movin' the bar in there next week."

"Thank the Lord!" said the same local.

"Yeah, well, it's bigger, has better parking and even comes with a few outbuildings. It seemed like the right thing to do, so we're doin' it." Then she added, "If any of you wanna help us move, we're startin' Monday morning and we'll keep at it 'til we're done."

Kurt said, "I don't really remember seeing anything down the road that I'd actually call a building. Do you?"

"Nothing comes to mind," I said, "but I guess we should check it out before we head back to the fort tonight."

"Okay," said Kurt.

"Hey, you want to offer to help Les & Dora with the move?" I asked.

"Sure, as long as they understand that it'll have to be when we're off duty in the evenings and next weekend, if it isn't completed by then," said Kurt.

"Okay, I'll go tell 'em," I said, sliding my chair back.

I walked to the bar and made the offer to Dora.

She looked genuinely surprised, but quickly composed herself and said, "That's mighty nice of you boys. We appreciate it." Off to the side, Les nodded in agreement.

"Glad to help," I said with a smile. I think that might have been the beginning of a real friendship.

That night we drove west and spotted what we realized must be the new home of Les & Dora's Place. Set back a little in a grove of the stunted oaks common to the area, it was a clapboard structure, thirty to forty feet wide by forty to fifty feet deep, with a storage shed near the east side and small shack up a little slope out back. "Well, it is bigger," I volunteered.

"Yes," said Kurt.

The following Monday evening, we did help with the move, but Les and Dora, like most Oklahomans, were extremely self-reliant so there wasn't much help needed by the time we arrived on scene at around 6:00 p.m. We hauled maybe ten cases of three-two beer and a couple of cardboard boxes filled with liquor bottles for them and that was about it!

By Tuesday afternoon, the new "Les & Dora's Place" was up and running and even boasted a larger sign!

Three-two beer is called that because it has a lower alcohol content than regular beer, 3.2% or lower to be precise. In the sixties, there were a number of states, most or all in the Midwest and West, with laws on the books that restricted drinking in general or drinking by younger adults between eighteen and twenty-one (sometimes nineteen and twenty-one) to so-called "low point" beer, meaning 3.2% or less. Oklahoma was one of them. I think state legislatures, in their collective wisdom, thought that consuming low point beer would make it more difficult for people to become inebriated. From the personal experience of one who drank a lot of three-two beer between eighteen and twenty-one (and at twenty-five at Fort Sill) I know you can get every bit as drunk on three-two as you can on alcohol of any other strength.

Tuesday night Kurt and I helped christen the new Les & Dora's Place and reluctantly headed back to our barracks around 9:30 p.m. The following Friday night, I was surprised to see a waitress working there. Her teeth weren't completely straight, and she looked a little thin for my usual tastes, but she was a blonde (or passing as one), had mostly green hazel eyes, and a damn nice figure. She was a pretty gal who'd fallen on hard times and looked a little malnourished to me. Her name was Alba León, pronounced lay-own, and she definitely got my attention. I spent a lot of time talking to her and learned that she was from a small town in North Texas and that part of her pay was made up by Les and Dora letting her live in the shack out back.

The holidays were two weeks away and the 4/30 decided that to maintain proper staffing half the command could take leave at Christmas and the other half at New Years. Partly because we'd just gotten there, Kurt and I both decided to take New Years' leave. That's how we found ourselves hiking along a trickling stream in the Wichita Mountains on December 20th, 1969. It was sunny and eighty degrees that day, beautiful! The narrow canyon through which the stream flowed was only about fifty to seventy-five feet deep and 100' wide at the widest and thickly wooded with oaks and cedars. By this time, we were becoming familiar with some of the area's history. It was rumored that Frank and Jesse James had hidden some of the plunder from their biggest robbery, a Mexican gold shipment, in the Wichita Mountains while passing through the area on their return to Missouri. About half-way through the canyon I looked across the stream and noticed a hole in the opposite wall. It was about fifty feet above the canyon floor and about twenty feet below the rim; impossible to reach without climbing gear or at least a length of stout rope. We talked about what an ideal hiding place that would be for stolen loot, but then again that it might just be one of the many artefacts left by abortive attempts to find gold during the mini-gold rush that occurred just after the turn of the century. By all accounts, Frank James was one of those who fueled rumors of gold, either in its natural state or in the form of hidden coins and bars. There is little if any evidence of gold ever having been found in the Wichitas, but due to the rumors Frank James and others made a bundle by selling picks, shovels and other things needed by miners. We resolved to come back some day to check out that hole in the canyon wall.

After our hike, we drove to the Meers Store and Restaurant in Meers, Oklahoma. Meers is a crossroads just north of the wildlife refuge. Somebody had told us they made great hamburgers there and they were right about that. Like darn near every other structure in this part of Oklahoma, the Meers store appeared to have been built over many decades using whatever scrap lumber was available at the time. The interior walls were almost covered with newspaper clippings dating as far back as the late 1800s. These offered a wealth of local history and lore to those who took the time to read them, as Kurt and I did. But the hamburgers were wonderful: steaming hot, bleeding a little, and as big as dessert plates. I had only tasted burgers that good once before, at Bert's Bank

Tavern in my hometown of Barrington, Illinois. The aroma alone made full men feel starved.

When we left, we decided to take roads that made their way to Medicine Park around Lake Lawtonka rather than back through the mountains. When we'd gotten a few miles north of Meers we turned east and, looking off to the west, noticed how imposing the view of the Wichitas was from this angle, from their northeast side. Many high ranges in the Far West like the Colorado Rockies, Utah's Wasatch Range, and the California-Nevada Sierras have one side or the other that rises so steeply from their bases that these places are referred to as "fronts." Hence most of us have heard of the Sierra Front, The Front Range (Colorado's Rocky Mountain front), or the Wasatch Front east of Salt Lake City. I had neither contemplated nor ever heard of the Wichita Front, but such a designation would be apt, if it were used to describe the northeast face of the Wichita Mountains stretching approximate twenty miles to the northwest from Mt. Scott near Lake Lawtonka. It's true that in terms of elevation the Wichitas pale in comparison to those higher ranges, but when seen from the northeast the Wichitas look very impressive, indeed. This is because the Wichitas break off in a long escarpment on their northeast edge. In aerial view from above it looks almost like the teeth of a saw with the highest points near the points of the saw blade, and when seen from below the escarpment rises very steeply over a thousand feet from rolling prairie to rocky peaks. But the illusion of great height is amplified by the barren peaks. I learned later that this is because the Wichitas are what are called Granite Dome Mountains. These are formed when molten rock bulges upward from deep below the surface and is eventually exposed by eons of erosion. Debris and loose rock are constantly eroded down the sides of the granite bulges, but the rock remaining on the tops is so hard and impervious and so lacking in soil and nutrients that vegetation simply cannot take root there. The Wichita Mountains are relatively unknown outside Oklahoma, but are majestic, beautiful, unique, and worth seeing. Kurt and I enjoyed exploring them.

The following week, whenever I made it to Les and Dora's, I began to develop a friendship with Alba. She was a nice girl and I liked her. She didn't talk very much about herself, but I was able to discover that she had come to Lawton with a guy with whom she thought she could have a real relationship. He turned out to be uncaring and abusive, which deeply hurt her. I asked how she'd gotten away from him. She said, "One night, I told him I was pregnant. That's the last I ever saw of him and that was a couple of months ago."

I replied, "That was an effective way to handle it, all right. But it's sad, too."

"Yeah," she sighed, "but it's for the best."

Exactly a week after our hike, on Saturday, December 27th (coincidentally my father's fifty-third birthday) Kurt and I were scheduled to fly out of Oklahoma City for our eight-day New Years' leave. We began the drive up I-44 at about 9:00 a.m. The temperature was around thirty and there was a light freezing rain beginning to fall. The weather didn't look good, but nothing was going to stop us from getting away for our leave. When we'd gotten about forty miles up the Interstate the temperature had dropped into the mid-twenties, half an inch of ice coated everything: trees, overhead wires, the faces of road signs, and the road itself. Being from Minnesota and Northern Illinois respectively, we knew a thing or two about driving in winter weather, so we pressed on... carefully. I found that a speed of thirty-five to forty-five was about right to maintain steering control on the relatively straight highway, but whenever we approached other vehicles or entered curves, I slowed even more. The worst of the storm was about twenty miles southwest of Oklahoma City, where between one and two inches of ice coated everything. Luckily, my car's heater was just barely able to keep the windshield warm enough to allow the wipers to keep most of it clear, but we each still had to occasionally roll down our windows and reach around to lift and slap the wiper blades against the glass to break off ice or use our fingernails to scrape the ice dams away from the lower corners of the windshield. It was stressful, but we made it.

Kurt and I flew together to Chicago's O'Hare Field and then I left for home and he caught a connecting flight to the Twin Cities. We planned to meet again at O'Hare for the flight back to Oklahoma City the following Sunday. My mother picked me up outside the terminal near the baggage pick-up and we drove the twenty-five miles or so back to the house. The weather was typical for the time of year: raw, gray, humid, and bone-chilling. The ground was covered in over a foot of compressed snow from numerous storms, big and small. As we pulled through the narrow opening between two oak trees that marked the edge of our property and dipped down the small slope, I felt safe and like there was still much good in the world.

My father had been seeing a patient at home that afternoon and couldn't make the drive to O'Hare, but by now he was back in weekend form, wearing shorts and a T-shirt and just finishing up popping a very large bowl of popcorn using the antique popper with the crank handle on top that was his preferred way to do it. He gave me a brief hug as I walked through the kitchen and said, "Hello, son. I'll be in as soon as I pour the melted butter on the popcorn."

"That sounds great," I said, carefully swinging my duffel bag through our tiny and very crowded kitchen and carrying it upstairs to my room.

I remember very little about that leave at home, except that I was comfortable there. I suppose I must have gone to town a couple of times and said hello to people who knew me, but I honestly can't remember. My high school girlfriend and I had broken up about four years before, so I had no female friends I wanted to see. My "home" now consisted almost solely of my family and my family's house. My sister Mimi was there, but my sister Julie had visited over Christmas and had already returned to Lexington. For the most part I was left alone to relax, which was all I really wanted. The following Sunday, Kurt and I met up again at O'Hare, flew back to

Oklahoma City and drove back to the fort without anything exciting or interesting happening.

Chapter 9 – Butt Sergeant; Plane Planner

Monday morning, I was put in charge of the "police calls" around the 4th of the 30th HQ building for the week. Just after sunrise, I'd meet up with a group of about half a dozen Private E-3s with an occasional Private E-2 thrown into the mix. Each man was given a cloth sack and a long stick with a nail in one end. I'd spread the men out from the front of the building to the street and start them walking clockwise all the way around it. When we returned to the starting point, I'd dismiss them. As I usually tend to do, I took my responsibilities seriously and would point out missed cigarette butts and bits of candy or gum wrappers to the nearest troop who'd missed it on his walk. When I did such things, there were some occasional mutterings and sighs, but no open complaints. I made sure that the sand filled urns near the front and back doors were cleaned out of butts and debris, though these were not used all that much since you could smoke inside the building and there were ashtrays on the desks.

Thursday morning was particularly cold and raw. About halfway through the police call, I told Private Emory he missed a butt.

He turned on me and snapped, "Get it yourself!"

I said, "Excuse me?"

"I said pick it up it yourself!"

I looked at him and said, "You know, this duty isn't that hard, and it doesn't take long to do it, so you should just get on with it."

"You have no idea how hard this duty is," he said angrily.

"What do you mean?"

"You're just outta shake 'n bake school and ordering us around on this shit detail," he spat out.

"Yes, I'm a sergeant, and that's my job at the moment."

"Well, you got any idea how that makes us feel? All of us have done at least one tour in the Nam and a couple of us have done two. Most of us have less than three months left in the Army. Some of us only have a couple of weeks left. Some of *us* were sergeants, too, only we got busted for one dumbass reason or another. We've been through hell, and now some 'instant NCO' who's never done shit is ordering us to pick up cigarette butts. Jesus, man. It ain't right!"

I looked Emory square in the eye. "You're right. I had no idea how you felt about this. And you're right that it's not right." I paused and looked around. As I suspected, most of the men were watching us. "Emory, there isn't anything I can do to make this right. Hell, if there's one thing I've learned about the Army in the short time I've been in it, it's that 'fair' and 'right' and 'logical' are not high priorities. Accomplishing missions is the priority. All I can say is I hear you and agree with you, but I can't blow off the detail. We still have to police our area. But what I can do is care how you feel about it and be less of a stuffed shirt and more of a fellow soldier. Together we can all get through this," I added, bending down to pick up the butt Emory had missed.

These were good men who had done their time in hell and just wanted the nightmare to be over.

Emory didn't look mad anymore; he looked sad. "Thanks Sergeant ... for listening." He held out his hand to take the butt from me.

That was the last trouble I had on police calls.

That Friday night I stayed at Les and Dora's until closing time. I gave Kurt my car keys and he headed back to the fort, but Alba took my hand and led me to her shack. It had barely enough room for a queen bed and a small bathroom. It was cold in there, but she had a dog that was friendly and wanted to be in the bed with us.

I'm a cat person, not a dog lover. Cats do as they please with very little input from people, but dogs are as demanding as an insecure child. Alba's dog drove me nuts. Eventually I gave up trying to be intimate, rolled over, and lit a cigarette.

"What's the matter?" Alba said.

"Your dog."

"He's jest bein' affectionate."

"I know, but so am I, and one of us has to go. I mean, let's face it, this place isn't big enough for the three of us!"

"Oh, I s'pose yer raht," Alba muttered. "C'mon Snuggles. C'mere, boy." She coaxed him into the bathroom and closed the door.

"Now that's more like it," I said rolling over to envelop her as she climbed back under the sheets.

* * *

Between romping with Alba and the near-constant yipping and whimpering of poor Snuggles, I got darn little sleep that night. But I was curiously refreshed in the morning anyway!

Kurt showed up about 10:30 and we headed out to the mountains. He doesn't ask for lurid details about other guys' escapades with the fairer sex, and I appreciated it. So basically, our conversation about Alba amounted to: I like her, she has a pesky dog, and she got rid of a bad boyfriend by telling him she was pregnant.

We headed to a place I'd spotted on a topo map called Charon's Garden. It looked interesting to me. There was a prominent peak, Elk Mountain, that could be reached by climbing up a steep crack on its southwest slope. After some trial and error, we found our way to the right spot, a dirt and gravel turnaround in a boulder strewn open area just southwest of Treasure Lake, about a half mile from the base of the crack. Such cracks are common in the Wichitas; they're usually ten to twenty-five feet wide with steep smooth bottoms, perpendicular sides ten to fifty feet high, and are usually filled with boulders of various sizes.

The first quarter mile was almost straight north on an established foot trail of sorts that paralleled the intermittent stream that fed Treasure Lake. Then we split off from the trail to the northeast and for the next quarter mile went up through a saddle until we reached a point where two upper canyons bent upward to the east and the west. The crevice or crack I'd spotted on the topo map emptied into the west branch just a few hundred feet away.

When we reached the base of the crack, we could see that it was packed tight with boulders ranging in size from bowling balls to Volkswagen bugs to tractor trailers.

We looked at the jumble before us and then at each other. "Wha'd'ya think?" asked Kurt, "Can we climb through that?"

"I have to admit that it doesn't look like it. Yet another example of how topographic maps don't reveal all the details of the terrain they cover."

"You can say that again."

"Just another example of..." I started.

"Okay. Okay!" Kurt exclaimed abruptly.

I chuckled and said, "Well, nothing ventured, nothing gained. I don't see any other way to get to the top, do you?"

"Nope. Let's give it a try."

So off we went. Not only was the crack very steep, about thirty degrees or sixty percent, but most of the spaces between the boulders were just barely wide enough for us to scrape and slither through. We were also very concerned that the angle was so steep and the weight so great above us that our movements could cause the whole jammed up jumble of boulders to shift, crushing or trapping us. We talked little, and wasted no time in pulling and pushing our way through this boulder chute in the aptly named Charon's Garden. In Greek mythology, Charon (pronounced Karon) was the demon who ferried the dead across the River Styx. When in it, imagining that chute as a gateway to Hades wasn't much of a stretch.

At last we began to see daylight above us and finally pushed our way out of the narrowest part of the chute into an upper canyon about 200 feet wide and 200 feet deep. This wasn't as steep, only about a ten to fifteen percent slope, and had fewer and more widely spaced boulders strewn along its length. After what we'd just climbed through, this nearly quarter-mile stretch was a piece of cake. Eventually, we reached the very top of Elk Mountain, which was relatively flat and nearly as smooth as polished marble with little pock marks in it, many of which held water because there was no drainage at all. We took a break; I smoked a cigarette (Kurt was smarter and didn't smoke) and we surveyed the view. It was awesome! In every direction rocky promontories poked up to about the same level as where we were standing, about 2270'. We felt like we'd really done something!

When I finished my cigarette, I wandered a bit farther over the peak to its north edge and was very surprised to see some buildings and a parking lot with several vehicles in it located very close below us to the northeast.

"Hey Kurt, come look at this!" I think he was expecting to see a rock formation, or a deer, elk or buffalo when he came alongside, but he quickly adjusted when he looked down on the relative metropolis below.

"Well, that's unexpected."

"Yes, you could say that. But the climb up here was still memorable!"

"That it was!" he agreed with a smile.

I looked this up later and realized that what we were looking at was the Refuge Headquarters at the base of a wide draw half-a-mile away and 700 feet below us, but at the time it seemed much closer and took a bit of the edge off our achievement!

We made our way back down using a much gentler and relatively boulder free route through a draw on the peak's northwest slope. That way we rejoined the hiking rail without going back through the boulder chute. It was a half-mile longer, but a heck of a lot safer!

When we got to the car we were famished, so I drove to the Meers Store where we each consumed one of the huge burgers in record time. While there we read the back of our menus and more of the clippings on the walls to learn more about the history of the Wichitas. For me, being there was an adventure and I intended to soak up all I could about the area. I think Kurt felt much the same way. To this day, I think of the place with fondness and like the fact that it remains a little known natural and social enclave.

* * *

We made it to Les and Dora's around 6:00 p.m. and I spent the evening drinking beer and exchanging smiles with Alba. In a pattern that continued throughout our time at Fort Sill, Kurt and I probably put darn near as much money in the juke box as we spent buying our own alcohol. It had a wonderful mix of great stuff. Some of my favorites were "Wichita Lineman" and "Galveston" by Glen Campbell, "Ruby" by Kenny Rogers, "Honky Tonk Women" and "You Can't Always Get What You Want" by the Rolling Stones, and "Get Back" by the Beatles, but there were lots of other wonderful songs on there. Being Oklahoma, most tunes were country western. Neither Kurt nor I had ever listened to much country music before or paid much attention to who performed it. Even now I couldn't tell you which more traditional country songs were on Les and Dora's juke box or who sang them, but at the time we really listened to them... eventually. CW was the preferred genre for the locals, and they put in almost as many quarters as Kurt and I did. We began to realize that CW lyrics, most of which dealt with being broke or falling on hard times, or men who'd cheated on their women and destroyed good relationships, and women who were loose and broke the hearts of their men, were musical descriptions of everyday life in places like Oklahoma, the Ozarks and Appalachia... or at least the way people there perceived their lives to be. So for us, being from the Upper Midwest, the songs had so little relevance that our minds normally tuned them out, but for most of Les and Dora's customers they were plaintive tales of their world sprinkled with valuable life lessons.

That night I asked Alba if she could get off a little early so we could spend some time in her bed before I drove Kurt back to the fort at closing time. She arranged it. Les and Dora, especially Dora, were very understanding and flexible about such things.

Sunday, we didn't go to Les and Dora's. Instead we spent the afternoon in a large bar in Lawton that catered mostly to soldiers. We did that because Kurt wanted to watch the Superbowl and the place had what, in those days, passed for a big screen TV, probably a twenty-seven-incher, set high up on a wall. Kurt's Minnesota Vikings were playing the Kansas City Chiefs and he was about as excited as I'd ever seen him when we arrived at the bar and got a table with a good view of the TV. Despite Joe Namath's Jets winning Superbowl III the year before, the AFL was still automatically considered a major underdog to the NFL, so the Vikings were favored by almost two touchdowns.

There are three things I remember about that bar. It had a concrete trench to pee into in the men's room, it was packed to the onion with soldiers which wasn't the atmosphere I really wanted to be in when I was off post, and it was the scene of one of Kurt's biggest disappointments. The Kansas City Chiefs never trailed in the game and soundly beat the Vikings twenty-three to seven. For obvious reasons, I hadn't really paid attention to professional football in the 1969 season, but watching that game made me a lifelong fan of Len Dawson, the Chiefs' quarterback and MVP of Superbowl IV.

Kurt had told me about his roommate, a fellow Staff Sergeant named Kinzie. He'd done three tours in Vietnam and was suffering in relative silence as he waited impatiently to be allowed to return for a fourth. I only met the guy twice, but he was a scary dude. As I recall, he'd been a Sergeant First Class on at least two occasions, but had been busted back down to SSG or below both times; I was reminded of SFC Smith, the combat veteran sergeant in charge of the POW camp in AIT who was busted to Sergeant E-5. At first glance, Kinzie seemed kind of calm and reserved, but he had a hair trigger and was completely devoid of ethical qualms about inflicting limitless bodily harm if something set him off. Some of the stories he told Kurt were hair raising. He also tended to have awful nightmares that often woke him up yelling and sweating. He had warned Kurt never to wake him by touching him because he might reflexively strike out hard. We had to be very careful around him, especially Kurt. Something had broken inside him in the Nam. This was a warning we both took to heart.

* * *

In mid-January I received a new task from Len. I was put in charge of creating loading plans for military air transport planes. I took on my new assignment with indifference, as just another tiresome office task. The objective was to maximize the amount of materiel that could be loaded onto the two most common types of military cargo aircraft, C-123s and C-130s. I was given a detailed itemized list of what was to be included in each load and its weight and dimensions. It was vital that the loads be placed so that the center of gravity was kept within a specified area. It was also essential that each pallet and vehicle be loaded in the correct order.

It was tedious and frustrating. The loading plans were complex problems that couldn't be broken down readily into constituent parts. In 1970, computers weren't even rumors in the office environment, so I drew scale outlines of every pallet and wrote their weights inside the lines. Then I cut them out and kept positioning and repositioning them on scale drawings of the aircraft interiors. It soon became apparent that the problem was even more complex, because certain pallets or vehicles couldn't be moved past others inside the cargo hold due to space constraints. In short, it was a nightmare. But when I realized what the planes' missions were, it bothered me even more on a personal level.

During the previous five summers, mass events of racial unrest had occurred in many of the country's major cities. In 1965 a routine traffic stop resulted in a riot erupting in the Watts section of Los Angeles. It was nationally televised every night for a week. The police were unable to stop the anarchy and eventually the National Guard was called in to restore order. Similar riots erupted in New York, Philadelphia, Cleveland, Omaha, Newark, Detroit, Minneapolis, Chicago,

Washington, and Baltimore. There was a heightened level of concern and fear on the part of some in positions of authority.

I asked Len and he confirmed my intuition. These loading plans, while including cargo, weaponry, and ammunition normally deployed to war zones overseas were, in fact, intended for domestic use by National Guard and Regular Army units, should they be ordered to a U.S. city for riot control. The loads included APCs, tanks, machine guns, hand grenades, and tens of thousands of rounds of ammunition.

There were many claims as to the underlying causes for this nationwide turmoil, but in my opinion it boiled down to two main factors: extreme poverty and unemployment compounded by discriminatory policies and governmental indifference. I didn't think it was appropriate to send such heavily armed forces into domestic service. My heart was not on board with it.

An incident had occurred in the summer of 1966 that changed my view of race relations in the United States every bit as much as witnessing the Selma March on TV in 1965. In the summer of 1966, I worked as a temporary mail handler for the U.S. Postal Service at the Air Mail Post Office at Chicago's O'Hare Field. The work was much harder than it normally would have been because there was a national strike of airline workers that summer. This caused us, the Postal Workers, to have to physically enter every plane carrying mail through Chicago. We unloaded incoming and loaded outgoing mail. In between the loading and unloading, we performed our usual tasks of emptying all the incoming mail bags onto conveyor belts, sorting every piece of mail to place it in the correct outgoing bins, and then re-bagging the sorted mail for distribution to wherever in the country it needed to go next. I calculated that on one particularly busy night, I personally lifted and slung about 90,000 pounds of mail. An important reason we could keep up with all this was that the Air Mail Post Office had an excellent night shift supervisor; a tall, black man by the name of William Otis.

On July 12th, about a month into my tenure there, race riots erupted in Chicago and continued for several days. On the night of the 14th, things weren't running quite as smoothly, and I noticed that Mr. Otis wasn't there. My first thought was that I hoped he hadn't been hurt in the riots. I asked the substitute supervisor where William Otis was and he answered, "Oh, he's a major in the National Guard and he's been activated to put down the riots."

I'm ashamed to admit it, but such a possibility had never occurred to me. I realized in that instant, that despite all my best intentions and sincerely held beliefs, I was a product of my society and had prejudices I'd failed to recognize or guard against. I've certainly not been perfect in such matters since, but acknowledging my shortcomings when it comes to personal prejudices and assuring that I constantly behave in ways that suppress or eliminate them was assured from that moment.

After weeks of working on the loading plans off and on while performing my other duties, I finished a workable plan for the C-123s. I never finished the plan for the C-130s, but I left my work in a file folder for the next poor bastard to complete.

Chapter 10 – CQ and Leave

Sometime in February, I had CQ duty on a Friday night. This wasn't the first time I'd had the duty, so I knew what to expect. Mostly it was just sitting behind a large desk looking official, though sometimes I signed leave or transfer papers for troops leaving the fort. This Friday night was different.

Around 2230 my reverie was disturbed when a black man in his twenties walked through the door and said, "My name is James Walters, and you're looking for me."

I looked through the papers on my desk. "I think you're mistaken. I don't have any information concerning you."

"I went AWOL twenty-six months ago, and I'm here to turn myself in," he replied.

"So you've been AWOL for over two years?" To say I was surprised would be an understatement.

"Yes. I took off before Christmas in 1967. I got back from the Nam in November, and I just had to see my wife and son for Christmas. I knew it was wrong, but I couldn't help myself."

"I see. What was your rank?"

"Corporal," he answered, then stated his serial number.

"Corporal, please be seated. I'll contact the MPs and we'll proceed from there. If you don't mind my asking, why did you turn yourself in after all this time?"

"I'm tired of running and hiding. It's time to put this behind me, no matter how long that takes, and make a normal life for my family."

I called the MP office, explained the situation, and read Corporal Walters' name, rank, and serial number to the clerk on duty there. It was clear that this was as unusual a situation for the MPs as it was for me. The clerk told me he would get back to me right away and we hung up.

Walters was a little antsy. "Sergeant," he asked, "would it be all right if I go outside and say goodbye to my wife? She's in the car parked right out front."

I hesitated for a second. "Yes, but when I call you, get back inside quickly."

As he walked through the door, I half hoped he'd keep going. I couldn't imagine how difficult this must have been for him and his wife.

A few minutes later, an MP corporal arrived and asked for Walters. I walked to the door and motioned for Corporal Walters to come back in.

"What was he doing out there?" thundered the MP.

"He asked if he could say goodbye to his wife and I told him he could," I answered calmly.

"You can't just let fugitives wander around free like that," he roared. By this time Corporal Walters was back in the office.

"I let Corporal Walters go outside to say goodbye to his wife because he turned himself in and I wasn't worried about him taking off again," I responded rather loudly.

"All right, but I'll take charge of him now." Facing Walters, the MP pulled out a pair of handcuffs and said, "Turn around!"

"Wait a minute," I said. "There's no need for cuffs; the man came in of his own accord."

"The cuffs are SOP," the MP said defiantly.

"I don't care. Under these circumstances, this man should be treated with dignity."

"I can't do that!" the MP practically shouted at me.

"Then call someone who can. There's just no need to make this more difficult than it has to be."

"I have to follow Army procedures," he answered.

"Let me put it this way, you're a corporal and I'm a sergeant. And I'm ordering you not to put cuffs on this man. Is that clear?"

"Yes, it's clear. I'm gonna call my lieutenant."

"You can use the phone in the colonel's office." I pointed the way.

Ten minutes later a lieutenant, clearly unhappy at having his evening disturbed, walked in and introduced himself. I suggested we go into the colonel's office to discuss the situation. The three of us went in and closed the door. I let the MP corporal say his piece, and then I said mine.

"Lieutenant, I know you have a job to do and I respect that. But here we have a man who of his own volition walked into this office and turned himself in, knowing full well the seriousness of his offense. All of us, including Corporal Walters, know how unpleasant his next several years are likely to be. I see no reason to treat him like an escaped prisoner while you walk him right past his wife, who's sitting in her car out front already scared about what's going to happen."

The lieutenant looked at me for a few seconds. "All right. Corporal, get the prisoner on his feet and walk him to the guardhouse without handcuffs."

"Yes, sir," the corporal said.

About two hours later, when my adrenalin levels had returned to normal, I felt pretty good about that shift.

During my last six weeks at Fort Sill, I spent more and more time with Alba. I'd like to say I was in love with her, but that wouldn't be the truth. She was my most effective escape. I needed her badly, and she enjoyed having me around for much the same reason. As is usually the case for a woman, she faced the hopeless reality of our relationship before I did and acted on the knowledge.

On a Friday near the end of my OJT assignment, I drove to Les and Dora's as usual. Alba wasn't there. I asked Dora where she was.

"She up and quit."

"When?"

"This morning."

Feeling suddenly angry and empty, I asked, "Did she say why?"

"Well, today is pay day. All she said after she got her check was that it was time to move on. Then she thanked us, grabbed her suitcase and dog, and hitchhiked out of town."

"Jesus. Do you have any idea where she's going?"

"Nope, but if I hear anything I'll let you know."

I drank more than I should have and ended up sleeping alone in the shack behind Les and Dora's. Even though I was off duty that Saturday, I was supposed to be back in the barracks the next morning. I didn't even wake up until 10:30, so at that point, I decided to stay there and hope for the best. I helped Les move around some heavy stuff and drank coffee at the bar most of the day. Finally, around 4:30 I decided to head back to the fort to find out how much trouble I was in.

When I saw Kurt I said, "I hate to ask, but am I going to Leavenworth?"

"No," he said in that way he had of sometimes turning short syllables into long ones. "No one asked where you were, and I didn't volunteer."

"Wait, you mean no one even noticed I wasn't here?"

"That's about the size of it."

"Well, I'll be damned."

"Probably. But if you disappeared on a workday, you'd be in trouble."

As we headed to the mess hall, I told Kurt that Alba left without so much as a word.

Around this time, Kurt and I decided that we'd start our one-month, pre-Vietnam leave together by driving to Arizona. Kurt had never been there, and I thought of the place, especially Tucson, as my second home. So the plan was to spend the first week or two there and then go home for the last week or two.

Monday after work, I went out to Les and Dora's and learned that one of Dora's regulars had stopped at a roadside bar about five miles west of Cache and seen Alba working there as a waitress. I drove straight out and found the bar. I ordered a beer. When I paid for it I asked if Alba worked there. The bartender was reluctant to say, but I told him I was a friend and wanted to say hello.

"She's sick today, but she's out back in the silver trailer."

It was a little hard to see in the moonless darkness, nestled in a grove of trees, but I made my way to the door and knocked.

"Who is it?" asked a voice with a bad cold.

"It's Jamie."

"What do you want?"

"I just want to talk to you."

"Okay, but I'm really sick, so you can't stay."

Alba opened the door, holding her robe around her, and then got back in bed.

"I wish you'd told me you were planning to leave," I said.

"I didn't really plan it. It just seemed the right thing to do."

I leaned over her, with my face just inches above hers. "It really hurt me that you didn't say a word." Her breath had that "cold" smell to it, but I didn't care. I wanted to kiss her, and more, to dissolve into her.

She sensed that and said, "No. I don't want to make love with you."

I could tell she meant it, but couldn't understand why. "Alba, you've got to explain this to me. I had no idea you wanted to leave. What in the world happened? Why would you do that?"

She hesitated. Then she half whispered, "I'm pregnant."

In a nanosecond, I recalled how she got rid of her last boyfriend by telling him she was pregnant. I felt used and abused, like I'd been thrown away when she was finished with me.

I jumped up and pulled my coat on. "I should have *known* you'd pull something like this!" Walking out, I slammed the door shut behind me.

It wasn't until years later that I wondered whether she actually *had* been pregnant. Then I wondered if I'd gotten her pregnant or if she'd been pregnant when she told her previous boyfriend that she was. I felt like the uncaring jerk I should have felt like at the time. But in late February of 1970, right before my tour of duty in Vietnam, it never entered my mind. From the moment I walked out of her trailer, I shut Alba out of my life and my thoughts. It's one of the biggest regrets in my life. Several decades later I asked Dora if she knew anything about Alba and whether she'd had a child after I left Fort Sill. She said she'd heard that Alba had a daughter around that time, but didn't know what time of year the child was born and had no idea where Alba might be. So that was that.

On Wednesday of the last week in February, a sergeant I knew walked over to me at lunch and said under his breath, "I thought you might wanna know we got a request from the XO to process paperwork for an Article 15 on you."

"What the hell for?" I asked.

"The charge says your personal grooming doesn't conform to Army regulations. Namely, that your mustache is too long."

"Oh, for chrissake. I bet it originated from a certain MP corporal. The asshole!"

"I don't know about that. All we can see is that it came from HQ. But does it matter?"

"No, I suppose not. Now that I think about it, there have been a few comments about my mustache." Thinking quickly, I said, "Is there any way you can slow down the processing?"

With a devilish grin, he said, "As a matter of fact, such things often get misplaced and could take three or four days to be completed and sent back to HQ."

"You don't suppose it could be delayed until next Tuesday, do you?"

"That's longer than usual, but I'll do it if I can. No promises, though."

Later, I explained the situation to Kurt and told him that if he didn't mind, we should plan to sign out for our thirty-day leave just after midnight on Monday night.

"Here's the deal," I said. "The CO and the XO are never in their offices late at night, and our orders say our leave starts on Tuesday. So if we sign out at one minute past midnight Monday night—which we have every legal right to do—the CQ can sign our orders and we can leave the jurisdiction that authorized my Article 15 before the paperwork gets there. Brilliant, right?" I smiled.

Kurt looked doubtful. "I suppose we could do that, technically."

"Damn right, because 'technically' is what matters!"

Monday was our last day at work. Right at midnight we strode into the HQ and handed the CQ our leave papers.

He looked unsure. "I don't know if I can do this."

"Sure, you can," I said with a broad smile. "Our leave papers authorize our leave to begin on the third. And it is the morning of the third, so it's absolutely okay. Heck, I'd do it if I were on CQ."

"I guess," he muttered as he signed and stamped the papers.

As we left Fort Sill, I felt a sense of relief that wasn't just about the Article 15. It was time to move on, literally.

We drove through the night and around mid-morning Kurt said, "How are you doing? I got a couple hours sleep, so if you need me to I can drive."

"I'm okay so far, but I'll definitely let you know."

Around 7:00 p.m. we pulled up in front of my old shared house on Euclid Avenue in Tucson. I introduced Kurt to everyone and then we left to eat. After we gorged ourselves on burgers and fries, we went to the Green Dolphin Bar for beer.

It was about 10:30 p.m. when I said, "Hey, why don't we go down to Nogales?"

"Why? What's so special there?" asked a tired and dubious Kurt.

"Well, it's got a red-light district and even if we decide not to partake, it's like stepping back in time."

"Man, I don't know; I'm beat. Bed sounds pretty darn good to me," said Kurt.

"Aw, hell. It'll be fun. C'mon, let's go!"

About halfway to the Mexican border, around midnight, loud insistent honking woke me just in time to see the cab of an eighteen-wheeler rolling over the front left corner of my engine compartment. My car scraped along the underside of the truck's cab, and I guided it, scraping and screeching, to the shoulder of the road. I immediately looked over at Kurt, who wasn't moving and appeared to be snoring a little.

I shook him urgently. "Are you okay?"

Groggily opening his eyes, he muttered, "Why wouldn't I be?"

"Because we just had a near head-on collision with a semi, that's why."

"Jesus!" said a now awake Kurt.

"Yeah, I know. Listen, stay in the car. I'll talk to the truck driver and make sure he's okay."

I felt sober and alert as I walked alongside the truck and met up with the driver as he climbed out of the cab.

"God, are you all right?" he asked.

"It's a miracle, but yes, we're both okay."

"Your friend must be drunk as a skunk! I honked and flashed my lights and he just kept veering into my lane."

"I believe you, but my friend wasn't driving. I was."

"Nah, don't protect him. What he did was damn serious."

"You're right, it's damned serious, but really, I was driving. I must have fallen asleep."

"Whatever you say," he said, still skeptical. "I radioed my dispatcher, and he'll get the cops here as soon as possible."

"Good," I said. "I'll go back and wait in the car."

About twenty minutes later an Arizona Highway Patrol officer arrived at the scene. After a lengthy discussion, showing IDs and proof of insurance, filling out some forms, explaining about our leave, and showing him my leave papers, he cited me for reckless driving. It could have been far worse. He clearly cut us some slack because he knew we'd be in Vietnam in a month. Once he got all the information he needed from the truck driver and called the wreckers, he drove Kurt and me back to Tucson. It was not my finest hour.

I called my parents the next morning and fudged the truth by telling them I'd fallen asleep at the wheel on the long drive from Fort Sill. They were upset, but mostly concerned about us. I assured them we were fine and that I'd be flying home after my appearance in traffic court. My father arranged for the Cougar to be towed to a repair shop in Phoenix from the Tucson impound yard. When I visited the auto repair place and saw the condition of that Cougar, I fully realized how lucky we'd been to survive the crash.

I admitted responsibility at the court appearance. The judge fined me fifty dollars and ordered me to pay for repairs to the damaged eighteen-wheeler. Surprisingly, the only damage to the truck was the loss of a gas tank strap my car had torn loose from the frame.

I stayed with my old roommates for the next week and met a girl named Julie Morse. Julie was a very nice girl, a freshman at the U of A. Of course, a real romantic relationship was out of the question. And frankly, she was both too young and too intellectually mature for me. But she was a wonderful companion and arm's length friend.

To my relief, I was greeted with warm hugs after flying home. Little was said about the accident, though it hung in the air whenever my father and I were alone together.

Chapter 11 – Leaving the World

Following an uneventful flight to San Francisco on April 1, 1970, I was transported by Army bus to the Oakland Army Base, where I met up with Kurt again. We were issued our first jungle fatigues, given sketchy maps of the base, and told to be in formation at 0700 the next morning. We changed into our fatigues—solid olive drab with deep baggy pockets in the jacket-like blouse and along the outsides of the thighs.

Pinching at a sleeve of his new jungle fatigues, Kurt said, "I strongly suspect that the real reason the Army requires us to wear these here is to discourage us from going over the hill. We'd stand out like sore thumbs outside the base."

"You're probably right. I guess we're stuck here for a couple of days."

For reasons that weren't at all clear at the time, there were seven to nine thousand soldiers at the base, instead of the normal one to three thousand. It takes time to process a soldier in transit, so our stay was much longer than the usual couple of days. By the end of our second day we'd established a pattern.

Every morning began with a huge formation at 0700. We were organized into blocks of 500 soldiers, and a senior sergeant used a bullhorn to call the name of every soldier, waiting for a reply before moving on to the next name. Following that process, information and special instructions were shared.

On one morning, IRS forms were handed out. In less than ten minutes we had each filed a federal tax return for calendar year 1969—or submitted a placeholder due to the exigencies of active military service. I was reminded of Benjamin Franklin's timeless saying that nothing is certain, except death and taxes. In our circumstances, both were in play.

In the evenings, we headed to the NCO club, which was big and bustling. Usually we were accompanied by Kurt's bunkmate Hal, even though he was a Mormon who never touched a drop of alcohol. He was as bored as we were and enjoyed coming along to observe the wildlife. He sipped soft drinks, while Kurt and I slugged down tap beers. We enjoyed his company and respected his religious beliefs but goaded him periodically about his abstinence.

"C'mon Hal, what's one beer gonna hurt?" I'd urge.

"Nope. I wouldn't feel right about it."

By the third night I could tell he was wavering. He'd seen that we were having as much fun as it was possible to have in our situation. He also knew that neither Kurt nor I were the devil incarnate.

I said, "Hal, you've never had even a taste of alcohol in your life. Is that right?"

"Yes," he answered simply.

"Well, don't ya think you oughta see what it is you're supposed to be avoiding? I mean, shouldn't you know your enemy, have at least an inkling of what it's all about?"

Hal hesitated. Kurt and I exchanged smiling hopeful glances.

"That does make a certain amount of sense," he said. There was another hesitation, then he said, "I'm gonna do it. Just one beer, though."

I called over our favorite barmaid, Angela. "Can you please bring this gentleman a draft on me?"

"Are you sure you want to do that, Hal?" she asked him.

"Yep. I'm gonna give it a try," he said with resolve. "But just one."

"All right," said Angela. "Comin' right up."

Hal took a tentative sip of his beer and found he liked the taste. He sipped it for the next half hour, but then a strange thing happened. Hal motioned Angela over. "We need another round here, and it's on me."

She raised an eyebrow, but said, "Right away."

Kurt and I looked at one another, but didn't say a word. Twenty minutes later Hal was quite drunk. He still had a swallow of beer, but we decided he'd had enough.

Kurt said, "Come on Hal, let's call it a night."

"Are ya shur?" Hal slurred.

"Yep, it's late," Kurt lied, "and we've got to get up for that darn formation in the morning."

"Yeah, I gesh sho," said Hal.

As we stood up, Angela glanced over and said, "You're doing the right thing."

I took one of Hal's arms as Kurt took the other. We steered him to bed and made sure he was asleep before walking back to the club, which wouldn't close for a couple of hours.

"I feel kind of bad about this," I said to Kurt.

"I know, but it'll be all right. Hal's a tough cookie and a really good guy. He'll learn from it and probably won't have another drink for the rest of his life."

I spent the rest of the evening flirting with Angela. God, I was horny. And there wasn't a damn thing I could do about it, restricted to the base as we were. But I just kept being my normal self anyway, despite the hopeless circumstances.

The next afternoon I read in the paper about a place called Fire Support Base Illingworth in Vietnam, which had been attacked on the night of April 1. Two dozen Americans were killed and over fifty wounded, but they'd managed to hold the base against an enemy force estimated at 400 NVA regulars. There was something ominous and personal about that story to me, something I could feel, but not touch.

That evening, Kurt and I sipped beers, nibbled on chips, and wondered aloud how long we'd be in this purgatory—halfway between the U.S. and Vietnam, peace and war, heaven and hell. Hal had politely declined to accompany us, and I still felt guilty.

On the night of the 5th, I flirted a lot with Angela and she seemed more receptive. It crossed my mind that it could be because she knew we weren't going to be there much longer. Anyway, I arranged to walk her to the bus stop at the main gate when the place closed that night.

As we walked out at closing, Kurt headed back to the barracks and I walked Angela slowly to the gate. It was a little past 2300 when we reached it. There was a single MP on guard duty there. Angela had Monday and Tuesday off and I was very sad at the prospect of maybe never seeing her again. I didn't want my time with her to end yet. The bus stop was a bench just outside the gate and about thirty feet to the right. The MP prevented me from walking Angela to the bench because it was outside the fence and I didn't have authorization to leave the base. I pleaded with him, that I'd be "just outside the gate," that he could "see me from your position," etc., etc.

To my surprise, young love won the day and against his better judgment, he said, "Okay, Sergeant. But don't go any farther from the gate and come right back when her bus leaves."

"I won't," I said with real gratitude in my heart.

So, Angela and I walked through the gate and sat together on that lonely bench. No one else was in sight, except a few cabs lined up across the street pointing in the opposite direction. We held hands and talked for nearly twenty minutes. At some point, I put my arm around her and eventually we kissed. It was warm and soft, comforting and compassionate. Suddenly, I decided that I just couldn't end things this way. I really LIKED Angela; she was kind, and pretty and just as lonely as I was. We needed each other.

With no preamble, I suddenly stood up, took her by the hand and said, "Come on!" urgently under my breath so as not to alert the MP. We ran hand-in-hand across the street and got into the back seat of the first cab in line. The driver folded the newspaper he'd been reading, placed it on the seat next to him, and said in a completely unconcerned tone of voice, "Where to?" I was amazed at how normal the situation seemed to be, even though I was more than a little shocked at my impulsive action and worried about the potential for bad consequences.

Angela told him her address and we were off. I didn't look back to see whether the MP had reacted or not. I didn't want to know.

Her apartment was across town. I felt awkward, but she took my hand and led me to her bedroom and nature took its course. We talked off and on for several hours. She was a sweet, kind person who needed me that night as I needed her. It was right. Finally, at around 2:30 in the morning we fell asleep in each other's arms.

Her head was still on my shoulder when her alarm woke us at 6:30. I knew that there was no way for me to get back to the base before the morning formation, so I hoped Kurt would cover for me. After breakfast, Angela and I turned our thoughts to getting me back on base without getting arrested by the MPs.

Angela did have a car thank heavens, so we could use that to get back. It then occurred to me that if I sat in the back seat, close to the left side – the side where the gate guard would be standing, and wore a civilian shirt over my army one, I might be able to pass through without any notice. Once inside, I could pull off the civilian shirt and immediately be back in uniform and then we could find someplace where I could exit the car unnoticed and walk back to my barracks. My greatest fear was that my name had been called for a flight to Vietnam at this morning's formation. If it had, there'd be hell to pay… or I'd have to come up with another plan for that!

As it turned out, she had a man's shirt that fit me loosely and everything went like clockwork. We drove around inside Oakland Army Base for more than twenty minutes, talking and holding hands, we both knew we'd never see each other again. There was a poignancy in the air as Angela gave me her full name and all her contact information and I gave her my name and home address. As I got out of her car in a deserted area behind some warehouses, she looked up at me with sad eyes and said, "Keep safe."

"You, too!" I replied with a smile. I hope her life turned out well, she was a good person.

Kurt, bless his heart, had covered for me by answering "Present" when my name was called in formation. The next day we received our orders, and the following morning at 0600 we packed our duffels and boarded buses. Since our names were close alphabetically, Kurt and I were assigned to the same bus, which drove us north to Travis Air Force Base. As we rode, the patchy fog and low-hanging mists gradually cleared.

In a little over an hour, we were boarding a Pan Am jet. I was surprised. I'd expected a flying version of the cattle trucks used to haul us around at Basic, but this was a normal passenger jet with flight attendants who served meals and brought magazines for us to read. The only differences—aside from our destination—were that no alcohol was served and two of the flight attendants were men.

We had an hour layover at the Honolulu airport, where we could deplane and wander around. Neither Kurt nor I had ever been to Hawaii, but we knew Pearl Harbor was nearby and recognized Diamond Head through the plane's window. Kurt and I found a shop that sold just about every kind of hard liquor you can imagine in those little bottles you normally purchase in-flight. Since we knew we couldn't buy booze on the plane, we stocked up on those little babies, about ten bottles each, transferring them to our deep thigh pockets in the nearest restroom. The shop had wrapped each one in paper, so they didn't clink around when we got back on the plane. We ordered lots of soft drinks throughout the flight and surreptitiously spiked them with appropriate choices from our variety of clandestine ingredients.

I was fascinated with the view from 37,000 feet. I thought I knew how big the Pacific Ocean was, but when I stared at it from that great height and saw no sign of human activity from horizon to horizon for hours at a time, its true immensity registered.

Our next stop would be Wake Island. Wake is a tiny hollow arrow-point of corral rising a few feet above the ocean surface. It was claimed by the United States as "empty territory" at the end of the nineteenth century and officially became a U.S. possession in 1898 when its status as a U.S. possession was included in the Treaty of Paris that ended the Spanish-American War. Its importance increased in 1935, when Pan Am developed it for use as a rest and refueling stop for its first commercial trans-Pacific flights to China, their famed China Clippers. Only in 1941, in belated response to Japanese expansionism, did the U.S. government decide to establish a military garrison there, but it was undermanned and poorly armed.

About half-way between Honolulu and Wake Island, I turned to Kurt and said, "Do you think we'll be cowards?"

"Damned if I know," he answered, taking another sip, "but somehow I doubt it."

"I don't know either, but we're about to find out," I muttered clinking my soda can against his.

On our approach to Wake, Kurt and I saw nothing but water as the plane dropped lower and lower. Neither of us said anything because we'd long since been conditioned to trust the judgment and skill of commercial aircraft pilots... but we were inwardly concerned. We didn't see any land until after the wheels touched down, but to our great relief we did land safely on terra firma.

At Wake, we again deplaned for an hour or so. The terminal building was a plain white rectangle, with enough chairs for maybe one plane load of passengers and a separate smaller room with a ticket counter. On the wall opposite the counter was a large framed list of all the military and civilian personnel killed in the Battle of Wake Island, December 8-23, 1941, and during the subsequent Japanese occupation, which ended September 4, 1945. I stood there reading the plaque and all the names on it and again felt that I was literally following the footsteps of our World War II veterans. It was a sobering moment. Were we being sent to complete a task left unfinished by our fathers and uncles?

Kurt and I bought sodas from a vending machine and loitered around, mostly inside the terminal building because it was as hot as Hades outside. Holding my can of Coke up, I muttered to Kurt, "You know, before the Army I never in my life called these things "sodas."

"You didn't?" He asked skeptically.

"Nope. Never."

"Well, what did you call them?"

"Whatever they were: Pepsi, Coke, 7-Up, root beer, ginger ale or, if I was referring to them as a group, soft drinks. In fact, I'd never heard anyone call 'em sodas. But I'm used to it now and probably doomed to keep using that term for the rest of my life!"

"Yep, you're doomed all right, but it has very little to do with what you call these," Kurt answered hoisting his 7-Up. We both chuckled at that! Before we knew it, we were taking off from Wake Island.

Many hours later, we landed at Clark Air Force Base in the Philippines, yet another place taken by the Japanese. The large airfield was surrounded by conical mountains that were obviously volcanoes. The mountains were clothed in deep green jungle from base to top and when we stepped off the plane it was even hotter than it had been on Wake, though not by much. Clark was a large base with a large terminal and cafeteria. We were served a late lunch there and then took off once again.

As the sky finally darkened outside the plane, I turned to Kurt, "We raced the sun all day and finally lost." We'd stood in our last formation at Oakland Army Base almost an hour after sunrise and our journey across the Pacific had been in daylight for twenty-five hours. The pilot came on the intercom and said, "We'll be entering Vietnam airspace in half an hour and have been advised that conditions at Bien Hoa are white."

"You s'pose that's good?" I asked.

"Hell, if I know. Let's hope so."

A bit later, the pilot came back on and said, "We're entering the War Zone now and the cabin lights will be dimmed."

There was very little talk. A few minutes later I noticed dim flashes ahead. I assumed they were thunderstorms, but as we got closer I realized the flashes were explosions—artillery, bombs, and even gunfire. As we got closer still and our elevation dropped, you could see that the flashes were mostly concentrated around widely scattered, roughly circular areas which we realized were likely American bases.

The plane landed smoothly and taxied to a stop.

"Please remain seated for the customs inspection."

"Huh?" I exclaimed. "You gotta be kiddin' me!"

But it wasn't a joke. The plane door opened, and a blast of superheated, steamy air flooded the plane. The heat was shocking. A handful of Vietnamese officials entered and asked each of us if we were bringing in any weapons or alcohol. Kurt and I had finished our last bottles of booze an hour earlier and chucked all the bottles into the restroom wastebasket chute. Numerous forms were duly filled in and checked, and we were allowed to deplane.

We reclaimed our duffels, and sat in rows of stadium-like seats in the terminal, awaiting whatever came next. A few minutes later we were ushered onto buses. Vietnamese civilian workers packed our duffel bags into the luggage compartments. For the first time, I heard Vietnamese being spoken. It didn't sound like a human language to me; it sounded more like a large flock of songbirds singing over each other. It was beautiful, but so foreign that I found it disconcerting—more proof that I wasn't even on the same side of the planet as Kansas anymore.

The buses hustled us from Bien Hoa Airfield to nearby Long Binh Army Base, together they comprised the largest U.S. military base on earth in 1970. It was so large the enemy had few weapons with ranges great enough to reach its center. After a short ride, we were unloaded at the 90th Replacement Battalion.

Our bunks were in a sprawling building with screened windows, but no air conditioning. It was hot and we were unsettled, like human versions of cattle being shunted through chutes on their way to the slaughterhouse. But we were also bone-tired, so we slept surprisingly well.

The next morning we learned we were required to take anti-malaria pills every day, starting immediately. One of my uncles contracted malaria in World War II and was still plagued by recurring bouts that rendered him feverish, delirious, and bedridden for days at a time. I'd seen the intensity of his suffering, so I never missed a dose.

Rumors were rampant in the 90th Replacement Battalion, and since we'd never been in Vietnam or any war zone before, we eagerly soaked them up—as a man dying of thirst might welcome the bitter water drops squeezed from a cactus. We knew nothing, but imagined a lot. One thing that was universally accepted was that no one wanted to be sent to Phu Bai. It was reputedly the most dangerous place in Vietnam.

We spent our days going on mock patrols in the sparsely wooded areas on the fringes of Long Binh. I admit to being quite alert. I wasn't sure how "mock" these patrols really were, but they did get us more acclimated to the heat and some of the jargon. We also attended orientation classes.

In the evenings, we went to movies, and of course we read *Stars & Stripes Pacific*—the military's newspaper for active duty troops—and kept an eye on the bulletin boards that listed our assignments.

On several nights, I was issued an M16 with two bandoliers of ammunition and assigned to four hours of perimeter guard duty in one of the large, rather widely separated bunkers (maybe fifty meters apart).

The guard bunkers were embedded in the ten-foot-high berm that encircled the base. Beyond the bunkers, mines, concertina wire (coils of sharp barbed wire), and trip flares surrounded the base for several hundred yards. Each bunker had an array of Claymore mines spread out in an arc in front of it.

Claymores are shaped like little car windshields, about four by eight inches in size. They're made of green plastic and have the words "Front toward Enemy" molded into their convex sides. Inside the mine is a layer of C-4 plastic explosive with steel balls pushed into it. Two pairs of folding metal legs allowed the mine to stand up on edge, facing the direction from which the enemy was expected to attack. In the top of the mine, a plug could be unscrewed, allowing a blasting cap to be placed inside with a wire protruding through its top. The plug was screwed back in place and the wire was uncoiled back to the guard position. Inside the bunker, the wire was fastened to a clacker—a green plastic device resembling a carpenter's stapler. When the handle of the clacker was squeezed, it generated an electrical charge that travelled down the wire detonating the blasting cap and mine.

Inside the bunker, clackers were arranged in an arc from left to right, corresponding to the position of the mines in front of the bunker. Each bunker's mines were carefully arrayed so that their fields of fire overlapped with those from the neighboring bunkers on both flanks. There's no doubt that Claymores are an effective deterrent to enemy attack, but timing is important, because once they're blown, the remaining defense consists of the men in the bunkers and their personal weapons.

On our sixth day in the replacement battalion, Kurt and I were assigned to the 5th Battalion, 7th Regiment, 1st Cavalry Division AM (Air Mobile) in Tay Ninh. We thanked fate that we hadn't been assigned to Phu Bai.

Ignorance was bliss then.

Chapter 12 – Tay Ninh

The next morning after chow, we were transported on a C-130 cargo aircraft to Tay Ninh. C-130s were not laid out with passenger comfort in mind. A web bench along the sides of the aircraft allowed troops to sit as they would on a hammock and hold onto the webbing lining the fuselage wall behind it. As we flew, the scenery changed from urban to agricultural to lightly scattered farms and villages to undeveloped jungle. We landed and reported for duty at battalion HQ.

"Welcome to the First Cav," said First Sergeant Horace Winter.

"Thank you, First Sergeant," we said in unison.

"Okay, the first thing is just call me 'Top' from now on. Got it?" We nodded. Top then went on. "Staff Sergeant Stephan, you've been assigned to Alpha Company and will be flown out tomorrow morning at 0730."

"Yes, Top," Kurt said in his calm, matter of fact way.

"Sergeant Thompson, you're assigned to Charlie Company, but can't be flown out for a couple days. Right now I want you both to go with my clerk, Corporal Simmons here, to store your personal items and get issued your weapons and gear. Just before you leave Tay Ninh, I'll give you the orders you need to report to your field units. Dis-missed!"

We picked up our duffels and followed Simmons to S-4 Supply, where he handed us over to a private behind a counter.

"These are sergeants Stephan and Thompson," Simmons said. "They're heading to the field for the first time, so they need the whole FNG package."

"Okay, you each get a pack frame and backpack, two canteens with covers, one canteen cup, one set of steel field utensils, four collapsible two-quart canteens, one M16A1 weapon, two bandoliers and fifteen M16 magazines, which you can load just outside," the private said as he placed a steel ammo box on the counter. "You also get a bottle of bug juice, a bottle of water purification tablets, a first aid kit, one helmet and helmet liner, one camouflage helmet cover, one elastic helmet band, one poncho, one poncho liner, one mosquito net, twenty yards of nylon cord, one inflatable air mattress, socks, t-shirts, skivvies, one bayonet with sheath, one entrenching tool with carrier, and one web belt." He took a breath and continued. "First, let's issue your weapons, because these are accountable and have to be documented by serial number and signed for."

The private took us to an area of the heavily sandbagged wood-frame building where hundreds of M16s stood on racks. "Pick out one you like, and we'll make it yours."

As I worked the bolts and checked the forward assist assemblies, I said, "Say, Private, what does FNG mean?"

He chuckled. "It means fuckin' new guy, but don't take it personally. Damn near every one of us started here as an FNG. I can't tell you when it'll happen, but I guarantee you'll wake up one morning and know beyond a doubt that you're not an FNG anymore. With me it happened in my third month with an AK round in a butt cheek. Hell, that's how I ended up doing this," he said, waving his arms around the weapons room. "I was kinda surprised, but knowing Army logic, I s'pose I should've known they'd reassign me to a rear job since I couldn't sit down."

Kurt and I both laughed. Kurt said. "Given the graduation requirements, I think we can handle being FNGs for a while."

We loaded our weapons and magazines, fastened our backpacks to their frames, and managed to stow everything into or onto our packs. We reported back to the HQ and Top walked us down to the eastern perimeter, which was only about 250 meters away. He led us to one of the sleeping bunkers and told us to find empty bunks. The bunkers were fifteen feet square and had eight bunk beds lining the walls, room for sixteen men to sleep inside. The only way in—and the only place air could get in—was a narrow sandbag stairwell with a ninety-degree turn. The sleeping area was below ground level. It was stuffy and hot. We dumped our gear on bunks and went back outside where Top waited for us.

"Top, what's that mountain over there?" I asked, pointing to the lone mountain just a few miles northeast, directly in front of the bunker.

"It's Nui Ba Den—Black Virgin Mountain. We have a base on top, but the whole damn mountain is riddled with tunnels controlled by the gooks," he said, using the slang term for NVA and VC. "Every once in a while, they bring out some mortars and drop a few rounds on us."

"That's a pretty impressive little mountain to be all by itself like it is," I said.

"Yeah," said Top, "It's over three thousand feet from base to top. It'd be damn nice if we could get the bastards cleared out, but so far nothing's gotten the job done." As he led the way back toward the HQ, he said, "It's supper time, so let's get you some chow."

We entered a wood-frame building that smelled like food and got in the chow line. Top went with us and we all sat. Top wasn't the most conversational of guys, but he extended the hand of friendship to us and we appreciated it. He told us we'd probably run into some grunts who resented that we'd gained our ranks so fast through NCO school.

"For some," he said, "the jury's still out when it comes to whether shake 'n bakes are real NCOs and deserve their rank. I want you to be aware of that, but I also want you to know I'm not one of those who doubts. I've been impressed with the caliber of service NCO school graduates have given. This is a hell of a war, gentlemen. It takes guts, smarts, and people skills to make it and to get the men under you through it. Never forget that you *are* NCOs and deserve the respect that goes with the rank, no matter what anyone might think about how you got it."

"Thanks, Top," I said.

"Have you two known each other long?" Top asked.

"We were in the same platoon in NCO school and the same headquarters in OJT," Kurt said. "So yes, we've known each other for a while; long enough to take each other's measure."

"I thought that might be the case. It's unusual in today's Army, but probably because your last names are so close alphabetically."

"That's what we thought," I said.

"Well, first you need to understand that there's a much greater need right now for "straight-leg" infantrymen than for operations and intelligence NCOs, so you'll be "grunts" in line companies in the bush and won't see each other much from here on," Top told us. "The way field tactics work, the same two companies aren't often in the same place at the same time. I suggest you make your way to the NCO-EM Club and have a last night of fun together."

When we left, Top pointed north up the track and said, "The NCO-EM Club is a couple of hundred meters up there and opens up at 1800. In the meantime," Top added, "there won't be any more training here while you wait. You also won't be pulling guard 'til you join your units, 'cause we only want experienced guys on the perimeter. So just try to relax and stay safe. Your time is your own 'til you leave for the field." Then he turned and headed back for the HQ.

"Thanks Top," said Kurt.

That night Kurt and I went to the NCO-EM Club. It was a hole in the wall, but it had a jukebox, booze and beer. "What kind of beer do you have?" I asked the corporal tending bar. "We have Black Label in closed cans and Black Label in open cans. What can I get you?"

"Hmm. I think I'll have a closed can. How 'bout you, Kurt?"

"Yeah, sounds good."

"Two closed cans, please."

"Comin' right up!"

We spent four hours drinking there, so the place served its purpose. Neither of us felt like it was goodbye forever.

"What do you think?" asked Kurt when we had a good buzz going.

"You mean about going to the field or the whole damn thing?"

"The whole thing, I guess."

"I don't know enough to know what the hell I think," I said. "I mean, I know it's hotter than Hell here, that it's going to be the experience of a lifetime—but hopefully not the last—and I know I should be scared. But for some reason I'm not. Feeling ignorant and lost, yes; but scared, no."

"I feel about the same," said Kurt, "but I'm not happy having to spend a chunk of my life doing something I'm pretty sure we shouldn't be doing at all."

"There is that," I said, hoisting my can of Carling Black Label in a toasting gesture. Kurt tapped his can against it and we both took long swallows. "You know, I'm not sure I've ever drunk Black Label before. It's not bad, but wouldn't be my first choice."

"It's pretty common in the Twin Cities," said Kurt, "but it's not a favorite. But getting back to the original subject, I have a feeling we're going to be all right in the end. I really want to get back into the sound business when I get home, so that's a big motivation for me to stay sharp and not do anything stupid."

"Well, personally I don't need any motivation to do that, other than just staying alive and in one piece. And I'm glad I don't have a major love interest to make my mind wander. You know, I'm not sure I've ever uttered those particular words before," I said with a laugh.

"It may be true that you don't have one girl on your mind, but random thoughts about several of them are floating around in there somewhere," Kurt said with assurance.

"Yes, but none are *the* one, and for that I really am grateful. I mean this is gonna be hard enough as it is, but it would be intolerable if I were pining away for my true love."

Back at the bunker, we noticed four or five guys sleeping on the sandbagged roof. However, we were FNGs and figured it was safer to sleep inside. We managed to find our bunks in total darkness, but it was so damn hot that within twenty minutes, comfort trumped fear. After a whispered conversation, we pulled our poncho liners out of our packs and found open spots on the roof. We were asleep in minutes.

When I woke in the morning, Kurt was gone. I didn't have a chance to say goodbye or to wish him luck.

I spent the day between meals leaning against buildings and bunkers. It's not good to have too much time to think ... especially when you're filled with uncertainty. I spent time looking at Nui Ba Den. Mountain views were the next best thing to being in them; they always seemed to set my mind free.

At 1800, I went to the NCO-EM Club and sat at the bar for a couple of hours talking to the bartender. He was a corporal who behaved like he'd rather be anywhere other than behind that bar. By around 2030, I was well lit and really bored. I'd loosened up to the point where I thought I could ask the corporal if he knew where I might be able to find some marijuana, something I hadn't even thought about since entering the Army. He looked annoyed.

Obviously, he was not into pot, but he said, "I don't know. Maybe you could head over to the ARVN area and ask one of them." ARVN was the acronym for Army of the Republic of Vietnam, the South Vietnamese Army.

"Where is the ARVN area?"

"Up the street half a klick and to the right."

I thanked him and wandered out. I walked along for what felt more like a full klick (one kilometer). I was beginning to wonder whether the barkeep had given me a bum steer, when I saw an arched sign in Vietnamese. I turned and walked under it. From the way the Vietnamese military personnel looked at me, it was clear that American soldiers never ventured into their camp. I began to feel uneasy, but was half drunk, so I kept on. Occasionally I asked one of the passing Vietnamese if he knew where I could find some pot.

Since none of them spoke much English, I spoke especially clearly and loudly and made smoking gestures. On my fifth try, a fellow took my arm and led me to a huge bunker, among the dozens I'd been walking around. He pointed down the stairs and said, "Number 1," which meant nothing to me.

I went down the steps and ducked under the low entry. In the back of the room was a second room—separated by curtains made of ponchos—which I realized must be the officers' area. I was surrounded by a dozen enlisted men who were busy cleaning their M16s, sharpening bayonets, or rearranging the contents of their backpacks. But in a corner of the main room, seated behind a small table with a map, was an ARVN officer.

The men's faces showed utter surprise at seeing an American in their midst. It was a bit tense. The officer looked annoyed and angry. He put his cigarette down and asked in broken English, "What do here?"

I figured I'd come this far, so I might as well go the rest of the way. "I want to buy some pot ... marijuana." Again, I made the puffing gestures.

He looked uncomfortable and even more annoyed. After a ten-second delay he spoke rapidly to one of the men and gestured to the room behind the curtain.

"You go him!" he said curtly, waving his arm toward the curtained doorway. The man he'd spoken to quickly stood and held the curtains aside for me. Once inside, he reached into a canvas bag and removed a cartoon of Winston cigarettes. He opened the carton, removed an unopened pack, and held it up, saying, "Two dolla."

I said, "No. No. Not cigarettes, not tobacco. Pot, *marijuana!*"

He nodded, again held out the pack of Winstons, and said, "Numba one!"

I was unsure of anything other than that it was time for me to get the hell out of that bunker and the ARVN camp so I said, "Okay," and gave him two dollars in Military Payment Certificates (MPC), paper money printed especially for use in war zones. He took the bills, handed me the Winstons, and ushered me out the door.

I put the Winstons in my pocket and headed toward the camp entrance, feeling relieved when I managed to find my way back to the NCO-EM Club. I stopped in for a last beer before closing time.

"How'd it go?" asked the bartender.

"Not sure. I ended up buying a pack of Winstons from an ARVN, so I guess that's better than nothing."

"Those might not be Winstons. But just be glad you made it back."

"Oh, I am. It felt weird over there."

"Yeah, there's hardly any contact between us, other than officers at staff meetings. The cultural and language differences are just too great. It's not right, but what're you gonna do?"

On the way to my bunker, it occurred to me that the bartender might be right. That pack might *not* be Winstons. I opened it the usual way and removed one of the cigarettes.

"Well, I'll be damned!" I muttered to myself after lighting it.

By the time I reached my bunker I was practically a zombie from the combination of alcohol and pot. I went inside to grab my poncho liner, then staggered up to a vacant spot on the lumpy sandbag roof and went right to sleep.

Half an hour later the loudest explosion I'd ever heard—accompanied by the sound of shrapnel zipping through the air and slamming into the sandbags all around me—shocked me awake. I found myself inside that bunker so fast I didn't even remember making the trip.

"Jesus!" someone said in the darkness. "What the hell was that?"

"A mortar round," said a nearly sober me. "It landed in the wire about twenty meters in front of the bunker."

"Holy shit. Is everybody okay?"

"I think so, but it's a goddamn miracle," I answered.

Just then, a second explosion sounded a hundred meters behind us. After that it was deathly quiet inside that bunker, and the heat no longer seemed that bad. I drifted into a fitful sleep.

About 0200 I awoke realizing that I needed to take a dump. *"Dammit, it'll just have to wait 'til morning,"* I thought. I forced myself to try to sleep, but within an hour I was lying in my bunk wide awake, knowing I had to go out and take a crap. I rationalized that it had been hours since the last mortar round, so I'd be fine. I eased out of bed and felt my way outside. It was the blackest night I'd ever seen, or not seen. I knew there was an outhouse fifty meters behind the bunker. But since I couldn't see anything, I decided the best thing to do would be to walk in ever wider spirals until I bumped into the shitter.

I kept widening my spiral for what seemed an eternity and was beginning to contemplate squatting where I was when I bumped into the rough wood exterior of the outhouse. I felt my way around, found the door, and swung it open. Inside I lowered my pants and was anticipating rapid relief when a mortar round hit close to where the first one had several hours earlier. "Jesus," I whispered, though why it was in a whisper, I couldn't say. It's difficult to describe the helpless feeling of being mortared. You can never be sure if or where the next round will fall. There's no warning unless the mortar tube is close enough to hear when it fires. But even then, there's no way to know where it will hit.

A few seconds later a second round hit a couple hundred meters farther inside the perimeter. Then a third round hit much farther inside. My first thought was of a headline I hoped would never appear in my hometown paper: LOCAL BOY BLOWN AWAY IN ONE-HOLER.

The next afternoon, Top gave me my orders and told me I'd be heading out to my unit the following morning. He also told me the third mortar round from the second salvo the night before had landed in the main part of the town of Tay Ninh, killing four civilians. I was saddened and sobered to hear that. I spent the rest of the day quietly, packing my gear and getting ready to join my unit. I didn't go to the club that night.

I didn't know what I was headed into, but I damn sure knew what I was headed away from.

Chapter 13 – Outpost on the Edge; First Patrol

The next morning after chow, I walked to the airfield. It was hot and dusty. Occasional dust devils spun their way zigzag fashion across the field, sometimes snaking skyward a hundred feet or so. It wasn't until about 1000 that my ride was ready. It was a Chinook helicopter, the kind that looks like a round-nosed semi-trailer under two large props. A crew member wearing a helmet with earphones and a mike, ushered me and about ten other guys up the back ramp, and told us to sit in orange web seats that were identical to those on the C-130 and stow our gear underneath. I picked a spot on the right side of the aircraft where I could see a little ahead out a window and settled in. There's a distinctive thumping rhythm in the sound helicopter rotors make. This was especially true of Chinooks. I'm not sure what caused it, but suspect it had something to do with air compression when the tips of the rotor blades passed closest to each other. The entire aircraft flexes to that rhythm. To passengers and crew, it feels like being inside a fast beating heart. It's not unpleasant, just different.

The crewman pressed a hand-held control and the ramp raised up 'til it was within a foot of closing. He left it in that position, I suppose to improve the ventilation and keep the temperature down. The Chinook lifted off, slanted its nose slightly downward, and accelerated rapidly. We quickly left the scattered agricultural fields around Tay Ninh behind and within five minutes began to traverse unbroken, verdant jungle. When we reached our cruising altitude, somewhere around 2000 feet, the crewman reopened the ramp door and left it open in a position parallel with the ground below. Apart from Nui Ba Den, which was rapidly receding from view out the rear, the country below us was remarkably flat. After perhaps twenty minutes, the ground began to show a few low undulations, but it remained the deepest green I'd ever seen. A few minutes later I looked to our front and saw a break in the green carpet. It was a large, irregularly shaped dry lakebed, perhaps two miles long by a half-mile wide. In its narrow northern end, I could see what appeared to be a circle. As we got nearer and dropped lower, I could see that it was a circular earthen berm. Inside it, OD tents and canvas buildings of varying sizes were jumbled about. And near its center a red, white and blue flag fluttered intermittently in the hot morning breeze. The similarity to a cavalry fort in Indian Country was undeniable. It was a 1970 frontier outpost on the ragged, far flung edge of American power and influence. I was awed that my country could exert its power so far from home. In fact, much farther would make it closer; this was the far side of the planet after all. But I also wondered whether, as a society, we'd progressed much at all since 1870.

After we touched down, I followed some guys who seemed to know where they were going and passed through a gap in the berm where a GI sat in a makeshift guard shack.

He looked me up and down. "Just reporting in, Sergeant?"

"Yes," I answered.

"Okay, head to the flag and report in at headquarters there."

At the flag I found the HQ and walked in, handing my orders to a Spec-4 at the desk.

"Okay, Sarge, have a seat and the XO will be with you in a minute." He disappeared into the next room and I waited.

In a few minutes a captain walked out and said, "Follow the specialist, and he'll take you to your new unit."

I grabbed my pack and walked with the specialist toward the berm on the west side of the firebase. He stopped in front of a lean young red-headed first lieutenant, who was writing a letter on an artillery ammo box.

Handing him a copy of my orders, the specialist said, "LT, this is Sergeant Jamie Thompson, newly assigned to your platoon." (LT, pronounced ell-tee, was the generic title given all lieutenants in the field.)

He stuck out his hand and I shook it. "I'm Lieutenant Sam Bowen, leader of First Platoon, Charlie Company, Fifth of the Seventh. Welcome aboard!"

"Thank you, sir."

"Listen, I know everything is new to you right now, but we'll get you squared away sooner than you think. This is my hooch," he said, pocketing his pen. He gestured to the open end of a corrugated galvanized steel half-culvert pipe with its other end buried in the berm behind him. It was covered in sandbags. "Leave your pack and weapon here for now, and I'll show you around."

I dropped my stuff and followed Bowen to a large screened-in rectangular structure. "This is the Mess Hall. Dinner is from 1130 to 1300, and supper starts at 1700 and runs to 1830. All the mealtimes are posted on the door," he said. Something I had trouble adjusting to was how the Army always referred to the midday meal as dinner and not lunch, and to the evening meal as supper and not dinner. It didn't feel right to me, but as the old saw went: *There's a right way, a wrong way, and the Army way.* I'm guessing that saying is translated from original Sanskrit.

Bowen showed me the aid station and pointed out the nearest shitters and piss tubes. Piss tubes were plastic pipes stuck into the inside lower slopes of the earthen berm, planted two feet deep at a sixty-degree angle. Urine directed into the top gradually soaked into the ground at the bottom.

When we returned to his hooch, the LT said, "Tonight, you'll share my hooch, but for now just wander around and get the lay of the place. Meet me back here after supper."

After "dinner" and spending the afternoon wandering and observing, I ate supper and found my way back to Lieutenant Bowen's hooch, where we sat and talked for a while. I smoked and he drank black coffee from his canteen cup.

"You're lucky you joined us the day we came into the firebase," he said. "It gives you a chance to get oriented better than if you joined us in the boonies."

"I can imagine. My friend Kurt Stephan joined his unit day before yesterday when they were resupplied in the bush."

"What company is he in?" Bowen asked.

"Alpha."

"That's a good outfit. He'll do as well there as he could anywhere. In the morning, I'll introduce you to your squad. I'm assigning you to First Squad, under Staff Sergeant Roger Campbell. He's good! You need to learn everything you can from him."

When it got dark, we crawled into the hooch and lay on our air mattresses, still talking. Lieutenant Bowen was from Willcox, Arizona, not far from Tucson, where a good part of my last several years had been misspent. We talked for hours, until he said, "We need to get some shut-eye now."

Finally, I drifted off to sleep, drenched in sweat and inhaling the smells of raw earth, vegetation, dust, gun oil, explosive residue, and other things best not thought about much.

At 0305, someone poked our feet with a rifle butt and whispered, "Time for the Mike-Mike," then moved on.

"What the hell was that about?" I muttered sleepily.

"It's called a Mad Minute," said the LT. "Most nights on firebases, every available man moves to the berm and fires into the tree line at pre-set random times—sometimes more than once in a night. It harasses the enemy and sometimes even disrupts an attack. C'mon, grab your weapon and bandoliers and follow me."

Within a minute, we were lying prone on the berm with our M16s pointed out into the darkness.

"When the first shot is fired, start firing, sweep the tree line in front of you, and keep firing for one full minute. Got it?" said the LT.

"Got it."

At precisely 0312 all hell broke loose. Damn near all the men on the firebase, over 300 of us, fired whatever weapons we had—M16s, sniper rifles, automatic pistols, .30 and .50 caliber machine guns, grenade launchers—for a solid minute. The tree line appeared eerily in flashing glows of gunfire and explosions. It was awesome. At 0313 all firing ceased, and we all went back to sleep or guard duty.

A surreal calm settled over the firebase as banks of gun smoke drifted across it, dispersing slowly into the steamy night.

At dawn I awoke and made my way to a four-holer. After completing my mission, I went to the mess hall and ate a hearty breakfast of scrambled eggs, bacon, toast, and several cups of hot coffee with reconstituted dry milk. As I ate, I looked around, absorbing the details of what I could see.

The mess hall was a canvas tent about thirty by seventy feet with sandbags stacked against its sides to a height of three feet. The cooking was done behind a canvas wall at the far end. Wooden frames were firmly lashed into openings in the canvas walls wherever screen doors were needed, and screened windows surrounded the eating area on three sides.

There were a lot of flies around, but only a few inside the mess tent. A particularly persistent fly kept landing on my eggs, but was never able to get a taste because I kept waving him away. It crossed my mind that his first stop of the day might well have been one of the four-holers scattered around the firebase. As I continued to chow down, my companion landed a few inches from my plate and waited for me to finish or drop my guard. I stared at that fly and decided it was exactly like the houseflies I'd seen all my life on the other side of the planet. I couldn't discern any detail that set it apart from American houseflies, and that surprised me for some reason. I mentally shrugged, absorbed the revelation, and finished my meal.

At 0730 I met Lieutenant Bowen and we walked to where a group of men were strung out along the inside of the berm, sitting on sandbags, ammo boxes, or packs. They were all busily cleaning their weapons and checking their gear. The LT introduced me to my squad leader.

"This is Sergeant Roger Campbell, leader of First Squad. Meet Sergeant Jamie Thompson, fresh from the World." The LT didn't say this in a way that implied anything negative or made me feel diminished, but I couldn't help noticing that none of the men did more than glance at me.

Campbell was a six-foot black guy, with an athletic build.

"Glad to meet you," I said, shaking hands.

"First Squad will be your new home, so Sergeant Campbell will finish the intros and get you oriented."

"Okay," said Campbell. "First, you need to make sure you've got full magazines. By that I mean make sure you have no more than eighteen rounds in each of your twenty-round magazines. Any more than that can cause it to jam. Trust me; you do not want that to happen in the boonies. The ammo is in boxes just over there." He pointed a few feet down the berm. "When you've finished, I'll get you to the next step."

After the ammo check, came the water.

"You need to make damn sure you carry enough water to last you three full days. Everybody's needs are different, so carry too much at first rather than too little. I suggest starting with seven collapsible two-quart canteens strapped to your pack and, of course, your two standard one-quart canteens on your web belt. When we're in the bush, try to make sure you always have water in the belt canteens. When you need it, you need it *now*, and you might not be able to drop your pack to refill."

I took to heart every word uttered by Roger Campbell. I was acutely aware that I didn't know shit from Shinola about fighting in Vietnam and that Roger—who'd survived seven and a half months as an infantry squad leader—knew damn near everything. I'd already realized that my main goal in Nam was to survive the experience and do my best to make sure the men I served with survived, too. I could see that Roger felt the same.

Roger and my squad mates gave me several tips that first day. Carry a machete with a sharpening stone and file if you could find 'em. (These weren't issued by the Army, so you had to get them from grunts leaving the field or have relatives mail them to you.) Strap an ammo can onto the pack frame under the bottom of the pack with its top facing straight back, so it could be opened without removing it from the frame. Ammo cans, steel boxes really, have a rubber gasket set into the top, making them watertight when closed properly. It was the only way to safely transport personal toiletry items like toothbrushes and toilet paper, as well as letters, photos, writing materials, and paperbacks.

As the day wore on, I added two and a half days of food: C-rations and LRRPs (Long Range Reconnaissance Patrol freeze-dried meals, pronounced "lurps"). I also packed one Claymore mine and one stick of C-4 plastic explosive, from which I would be using small pieces to heat my meals.

On my belt, I carried the one-quart canteens, a bayonet/knife in scabbard, and a first-aid kit. I couldn't find a machete, file, or sharpening stone.

When the pack was full, I hung the collapsible canteens all over it. I was to wear my two bandoliers with seven magazines of M16 ammo in each, crossed over my shoulders and chest. And I snapped together two 100-round belts of machine-gun ammo, which I crossed over my shoulders over the bandoliers. With each member contributing this way, a squad carried one to three thousand rounds of ammo for the machine gun (depending on squad strength at the time) in addition to the ammo carried by the gun team.

I'd left the battalion rear in Tay Ninh with my pack weighing twenty pounds, but by the end of my first day in First Squad, it weighed about sixty-five pounds.

The pack itself was, of course, olive drab in color, composed mostly of Nylon fabric with leather fittings. All the pockets on the outside—there were quite a few—had covers with adjustable buckle fasteners that snapped in place, and there were Velcro fasteners here and there to assure that covers remained fully over their respective pouches. The main pack bag consisted of a rubberized "waterproof" interior, with drawstrings at the top. The drawstring closure was covered by a Nylon flap secured with two adjustable quick-release squeeze snaps like the ones on children's car seats. The poncho and air mattress were normally rolled tightly and tied down hard over the top of the drawstring but below the top flaps; this improved the water resistance of the bag and assured quick access to the poncho during sudden rains. The ammo can was strapped so tightly to the frame that it provided a flat, stable base, enabling the frame and pack to stand upright on the ground.

At 1600 hours, the LT told us Charlie Company would be going on patrol outside the wire the next morning. "It'll just be a one-day deal. We'll work our way through the bush to Fire Support Base (FSB) Illingworth, about two and a half klicks south. We'll stay in the cover of the tree line as much as possible, inspect the place, and then return. This'll be light gear only. First Platoon has point."

No one said anything, but we all knew what had happened at FSB Illingworth a couple weeks before. What I hadn't realized was that the battle I'd read about back in California was only a mile from where I was now. I've never been a believer in ESP, precognition, or premonition, but once in a great while strange things do happen. I remembered the odd sense of foreboding I'd felt when reading about the Illingworth battle.

That night I slept with squad mates in one of the bunkers not far from the LT's hooch. First Platoon was nearly at full strength, consisting of twenty-five men divided into two squads. First Squad had eleven, counting our squad leader, Roger Campbell. Four men—Platoon Leader LT Bowen, Platoon Sergeant SFC Elroy Crippen, Platoon RTO Cpl Bob Berning from Kentucky, and Platoon Medic Cpl Henry Jacobs from Colorado—were not assigned to either squad. The guys in my squad were nice enough, but not overly friendly. This was a fraternity I had to earn my way into. I wasn't one of them yet, and had no idea how long it would take to be accepted, if I ever would be.

Roger Campbell filled the role of combat infantry squad leader to a T. We had two black guys in addition to Staff Sergeant Campbell: Nathan Ardmore, a rifleman from Detroit and Emory Blaine, a rifleman from Alabama. José Fuerte was a rifleman from Texas and chose to carry grenades. A wiry little Filipino named Ferde Salazar was the squad gunner, who carried and operated our M60. His assistant gunner was Herman Bauman, a German American kid from Ohio. Albert Dread was a taciturn, hard-bitten type from Kansas, who'd been in-country for over ten months. Howard Forman, Dread's constant shadow, seemed jittery, possibly from his ten months in the boonies. Our chunker man (who carried the grenade launcher) was James Billings. He looked so much like Clark Kent that everyone called him Superman. Chuck Stadler was a PFC rifleman. He seemed perpetually angry and I found out he had a hard-on for shake 'n bake sergeants or anyone else who outranked him. His father was an Army lifer, and he apparently thought he deserved more rank by osmosis than he'd earned. And then there was me, the only shake 'n bake NCO in First Squad.

I was awakened at 0137 for the Mad Minute, and again at 0330 for my hour and a half stint on perimeter guard duty. It felt like I'd barely closed my eyes when we were all rousted at 0630. Time to begin another day in the Nam. This was going to be my life for as long as I was there, so I knew I'd better get used to it.

I had breakfast with my platoon mates and then learned how to put together "light gear," which consisted of all weapons-related gear—except Claymores and clackers—one meal, and as many canteens as we thought we would need. We could forgo the pack altogether and just strap whatever we needed over our shoulders and on our belts or shove it into the deep pockets in our pants. Or we could wear the pack and remove unnecessary items to reduce the weight. I wasn't sure what I'd need, and I opted for using the pack so I could lug plenty of water. I decided on six quarts of water. We all still carried the two loops of machine-gun ammo. All told, the light gear weighed at least thirty pounds.

We were doing final weapons and gear checks when Campbell returned from meeting with the LT and told us to "saddle up," a term held over from horse cavalry days. It meant "get your gear and weapons ready and prepare to move out."

After some clicks and creaks as magazines were shoved home into M16s, packs were slung over backs, and ammo belts and bandoliers were shouldered, we rose, bending forward slightly under the weight. We followed Sergeant Campbell toward the main entrance and through the berm, where we were joined by Second Squad, and then by Second and Third Platoons. Our Mortar Platoon stayed on the firebase.

After glancing at the LT, who nodded, Campbell said, "I'll take the point. Blaine, you're my coverman." At that, he moved out to the right toward the tree line."

Campbell and Blaine shifted their right hands from their M16s' carrying handles to their pistol grips and used their left hands to support them by their heat shields under the barrel. Then Campbell set off at a moderate pace. The men in Charlie Company spaced themselves with three meters between every man. Once we were beyond the concertina wire, Claymores, tripwires, and barrels of fougasse, Campbell made directly for the closest edge of the tree line.

The sun beat down relentlessly from a cloudless blue sky as we crossed the 200 meters of flat, dry lakebed to reach the trees. Puffs of dust swirled around our boots as we walked, leaving a shifting contrail to mark our passing. Sweat poured down from beneath my steel-pot helmet, running down to my chin and dripping beyond. I was overheated, just in the first few minutes with light gear. I thought, *"Forget about the enemy, I don't know if I'm going to be able to survive the heat!"* I was glad for my six quarts of water; I just hoped it would be enough.

We reached the tree line, and seventy-five men slithered silently into the steamy green. We continued straight into the tree line for 200 meters and then turned south to parallel the edge of the lakebed as we worked our way to Firebase Illingworth—or where it had been. After a few hundred meters, we reached a cleared strip in the jungle with a dirt road in its middle. We halted in place at a hand signal from Campbell. The LT went forward to take a look and sent word back to the CO, Captain Robert Osgood, that the last squad in the line should send up four men to watch the flanks as we crossed the strip. That was done in short order and the company moved ahead. The eerie silence continued; not one word or sound that was not essential to our mission had been uttered since we left Firebase Wood.

We entered the trees on the far side of the road, the flankers rejoined us, and we continued for 500 meters until the LT passed the word in whispers from man to man down the line to take ten in place. We slowly seated ourselves on whatever was handy and drank liberally from our canteens. I wolfed down a packet of crackers and what passed for a chocolate bar from the scant rations I'd brought along.

"I wish I had some salt tablets," I whispered to Superman, who was sitting closest to me.

"Yeah, they'd come in handy all right, but I haven't seen any in Nam."

Sooner than any of us liked, we were off again. I was still sweating like a Roman mule, but I wasn't dwelling on it anymore. It was already one of those things I had the wisdom to know I couldn't do anything about. After another 500 meters, we set up in a loose circular formation with guards at the periphery for our thirty-minute lunch break.

After lunch, we moved south for another 500 meters and then southeast, slowly making our way toward FSB Illingworth. We'd moved 200 meters when Campbell held up his hand and motioned for the LT to come forward. He was standing just a meter from the edge of a dry lake as he pointed to the remains of Illingworth less than 200 meters ahead. Four men from the rearmost platoon served as moving flankers as we moved out onto the lakebed and over the flattened berm.

Scars in the earth marked what had been bunkers and perimeter guard positions. A few pieces of bent metal and broken wood were scattered about, but nothing to indicate that a major battle had taken place less than a month before. We inspected the place, speaking only in hushed tones out of respect for the comrades who'd fought and died here.

After twenty minutes of milling about, we set off on our return to Firebase Wood. With Wood in sight at the other end of the dry lakebed, Campbell had Blaine take point as he drifted back to the middle of the squad. It was even hotter now, but I wasn't thinking much about that.

Chapter 14 – What It Means to Be a Grunt

The next morning before chow, the LT told us that First and Second Platoons would move out in light gear within an hour, to provide "security for a road clearing operation near Tay Ninh." That sounded pretty tame, especially since we would be transported by Chinook.

Dread mumbled, "This ain't been much of a stand-down."

I gathered that when field units came into a firebase for a few days, they didn't do much more than burn shit, pull guard duty, and lounge around. In short, it was supposed to be a rest from the constant humping in the boonies.

Pretty soon, we heard the distinctive whap, whap, whap of two approaching Chinooks. The sound got deeper and sharper as they slowed and lost altitude. Their twin rotors sent up rolling clouds of choking dust. The rear ramps lowered, several GIs exited, and various crates, pallets, and bundles were offloaded. As soon as this was completed, each platoon filed inside a Chinook and we were off. Nobody talked much. It was loud inside helicopters, so even if we'd been inclined to talk it would've been difficult.

Twenty minutes later, the Chinooks landed on a wide dirt road in a 500-meter-wide strip cleared of vegetation. We jogged down the ramps and the Chinooks lifted off, the sound of their rotors quickly fading to the utter silence of abandoned countryside.

Nearby, soldiers stood around a couple of deuce-and-a-halfs.

The captain in charge of them walked over to Captain Osgood, our company CO, and said, "Good morning, sir. Glad to get your help. We need to clear mines from this stretch of road, and we have two minesweepers to do the job. My minesweepers will form the points of two Vs, with your men flared out behind them to either side, forming the legs of the Vs. We're clearing two klicks. When the road is cleared, your men will set up guard positions on both flanks until a convoy passes through. Following that, you'll await transportation back to your firebase by deuce-and-a-half. Any questions?"

"No, sir. That's clear," said Osgood. "Position your minesweepers and we'll form on them."

The road was about forty feet across. One minesweeper walked the road about ten feet in from the right side, and the other about ten feet in from the left. Each leg of the Vs was formed by one squad, with our squad being the leg to the right of the minesweeper on the right or northeast side of the road. Each V covered about thirty feet in width, with the last men in the outer legs about five feet off the road shoulders and the last man in the inner legs at the center of the road.

It was early, but the heat was already approaching unbearable levels. There was no breeze as we slowly walked at the pace of the soldier swinging his mine detector back and forth in front of him. At first, I strolled along not thinking about much of anything. I was the third man back on the right and idly watched the almost hypnotic sweeping of the mine detector from left to right, right to left, left to right as I put one foot in front of the other. The road was so dusty, I felt like I was walking on talcum powder. I began to study the minesweeping to keep my mind occupied. Then it hit me.

The detector's arc covered a width of only twelve feet. Its sweeps never reached as far to the east as I was walking. When I looked around and thought it through, I realized that the sweeps of the two mine detectors were only covering the paths of about two-thirds of the men in our two platoons. *"Jesus,"* I thought, *"WE are the minesweepers."*

Forman was in front of me, just inside the detector's arc of coverage, Dread was in front of him, right on the minesweeper's ass.

"Hey, Forman," I said in a loud whisper.

"Yeah?" he answered.

"Did you know most of us are walking across uncleared ground?"

"Welcome to the infantry," he muttered, while spitting some dust out to the side of the road.

For the next hour, I knew that every step I took could be my last. I didn't like what that said about the regard in which grunts were held by higher command. Hell, even the name "grunt" probably came from the same mind-set. I focused on how similar the dirt looked to the red soil I'd seen in parts of the American South. The heat continued to build. Eventually, the minesweepers halted, and we were told to string back along the road and establish guard positions.

Almost unnecessarily, the LT told us, "Try to find some shade, if you can."

The wide strip cleared of jungle was almost devoid of vegetation of any kind, even grass or weeds. It had obviously been cleared recently with large dozers because the tree lines were edged with piles of tangled trees, brush, and rocks. It was a corridor of sun-scorched desert in the midst of the jungle.

First Squad, led by Campbell in consultation with Dread, headed for one of the few places with any vegetation at all, a place where several piles of dirt, maybe fifteen feet high, had been pushed together with a few saplings and some brush. It was 150 meters from the road, but it was worth the trudge. When we got there, we found almost no shade, but *almost* was better than *none*. Guys took up spots all over our little island of man-made hummocks and uprooted brush, looking for personal refuge.

Campbell said, "Salazar, set up the gun in that little dip with your field of fire toward that tree line behind us. The rest of you keep watchful eyes on the tree line, too."

Once hunkered down in our various nooks and crannies, we watched and waited.

Before long, Dread started holding court. "You fuckers don't know how lucky you got it. Last year we were in the shit all the time."

"Amen!" Forman chimed in. "Remember in September when we got hit twice in three days?"

"Yeah, that's what I mean. Now all we do is wander around and sweat. Not that I'm complainin'. We ain't lost a man in months, and that's a good thing. But it ain't natural in the Nam."

From a few feet away, Campbell added, "God knows how long we'll be stuck out here. Find what shade and comfort you can, eat some chow, and try to get some rest."

Some of the men adjusted themselves a bit more so they could see that tree line, but Dread, Forman, Stadler, and Fuerte stayed together on the side of the berm facing the road.

Dread pulled out a deck of cards and said, "Spades, anyone?"

"Sure," the three guys near him said.

Forman smoothed a small area in the dirt to use as a card table, Stadler took a notepad and pen from his ammo can, and the game began. From my chosen spot, just over the top of the dirt piles on the tree line side, I could look down on the game. I'd played hearts and euchre, but never spades, so I was interested in learning.

After a while I sat down near Campbell and said, "Can I ask you something Sergeant?"

"Anything, anytime," he said with a smile.

"I was wondering why you walked point yesterday. I mean if I remember right, we were trained that a squad leader should assign that to someone else and stay near the center of his squad."

He looked at me as if I was a well-meaning child and said, "If you become a squad leader, you'll know."

About 1230 we saw movement on the road, approaching from the direction of Tay Ninh. Through shimmering heat waves, the movement slowly resolved itself into a few kids on bicycles and on foot.

I asked, "Wha'd'ya make of that?"

"Not much," Dread muttered through the corner of his mouth as he swept up another card trick. "You're an FNG, so you don't know how things are over here. Hell, last year up north, we stayed in the same base camp for three weeks and had mama sans livin' there with us. They cooked, cleaned, did our laundry, and fucked for us whenever we liked." He grabbed another trick. "Shit, all we had to do was give 'em some cigarettes and candy, or sometimes a little MPC. Life was good!"

"Yep, them was the days, all right," said Forman with a huge grin. "REMFs have got it made in the Nam."

"So ... not to worry then?" I asked skeptically.

"Oh, we'll keep a sharp eye on 'em, but I doubt they'll be a problem," said Campbell. "In fact, they might bring us some goodies," he added as more kids appeared on the road, and a few small groups peeled off and headed straight for us.

I didn't want to embarrass myself, so under my breath I asked Campbell, "What's a REMF?"

"It's an acronym for rear echelon mother fucker. Basically, it's how we describe anybody in the military who's not in combat and never has been," he explained. "Needless to say, it's not a complimentary term."

"Thanks, Sergeant. I gathered that last part," I said with a grin.

In a few minutes, the first bike kid arrived at the foot of our hillock. He dismounted, smiled a huge smile, and said loudly, "GIs numba one!"

He pulled plastic bags from his basket and held them high. They were full of watches and trinkets, which the veterans quickly dismissed with hand gestures and strong statements of "Nah. Number ten, number ten." After a brief attempt to change our minds, the kid put the trinkets back in the basket and opened the lid of the ice chest fastened behind the seat. In it were bottles of Coke buried in ice. He grabbed a couple and said, "GI want Coke? Jus' one dolla MPC. Jus' one. GI want?"

I'd heard all the stories on TV about how even the kids and pretty girls in Vietnam couldn't be trusted not to frag American soldiers, so I hung back. But damn! It was hot as hell. And those Cokes looked like the real thing. The kid only had a dozen and after Dread talked the kid down to "fitty cen," we bought 'em all. It only took a minute or two to pass them out to the entire squad. To this day, no Coke has ever tasted as good as that one did. It was the nectar of the gods, and it didn't hurt that it also cut the dust that I hadn't realized was coating the inside of my mouth and throat.

As quickly as they materialized, the civilians melted away down the road, back toward Tay Ninh. We were again alone with the heat and the cards. Five minutes after the last civilian disappeared, a U.S. tank rolled up from the south. It seemed Vietnamese civilians had better intelligence and communications than we did! Behind the tank was a long line of deuce-and-a-halfs with a few APCs mixed in and more APCs bringing up the rear.

"Now we know why they wanted us to sweep the road," said Campbell.

However, the convoy pulled about fifty feet off the road and moved parallel to it at ten miles per hour until they disappeared into the distance. We watched the convoy driving well to the side of the strip we'd cleared. No one said a word until the sound of the convoy faded away; even FNGs understood that such things were "the Army way."

"Well, ain't that somethin'," muttered Dread.

Wiping sweat streams off my forehead, I silently agreed. Campbell merely grunted.

A little later, the LT called us in with a hand signal and two deuce-and-a-halfs pulled up to drive us home. The trip was uneventful, and the breeze helped dry the sweat.

After chow, I took a shower in an area with a couple of wooden pallets surrounded on three sides by ponchos tied to poles. I heated my water in a canteen cup over burning C-4, then mixed it with ambient temperature water in my helmet. Pouring it into the field shower, I was ready to go—or at least ready to remove the top layer of filth from my long-suffering body.

Chapter 15 – Into the Boonies

The next day we burned shit in the morning and lounged for the rest of the day. I adjusted, tightened, and reorganized my backpack, making sure I had everything I was supposed to have. Carrying fragmentation grenades was optional and I decided not to do it; I still had concerns that a grenade could catch on a branch and get both its pin pulled and its safety clip snagged off. The odds might be slim, but the benefits didn't outweigh the risks. Besides, there were three or four guys in the squad who did carry them.

We knew we were headed to the boonies the next morning, so that night I was tense. I felt like I was drifting in a current over which I had no control. A couple of the guys managed to get drunk somehow, but I had no interest in adding a hangover to the exhaustion I already felt. Sleep deprivation was taking a toll on me, and I hadn't spent a single night in the field yet.

Shortly after morning chow, I anxiously waited for my first CA (combat assault by air) to begin. A low sun glared off the dust and dead grass into our narrowed eyes. It was warm, but there was a promise of high heat in the still morning air. We clustered together by platoons outside the berm as the thrumming of approaching slicks reached our ears. I looked toward the sound as five Huey helicopters came into view. The most familiar symbol of the Vietnam War, the helicopter was called a "slick" because it had no weapons permanently fixed to its smooth exterior.

The choppers flew and landed in two off-set lines. First and Second platoons—along with Captain Osgood and his RTO—clambered aboard and lifted off in swirling, blinding dust that enveloped the troops remaining on the ground. The slicks would return for the rest of the company after they dropped us at our temporary LZ (landing zone).

I was on the floor, squeezed between squad mates near the middle of the helicopter as it achieved just enough altitude to tip forward and make its sprint to the boonies. The entire world seemed to vibrate in tune with the thrum of the rotors. The side doors were left wide open, and the rapidly moving air was a welcome break from the relentless heat and humidity on the ground. I didn't like being in the middle and resolved to take a window seat whenever possible, which meant I would be sitting on the floor with my legs dangling in open air.

A crew member whose helmet earphones were wired to the pilot and copilot, manned an M60 machine gun mounted on a sling at the left door. His eyes constantly swept the jungle below for any signs of movement. After ten minutes, the slick's nose tilted up and back as the tone of the rotors took on a thwacking sound, and the formation dropped rapidly into a clearing barely large enough for the five helicopters to land together.

I mimicked those around me, leaping to the ground and running bent over until I was outside the reach of the rotor blades. Then we ran to the nearest tree line and took position to fire into the jungle—should the need arise to protect the LZ. There was no time for fear or worry, only action.

Lieutenant Bowen conferred briefly with Captain Osgood and then with Sergeant First Class Elroy Crippen, our First Platoon sergeant, who was a quiet, efficient, no-nonsense Army lifer. He spoke briefly with the two squad leaders after which our squad leader, Sergeant Campbell, assigned rough positions to each man, with special attention given to where the gun (the M60) was placed to assure overlapping fields of fire between both squads' guns. The rest of us ordinary riflemen spread out between and to either side of the two gun positions so that the extreme ends of our formation curved halfway around the clearing. When the second lift arrived, the other two platoons faced the jungle on the opposite side of the LZ, forming a narrow oval, bristling with firepower. From this formation it was relatively easy to move quickly away from the LZ in a single file.

The silence after the slicks disappeared was absolute. Second Platoon's First Squad, took the point, followed by Second Platoon's Second Squad. Third Platoon came next followed by the Mortar Platoon, which never walked point and always had either second or third position in a company size formation. Then came my platoon's Second Squad, followed by my squad which brought up the rear. This order seemed confusing at first, but I soon realized the order for the three rifle platoons was determined by the sequence in which the squads had the point. Since my squad—First Platoon's First Squad—had point when we reconnoitered Illingworth, we rotated to the back and moved forward as other squads took their turns. In theory, the third position was the safest, and being there allowed the CO to move quickly to whatever part of the formation made the most sense in the event of a firefight, and it made it easier for the rifle platoons on either side of it to protect the mortar platoon as it set up firing positions for its mortar tubes.

I had only the vaguest idea where we were. There were no roads, no trails, no paths. I was surrounded by a cloying green hotness, with natural scents of freshness and decay suspended in the still air. Occasionally, I heard muted thwacking as the first few men in the formation used machetes to cut a narrow slit through the layers of leaves, branches, and vines that enclosed us. There was no other sound as one hundred heavily armed men scoured the jungle with sharp eyes. A sense of pride welled up in my chest.

After an hour and a half, a whisper was passed along the line to break in place for five minutes. I sat down and eased my arms out of my pack straps, glad to get the weight off if even for such a brief time. I took a long drink and checked to make sure my pack was holding everything in place. I adjusted the top flap and then leaned back against the pack. The sky was only visible in tiny slashes and spots of blue through the dense vegetation. Before I knew it, the word was quietly passed to saddle up.

Slipping into my pack straps and standing up, I whispered to José, "You know, Custer commanded this regiment, the Seventh Cavalry, at the Little Bighorn Battle in 1876."

He looked over at me and said, "Yeah, we try not to make too much outta that."

"Prob'ly wise," I muttered, and then we were off again, silently filing through the bush.

At midday, we broke for chow. I was soaked to the skin and now understood why every grunt wrapped a towel around his neck. Sure, it helped cushion the pack straps over the shoulders if you remembered to put it on before the pack, but mostly it soaked up the sweat that constantly flowed from under our steel pots. It was also handy to grab a dangling end and wipe sweat out of your eyes before it blinded you. We did try to keep one of our towels clean enough for shaving and infrequent showers, though.

I was so exhausted I didn't feel like eating, so I just snacked. I used my P38—a folding can opener about the size of pull tab on a soda can—to open a couple of my C-rations (noting that they'd been canned in 1955) and pulled out another of those things that served as a chocolate bar. A little later, I opened a tin can that looked like an olive drab version of a tuna can. It was marked Pound Cake on the lid and sure enough, in it was a fifteen-year-old pound cake. The chocolate bar tasted more like cardboard than candy, but the pound cake was darn good.

We never smoked while we moved—in the wilderness, tobacco smoke was like a siren going off—but during chow we had guys on guard, so we smoked. After finishing my snack, I leaned back and lit a Camel. It tasted wonderful and relaxed me as I watched the smoke float lazily in the steamy air and take forever to dissipate.

My squad mates relaxed in their own ways. Dread, who had his back to me, was doing something that caused him to nod his head a lot and snicker. As always, Howard Forman was next to Dread. He smiled and occasionally shook a clenched fist, saying, "Yes!"

"What's Dread doing?" I asked José.

"Oh, he likes napalming termites and ants, but especially termites."

"How the hell does he do that?" I asked.

"When he's done eating, he lights his plastic utensils on fire and tries to drop melted plastic on passing bugs. It works good," José added with a big smile.

"That's ingenious," I said.

"I'm sure he didn't come up with it himself, but it's a satisfying way to pass the time, all right. When you've been out in the field a little longer, you'll hate the damn bugs as much as the rest of us. And believe me, if you're ever bitten by a termite you'll remember it."

Too soon, we were off again. We'd been moving for about ten hours when the word came to halt and set up a night defensive perimeter (NDP). Each of the three rifle platoons was assigned one-third of a circular perimeter to guard, while the company command post (CP)—consisting of our captain, first sergeant, RTOs, and Mortar Platoon—was set up in the center.

For a company-size element such as ours, this meant creating an NDP roughly fifty feet across with a circumference of about 165 feet. Each of the six rifle squads provided a guard position, so the six guard holes were spaced about every thirty feet. Of course, no one measured this out or used a slide rule to mark these positions; it was done reflexively, quickly, and efficiently. As soon as the areas of responsibility were assigned, squads worked in coordination with the squads on their flanks to assure that spacing was uniform and that fields of fire overlapped. Adjustments were made for terrain and vegetation so that the fields of fire were as unobstructed as possible. This was important; geometric precision wasn't.

Along with everyone other than the officers, first sergeant, RTOs, and medics, I took my turn digging guard holes. The first foot was hard because it was the dry season, but after that the clay soil was easier to excavate. We used the waste dirt to create a berm in front of the hole. When finished, the hole was approximately three feet deep by three feet from front to back and four feet side to side. Two men could fit side by side, and the depth allowed a soldier to squat, kneel, or sit on his steel-pot helmet with his view to the front just above the little berm. While some dug, others placed Claymore mines at strategic locations. Since each of us carried one, there were about ten available for each guard hole. As on the Long Binh perimeter, the clackers were carefully positioned along the front edges of the holes.

In open terrain, an exploding Claymore sends its 700 eighth-inch steel balls in a sixty-degree arc that spreads to fifty meters across at fifty meters distance from the mine at no more than the height of a man if it's positioned correctly. At close range, it can cut down trees up to six inches in diameter and it can kill a man at 100 meters. Like the fields of fire from rifles and machine guns, the Claymores were positioned so that their effective ranges overlapped each other and the Claymores from adjacent guard holes.

Once all guard preparations were complete, we set up our individual shelters. This was an adventure for me, since I'd never had any training in creating a hooch. José was helpful, and I observed my other squad mates as well. The first step was to find two upright trunks—or rig up two sticks and stake them upright—tying a cord between the two supports. This formed the roof ridge. Cords were tied to the mosquito net, positioning it to hang loosely to the ground with no gaps on the sides or ends. The poncho was placed over the mosquito net and tied at the same points, and all four corners of the poncho were tied to anchor points to stretch it tightly so it would shed rain. Heavy items were placed on the inside edges of the net to hold it out and down just inside the drip lines of the poncho. After that, the air mattress was blown up and slipped inside, and finally, the poncho liner was arranged on top of the air mattress. It was important to find a level spot without sharp sticks or roots. The finished hooch was large enough for one man to comfortably lie down or sit up in and for two men in a pinch, and it kept the worst of the bugs and weather away.

When the hooches were completed, our squad leader, Sergeant Campbell, assigned guard shifts. Dusk to dawn was about twelve hours, and we had eleven guys available to pull guard, so everyone stood a one-hour shift. Being an FNG, I was assigned the 0200 to 0300 slot, which was considered the worst since it fell when people were most deeply asleep.

When in a company formation, the man on first shift took the "prick twenty-five" radio (PRC25) from Platoon RTO Berning and placed it beside one of the guard holes. If something bad or suspicious happened, we could notify the on-duty RTO at the CP (command post) without leaving the hole. Guards reported in once each hour by requesting a commo check. If all was well, the guard and the RTO confirmed that they could hear and understand each other by saying, "I hear you Lima Charlie," meaning loud and clear. The four platoon RTOs and the company RTO divided the duty of monitoring commo checks among themselves. I don't know how they managed to function, having their sleep interrupted so much every night.

With our immediate duties completed, things relaxed. Some guys sat on the ground against their rucksacks. Some read tattered paperbacks they carried in their ammo boxes, some wrote letters, others just stared off into the jungle—which effectively limited their view to less than ten meters—and two groups of four partnered up to continue the never-ending games of spades.

I was bone tired. At first, I leaned back against my rucksack and smoked. I felt the heat ... and the humidity ... and the wildness soaking into me. I turned to José and said, "You know, this place makes me feel more like I'm swimming than like I'm in open air."

"Yeah," he said, "It gets worse, believe me. No one *ever* gets used to it. After a while we start tolerating it and stop thinking about it."

"How long you been here, José?"

"Four months and seventeen days," was the instant reply.

"How long did it take you to stop thinking about the heat?"

He laughed. "Well, I guess I've never *completely* stopped thinking about it, but I'd say after about a week, it was no longer important. There's a saying among us grunts, 'Fuck it; it don't mean nothin'.'"

"What's that supposed to mean?"

"It means, if it don't kill you, it don't matter. Not at all. Not spit!"

"There is that. Thanks, José."

"For what?"

"For helping this FNG get his bearings."

"No hay problema, amigo."

I wandered over to watch the spades game where Dread was holding court. It reminded me of euchre, which I played when I was a boy. I loved that game, but hadn't played it in probably fifteen years. I continued to watch, trying to figure out the rules and the nuances.

My thoughts drifted to my Great Aunt Cody, who'd taught me euchre. Her real name was Cora Tyler, but in the mid 1880s as a young girl of nine or ten she'd spent several years at a stage stop operated by her aunt and uncle in Dayton, Wyoming Territory, not too far from where the town of Cody was founded fifteen years later, so the nickname stuck.

From the age of three, when I visited my grandparents Brayton and Marjorie Castle in Terre Haute, Indiana, "Cody," who was Marjorie's half-sister, had been my best friend and constant companion. We used to go for long walks of several miles around the fields of corn silos across the road from the family home my great-grandfather John Tyler built with his own hands following his return from service in the Union artillery during the Civil War. Aunt Cody shared wonderful stories with me on those walks, but the ones I remembered best took place during her time in Wyoming.

My daydreaming was interrupted when Dread bid "double nil." This meant he couldn't take a single trick. If he pulled it off, he'd get 200 points, but if he didn't, his opponents would get 200. When someone bids Nil, their partner makes an independent bid and gets scored separately. Of course, the partner can help him to lose tricks, but he has to be careful not to jeopardize his own bid by doing so. It was tense, but Dread did it, and when the last trick was lost, he exclaimed, "Fuckin' A, man!" and reached across the makeshift card table (a folded poncho liner) to slap hands with Forman.

The excitement over, my thoughts returned to a particular story Aunt Cody had shared with me. "The stage stop was near the base of the Bighorn Mountains and it was cold there in the winter, much colder than here," she said in her gentle, slightly shaky, high-pitched voice, "but my aunt and uncle always kept a fire blazing in the large stone fireplace, not just for us, but for stage passengers and other travelers who stopped by." Her gray-blue eyes glittered at the memory, as she went on.

"One especially cold January night, as we were eating dinner at their big pine table, we heard a soft tapping on a windowpane. When I turned toward it, I saw an Indian man with long graying braids, probably in his fifties, though it was hard to tell. There was a scarf or bandanna tied over his ears, and he had no gloves on the hand doing the tapping. He didn't say anything. He just pressed his nose to the glass. My uncle gave an affirmative nod to my aunt, who quickly wrapped some bread, butter and slices of elk meat from the serving plate, in a cloth napkin. 'Better give him some more,' my uncle said, 'I s'pect his family's out there, too.' My aunt tripled the original portion, folded the napkin over it and handed it to my uncle. 'Stay at the table, now,' he said to us reassuringly as he stood and walked to the door. He opened it a crack, nodded, and handed the food to the Indian without a word being spoken. When he returned to the table, he shook his head and, with a sad expression on his face, said, 'Poor devils.' Then we continued our meal. This happened from time to time," she said with a warm smile and crinkled eyes, "My aunt and uncle were kind people." This all happened ten years after Custer's Last Stand and fifty miles south of the battlefield. I loved my Aunt Cody. She'd died a decade before.

After about an hour, I wandered back to my hooch and pulled out a LRRP: beef stroganoff. My mother was a good—not great—cook, but her stroganoff was unbelievable. I guess I was yearning for some of that home cooking, as they say. I pulled a small piece off my bar of C-4 and lit it to boil some water. This was just one of the countless "field expedients" that combat troops developed to keep themselves safer, better fed, and better protected from the elements.

I opened the stiff, canvas-like, freeze-dried packet and poured in the boiling water. I then folded the top over a couple of times and sloshed the contents to mix the dried food with the water. Satisfied, I stuck a split stick over the folded top to keep it reasonably shut while I waited for the contents to completely hydrate. When the time was up, I opened the bag with low expectations. It was good! It wasn't my mother's stroganoff, but it was damn tasty. I ate slowly, which was hard since I was starving, but I wanted to savor every morsel. It was an escape into a private little ecstasy while it lasted. I was learning to appreciate the tiniest pleasures more completely, more thoroughly, than ever before.

After eating, I opened my ammo box and pulled out a photo of Julie Morse, the girl I dated briefly just before I left for Vietnam. Thinking about her made me feel warm and a little empty inside, as though there was a void that needed filling. Truth be told, she was too good for me, probably too young chronologically and too mature intellectually. While we liked one another, we weren't romantically interested. But when I asked if I could write to her, she said yes. I scrawled a few opening lines, but I was so hot and tired I couldn't concentrate. Besides, it was getting dark. I crawled into my hooch, took off my boots, and wrapped my GI towel around my shirt for a pillow. I was asleep in minutes.

Before I knew it, Superman was shaking me. "Wake up; it's your turn for guard."

"Okay, I'll be right there."

It took longer than I expected to find my boots and get them on. I'd have to work on that. I grabbed my M16, bandoliers, belt with one-quart canteens, and steel pot. Pushing my way under the mosquito net, I made my way toward the guard hole. Outside, it was the deep black I'd only once experienced before the Tay Ninh episode—on a tour of Carlsbad Caverns when the tour leader turned off the lights. In other words, I was blind.

When I thought I was close, I whispered, "Superman?"

"Yeah, right here," came a muffled response.

I made my way to the hole, where we exchanged places. "Make sure you feel for all twelve clackers, so you know where they are. Their positions are your best guide to your fields of fire, too."

"Right. Thanks, man."

"No problem," he muttered as he slunk back to his hooch.

I felt for the clackers. Then I took off my steel pot, turned it upside down and sat on it. It was uncomfortable, but better than squatting. There was no sound at all. That seemed strange to me. At night in wild country back in the World, there were almost always sounds: the rustling as wildlife moved about; distant calls of coyotes or night birds; even the sounds of beaver tails slapping the water, muskrats diving, small critters scuffling about, or fish jumping. But here there was nothing, sound was as absent as light.

I remembered something my father told me about brainwashing techniques the North Koreans used on their captives. They immobilized a prisoner in a tank of body-temperature water inside a dark soundproof container. Under those conditions—weightless, sightless and soundless—even a trained psychiatrist would begin to hallucinate in minutes. The prisoner's only contact with the outside world was irregular, infrequent, and always through the same handler, who would perhaps offer a morsel of food or a swallow of water and utter a simple phrase like, "Communism is good." After a surprisingly brief time, many prisoners were putty in the hands of these handlers. It was insidious, and in my present circumstances I could well believe that it was effective.

I kept my eyes wide open and listened as hard I could. Sometimes I thought I could make out barely audible rustling. Insects, I guessed, but I couldn't be sure I'd heard anything at all. I wasn't afraid, but I was alert. Time passed slowly, but it did pass. When I thought an hour had passed, I called in my commo check and asked what time it was. The RTO said it was nearly 0300, so I made my way to José's hooch. I woke him, returned to the hole, and waited. When he arrived, I went back to my hooch and caught another couple of hours of much needed sleep.

At dawn, the men began to stir. In ones and twos they stepped out past the guard holes to relieve themselves. I opened a C-ration of scrambled eggs dated 1953 and smelled them.

"They're fine," joked Superman. "Eat hearty!"

"Hey, why not." I smiled. "It don't mean nothin'. Right?"

"Right. You catch on quick."

After this, there were more trips outside the perimeter, some of which were to retrieve the Claymores. Then we punched extra holes in the C-ration cans we'd opened to prevent the enemy using them for explosive devices. All the plastic and metal waste was dumped into the guard holes, which we filled by pushing the berms back into them. We packed down the disturbed ground and scattered leaf litter to conceal the location. When we finished and packed our gear, the order was given to saddle up.

I put on my gear and slipped into my pack straps. Standing up, I crossed my two loops of machine gun ammo over the bandoliers and pack straps, and grabbed my M16.

As we were swallowed up once again by the bush, our silence merged gently with the wilderness. All was quiet … and watchful.

ABOVE - Setting up a two-man hooch in an NDP.
(photo 15-2)

LEFT - Saddled up and ready to hump.
(photo 15-1)

Chapter 16 – Humping Begins; Bees

That afternoon, the company split into three elements. First and Second Platoons each moved out alone, while Third Platoon accompanied Mortar Platoon as the third element. The theory was that the Mortar and Third Platoons would be Charlie Company's mobile reserve and fire support force if either of the other platoons made contact with the enemy. But at the time all I really knew was that twenty-five of us were going to be alone, somewhere in a hostile wilderness on the far side of the planet.

We were always alert humping through the boonies, but the level of alertness notched up a bit in a platoon-size element. My eyes constantly swept both of my flanks, the ground I was walking on, and the trees above me. I realized how essential it was not to miss anything, so I trained myself to focus and really register everything in my view. Throughout my tour, this intense awareness continually increased and never slackened. I found it addictive and intoxicating. It made humping through the boonies anything but boring. I began noticing how quickly time passed when I was so focused.

Before I knew it, it was time to set up our NDP. Although we'd split from the rest of the company, I figured we were still pretty close to each other. In such an impenetrable wilderness, however, one klick might as well have been ten. If the shit hit the fan, it was uncertain how effectively we could support one another. But *"Fuck it; it don't mean nothin',"* I thought. It was dawning on me what a useful and appropriate saying that really was!

It took me a lot less time to get my hooch up and make dinner. I was like a human sponge, not just because sweat was constantly being wrung out of me, but because I soaked up every drop of knowledge by watching everyone and everything. I figured it would increase my survival odds, so it wasn't as if I really had a choice. I was getting an education in adapting to an alien environment, and I'd automatically placed survival above all other priorities. Usually we don't have to consciously do that, but in a combat unit in a shooting war, it's at the forefront of consciousness all the time. For me, it wasn't just *my* survival that occupied that top spot on the priority list; it was *our* survival, every damn one of us. Maybe I'd always felt that way but never had occasion to crystallize the thought before then.

After dinner, I watched the spades game and began to catch on to more nuances. It was a game that kept the mind sharp while offering the closest thing to a true escape—though brief—from the constant physical demands of the hostile green steam bath we trudged through endlessly.

Campbell had again assigned me to the 0200 guard shift. I inspected my guard hole and then sat down outside my hooch, leaning against my pack. I smoked a cigarette and felt the exhaustion setting in.

"I'm just getting started at this and I'm dragging already," I told Superman, who was set up nearby.

"Join the crowd, man. It gets worse before it gets better, but you know ... fuck it; it don't mean nothin'!"

I had trouble rousing myself when Superman woke me for guard duty. Somehow, I made it to the hole and arranged myself on my steel pot. Shifting position amounted to moving the center of my butt a little to one side or the other atop the helmet. This alternated putting most of my weight first on one butt cheek and then on the other. It sure wasn't a La-Z-Boy, but at least my ass had been asleep most of the night.

On the third day out from Firebase Wood our food and water were getting low. I still had five quarts of water, but the consequences of running out in this heat were unthinkable. Of course, the upside of using up my supplies was that my load was lighter, and the humping was easier.

We headed for a spot the LT found on the topo map. With a little effort, it could work as an LZ for our resupply chopper. We reached it around 1000 hours, set up the two machine guns, and secured a circular area about 100 meters in diameter. Two men from each squad cut down trees and tall brush in the center so helicopters could safely land and take off.

When the work was done, we moved to the tree line perimeter and took up guard positions, in the shade if possible. We then pulled out clothing, boots, towels, and other expendable gear that was worn out or damaged. An itemized list had been radioed to battalion HQ earlier, and they stuffed replacement items, if available, into large plastic bags and loaded them onto our resupply chopper. This process was called direct exchange or DX. The term DX came to be commonly used to refer to anything that needed to be gotten rid of, exchanged, or improved—sometimes including officers or fellow grunts. Each squad gathered up all its DX items and placed them in a pile.

As often happened, our chopper was late. Finally, around 1500, we heard the slick approaching. Guided down by a smoke grenade popped in a pre-arranged color and hand signals from Platoon Sergeant Crippen, it landed and powered down its rotors. Our squad unloaded it, moving most things beyond the whirling rotor blades. Exceptions were the large blocks of ice brought to cool our beverages and the opaque rubber bladders filled with water (three to four feet long by ten to twelve inches in diameter); these were just pulled off the slick onto the ground beside it. One end of a bladder was held at waist level and sliced open; as the water gushed out, canteens were held under the flow to fill them. The procedure may have wasted a lot of water, but it was fast and did the job.

There were also clear plastic bags full of C-rations, LRRPs, and other goodies. Among them were cartons of cigarettes, rolls of toilet paper, beer and soda for each man, and candy bars or other feel-good items sent by well-wishers back in the World. Sometimes we even got a few paperback books. Each box of Cs included a small bundle of GI toilet paper banded with brown paper. Since this wasn't very absorbent, the rolls of back-in-the-world TP brought out on resupply days were highly valued! As the unloading continued, the bags with replacement items were emptied, and our discards were stuffed into the bags and tossed in the helicopter.

The chopper lifted off and another landed in its place. The second chopper had folding tables, insulated containers of hot food, and two guys who jumped off to serve it to us. This was unexpected for me, but it was First Cav SOP to give its infantrymen one hot meal every third day.

Each man also got two cans of soda and one can of beer. When someone wanted a cold soda or beer he placed the can on its side on the block of ice and spun it. The first few cans took a bit of coordination to prevent them flying off, but indentations quickly deepened under the spinning cans, and the beverages cooled rapidly. This method could chill a can in about a minute. Most of us traded our one beer for a third soda, which we usually packed for a treat at a later time. As much as I enjoy a cold beer, I really didn't feel like engaging in four hours of strenuous activity in sweltering heat immediately after downing one.

For the next week, we stayed in our platoon-size element and kept moving. I played spades a few times and gradually improved my skills. It was a good way for grunts to get to know each other in a non-military, non-war way. To be sure, the stark reality of our circumstances was all around us and as ready to hand as our ever-present M16s, but our concentration was on the game and the people playing it. Scores were carefully tallied, and games could go on for days. We looked forward to a game more than to any other thing we did on a regular basis. In a sense, it was a metaphor for our lives as combat infantrymen: we concentrated on the hands we were dealt and very little else.

I learned a lot about my squad mates in and around the spades games. I also discovered that there were a few traits that weren't tolerated, one of them being whining. Sure, we were expected to mock the military—specifically the Army—and grouse about this duty or that requirement, but truly feeling put upon or mistreated was not acceptable. There was no time for self-pity. Everyone was in the same boat, and to make it out alive we had to depend on each other. Whiners set themselves apart as petty and undependable and were outcasts to all but other whiners. I quickly learned that Private Stadler was our only whiner. Because his dad was a master sergeant—which he mentioned often—he seemed to feel it should give him a special status. He was tiresome and damned unpleasant to be around.

Eventually, we reached the Prek Kampong Spean, a good-sized river thirty to fifty kilometers to the west-northwest of Tay Ninh that formed twenty kilometers of the boundary between Cambodia and South Vietnam. This river is navigable and provided a transportation route for NVA and VC men and supplies from the Ho Chi Minh Trail in Cambodia to the most heavily populated parts of South Vietnam. But at the time, all we knew was that we were humping parallel to a wilderness river and that the far bank, less than 200 meters away, was Cambodia, which was off-limits to the U.S. military and considered enemy territory.

At one point, I heard a single-engine airplane passing repeatedly back and forth over the river. I caught a few glimpses of it through breaks in the canopy near the river's edge. It was no bigger than a Piper Cub.

"Is that one of ours?" I whispered to Campbell.

"Yeah, it's an FAO, forward artillery observer. They must think something's up along the border here."

The sound of the plane continued for an hour, then faded away. We were again enveloped by silence ... and the jungle.

Three hours after the plane disappeared, we found a circular area about twenty meters across and relatively free of vegetation and tree trunks—an ideal place to stop for the night. As always, gun positions were set first. As I began to look for a good place to set up my hooch someone on the opposite side of the clearing let out a loud yell. I was shocked. The near total silence we maintained on patrol was *never* broken, and even in an NDP noise was kept to a minimum. I turned around abruptly and saw men shouting and running in all directions, many without even remembering to grab their weapons.

Someone yelled, "Bees!"

I grabbed my M16 and a bandolier of ammo and moved ten meters back toward the river. I was stung a few times, along with everyone else, but I focused my attention down our back trail as things began to calm down. Superman joined me.

"What the hell happened?" I asked.

"Some guy in Second Squad started digging their guard hole right into an underground bees' nest."

"Jesus. Been there and done that. I guess we now know the best way to disrupt a well-oiled military machine," I joked.

The LT came over and said, "Move slowly and gather up your gear. Looks like we're gonna have to move a little way upriver."

"LT!" shouted RTO Berning. "LT!"

"Calm down, Bob. What's the matter?"

"It's Roger. He's down. We don't know what's wrong with him."

"All right. Let's check him out. Men, secure the area as best you can until we sort this out."

I followed the LT and could see that Campbell was unconscious and blowing up like a balloon.

"It's anaphylactic shock, LT," I said without thinking.

Our platoon medic, Corporal Henry Jacobs, was already bent over Roger, tearing free a syringe. "I agree with Sergeant Thompson, LT. Roger's been stung pretty bad, and I'm giving him a shot of Benadryl. But we need to get him a medevac ASAP. He's already unconscious and swelling up."

"All right! Bob, request an immediate medevac for Staff Sergeant Campbell."

"Yes sir," replied Berning.

"Sergeant Thompson." Lieutenant Bowen turned toward me.

"Yes, sir," I answered.

"You're now the squad leader of First Squad."

"Are you sure you want to do that?" I asked in surprise.

"I'm sure," he said firmly. "Now get your squad together and find us a spot close by where we can set up an NDP. I'll keep the rest of the platoon here to secure Roger for the medevac."

"Yes, sir," I said. "Okay, men, you heard the LT. Grab your gear and follow me."

We silently moved upstream along the river. Within 200 meters we found an area. I sent two men twenty meters farther along to guard that approach, two men back to the get the rest of the platoon, and the rest of us fanned out around our new NDP. I stayed to set up our temporary gun position and choose a location for our guard hole. There was no repeat of the bee incident.

The medevac chopper hovered over our previous position and used a jungle penetrator—essentially a chair on a cable—to lift Campbell and two other men from Second Squad out. Shortly after, we got word that it was a close thing, but Roger and the others would be all right. The rest of the platoon joined us and closed the perimeter on our new NDP.

"Roger and the other two men will never be allowed back in the field again," the LT told me. "It's just too risky. So First Squad is yours now." I know I looked dubious on hearing that, but the LT said, "Just be yourself and you'll be fine."

There were times when the LT looked much older than his twenty-five years. This was one of them. His voice was tired, and his face bore a serious expression. "Jamie, this damn place can hurt and kill you in a lot of ways that don't have anything to do with the NVA or VC. Remember that!"

That night, I assigned the same guard shifts including my own that Roger had assigned since we'd left Firebase Wood, only longer of course because we were down a man. I could tell the men were surprised, but it was the right thing to do. I might be a squad leader, but I was still an FNG.

My squad had point the next day and I assigned Forman the job. He wasn't happy, but he did as ordered. He had experience and he wasn't quite as "short" as his buddy Dread. I realized that when the time a grunt had left in Vietnam was short, his nerves often got to him. Why the risk of death would seem closer at such a time than it did at any other was a mystery to me, but there it was. Dread walked cover right behind Forman. Then came José, then me, and then the gun crew, with Stadler bringing up our rear.

Our new azimuth, the compass direction we were to initially follow, turned us to the southeast, away from the river, back the way we'd come, though by a different route. The day was uneventful, which was good for me.

That evening I picked the location of our guard hole and assigned the same guard shifts. I detected a change in the way my squad mates interacted with me, but nothing dramatic. While I understood that with command, a certain distance was required, I did not believe it made me more entitled to privilege than anyone under my command. I played spades that night with Superman as my partner. We lost the first game, but won the second rather handily over Dread and Forman. We were happy about it, but didn't gloat … visibly at least. It had been clear from the beginning that Dread and Forman intended to put their FNG squad leader in his place when it came to spades.

After the game, I spent a few minutes talking to José.

"How'd it go for you today, Sarge?" he asked.

"It was okay, but between you and me, it'll take a while before I settle into the job. There's a lot I don't know that only experience can teach me."

"That's true, my friend, but at least you *know* you don't know shit. That's important, and it's important that all of us know you know it. This is a hard thing, and we've all had close calls and lost friends here. It's a brotherhood, man. In a way, we've earned our survival and we share a bond that's stronger than any other. When you've earned yours, you'll know. In the meantime, respect us and learn what we know, and we'll return that respect."

"José, you're a philosopher!" I said.

"No, mi amigo, I'm a survivor. And you must be, too."

I put out my cigarette and field-dressed the butt—tearing open the paper and sprinkling the remaining tobacco over the ground. Then I rolled the paper into a tight ball and flicked it off into the brush. I lay awake for a while before drifting off. My thoughts were tightly focused on what must be done the next day, but my exhaustion was reaching levels I'd never experienced. My body's need for sleep overpowered my mind's need to plan, but perhaps I'd been over-thinking anyway.

Chapter 17 – Claymores and Arc Lights

When Superman shook me for my guard shift, I again had trouble waking up. The night was black as coal, and there was no sound. My mind meandered through memories and images. Among them was Julie Morse. Visualizing her, I felt warm and affectionate. *"What a good person she is,"* I thought idly. I resolved then and there to finish my letter to her the next day.

After my shift, I slept deeply until the sound of men moving around awakened me. My first thought was how badly I needed to take a shit. I grabbed my M16, bandoliers, and entrenching tool, and made sure my men knew where I was going. I found a moderate diameter fallen tree trunk, made sure there were no bugs on or under it, dug a small shallow hole on the back side of it, and sat with most of my butt hanging over the hole. It was awkward, but when you gotta go, you go. I'd used the last of my real TP the day before, so I used a packet of the GI toilet paper, then covered the hole and scattered leaf litter over it. Most of the time I just squatted without any tree trunk. If nothing else was true of jungle warfare, this was: we returned to a state of existence that predated civilization, a state our distant forebears adapted to and survived in for far longer than civilization's eye blink.

The pattern of humping, setting up, guarding, and saddling up went on and on. The physical toll of carrying eighty-pound packs, making our way through thick vegetation in sweltering heat and humidity, and remaining alert despite perpetual sleep deprivation wore heavily on all of us. We were in a state of ultra-heightened alertness while otherwise functioning on autopilot.

One day merged seamlessly with the last and into the next. Other than the here and now, the passage of time was blurred and irrelevant. This unique state of "gruntness" only faded fleetingly, in the intervals between setting up the NDP and sleeping, and between waking and saddling up. But even in those intervals, total alertness was only an eyelash away.

During our next resupply day, my squad got Woodrow Myrick to replace Sergeant Campbell. Woody was a lanky kid from Mississippi. His appearance and slow way of talking reminded me a lot of the Sergeant York character played by Gary Cooper in the movie of the same name. I can't say for sure that Woody could shoot the eye out of a squirrel at a hundred yards, but I just kind of assumed he could. I took an instant liking to him.

One afternoon we set up in the tree line at the edge of an area of less dense vegetation. Because of the exposed lay of the land, the LT decided to set out an Alpha-Alpha (automatic ambush) that night along a likely approach route where we'd found a narrow trail. It was my squad's turn to set out the Alpha-Alphas and since only NCOs or officers were authorized to set them up, it fell upon me to do it. I'd never done it before, and neither had the three men I took with me.

About 200 meters from the NDP we found a good spot to conceal a Claymore mine and I strung a trip wire across the trail. I had my men watching the jungle around us as I worked. Because I'm careful by nature, I made *very* sure the mine was facing exactly the way I wanted it to, at the right declination to assure maximum damage over maximum range. I then made certain all the men were behind not only the Claymore, but the battery, which was thirty feet behind the mine, before I attached the wires to the battery.

It's a damn good thing I did this, because when I connected the wires the mine exploded. Electrical connections have never been my long suit, but this was embarrassing. Undaunted, I found a new location for a second Claymore, and when I connected the wires, that one blew, too. Third time was a charm, thank God. By then I'd realized that I was making the gap between the electrical wires that would be closed when the trip wire was tripped too narrow. In other words, my conscientious effort to make sure everything worked right had been counterproductive! The electricity was jumping the tiny gap as soon as the wires from the battery went live. If the enemy was near enough to have heard the debacle, he would likely think the explosions were from artillery fire rather than mines and avoid the area, believing it was a zeroed-in firing point for our big guns. That night, I was the butt of good-natured ribbing rather than mean-spirited ridicule. No one was happier about that than I was.

There were several good things that came out of this incident. First, my men and I had two opportunities to see firsthand the destructive power and range of Claymore mines in dense terrain. Within twenty feet of the detonation tree trunks five inches in diameter were shredded, but damage was limited to a maximum range of only forty feet. This lesson ensured that we always placed Claymores properly when setting them up as Alpha-Alphas or as perimeter defense. It also let everyone know I had a sense of humor.

The following morning, I retrieved the Alpha-Alpha without incident. When doing this, great care had to be taken. Obviously, I didn't want to trip my own device by walking past the hidden battery into the trip wire, but also the enemy was known to sometimes discover Alpha-Alphas and reposition them to blow away the people who'd set them.

One thing of note during this time was that I decided to take the point myself. I did it for two reasons: I didn't like ordering someone else to do the most dangerous job in the infantry, and I trusted my own senses and abilities more than anyone else's. It was a fairly unusual decision, but it was also what Roger Campbell had chosen to do. The SOP was for squad leaders to choose others to walk point while they took a position near the center of the squad to provide command and control if the shit hit the fan. But it seemed to me—given our single-file formations and the dense vegetation—that being three to five men back from the point was too far away to effectively command and control the action. Lieutenant Bowen supported my decision, and my instinct proved to be right. I chose Woody as my cover man. His vision was as good as mine, maybe better, and his outdoor skills were excellent and instinctive. Also he was new. Next to point, cover was the most dangerous place to be, so it was only right that the guys who'd done the most time in hell got a break now and then

On one of many seamless platoon-size humping days, the LT passed the word that we needed to find cover ASAP because an Arc Light was going to take place nearby. An Arc Light was a bombing strike by B-52s, each plane carrying 54,000 pounds of explosives. A typical strike used three planes flying in an arrowhead formation and destroyed an area three miles long by a half mile wide. Normally, Arc Lights were not allowed any closer to our troops than three klicks, but for reasons unknown, this one was going to be closer. We needed no encouragement to seek shelter and found some deep bomb craters, no doubt caused by Arc Lights in years past.

Our crater was twenty-five feet across and ten feet deep, with a puddle of muddy water in the bottom. A downed tree trunk, two feet in diameter, lay across the center of it. We got into prone positions around the sides of the crater with our heads just below the rim. We would have no warning before the bombs impacted, since the B-52s flew at 30,000 feet and would be neither seen nor heard.

As we waited, the men began smoking and joking among themselves. After a few minutes, I noticed that the shady underside of the fallen tree trunk was populated by between six and ten scorpions. They were of three types, some were brown and small (two inches long), and the others were either black or kind of bluish and larger (five to six inches long). Having lived in Arizona, scorpions were no strangers to me, but I still found them damned unpleasant to look at, let alone to have close by.

While the big black ones certainly looked the most dangerous, I couldn't help remembering that in Arizona it was the small pink ones that were the most poisonous. "Look at that," I said to Dread as I pointed.

"Yeah. Nasty little critters, ain't they?"

"You can say that again!"

I noticed that the scorpions were not moving at all. I supposed they were nocturnal and just trying to stay out of sight during daylight. "Well, it's live and let live. Let's leave 'em alone," I said.

"Works for me," said Dread.

Time seemed to drag, but I suppose it was less than half an hour before the ground began to shake. Concentric ripples radiated outward from the center of the puddle at the bottom of the crater. This continued for a few seconds before the sounds of terrifically powerful explosions reached us. The shaking and thundering stutter of exploding bombs went on for half a minute. We gave the Arc Light no more thought as we humped away.

That evening we rejoined the rest of Charlie Company, and things returned to normal. We kept humping longer than usual the next day and weren't able to set up the NDP until close to dark. I was so exhausted I decided to change the guard shifts and give myself the last shift before dawn. That would give me a chance for a longer period of uninterrupted sleep, which my body was telling me I needed badly.

In the middle of the night I became vaguely aware of explosions in the distance. I don't know whether I was sick or just so exhausted I wasn't able to wake fully, but I continued to sleep fitfully through it. When José came to wake me, I told him I was awake, and he should go get some sleep. It was true, but I made the mistake of closing my eyes ... just for a second.

I awoke with a start and realized it was almost dawn; I'd slept through a good part of my guard shift.

My first thought was that men had been shot for such things in other wars. I was angry and ashamed. Gathering myself, I crawled to the guard hole. I was lucky. No harm had come to us, and no one was aware of what I'd done. From that time on, I insisted that when a man woke his replacement, he always returned to the guard hole until relieved.

After morning chow, we were told we'd move back along a road to be picked up for transport back to Firebase Wood. This was highly unusual. When we reached the road, we put flankers at its edges and moved east. I knew this was just not done. Normally, grunts avoided moving directly on *trails*, let alone on roads. The risk of mines, booby traps, and punji pits—or being sniped at or ambushed—was just too great. But now we were being ordered to do just that.

"Something's up," Dread whispered to me.

"Yeah, I was thinking the same thing." I was beginning to realize that Dread was a force to be reckoned with when the going got tough. I was glad we'd reached a condition of mutual respect. Thank God for spades.

We moved quickly down the road for about a klick, until a nearly impenetrable tangle of broken trees, rocks, and dirt completely blocked the road for an indeterminate distance ahead. The late morning sun was wickedly hot, and I had the strange thought that we were out of our element. The multi-canopy jungle was our friend.

As we approached the tangled mass, a sickly-sweet smell assaulted our nostrils.

"Hey, LT. Take a look at this," said Sergeant Crippen.

"What is it?" the LT asked.

"It appears to be a foot."

The LT bent over and looked deep into the pile of twisted trees. "I agree, Sergeant. That explains the stench. This must be where that Arc Light was dropped a few days ago." The LT straightened up. "All right, men, try not to let the stink and the sights get to you. We'll get through as fast as we can. Move out!"

Never have I smelled anything as bad as that twisted stretch of dead trees and dead men. As we moved over, around, under, and through the mess, it became evident that the enemy had carried away all major body parts. It was their habit to haul off their dead, both to give them decent burials and to reduce our ability to know what damage we were inflicting. Some of their combatants had handles attached to their bootheels that folded up against the back of the ankle for walking, but made dragging their corpses off the battlefield easier and quicker. As we moved through the seemingly interminable stretch of carnage, Vietnamese ears, noses, eyeballs, hands, feet, fingers, toes, and lengths of intestines were occasionally visible in the debris. We didn't stare or linger; we moved along as quickly as we could.

After about a klick we again came to open road. But the stench of rotting human flesh remained in my nose and on my tongue no matter how far I moved from the Arc Light strike or how often I rinsed out my mouth. Half a klick farther along, five deuce-and-a-half trucks waited for us. About thirty seconds into our ride, I felt much like I had when a friend gave me a ride in his brand-new Corvette. I was traveling in luxury.

Half an hour later we entered the dry lakebed where Firebase Wood was located and were unloaded in almost the same place where we'd piled into slicks two weeks earlier.

Chapter 18 – Wood; Bu Dop; The Dunes

Wood was a hive of activity. We formed up and Captain Osgood told us that Wood had been hit the previous night by a large NVA force.

"That explains the explosions I heard," Superman whispered.

"This morning seventy-three enemy bodies were found, and we know more were hauled off," the captain continued. "We had thirteen men wounded but no KIAs. It would have been a hell of lot worse without that Arc Light."

"That's for damn sure," I said.

"Okay, men, get some chow, top off your supplies, and be back out here ready to hit the road in these trucks in one hour. Dis-missed!"

As we walked through the gap in the berm, I saw Gordon Castro, one of my fellow candidates from NCO school. His left arm was wrapped in a field dressing and sling.

"Hey, Castro. What the hell happened?" I shouted.

"Jesus, man. It's good to see you. Christ, all hell broke loose last night. We went to the berm a little after 0300 for a scheduled Mad Minute and got return fire. It was crazy. I mean the whole goddamn tree line lit up with AK and machine-gun fire. And then they started lobbing in those damn mortars. It's a fuckin' miracle none of us were killed!"

Castro was pretty shaky, and I didn't blame him.

"We were a few klicks away and heard the fight, but didn't know what it was," I said. Then I told him what we'd seen in the wreckage of the Arc Light.

"God, it's a good thing they hit those bastards before they made it here, or I might not be talking to you right now." Castro grinned when he said it, but his eyes were serious.

"So tell me what happened to your arm," I said.

"I'm not sure. I was either hit by shrapnel or grazed by a bullet. I didn't even know I was hit 'til after the battle when a medic noticed the blood."

"You might be the first from our NCO School platoon to get a Purple Heart," I said.

"Holy shit! I hadn't thought about that. I guess I *will* get a Purple Heart." Castro's eyes were wide, as the reality of being wounded hit him for the first time.

"No doubt about it," I said, gently squeezing his other shoulder. "Hey, I want you to meet Superman and José from my squad."

"Glad to meet you," Castro replied. "Hey, wha'd'ya mean, *your* squad?"

I told him how greatness had been thrust upon me by a nest of angry bees.

"I guess that makes you and Kurt the first to get commands, such as they are," he said.

"You've seen Kurt?" I asked.

"Yeah. His company was on Wood last week. He's the leader of Second Squad, First Platoon, Alpha Company."

"How did he seem?"

"He was good, but you know Kurt, he's not much of a talker, so I'm reading between the lines."

"Yeah, but he seemed all right to you?"

"Yeah, Kurt's a solid guy. He handles this shit better than most."

We excused ourselves to get to the mess hall. While eating, Superman said, "Hey, did ya hear about Cambodia?"

"No. What about it?"

"We invaded the place."

"What the fuck!" I exclaimed. "What units?"

"I think it's just the 11th Armored Cav," said Superman.

"Maybe, but something tells me we won't be far behind."

"Yeah. That would explain the weirdness lately. I mean like the close Arc Light and the ride back to Wood."

"You're right... unfortunately." I looked around at my squad mates and added, "You know, I think the Army has a corner on the chipped beef market. I can't remember seeing any of this stuff for years in the civilian world."

"Me neither," José said.

We cleaned our plates, washing the beef chips down with the Kool-Aid du jour.

Fed and watered, we sat on our packs at the departure point, BSing about the Cambodia thing. The LTs formed up the platoons and Captain Osgood addressed us again.

"Men, as you may know, a few days ago a major offensive began inside Cambodia. We're being trucked to a Special Forces camp that has a fixed-wing airstrip. We'll set up there for the night and tomorrow we'll be flown to a second Special Forces camp farther north called Bu Dop. From there we'll CA into Cambodia, an area called The Fishhock. So grab your gear and climb on your trucks. Let's move out."

We scrambled onto the trucks, small cogs in a military machine that churned and turned with a life of its own. If we were apprehensive, we hardly noticed. I mean, what were they going to do, send us to the Nam? Oh, that's right, they already had.

I felt a swell of pride that our country had the raw power and wherewithal to transport half-a-million young men to the far side of our planet; clothe, feed, and supply them there; and provide them with powerful weapons to enforce its national will in a place as foreign as any on earth. I knew things were not as simple as that, but I was still awed by the power, capability, and audacity of the United States.

We got to the camp around 1500 hours and found that a good part of our battalion was already there. We were told to stay where we were, a sparsely vegetated area southeast of the road we'd come in on and just to the southwest of the camp, and wait for further orders. I took this as an opportunity to explore a little. Alone, I left my pack in the care of the squad, threw one bandolier over a shoulder, picked up my M16 and walked toward the camp. I soon passed under a ragged plank stretched between two tall posts that I guessed was the entrance to the base itself. It reminded me of a makeshift copy of the kind of gates you see over ranch roads along highways in the West. On it was scrawled, "You Are Entering Prek Klok, Abandon All Hope!" or words to that effect. The berm was low, but well sandbagged and the interior sandbagged structures were few, far between, and lower than regular Army firebases. In other words, they were partly dug in below ground. There was no activity and I saw very few troops. The place had a forlorn and forgotten feel to it that made me vaguely uneasy.

I spotted a structure that was clearly the local watering hole, so I made a beeline for it. It was only about fifteen feet across and maybe twenty-five feet long, with triple layers of sandbags for walls and a roof made of PSP and four layers of sandbags. PSP was the acronym for Perforated Steel Plank, thick, stiff steel plates with holes to reduce weight and allow water, dirt and sand to pass through. The plates had protruding 'L's on one long edge and slots on the other that allowed them to be locked together side by side. When laid in a staggered pattern, large areas could be locked together. It was used for all kinds of things, but mostly to construct landing pads and runways in the field. There was also a variety that was not perforated, which was great for leak proof bunker roofs that allowed layers of sandbags to be placed on top of them. The holed sheets were about a foot-and-a-half by twelve feet and the solid ones were about two feet by fourteen feet.

There was a Playboy Calendar pinned to the sandbag wall behind the small bar at the east end, and six small tables with four chairs at each filling the rest of the space. Two Special Forces guys sat together at one table and another was behind the bar. They all looked at me, or really through me, but no one said a word. All three of them reminded me of Kurt's roommate at Fort Sill. These guys were killers and I was a pansy grunt, less to them than the dirt under their feet. Their contempt was a tangible thing in that bunker bar. I was an unwelcome visitor to their very private, very hidden, very secret war. At least that's the impression they gave me.

I stepped to the bar and said, "Can I get a beer?"

"Two bucks," came the terse response from the surliest bartender I'd ever seen. One look at the guy told me that bartending duties at Prek Klok were rotated among the combat troops; this guy was hard as nails. Two dollars was four times the going rate, but I handed him a five-dollar MPC note and he pushed three ones back across the bar, opened a cold can of Miller High Life and clunked it down in front of me.

"Thanks," I said in a firm but friendly way as I looked the guy straight in the eye. I turned and sat at a table. There was nothing to do in the place and no one to talk to, but I appreciated being out of the sun and drinking a cold beer that wasn't Carling Black Label. I looked around and noted that symbols and macabre sayings had been carved into every available piece of wood, especially the tables. One carving said, "Jodie got my girl, good fuckin' riddance!" Another said, "Prek Klok – shithole to some, paradise to us." I took as much time finishing my beer as I could stand, but was outta there in about five minutes.

"Thanks," I said to the bartender as I opened the screen door to leave.

He merely grunted through his nose.

His condescending, more macho than thou attitude might have resulted from some personal hell unknown to me, but it was wrong to treat fellow line troops this way. I had no time for it. *"Fuck the asshole,"* I thought.

I got back to my squad and joined in the group wait. Finally, at around 1630, we were formed up and told to spread out into the brush along the southeast side of the road to set up our NDPs. Charlie Company dropped off to the flank within about 100 meters of where we'd been waiting for hours. It was a very strange place to set up any kind of defensive position. It reminded me of White Sands. The terrain consisted entirely of hummocks of sand between five and ten feet high separated by very narrow dips. All the hummocks were covered with deeply-rooted, tough-stemmed plants, some similar to sagebrush but with larger leaves, and some more like manzanita. The dips were sparsely vegetated with a mixture of what looked to me like forbs and isolated blades of grass. I guessed it was an area that had been repeatedly sprayed with Agent Orange to provide better fields of fire for the Prek Klok camp. We did the best we could to find an area we could guard that offered enough hooch-size spots for all of us. For the remaining daylight, I set the squad gun up in a small notch near the top of a higher dune pointing to the southeast away from the road and designated the guard hole just behind it; after dark the gun would be pulled back and riflemen would pull guard there. Between my shifts digging the hole, I set up my hooch in a completely unsuitable spot near the base of a dune. I cleared barely enough space to set it up by using my entrenching tool to hack away some of the brush at the base of the dune and then chopping the ground up under it to soften the hard-packed sand. When I was finished, I made an inspection of my part of the perimeter and judged it adequate under the circumstances. But as I checked our guard hole, I thought I heard something.

"Do you hear that?" I asked Dread whose hooch was nearby.

"You mean anything beyond all the complaining about the shit-for-brains idiot who decided to have us set-up in this abandoned prairie dog town?" he answered.

"Yeah, beyond that," I said with a smile of agreement.

"Nah. I ain't heard nothin'."

"Okay, but just in case, I'm gonna go check it out. Spread the word so nobody blows me away out there."

"You can count on me, Sarge!" he said a little too enthusiastically. But I knew beyond doubt that he would have my ass covered.

I took a bandolier and my M16 and walked past our perimeter – such as it was – and just as I stepped past the Claymores, I was sure I heard muffled talking. Because of the damn dunes and brush, I couldn't see anything more than about five meters to my front. I very cautiously moved a bit further until I was almost positive I was hearing American voices. I stepped through a gap between two higher dunes and could see a GI camp in a swale about thirty feet away and a dozen feet below me.

"Hello, the camp," I called out in a loud but gentle tone.

Several grunts who were seated around the center of their NDP looked up at me and said, "Come on in." One of them waved me down with his arm. "Hey, you want a cup a coffee?"

"Sure, that'd be great!" I said as I joined them. "What a cluster fuck this is. My company is set up about forty meters behind me and we had no idea you or anybody was to our front."

"We didn't know you were there either!" said the arm waver as he handed me a canteen cup of hot coffee. "What unit are you with?"

"Charlie Company, 5th of the 7th, 1st Cav," I said.

"We're in the 25th," he said. "I'm Sgt Tom Alderson by the way. Leader of this motley bunch." I noted that the men who heard him all looked over with big smiles. I liked this guy.

"I'm Sergeant Jamie Thompson, leader of our 1st squad, 1st platoon. Have you got any idea what's going on here?"

"Probably no more than you. I guess you're going north into Cambodia and we're moving southwest to take over your old AO [Area of Operations] and move into Cambodia from there."

"Well, that second part is something I didn't know," I said taking a pull on the coffee. "I think we need to accommodate ourselves to this situation. I'll tell my men to move their fields of fire to either side of your location and to be damn careful before firing at anything out this way. I'd appreciate it if you'd do the same."

"It's a deal!" he said sticking his hand out for a shake. "That should work, since we're kind of the far edge of a company-size circular NDPs.

"Actually, our set up is a little different. Our whole battalion is strung out in a rough line parallel to the road just beyond our position."

"Okay, I'll make damn sure our guys know where you are and I'll spread the word to the rest of the company," said Tom.

"Thanks. You know, Tom, it might make more sense if we both just left our facing positions unguarded tonight."

"I agree. Besides, God knows we need the rest!"

"Same with us."

"Can you tell me what your old AO is like?" asked Tom. At that, several of his men moved within earshot.

"Most of the area is wilderness," I said, "no villages and very few trails or roads. There's a river at the Cambodian border that's used by the NVA and VC to ferry men and supplies into Vietnam and one main road leading from it to Tay Ninh and on to Saigon that I'm sure the enemy would dearly love to use, too!"

I told Tom about the bees and said, "So you see, I owe the success of my military career to a bunch of angry bugs." This got a laugh out of Tom and our audience.

We compared notes on the details of our operations. Tom said, "We get hot meals and resupply every other day..."

"Wait!" I said, "every second day?"

"Yeah, isn't it the same for you guys?"

"No. For us it's every third day. I guess there are only so many helicopters to go around," I lamented.

"Isn't that just like the fuckin' Army," said Tom. "The 25th doesn't have any helicopters in it, and the 1st Cav does. So naturally, since we don't have any of our own, whenever we need one we have first call on using yours!"

"And we, since we have hundreds of 'em, suck hind tit!" I finished for him.

"That sums it up quite well," Tom said with a smile.

"You know, Tom, this is kind of a big deal. It means we're forced to carry one-third more weight in water and food than you guys."

"True, but think of how much better shape you guys are in because of it," he joked.

"There is that! I guess..."

"Listen guys," I said more seriously. "Most of the time our old AO was just boring humping and lots of sweat, but you should be aware that in the past six weeks there have been two major attacks on firebases that flank that road. The most recent was last night at Firebase Wood. Our guys lucked out for two reasons. First, the attack was disrupted just before it was due to begin by a Mad Minute, and second, an Arc Light two days before that landed right in the middle of an NVA battalion on that same damn road. We walked through the aftermath and it was some nasty shit."

I was really enjoying this interlude with Tom and his men, but the sun was about to set and no matter how conscientious Dread had been in letting everybody know where I was, I had to get back to my NDP before that happened. I placed my borrowed canteen cup on the ground, stood up and said, "Tom, it was a real pleasure meeting you and your squad. I've gotta get back. You be careful out there!"

"We will," said Tom, extending his hand again. "You be careful, too!" he said with feeling. One of his men said very seriously, "Thank you for the info, Sergeant."

"No problem," I smiled back. Tom and I looked at one another long and hard, nodding with narrowed eyes as I turned back toward my NDP and disappeared into the hummocks and brush. Two strangers who could have been life-long best friends; we knew we'd never meet again.

When I got back to my squad I first talked to the LT and explained the positioning of Tom's squad from the 25th. He agreed that the safest plan was to leave our guard positions set up but unmanned, so that's what we did. This was welcome news. It meant that everyone in the squad got the first uninterrupted night's sleep in many weeks.

The next morning the field elements of the 5/7, somewhere near 500 men, packed up and moved out to one end of the airstrip. Naturally, no aircraft were to be seen, so we spent our time playing spades and shooting the breeze.

"Not much of an airstrip," said Dread.

"No, and not much room for error either," I said, motioning to the ditches paralleling both sides of it.

"Fuck it; it don't mean nothin'," Forman contributed.

"True," I said, taking another trick.

"Hey Jamie, wha'd'ya think of all this?" Superman asked.

"You mean about this particular shit hole or the Cambodia thing?" I asked

"Cambodia."

"Well, one thing's for sure. It's gonna raise a hell of a stink back in the World. But that won't make one iota of difference to us. It'll just be more of the same, only worse, maybe. I mean, your guess is as good as mine about how much contact we're likely to run into, but it's bound to be more than we've seen."

"I agree," said Dread. "We haven't been in the shit since last fall, and the odds are against us."

"Jesus, Dread, how much time have you got left now, anyway?" I asked.

"Forty-three days."

"Have you heard anything about the Army pulling you out of the field."

"Nope, but I guess I got lost in the shuffle of the firebase attacks and the Cambodia thing," he said, more somberly than I'd ever heard him. "Made it!" he said as he swept up his eighth trick.

I was tired of sitting in the increasing heat, so I left the game and sought out the LT. "You know, LT, Dread is really short. Only forty-three days left. Maybe he shouldn't even be going into Cambodia."

"He's certainly close to getting pulled out of the line. I can't do anything about it right now, but I'll work on it when we get on the ground in Cambodia. In case you hadn't noticed, things aren't exactly running smoothly right now."

"I've noticed. All the men have."

There were still no planes at noon so we broke out our Cs and LRRPs and had lunch. Finally, at 1400 the first C-130 landed. Eighty guys hurried aboard, and the plane was airborne in a few minutes. From that point on, the planes kept coming. Soon enough, it was our turn. We squeezed most of Charlie Company into the aircraft, stowing our gear beneath us.

Twenty minutes later, we set down on a larger airstrip at Bu Dop Special Forces Camp near the Cambodian border. We made our way outward, past the gradually evolving NDPs of the already arrived troops, and ended up at the northern end of the large, temporary camp.

We dug our guard holes and set up fields of fire. After that it was back to eating, spades, and sleeping. At dusk, as I crawled into my hooch, I thought, *"There's something to be said for carrying everything you own on your back. Something, but I'm not sure exactly what."*

Guard duty that night was uneventful. We were basically on the edge of a metropolis by infantry standards. Ours wasn't the only battalion set up at Bu Dop that night. I figured there were well over a thousand men within a stone's throw of my guard hole, all of us armed to the teeth. It was as safe as a grunt could ever be in the Nam.

The next morning, the LT showed us a topo map. "As you can see, there's a large dry lakebed here. The slicks will drop us off and we'll set up a firebase on the northwest edge of the lakebed. Got it?"

"Got it," we answered in unison.

I returned to my pack and was gearing myself for another long wait, when the LT yelled at me and waved me over.

"Someone fucked up," he said without preamble. "There's no one assigned to ride in the first slick. So grab your gear and five of your guys and get to the runway. The choppers will be here any minute."

"Yes, sir," I said, much more formally than usual.

I rushed back to my squad and picked Superman, Stadler, Ardmore, Fuerte, and Blaine. "Grab your gear and saddle up. We're heading out now!"

Seconds after we made it to the edge of the runway, we heard the distant thrumming of helicopters, but it was unlike anything we'd heard before. From our vantage point, we had an unobstructed view down the length of the airstrip. The sight was jaw-dropping. Three staggered lines of slicks flying in perfect formation appeared in the distance, descended toward the airstrip, and landed in formation—simultaneously. The noise and the sight vibrated the soul.

The lead helicopter—closest to us—was the point chopper for the entire formation of fifty slicks. We ran in a crouch to the open door. I noted that the door gunner was manning a minigun, not the usual M60 machine gun. (A minigun puts out up to 6,000 rounds a minute.) I positioned myself next to the door gunner with my legs hanging out the door. My men scrambled past me and arranged themselves in the aircraft.

Chapter 19 – The Parrot; Into Cambodia

The formation sped northward, flying 200 feet above the ground at 120 mph. The noise was intense, but I relished the cool feel of the wind above the jungle. The usual sea of green flowed beneath us, though I couldn't help noticing that this sea was unbroken by any signs of destruction or development.

A few minutes into the flight, I saw a large multi-colored parrot flying just above the trees below us. I tapped the door gunner on the leg and pointed to the parrot. He looked where I pointed and nodded. As we crossed the international boundary into Cambodia, the formation gradually dropped until we were flying at tree-top level. Occasionally, the landing skids brushed the uppermost leaves of the jungle trees. At over 100 mph, this was interesting. I understood that, as counterintuitive as it may seem, a fast-moving helicopter flying low to the ground was much harder for enemy fire to hit than one flying higher. That's because he'd have less time to react and aim at a lower flying one.

Being aware that we were part of history, I yelled to the gunner, "I've never invaded a country before. How 'bout you?"

Because of the noise and his radio equipped helmet, he spread his hands apart, indicating he couldn't hear. So I tried again without success. Then he tilted the helmet away from his left ear and leaned down. I stretched up and yelled as loudly as I could.

The gunner replaced his helmet and looked down at me rather disinterestedly. "Oh, hell, I've been in Cambodia lots of times."

That kind of deflated me, but I realized it was not mere chance that this slick was the point and that it had a minigun rather than an M60.

A dry lakebed came into view and the door gunner opened up with the minigun, spraying the tree line back and forth for about a minute. The sound was a scream like a mythological banshee, rather than a rapid series of gunshots.

The gunners in slicks landing beside us sprayed lead into the opposite tree line. The instant the skids touched ground we jumped out and ran crouching to beyond the tips of the rotors. In seconds, the choppers were airborne, turning back for the next lift. As the dust drifted away, I realized we were in the southeast corner of the dry lakebed, nearly two klicks from the northwest corner where we were supposed to meet the rest of Charlie Company and set up our firebase.

We were completely exposed and needed to get to cover. The closest tree line was fifty meters to the east, so I led the men there in a crouched run. As soon as we reached concealment, I told them we needed to make our way around the edges of the lakebed to meet up with Charlie Company. It was a long way, perhaps three klicks. I took the point and we stayed twenty meters inside the tree line, working our way around the south end and up the west edge.

At one point I saw what appeared to be a primitive trail. Concealed beneath low, overhanging branches was a bamboo triangle about twelve inches on a side with its apex pointing ahead of us along the path. I knew from my training that this symbol was used by the NVA and VC to indicate booby traps ahead.

"Stay to the right of the path and follow me," I said. We saw a few other signs along the way, but less obvious: sticks broken to form one-sided arrowheads and the occasional machete slash in a tree trunk. Hours later, exhausted and hungry, we reached our destination.

By now our new firebase, named Brown, was bustling. I found the LT, who seemed relieved to see us. I explained what happened, and gave him the locations of the evidence we'd discovered along the way.

He put his hand on my shoulder. "I'm glad you made it. Get something to eat. We'll be moving out in half an hour."

He left to share our information with Captain Osgood, while we rejoined the rest of the squad.

"I get the impression we were given up for dead. Am I right, Dread?" I asked.

"Let's just say the LT was lookin' around for another shake 'n bake to fill the void," Dread said with a wink and a smile.

I laughed, but I knew he was only partly kidding. "You can't get rid of me that easy."

Dread nodded and went back to cleaning his M16.

Twenty minutes later, we moved out of Firebase Brown. We never saw the place again. Clearly, the army had decided that the job of the 5/7, or at least our part of it, was to search out and destroy the enemy, not build firebases.

That night we set up an NDP beside a rutted two-track dirt road that was a main branch of the Ho Chi Minh Trail, setting out Alpha-Alphas across likely avenues of approach to our position. Two hours after dark, we heard the thud as one of them went off. In the morning, we found blood pools, a human leg, and two left feet where the AA was tripped.

For the next several days, we humped and sweated, but made no contact with the enemy. The country was more pristine than Vietnam, with no bomb craters and few broken trees. The vegetation was dense, but the going was a bit easier for us. Our first resupply in Cambodia saw Ferde Salazar go in on the chopper for his R&R. Being Filipino, of course, he'd put in for Manila. Chuck Stadler took over the gun, mainly because he wanted to and Bauman didn't.

The next week was routine: humping, sweating, cursing, and playing spades. We separated into platoon-size elements and fanned out to cover more area.

One day during lunch break, I heard a grunt say, "Jesus, look at the size of that centipede!" A multicolored centipede about a foot long and two inches in diameter scurried across a small clearing. Another grunt ran up and chopped it in half with his machete. That just made it worse. Both halves continued to run around separately. More grunts joined the fray, using crude clubs to mash the pieces of the monster into slime and goo.

"Well, that was entertaining," I said to Superman as I returned to my lunch.

"I suppose, but I prefer dancing girls," he said. "Have you ever seen Joey Heatherton?"

"Of course! She's definitely USDA Grade A Prime."

"That she is."

"What made you think of her?"

"Just trying to turn a nightmare into a dream," he said wistfully.

"Well, it worked. Thanks," I said dazedly.

The next day, we humped four and a half klicks and cleared a small LZ so we could be resupplied the next morning. As always, I designated the positions for the squad's guard hole and the gun. Then I led a patrol out to set up an Alpha-Alpha.

Coming back, I smelled marijuana smoke. I was furious. I followed my nose straight to the gun position, manned by Stadler and Bauman. Bauman lowered his eyes, but Stadler went on telling jokes and sucking on his lit number.

"Put that out *now*," I said firmly.

"What the fuck, man?" Stadler said.

"I said, now!"

"Shit, man. You're not a juicer, are you?"

"No," I said, "I smoke pot where it's safe and doesn't matter, but not out here in the boonies. Why? Because the gooks don't smoke pot; they smoke opium. They can smell pot a mile away and know exactly where you are and *will* find you ... like I just did!"

"Fuck you," said Stadler.

"Listen very carefully, Private. You will put that number out right now, and you will never light another one in the field again. If you do, I'll court-martial your ass. Do you understand?"

"I'd tell 'em you smoke pot, too!"

"I don't give a shit. Do you understand me?"

Silence.

"DO YOU?"

"Yes, Sergeant."

"Good. Now move the gun to the place I told you to put it an hour ago."

"But it's in the sun over there," he whined.

"I know that. But the reason I placed the gun there is because it's the only spot in our part of the NDP that has a full range of fire. Look where you moved it. Yes, it's in the shade, but it's right next to a tree trunk that obstructs both the movement of the gun and your ability to see to your right. In the future, I will not be explaining the reasons for every order I give. Now *move* that gun!"

"Yes, Sergeant."

Stadler didn't like it, or me, but he moved the gun. This incident was damned unpleasant, but it was the last time Stadler and I had words, mainly because he gave me a wide berth.

We were tired and dirty. It had been over three weeks since we'd been able to shower. It was an interesting experience. The first couple of weeks of constant toil and heavy sweat made everyone very stinky. I'm sure the NVA could smell us a good way off, that is unless they were as dirty as we were. But after about three weeks, the body accommodates. The constant sweat literally sluffs or erodes the dirt and body cheese to the extremities. I realized that my hands and fingers and feet and toes were stained a deep red color. We so seldom saw exposed soil without any plant cover, that I hadn't realized that the jungle dirt was red clay almost everywhere. Anyway, after three weeks or so the human stench lessened, and we became part of the environment. Or perhaps it just seemed that way to our overloaded olfactory senses. Oh, we tried to take sponge baths using our limited water supply and GI towels, but that did little more than hasten the natural sweat erosion a smidgen. We did wash our faces and brush our teeth every day, but the flow of sweat, salt and grease from steel-pot-encased heads undid the job in minutes as we humped on and on.

If the bugs were even worse than usual and we thought about it, we might smear a little bug juice on our exposed forearms, faces and necks, but our sweat sluffed away the repellent in short order, so we didn't use it often. The little plastic squeeze bottles of bug juice were secured under the elastic bands on our helmets. The band's designed purpose was to hold the camouflage helmet cover tight against the steel pot just above the flange, but they were very handy for carrying small items like the bug juice, cigarette packs and matches.

In the morning, we secured our LZ and waited for the choppers. It was, relatively speaking, a lazy day for us. Around 1100 hours, the first chopper landed. The crew shoved off a water bladder, clean clothing, a couple cases of ammo, some grenades, Cs and LRRPs, care packages from home, a red bag with letters from the World, and an FNG.

Lieutenant Bowen called me over and introduced me to the FNG. "Sergeant Thompson, this is Private Krolicki. He'll be joining your squad. Can you get him situated?"

"Yes, sir. Welcome to the boonies, Krolicki. Follow me and I'll introduce you to the rest of the squad."

He looked even younger than most of us, but I marked that down to my turning into a grizzled old grunt. "How old are you, Private?"

"Just turned eighteen, Sergeant," he said.

"You joined up right outta high school?"

"Yep, my dad told me it would make a man out of me, so he gave permission when I was seventeen," he said, his eyes darting from side to side.

"Is it working?"

"Is what working?" he asked.

"Is the Army making a man out of you?"

"I ... I'm not sure, Sergeant," he stammered.

"It's all right," I said, "We'll work on that. What's your first name, Private?"

"It's Merton, Sergeant."

"Well, Merton, these sorry excuses for soldiers are your squad mates," I said, introducing him around. "Get to know each other. I'm heading to mail call."

I sauntered over to where Crippen was just opening the mail bag. On this day, he read out my name three times. That was very rare. One letter was from Julie Morse, another was from my barber in Tucson, George Keahey, and the third item was a heavy flat package from my parents. In it was a nice letter keeping me up to date on things at home, but of even more importance at the time were the machete with sheath, long steel file and large sharpening stone they'd sent along with it. As soon as I'd realized how vital these things were, I'd written to see if they could send them to me. They'd wasted no time doing it, and I really appreciated it. I stuffed the letters in a pocket to read later and rejoined my squad. I secured the file and sharpening stone in a pocket of my rucksack and attached the machete scabbard to the back of it where I could reach over a shoulder to grab the machete's handle and pull it free in a hurry when needed.

The same chopper returned about forty-five minutes later with our hot meal and the cooks. Hoping for prime rib, I sauntered over to the chow line and asked, "What's for lunch?"

"Chipped beef on toast or spaghetti 'n meat balls. We also got mashed potatoes with gravy, sweet potatoes, noodles, and green beans," said the first cook. "Oh, and cobbler for dessert."

"I can't believe I'm saying this, but I'll take the chipped beef and mashed potatoes, please."

He scooped generous portions onto my plate, and when I got to the other cook, I opted for cherry cobbler and raspberry Kool-Aid.

As I ate, I turned to Woody. "You know, this isn't my grandmother's cobbler, but it's not bad."

"I was thinkin' the same," Woody said.

"Hey, Merton," I called, "Have you had chow yet?"

"No, Sergeant," he said.

"Well, head over before they close it down."

"Yes, Sergeant." He jumped up and hurried to the line.

I shook my head at how lost he seemed to be.

We ate in silence, and afterward I took out the envelopes and opened them. Julie was nice to write me, and I appreciated it; I'd finally sent her a letter the week before. She told me the monsoons in Tucson were trying to get started and how hot it had been—which I got a real hoot out of—and enclosed a photo that her dad had taken of us standing under a palm tree in front of her house. It choked me up, so I quickly put the letter back in the envelope and put it in the ammo box fastened to my pack frame.

Next, I read the letter from George Keahey. George was as fine a man as any I've met in my life. He was a slim old fellow with clear blue eyes, a sparkling personality, and an uncanny way with people of all ages, backgrounds, and personalities. George was one of the few people outside my family who wrote to me in Vietnam and Cambodia. I think Jamie sounded effeminate to him, so he called me Jim, the only person who ever has. George worked hard for everything he had and was proud of what he'd achieved. I liked and admired him.

Hey Jim, hope you're keepin' your powder dry in that damn jungle. Summer school just started so I've got a few first timers in here from them big cities, you know the type. Oh. I forgot you ARE the type. Ha ha.
Listen, you take damn good care of yourself over there. You're missed.
Your Friend, George K.

This got to me, too.

Superman walked by just then and said, "You okay?"

"What? Yeah, I'm fine. I was just thinking how much can be said in just a few words. You know what I mean?"

I'm not sure he did know, but he said he did.

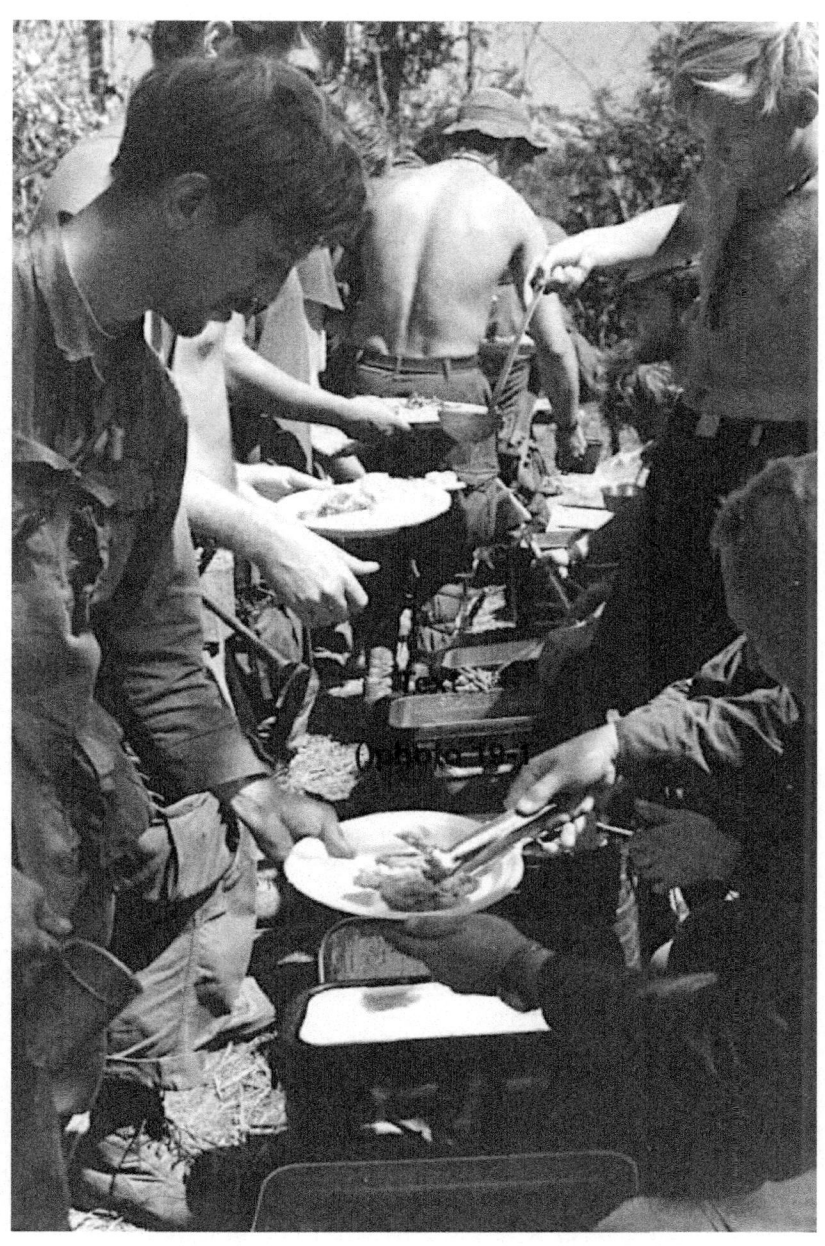

Resupply Day - Hot meal in the field.
(photo 19-1)

Chapter 20 – Ambush; Tickets to the World

The next morning, having used the water left over after filling all the canteens to take sponge baths, we felt a bit cleaner and a bit more refreshed. And we were wearing cleaner uniforms. It felt good, especially the socks. At first light, we got word we'd be flown to a new location ten klicks southwest. That was a nice surprise. We weren't usually CAed on such short notice, so I figured it was based on intel of suspected enemy activity. We humped for six hours, skipping our mid-day meal break, to reach the LZ designated for pick-up. First Platoon was on the first lift, partly because our Second Squad had point that day and partly because, well, we were the *First* Platoon. We set down in a meadow surrounded by thick jungle. A stream flowed near the meadow's north edge, and in the jungle off its northwest edge a steep hill rose a hundred feet above it.

We humped to the base of the hill and took a late break for chow. After finishing my beef stew, I entertained myself by doing what I'd learned from Dread—setting my plastic spoon on fire and dripping melted plastic on passing ants and termites. I fleetingly thought it wasn't a very civilized way to pass the time, but then I glanced around me at seventy-some men bristling with rifles, grenade launchers, machine guns, mortars, hand grenades, and plastic explosives, and went back to napalming the local insects.

After an hour, Osgood had the company form up behind First Platoon and ordered Bowen to have us drop our packs and assault the hill. He was almost apologetic when he gave the order. We exchanged glances with one another, but no one said what we were all thinking: we *never* charge hills. There's a saying in the infantry: "The difference between the Infantry and the Marines is that the Infantry shells a hill first then assaults, but Marines assault a hill first and then shell it." None of us had ever assaulted a suspected enemy position on higher ground. Our preferred MO was stealth.

But orders were orders, so Second Squad formed two skirmish lines of four or five guys each and I did the same with First Squad, right behind them. The LT positioned himself between the squads, along with Sergeant Crippen and the RTOs. I kept Merton Krolicki next to me as the command came to charge.

That hill was damned steep, but we scrambled up in short order, moved across the top, and secured the far lip. Second and Third Platoons secured the remaining perimeter of the hilltop, while the Mortar Platoon set up in the middle. We began digging guard positions to establish our NDP there. As the holes were being dug, word was passed that the men should go down in twos and threes to retrieve their packs.

Almost at dark, Krolicki came up and told me he didn't have a hooch because he didn't have his pack.

I exploded. "You mean to tell me, that your pack is still at the bottom of the hill?"

"Yes, Sergeant," he said shakily, staring at the ground.

"Jesus H. Fucking Christ! How the fuck did that happen?"

"I didn't know I was supposed to go get it," he stammered. "Should I go get it now?"

"Absolutely not! It's too dangerous now. What the fuck were you thinking, Private? Your pack has C-4 and a Claymore in it, for chrissake! You better hope to hell it's still there in the morning and hasn't been dragged off by the gooks, because if it has, it'll be your ass!"

"What should I do now, Sergeant?"

"Bunk with me tonight. You can squeeze into my hooch, but you'll have to sleep on the ground."

"Thank you, Sergeant," he said quietly.

At that moment, it fully dawned on me that Merton was scared nearly out of his mind. He was a frightened child in a terrifying situation. I was still mad as hell, but also felt responsible for him. He needed me to protect him. I understood that, but it was untenable because I was equally responsible for every one of my men, no one of them more than any other. It occurred to me that Merton was too shy to ask any of the other men if he could go with them. I calmed down, took Merton to my hooch, and asked if he had any water in his belt canteen.

"A little bit," he answered.

"Fill it up from one of the canteens on my pack. You need to stay hydrated."

"Yes, Sergeant. Thank you, Sergeant," he said rather crisply.

"You stay here, and make yourself as comfortable as you can on the left side of the hooch. I have to check the perimeter."

As I made my way to my guard hole, I thought, *"Christ, this is the real thing, but the kid is talking to me like it's Basic and I'm his Drill Sergeant."*

I joined Superman in the hole, and we looked down through the jungle. It was rapidly getting darker.

"What do you think?" he asked.

"I think we're damn lucky there weren't any gooks up here when we charged the damn hill. Did you notice all the fléchettes stuck in the trees?" I asked.

"Yeah. That's why no one was here."

"That's certainly true, and it also tells us HQ thinks there's a force here. Or they wouldn't have sent in an airstrike and then us to check it out." Still scanning the area, I said, "We need to keep our eyes more open than usual tonight." I could just make out Second Squad as they silently left the perimeter and headed down the hill to set out the Alpha-Alphas. I turned to Superman. "If you ask me, it's already too dark to put out the Alpha-Alphas."

"Yeah, I agree."

As we watched, Second Squad merged with the jungle shadows, and our attention turned more directly to our front. That's when weapons fire erupted. It was impossible to tell exactly where the first shots came from, but without a break, our entire south perimeter fired everything they had.

I realized most of our fire was pointed too close to Second Squad, and yelled, "Cease fire! Cease fire! God dammit, *cease fire*! Second Squad's out there!"

It took less than ten seconds for the firing to cease, but it seemed like an eternity when bullets were flying.

"Follow me!" I yelled, as I grabbed my M16 and bandoliers and ran directly down the hill toward where I thought Second Squad was. I got there in seconds and could barely make out the prone men flattened into the jungle floor. I directed Superman and José to move through the men and secure the front.

"Is anyone hurt?" I shouted. No one made a sound. They were scared shitless and I didn't blame them. "All right, look around and check each other. Is everyone moving and accounted for?"

Second Squad began to sound off to indicate they were okay. But a few feet in front of me, there was one man who didn't move. Down in that swale, it was nearly too dark to see. Our medic was just behind me and I said, "Check him out, Doc."

Jacobs bent down and began to gently prod the man. "I can't see anything wrong with him, Sarge."

For a second, I hoped the man was just stunned. I stared and squinted, and it looked to me like a spot on the top of his head was a little darker than everything else. "Check out his head," I said. "The top of his head."

"Oh, Jesus," said Jacobs. "He's been hit, but I can't tell how bad in this light."

"All right," I said, "whoever's got their machetes, cut down some saplings to make a field stretcher. Now! And someone run up and get a poncho ASAP!"

Lieutenant Bowen joined us, but I barely noticed.

"Is he the only man hit?" I shouted. "Is he the only one?" I shouted a bit louder.

The LT looked at me and said angrily, "Shit! Isn't one enough?"

"One is *more* than enough, sir," I said softly, "but I want to make damn sure no one else is lying out here wounded."

He looked away then. I knew he wasn't really mad at *me* ... and so did he. We were both mad at the damn war.

With the makings now in place, I bent to the task of building a field stretcher. I could now see that it was an RTO who'd been hit; it was Corporal Marc Belon. In less than two minutes he was on our field stretcher and we were moving quickly up the hill toward the perimeter. I was holding the left front end of the stretcher and the LT was holding the right front.

"Clear the way!" I yelled. "Make a path or we'll make it for you. We have a wounded man here!"

As we reached the perimeter, I saw that no one had done anything to clear the way. It was as though the men were paralyzed, so I stomped down the corner of a hooch that was in our way. We placed the stretcher where we were told to, in the center of the perimeter where the medics could dare to use a little light to examine the wound.

Just then, a driving rain hit us as though a faucet had been turned on directly above our little hill in the jungle. I went back to my guard hole and was joined by Superman. We resumed our watch out into the night. Neither of us spoke. I wondered if the medevac chopper could get to us or even find us in this deluge, but I knew they'd sure as hell try.

There was a constant roar from the pounding rain. The guard hole quickly accumulated six inches of water soaking our feet through the breathing holes in our jungle boots.

Bob Berning, our platoon RTO, came over and said, "Thought you'd want to know, the medevac bird is a coupl'a minutes out."

"How're they gonna find us, Bob?" I asked.

"When they're close, we'll talk 'em in by the sound of their engine, and when they're close enough, we'll shine a flashlight straight up above the extraction point. It might work."

He stayed with us, sitting on his haunches just behind the hole. In a few minutes, we heard the helicopter hovering above the center of our position. It dropped a cable through the treetops with a jungle penetrator basket attached. Corporal Belon was quickly secured to it and hauled up to the chopper.

Before the sound of the chopper faded, we heard the medic on board say over Bob's radio, "I suppose you know you have a line one here?"

Captain Osgood answered somberly, "We thought we might. Thanks."

The chopper, and Corporal Belon, disappeared into the black rain.

"Bob, what's a line one?" I asked.

"It means he's dead," said Bob. "The casualty form has boxes to check. Line one is KIA, killed in action."

"Shit!" I said.

Later, I crawled into my hooch next to Merton. I didn't know if he was asleep or not, but I didn't feel like talking.

At 0200, José woke me for my guard shift. The rain had stopped, and I used my steel pot to bail out the last of the water in the guard hole. As I stared out into the blackness, I saw nothing at all. I listened hard and heard nothing. But I felt a lot. I was angry, I was sad, and I was glad: angry at the war, not at the enemy; sad about a good man dying for something we weren't too sure we understood; and glad it wasn't me who'd gotten blown away. It was difficult to deal with three very different and very powerful emotions at once.

In the morning, Merton looked at me like he was afraid of me. I headed back toward the guard hole. On the way, I saw Superman and we talked about Belon. I barely knew him, but he and Superman had joined the platoon together.

"He was all right, Jamie. I know it doesn't really matter, but I hope he was killed by the enemy and not by us."

This was the first time Superman had used my first name. I returned the favor. "Jim, it doesn't matter to Marc, but it matters to us because we don't want to feel worse than we already do!"

"God, you're right about that. But what do you think happened?"

"I think the first shots were from an AK and came from the right front of Second Squad. I think they were ambushed. And I think there's something nearby that the enemy doesn't want us to find. However," I added, "that doesn't guarantee that Marc was hit by enemy fire. Look at it this way: if the enemy initiated contact by ambushing the squad, we were right to be firing even if our fire hit him. My problem at the time—the reason I yelled cease fire—was because it was clear that not all our guys knew where Second Squad was, not because we shouldn't have fired at all. Either way, Marc's death occurred during contact with the enemy, so if there's any justice in the world it will officially be declared as due to enemy action."

"I hope so," said Superman.

I joined Forman in the hole and was looking down to our front when I saw a Vietnamese man with a rifle move slowly in a crouch from one tree to another.

"Did you see that?" I whispered.

"No, what?" he asked.

"I just saw a gook down there."

"Where?" he said excitedly, pointing his M16 to the south.

"You see that tree a hair to the right of straight out? With the broken limb about twenty feet above ground?" I asked.

"Yeah. Yeah, I see it!"

"He's right behind it. Keep it covered, but don't fire. I want to make damn sure we don't have any Kit Carsons out there." Kit Carson scouts were former VC soldiers who had changed sides and worked with us now. "I'll go talk to the CO and see what he wants to do. Just watch that tree. And if he moves, track him but don't fire. I'll fill in the guard positions on either side of us."

"Okay," he said a bit doubtfully.

Bowen and Osgood confirmed we had no KCs outside the perimeter.

"How do you want us to handle this, sir?" I asked Captain Osgood. "I know exactly where the gook is."

"Do not open fire unless fired upon," he said. "We CA out of here in an hour, and I'm pretty sure they'll call in an Arc Light in short order."

"Sir, this gook was likely involved in last night's ambush. Some of the men won't be happy about not blowing him away."

"That may be, Sergeant, but there is no military need to put any more of our men at risk here. Make sure they understand that."

"Yes, sir."

When I got back, I said just loudly enough to be heard by the whole squad, "Okay, here's the deal. We are not to fire on this gook unless fired upon. An Arc Light will be called in after we leave."

"When are we leaving?" asked Forman.

"In an hour," I said, "so I suggest you take turns watching for movement outside the perimeter and packing up your stuff."

An hour later we humped back down the hill to the same LZ we used the day before. Along the way, I stopped at Krolicki's pack and checked it for booby traps. Luckily, it hadn't been found by the enemy.

After a short wait, a single lift flew us away. I watched the sea of green flow by below as we moved to our next patrol area in Cambodia.

It was May 14, 1970.

* * *

Three days later, we crossed a stream and made our way through thick vegetation to the top of a small hill. My squad was at the rear of our platoon, and our platoon was the third back from the point. Suddenly, the sound of automatic weapons fire broke out to our front. The LT sent word that I should work with Second Platoon (positioned behind us) to establish a secure rear perimeter, which I quickly did by coordinating gun and guard positions. The LT and our platoon's Second Squad moved through the Mortar Platoon toward the sound of the gunfire to reinforce Third Platoon on the point. Within a few minutes the firing tapered off and stopped.

Word came back from the point platoon that LT Bowen had been shot in the knee and two sergeants in Third Platoon had been shot up pretty badly. A medevac was called in and at the same time a request was made for an emergency ammo resupply. I was sad and mad at the same time until I thought, *"The LT is gonna live through this shit,"* and felt a little better.

Twenty minutes later we heard the medevac chopper fly over us, hover for a few minutes, haul the three men up on a jungle penetrator one at a time and head back the way it had come.

"Good luck, LT," I said to the air.

"Amen," said Blaine.

Dread quietly added, "They got their tickets to the World, boys, and they're still breathin'; that's a good thing."

Five minutes later another slick approached bringing the ammo. We were in rough terrain and dense jungle, so landing wasn't an option. A smoke grenade guided them to a location about ten meters to the west of our position. The chopper radioed that we should watch our heads because they were going to kick out one crate each of M16 and M60 ammo. We could barely see the slick above us, so we had to jump out of the way as the crates were deflected by tree limbs on their way to the ground. It was a close thing. Each crate weighed over 60 pounds so being hit by one could be fatal. The sturdy wooden crates popped open a bit on impact, but the metal ammo boxes inside and the ammo they contained were undamaged. We pried open the crates and passed the ammo boxes forward; 1600 rounds of M16 and 600 rounds of M60 ammo quickly made their way forward to replace the ammo expended in the firefight.

After another half-hour, knowing we were short of water and couldn't be resupplied that day, I ordered Stadler and Ardmore to gather up everyone's one-quart canteens and go through Second Platoon to fill them at the stream.

"Make damn sure the Second Platoon guys know you're there, and keep your eyes open," I said.

They slid sticks through the looped straps that secured the caps to the canteens, and slipped away.

We all noticed it was hot as hell—not that it wasn't always that way. But when you're under stress, forced to remain in one place, and frustrated that there's nothing you can do to make things better, you notice things like that more.

"Hang in there, guys," I whispered. "The water will help."

Tired, serious men glanced at me and nodded.

Ardmore and Stadler returned and distributed the canteens. It briefly dawned on me that we were not necessarily getting back the same canteens we'd used for the past many weeks, but I shrugged it off as one of those "fuck it; it don't mean nothin'" things.

I stood up and said, "I know we're all thirsty, but put one or two iodine tablets into each canteen and wait a full thirty minutes before you drink. And shake it up off and on while you're waiting."

Expressions indicated grudging agreement, and I sat down to dig some iodine pills out of my first aid kit. I opened my first canteen and dropped in a tablet. When I unscrewed the cap on the second one, a moss-covered twig poked out. I gave Superman a what-are-ya-gonna-do shrug, pulled it out, and dropped two pills into that canteen. Then I unscrewed the first one again and dropped in a second pill.

That night we got word that one of the sergeants didn't make it and the other was in bad shape, but that the LT would recover. I had trouble falling asleep. I would miss Lieutenant Bowen, and it saddened me that I hadn't seen him before he was medevacked—and would likely never see him again.

The next morning, with Sergeant Crippen in temporary command of the platoon, such thoughts quickly fled as we continued our endless patrol through the hostile wilderness. We were in full survival mode, a condition that—despite appearances sometimes—never left me during my entire tour. Our soundless movement as we slithered through nearly impenetrable terrain reminded me of that timber rattler back in Georgia, only we weren't lethargic. We were poised to strike.

A couple of days later, Jacobs came to me and said, "I thought you should know, the other sergeant didn't make it either."

"Fuck!" I blurted out.

"Yeah, I know," said a very somber Jacobs.

It was May 20, 1970.

Chapter 21 – Neal; A New Friend; Montagnards

After a few more days, we emerged from the jungle onto a well-maintained dirt road that led to the north up a high hill. The heat was made worse by the steep grade of the road and because we were moving up a south-facing slope.

For several days, I'd had a pain in my left heel that was becoming more and more severe. I'd ignored it, but it was getting harder to do, especially as I trudged up the hard-packed surface.

Soon, on the right side of the road we saw a simple wooden sign on a thin post written in Khmer, the native language of Cambodia, and in French; it said "Phumi Phum Krang," which we took to be the name of the place. As we walked past the sign, we entered the largest village we'd yet seen. The vegetation had been cleared and irregular rows of small huts paralleled the road, mostly on the left. To the right, we could see many rows of banana trees, most of which were twelve to twenty feet tall. It had the appearance of being a going place, but it was totally deserted with not one soul in sight. As we reached what we thought was the crest of the hill, we saw that it was one of three crests. Ahead of us was a dip that dropped about a hundred feet to a swale between the other two crests. One to the east and one to the west of the low point. Each platoon was assigned to secure one of the crests, with our platoon sent to the highest and flattest one, to the west.

Once we'd established a perimeter and secured the area, helicopters began to arrive with all the equipment, supplies and specialized personnel needed to construct a firebase. This one was named Neal and would be our main base for the remainder of our time in Cambodia. The site was excellent. Neal sat on the crest of a foothill about 500 feet above the surrounding wilderness. At sixteen klicks from the border, it was farther inside Cambodia than any other FSB.

We stayed at Neal for several days, providing security as the berm was constructed to a minimum height of six feet.

Only two gaps were left, one near the southwest corner to allow ingress and egress to the new helipad and another on the east side accessing the road we walked in on.

"Hey Jerry, how goes it?" I shouted, seeing a familiar face emerge from the battalion HQ bunker.

"Well, Jamie, good to see you," Jerry Pickering said with a smile. "What unit are you with?"

I told him and asked him the same thing.

"I work in S2/S3 here at the battalion field headquarters," he said.

"My God, a Foxtrot NCO School grad actually working in Operations and Intelligence. Amazing!"

"Yeah, I'm surprised, too. As far as I know I'm the only guy from our class doing it."

"Well, if you get a chance, look me up at the northwest part of the berm."

"I'll do that," he said. "See ya later!"

During a break from perimeter guard I spotted some grunts in various states of undress, loitering down in the swale a few hundred meters east of the firebase. Curious, I wandered down there.

"What's goin' on?" I asked a soaking wet grunt.

"We found this well with good clear water, and everybody's gettin' clean!"

I walked to the well and looked down. Nearby were a couple of buckets on ropes, so I threw one in and pulled it up. The water was crystal clear and cool. I stripped out of my uniform, leaned my M16 on a bush, and poured the water over my head.

"Geez, that's cold!" I shouted.

"Yeah, it's wonderful, ain't it?" said a nearby grunt.

Somebody had put a big GI bar of soap on a rock nearby, so I lathered up and went back to the well. I spent a good forty-five minutes, dousing myself with buckets of cool, clean water. It was a little bit of heaven in the midst of hell.

A Spec-4 in a cleaner uniform than I'd seen in a while wandered over and started bathing. "God, that water feels good!"

"Yeah. It's amazing how the simplest thing can feel like a luxury out here," I said. "What unit are you with?"

"USARV headquarters, actually. I'm an Army reporter, here to cover the Incursion," he said. USARV stood for U.S. Army Republic of Vietnam, the most rear echelon and highest Army command in Vietnam.

"Hell of a place to be ordered to do a story," I said.

"Oh, I wasn't ordered here. Believe it or not, per some dumb-ass regulation, the Army can't order its reporters into combat zones. I volunteered. This is where the war is happening now."

"I admire you for that," I said, my opinion of him changing. "I'm Jamie Thompson, squad leader of First Squad, First Platoon, Charlie Company, Fifth of the Seventh, First Cav." I extended my hand.

"Glad to know you. I'm Steve Warner," he said, shaking my hand. "Actually, I'm hoping to hook up with an infantry unit to see what this war is really like."

I was quiet, thinking about what "really like" meant. "If you're sure that's what you want, my unit's heading out in a couple of days. You're welcome to come with us. I can always use a hooch mate."

"It's a deal. I'll work out the details at HQ. Where can I find you later?"

"Northwest perimeter with my unit. By the way, when you're at the HQ ask for Sergeant Jerry Pickering. Tell him we talked and I'm fine with it. Maybe he can grease some wheels."

That night, Steve and Jerry found me. I introduced them to SFC Crippen and left them to handle the technicalities. Later, Steve and I set up a double hooch and talked for hours. He was from New Jersey and had graduated from Gettysburg College with a degree in journalism. I took an instant liking to him. There was nothing phony about him. It also didn't hurt that he was smart as hell. Steve was a kindred spirit and not someone I commanded or was commanded by. He was a breath of fresh air.

The next day, we went back to the well. A couple of grunts were pulling up a basket with half a dozen glass bottles in it.

"What've you got?" I asked.

"It looks like booze! I saw this rope wedged in a crack a couple of feet below the rim and started pulling. This is what came up." He carefully lowered the treasure to the ground and grabbed a bottle. "Boy. It's cold!"

None of us could understand the language on the label, which read *"Nước Mắm,"* but it seemed quite the prize. After a frustrating and unsuccessful attempt to open the bottle by digging at the cork with a bayonet, the grunt broke the top of the bottle on the edge of the well. He stopped in mid-lift when our noses were assailed by the stench of rotted fish.

"Oh, my God!" he shouted. "What the fuck is this stuff?"

None of us knew, but it sure as hell wasn't booze. Later, we learned it was a traditional sauce made by fermenting salted dried fish for a year or so. Let's just say it's an acquired taste that none of us had acquired.

The next day, Jerry Pickering found me and asked, "Want to visit the Montagnard village at the bottom of the hill?"

"Does a grunt shit in the boonies?" I said. "Hell, yes."

"The Montagnards are our natural allies. They hate the VC and the NVA. Plus the NVA took over that old French banana plantation a couple weeks before we got here, tortured a lot of people and killed a few. They left the Montagnards alone, but let's just say they didn't make any friends among them. We've already killed three Montagnards accidentally with artillery fire and need to make sure they concentrate their people from the surrounding area into the village. By the way, they carry crossbows," he explained. "Anyway, we want to prevent any more deaths."

"This has got to be hard on them," I said.

"It is, and it'll still be hard when they concentrate their people in there, too. We've flown in some rice we captured, but we need to do more. That's another reason for the visit. We need to work out the logistics of how we can feed the extra people."

"That's mighty decent of us," I said.

"Yeah, but we didn't have anyone who spoke their language," he said, "until we borrowed a Marine, and he'll be here in an hour or so."

"Wait, you mean to tell me we invaded their country and not one person in the whole damn First Cav speaks Khmer?" I asked.

"Well, not anyone in our brigade anyway. But the Marine translator will be here soon, and he doesn't want more than two or three people down there. HQ chose me and I suggested you and Steve. I pointed out you're an infantry NCO with combat experience, so they agreed. Your Platoon Sergeant agreed, too."

"What gear should I take?"

"Just your weapon, bandoliers, and web belt with canteens. We don't want to appear any more aggressive than we have to."

I spent the next hour cleaning my M16, making sure all the magazines were clean and full, and filling my belt canteens with water. At the mess hall, Steve and I ate a lunch of chipped beef on toast, then waited outside the HQ bunker.

Pickering came out with a guy wearing Marine fatigues with darkened E-9 patches. It was dangerous to make it easy for the enemy to identify officers and NCOs in the field. That's why rank identifiers like captain's bars and sergeant's stripes were darkened and why we didn't salute officers in the field.

Jerry said, "Master Gunnery Sergeant Ellis Conway, this is Sergeant Jamie Thompson, leader of First Squad, First Platoon, Charlie Company, and USARV reporter Spec-4 Steve Warner."

"Glad to meet you, Sergeant Thompson, Specialist Warner, call me Ellis, please," he said with a smile. "Do you mind if I call you Jamie and Steve?"

"Not at all Mas— I mean, Ellis," I said.

"That's fine," said Steve.

"I know it's hard to use first names, but we need to project calm, friendly demeanors. I think that will be easier if we treat each other as people first and military personnel second. So let's do our best with that," Ellis said.

We walked to the west, across the south end of the helipad, down a two-track dirt road flanked by jungle on both sides. At first it was damn hot, but as we got lower, the trees got bigger and gave enough shade to make things more bearable. Then, gradually, the trees thinned, and I could make out thatched huts ahead and the movement of scantily clad people. As we came within earshot, Ellis called out a greeting. This was acknowledged by a young man with a crossbow. He spoke to another young man, who nodded and hurried deeper into the village. Then he told us to follow him to a shady spot under a tree.

"What did you say to them?" asked Jerry.

"I told them who we are and that we'd like to meet with the chief to discuss how we can best live near each other. The guard asked us to wait, so here we are," he explained.

Five minutes later, the messenger returned and escorted us to the center of the village, where an old man sat cross-legged on the ground with a young woman wafting a palm frond over him to keep him cool. There was a tree a few feet to my left, and it dawned on me that I should lean my rifle against it before I sat in front of the old man. I had never been out of reach of my weapon in the field since arriving in Southeast Asia, but this seemed a gesture worth risking in the circumstances. Jerry did the same, and we sat down to face the old man.

Ellis placed his palms together with the fingertips pointing toward the old man and simultaneously dipped his head and the fingertips downward. Then he straightened and the chief asked him to speak. They spoke for perhaps five minutes as I watched with great interest, though in total ignorance. Then Ellis again made the hand and head gestures and told us to follow him.

We went to a small bamboo corral where rice was being distributed. There was no talking as varying portions of rice were doled out to each individual. After watching how the village shared the rice we provided, I had a true epiphany. Everyone in the village, including the new refugees, knew exactly where they stood in the pecking order. And the men distributing the rice knew exactly how many people each person was responsible for feeding. I was struck by how comforting that must be for them. At first blush it would seem to be so limiting, so constraining, as to be anathema. But when I saw it in action, I could understand the kind of inner peace such a society must engender in its members, something Westerners would never know. Such a thing is unimaginable to an American.

We then toured the village. Steve and Jerry took a few photos, but only when people were comfortable with it. A young man went with us to grease the way. We entered one of the large huts on stilts, which superficially made me think of an Iroquois longhouse. The central roof extended four or five feet beyond the end walls over open doorways at each end. Clay pots full of fresh water and gourd ladles hung from the rafters above the sheltered entrances. The floors of the huts were four feet above the ground which protected them from water damage, but perhaps more importantly kept the people above most of the insects and snakes. The structures consisted entirely of bamboo poles, woven reeds, and roofs of thatched palm fronds. The walls were woven and ended a foot or two below the roof to allow for the free flow of air. They were clearly well protected from rain and were surprisingly cool and breezy inside. As we walked through, some people were busy weaving, and several pairs of women were combing each other's long black hair, but most were simply lying down relaxing through the heat of the day. The huts had a central aisle six to eight feet wide and what might be called enclaves lining both sides. Each enclave consisted of one or more woven sleeping pads and perhaps a very low table/platform or two. I noted that most had shallow bowls with several combs, made of shell or horn placed in them. The small amount of personal clothing and other items were simply arranged neatly in piles wherever they could be placed out of the way.

I was fascinated by the differences in the appearance of the women. Some were clearly of Chinese ancestry, while others were Indian—even to the point of having caste marks on their foreheads. Ellis told us that women were commonly traded among various cultures in Southeast Asia, sometimes over vast distances. The only clothing worn by both sexes were loin cloths and sandals. We were careful not to stare or comment in anyway.

With two minor exceptions there were no manufactured items of any kind anywhere in the village. Everything was made with their own hands of natural materials. I'd never seen such a thing before and knew I likely never would again.

One exception was a huge GI soup can, about eight inches in diameter, they had incorporated into their noodle making machine. The can was open at one end and punctured with about a dozen holes at the other. Soft dough was placed in the can and a bamboo lever would be pulled down forcing a round, flat stone downward onto the dough. This pushed the dough through the holes directly into a large clay pot full of boiling water. It cleverly made the noodles, kept them separated, and cooked them all at once. Every part of the machine other than the GI soup can was made of natural materials.

The other exception was the armbands worn by both sexes. Most armbands were made of woven natural materials or of copper, but a few, and clearly the most prized because of their rarity, were fashioned of aluminum. I asked Ellis to find out how they got the aluminum. He was told it had been salvaged from the casings of flares that had been dropped by

U.S. aircraft at night. Some were plain and others were decorated with beautiful hammered designs.

We made our way back to the chief and again sat down in front of him. Ellis made the greeting gestures and they began conversing. When the business of our visit had been concluded and there was a lull in their conversation, I bent toward Ellis and quietly said, "Can you ask him if anyone from the village has ever visited Phnom Penh?" He did that and then turned to me with the Chief's answer, "He says, he doesn't think so." But just then the Chief motioned to get Ellis' attention and added that, "His eldest son might have gone there once."

I found this amazing, since Phnom Penh was only about 145 miles away down the very dirt road that led out of the village to the southwest. As a follow-up, I then asked Ellis if he could ask the Chief how long the village had been here, which he did. "What did the Chief say," I asked.

'Since Buddha was born.'

"When *was* Buddha born?"

"Well," said Ellis, "in Khmer, that means 'forever.'"

This answer sent chills down my spine. I realized what a rare and vanishing opportunity I was experiencing by being here and felt deeply honored.

As I looked closely at the Village Chief, I realized that he was probably only in his fifties, if that. But the responsibility he alone bore for the welfare of all the people in his village, was greater in its way than that borne by perhaps the president of General Motors in our society. That responsibility had wrinkled his face and forehead giving him the countenance of a man of importance, an appearance that is universally recognized across all cultures.

We bent to retrieve our M16s and left the way we'd come. On the way back, Ellis told us the chief agreed to move his people into the village, which would roughly double its population to twelve hundred. Ellis promised enough rice to feed them. Up to now, slicks had flown a few bags at a time to the village, but that would no longer be sufficient, so the chief agreed to send villagers once or twice a week to get the rice we'd stockpile at Neal for them.

Spc Steve Warner, USARV Army Reporter, in the field with grunts.
(photo 21-2)

Sgt Jerry Pickering, S2/S3 NCO 5/7 Field HQ at FSB Neal Cambodia June 1970.
(photo 21-1)

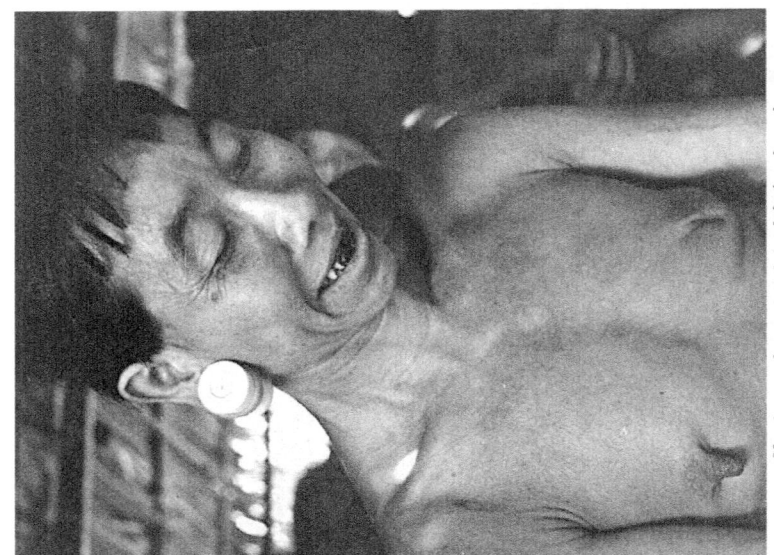
Montagnard woman at work in her hooch.
(photo 21-4)

Family in the Montagnard Village.
(photo 21-3)

Firebase Neal, Cambodia, May 1970. LEFT - 155mm Howitzer to the left and newly built hooches. RIGHT - 8" Gun.
(photo 21-5)
(photo 21-6)

Chapter 22 – Trumpets; Wilderness AO

That evening, Crippen told me to take my squad on patrol two klicks north first thing in the morning. "As far as we know, there's nothing up there but bush. But HQ needs to know for sure, so you're elected."

"Okay. I'll do that little thing," I replied with a glint in my eye.

On paper, it looked like a fairly easy patrol. According to the topo map, a couple hundred meters north, the mountainside split into two ridges on either side of a ravine that eventually reached a depth of a hundred meters. I decided the best route was to stay about halfway between a ridgetop and the bottom of the ravine. When we'd gone far enough, we'd climb to the top of the ridge and follow it back to the helipad.

That night I kept thinking about the Montagnard village as I drifted off to sleep. They were smart, capable, and organized. I was glad they were on our side.

At dawn we moved out. I did not take Steve along. I took the point, as usual, and gave Woody a break by choosing Emory Blaine to be my cover man. As we crossed the helipad, I flipped the selector switch on my M16 from "Safe" through "Fire" to "Auto" and carried it by its pistol grip in my right hand. Within fifty meters of leaving the cleared pad, the silence of the jungle enveloped us. We could as easily have been fifty miles from any clearing or other GIs. At first the going wasn't too bad. When the ravine began, we kept to the left side slope. The vegetation was heavier here, and we slipped and slithered around massive trees, clumps of brush, and tangles of vines. I had to use my machete, which I disliked because it was impossible to use it silently. Luckily, the farther we got from Neal the less brush there was, so I put the machete back in its sheath and pushed through with almost no sound at all.

My eyes ceaselessly swept the area to my front from the ground to twenty feet above it, side to side, sweeping upward and back around, again and again; my M16 always pointed where my eyes looked. I knew Emory was doing the same behind me, but his gaze swept higher and farther out to look for snipers and other signs that I might miss. My ears were attuned to listen for the slightest unusual sound. I was a hunter, doing much the same thing our earliest hominid ancestors did when territory was potentially filled with human and animal enemies. I focused on the here and now, in hopes of surviving until the there and then. Nothing else intruded on my thinking when I was on point, nothing. It was primitive, pure, and highly addictive.

We took great pride in our stealth. No words were spoken as we meandered silently in single file. No one farther than ten feet away would have heard us pass.

Gradually, the going got much tougher. At one and a half klicks, the area was littered with huge fallen trees. The broken ends of limbs stuck out from the trunks, forcing us to move to one side or another rather than over or under them. This was virgin old growth forest, as attested by the fact that there were no flat-topped or angled stumps, as would be the case if trees had been cut down by man. Instead, every stump—and there were many—was topped by jagged and torn points of wood. It was clear the area had experienced a strong windstorm.

There were fewer broken trees lower down, but moving deep into the ravine was not smart. We'd be at a severe disadvantage if we made contact in a place with higher ground on two sides. When we reached two klicks, it was 1100 hours, so I motioned everyone to stop for a chow break. We ate in silence in a rough circle with everyone facing out.

After twenty minutes, I softly said, "Okay, let's saddle up."

In less than five minutes we were moving north again. We worked our way around an especially long and gnarly tree trunk, and as we regrouped on the other side, I heard a sound in the near distance.

"Did you hear that?" I asked Emory.

"I sure did," he answered with a concerned look.

"I'm sure that's an elephant," I said.

"I agree wit' ya," Emory said.

I motioned the squad to move closer. "Men, there's an elephant somewhere ahead of us, and my M16 is looking mighty small right now. We're gonna move a hundred meters farther and then curve up to the ridge top. We've come a bit farther than our orders required anyway so we're good."

There were nods and mutters of agreement. A few minutes later, we again heard an elephant trumpet. I guessed it was within half a klick of us.

When we reached the ridge top, I turned to the men and said, "You know, it occurs to me that here and now we may be deeper inside Cambodia than any other U.S. ground combat troops."

Panting and sweating from the climb, they looked at me like I'd just said something they really didn't need to know.

So I added with a smile, "Don't let it go to your heads!"

The trek back was uneventful and rather easy. The blowdowns at the ridge top had fallen downhill to one side or the other, but mostly to the east, leaving a relatively obstruction-free route along the crest. We had to wind around some huge masses of roots here and there, but it was small potatoes compared to the walk out. We emerged onto the helipad around 1500 hours. I dismissed the men and made my Elephant Patrol report to SFC Crippen. He got a kick out of it and dutifully reported it on up the chain of command. He also told me that Ferde had just returned from his R&R in Manilla and seemed to be in good spirits. I was very glad Ferde would be taking over the gun again.

That evening, Crippen told me that Woody had gotten a letter from his mom telling him that his dad was sick back in Mississippi. "That's the shits," I said.

"Yeah, it is. We're sending word to the Red Cross to look into it. If it's bad enough, he might be granted Emergency Leave to go home, it's rare, but it could happen."

"Thanks for the information. How long 'til we hear from the Red Cross?"

"Likely a coupl'a weeks. We'll let you know as soon as we hear anything."

* * *

The next morning right after chow, Charlie Company walked away from Neal to the southwest, staying just out of sight of the Montagnard village. Steve Warner walked near me at the start but later moved back and forth in the company formation, getting to know as many grunts as possible.

Our AO as infantrymen was limited to the range of the biggest howitzers on our firebase. Depending on local conditions, firepower availability, and targeting priorities, artillery fire support could vary from the 81mm mortars our mortar platoon carried with us to eight-inch guns on a firebase. Typically, when operating out of a semi-permanent FSB, we were supported by howitzers with bores of 105mm, 155mm, or eight inches. This artillery was the reason the bases were called fire support bases—or firebases for short. Neal had all three types of howitzers.

On level terrain, the 105mm howitzers could fire thirty-three-pound, high explosive (HE) rounds about seven miles. The 155mm howitzers fired ninety-five-pound projectiles a little over nine miles, and the eight-inch howitzers fired 200-pound projectiles slightly more than eighteen miles. Since Neal's elevation was 500 feet above the surrounding terrain, its effective ranges were greater. Coupling these differences with the increased rate of fire of the smaller canons meant that if the shit hit the fan, we could depend on fire support of increasing effectiveness the closer we were to the firebase.

We patrolled the area that extended around Neal for a radius of approximately twenty miles. This translated to an AO for our battalion of just over 300 square miles. Considering that our battalion went into Cambodia with four line companies of eighty-five men each, and one with about forty, that meant—in theory at least—that each one of the 380 of us was responsible for nearly one square mile. However, this doesn't give a true picture of the situation, since we weren't distributed evenly in the AO. When operating in company-size elements, there were no U.S. troops at all in 298 of the 300 square miles. Even when we operated in platoon-size elements, it still left 97.5 percent of our AO empty of any U.S. ground presence.

The simple truth was we were deep in a wilderness in a country none of us ever expected to see. It was a bit of a challenge. Our topographic maps sometimes helped us anticipate terrain features like hills, valleys, and rivers, or man-made features like roads and towns. But since many maps were based on aerial photography and hadn't been ground proofed—especially in Cambodia—the terrain information was sometimes quite wrong. Most of the time only the officers and platoon sergeants knew where we were—or where we thought we were—in relation to the firebase. Ordinary grunts and lowly sergeants had no specific idea where they were. Truth be told, if you weren't in charge of the element, it wasn't important to know. Other things were far more important, like making sure the men under you had enough water and ammunition, were doing their jobs, and were protecting each other. My focus was on keeping my men alive. Period.

The area we were in was as close to primeval wilderness as anyplace I'd ever seen. We patrolled for days without finding any evidence of the hand of man. It was eerie and beautiful. At the same time, we were acutely aware that we were in the enemy's stronghold and remained on high alert all the time.

Steve Warner spent his days moving among the platoons, but each night he set up a double hooch with me and we'd talk in whispers. I shared my thoughts and insights, and he did the same. There's really no comradeship akin to that built on shared danger and physical challenge. We felt closer than we would have if we'd known each other for years back in the World.

The terrain for the next four or five days was especially rough, with broken limbs and tree roots scattered everywhere underfoot. I've always prided myself on being sure-footed and well balanced in rough terrain, able to move quickly when necessary. But by this time, my left heel was so painful I could barely walk. Our medic noticed and asked to take a look. He couldn't feel any breaks, but noted redness at the back of the heel. Slight thumb pressure caused sharp pain.

"Ever had anything like this before?" Jacobs asked.

"Well, now that you mention it, I did have a stress fracture in Basic. They put me on a three-day profile, and I got over it sort of. Besides that's ancient history."

"Maybe not," he said, looking pensive. "I want to look at it tomorrow before we get resupplied. If it's as bad as it is now, you're going to the aid station at the battalion rear."

"Okay," I said rather dubiously.

The next morning my heel was worse, so Jacobs talked to Crippen and told me to get on the resupply chopper and get back to HQ at Tay Ninh. I had mixed feelings. Only a fool would stay in the field if there was an honorable alternative, but I was responsible for the men in my squad and didn't want to leave them. But the reality was that I could barely walk, especially under the weight of my pack and gear.

I told Crippen that I thought Dread should take the squad in my absence and he agreed. When the chopper landed, Crippen received orders for Woody. The Red Cross had confirmed that his dad had suffered a heart attack, was hospitalized and that it wasn't certain that he'd survive. "Go get Woody and tell him he's got five minutes to get his gear together and get on that chopper, you two can keep each other company as far as Neal," he added.

"Will do," I said.

I shook hands with Steve, found Woody and explained the situation, and the two of us boarded the resupply chopper. It lifted off immediately after we scrambled aboard. A few klicks out, the door gunner thought he saw movement in a five-acre patch of tall grass, so the pilot began making tight circles within thirty feet of the ground trying to scare out anyone who might be hiding there. At times, we came perilously close to the tree line encircling the grass. This was a thrill for me because I was sitting in my usual position, with legs dangling out of an open door. Luckily, I was on the side that was on the inside of the tight loops. At times, I found myself looking straight down at the ground, but the centrifugal force kept me firmly seated on the chopper's floor despite not wearing any kind of restraint. I wasn't too worried about it but was relieved when the pilot and door gunner agreed that it must have been a false alarm, and the slick climbed a bit and moved on at speed.

We were dropped off at Neal, explained the situation to the powers that be, and received written orders, me to Tay Ninh and Woody to Bien Hoa. They told us to ask whatever slicks came in if they were headed that way and could give us lifts. Woody caught a ride right away, but it took three tries for me to hitch a ride to Tay Ninh.

Tay Ninh base was all but deserted. I walked to the battalion HQ and found Top there with Corporal Simmons. Obviously harried, Top looked up from a stack of papers and said, "What the hell are you doing here, Sergeant?"

I explained the situation and he said, "Well, as you can see, Battalion HQ is no longer here. Simmons and I have to clear up a few final details and then we'll be heading to Song Be to set up the new HQ. You need to get your ass to Song Be and get that foot taken care of."

"How do I manage that, Top?" I asked.

"Simmons'll give you an in-country transit slip." He looked at his watch. "Get some chow and go down to the airstrip and wait for a fixed wing flight to Song Be. Report in when you get there."

"Okay, Top. Sorry about the screw up; nobody told me HQ moved," I said.

"It's okay, son. I've seen a hell of lot worse screw-ups in my time in this man's Army. Now get on outta here."

As I turned around, Simmons handed me the slip and said under his breath, "Don't worry about it, man. It don't mean nothin'."

After chow, I limped down to the airfield and checked in. Around 1400 hours, a C-130 landed and rolled to a stop about fifty meters in front of me. It turned off its engines and lowered its rear ramp. Two crewmen walked out onto the field as a jeep pulling a couple of flatbed trailers appeared. Each trailer held six aluminum coffins. The two crewmen secured an American flag over each coffin and supervised as it was carried up the ramp and loaded onto the plane. When the last coffin was loaded, the ramp closed, and the plane took off.

I realized I hadn't moved during the entire operation.

I walked around the building to find someone and asked, "What unit were those coffins from?"

"The Twenty-Fifth. They're transported from here to Bien Hoa and then back to the World."

A second C-130 landed and the same procedure was repeated. I wanted to cry, but couldn't. I was as hard as granite inside and getting harder. I was thinking of my friend from the sand dunes, Sergeant Tom Alderson, whose unit had been sent into our old AO. I've never prayed in my life, but my hopes for him and his men were sent as powerfully as any could ever be.

Chapter 23 – Jamie's Hooch

About an hour later, the C-123 that was to take me to Song Be rolled to a stop. I wasted no time clambering aboard. My mind was grayed out during the flight, but I cleared it when we landed.

Song Be was hopping compared to Tay Ninh. I checked in and was directed to the aid station, where my heel was x-rayed. An hour later a doctor came out to talk with me.

"You've got a pretty bad stress fracture in the left heel, Sergeant." Handing me a piece of paper, he said, "Here's a fourteen-day profile. There's no treatment for this except giving it time to heal. For the next two weeks you have to take it easy on that foot. Got it?"

"Got it, sir." I heaved my pack onto my shoulder and headed back to the airfield.

On my next ride, I read the profile. I chuckled as I read "No heavy lifting, no prolonged walking or standing, no heavy exercise for fourteen days."

I knew it wouldn't be possible to adhere to the letter of the profile. By nightfall, I was back in Cambodia at Firebase Neal, setting up my hooch in an empty area. There was so much going on at Neal, so much equipment going this way and that, I was worried about being crushed during the night. Since there was nothing I could do about it, I hit the sack and hoped for the best.

The next morning, I made sure my unit was notified of the profile. Right after that, I determined to build myself a better place to spend the next two weeks. I made a complete circuit of the firebase and determined that the most open and least underfoot area was just inside the west berm about fifty meters north of the gap leading to the helipad.

Because they were heavy, it occurred to me that as a foundation I could use some handy boxes of Bangalore torpedoes that appeared to have been abandoned, then pile empty artillery round boxes on top to build my temporary shelter. Common practice was to empty large numbers of these boxes, stacking the loose artillery rounds in pyramids near the gun emplacements. The empty boxes were filled with dirt and used like oversized bricks to create the framework for bunkers, mess halls, and other structures. I asked an artillery sergeant if I could have some empty boxes.

"Take as many as you need. After a while, we have trouble getting rid of the damn things," he said with a grateful smile.

I thanked him and looked for empty 105 boxes, which were two feet by eighteen inches by twelve inches. I spent the next few hours dragging boxes to my spot. It would have been safer and more structurally sound to fill them with dirt first, but I was on a profile and in a hurry, so I didn't bother. It took several more trips to accumulate enough boxes to make a rectangle of walls large enough to sleep and stand in. I left the west end open because it shortened the trip to the berm in case the shit hit the fan. When I was satisfied, I stretched my poncho over the top and moved six more boxes inside to serve as a bed and two more boxes to serve as a table.

My little project had attracted a lot of interest. Grunts helped me work on it, and I'd offer them a beer or a soda, which reminded me of Huck Finn getting his friends to help him whitewash a fence. It quickly became apparent that I'd have to expand to make room to play spades or just bullshit in comfort. The next day I managed to get a second poncho and enough ammo boxes to widen the hooch, make a bigger table, and add benches.

As I was engaged in my expansion project, a backhoe and a dozer rolled over to the area south of my hooch. A captain in the Engineers pointed and gestured as he gave instructions to the operators.

I was concerned, so I walked over and asked about it.

"We're digging a pit to hold some of the weapons and ammo we're finding around here."

"How big is it gonna be?" I asked.

"Well, for now, it'll be fifteen by forty feet and ten feet deep."

"That's pretty big," I said.

"Yeah, well we're finding a *lot* of stuff, Sergeant. Why do you ask?"

"I have a hooch about ten feet beyond the pit and was wondering if I need to move it."

"If you don't mind being next to tons of enemy munitions, you should be fine," he said with a twisted smile.

Since the base of my hooch already consisted of Bangalore torpedoes this didn't change my circumstances any, so I said, "Thanks, I'm relieved to hear it!"

The strange thing is that I really *was* relieved. If there's one thing you learn very fast in a war, it's that danger is a relative thing. If you're not in immediate mortal danger, your situation is far better than it could be. So I was fine with living next to enough explosives to destroy a good chunk of Firebase Neal, especially if it meant I didn't have to relocate my hooch.

Over the next day I refined the hooch and added amenities, like candle holders from C-rat cans. I removed the roof ponchos and used the thick plastic sheets that came with some of the artillery rounds to make the hooch more waterproof, placing the ponchos back on top of the clear plastic to keep the sunlight out. I found a torn poncho for a door flap. And I stretched plastic sheets over the outside walls to keep the wind, dust, and noise down. Unfortunately, on the third day the engineers reclaimed their "abandoned" Bangalores and I had to rebuild the hooch from the ground up using empty 105 boxes. But that was okay, 'cause with lots of help, I made it bigger and better than before.

I folded a plastic sheet to four thicknesses to line a bigger ammo box for an ice chest that could hold one of the ice blocks the Army shipped to field units. The only problem was that I wasn't on the list to receive one. I scrounged the remnants of blocks from other places, enabling me to cool down quite a few beers and sodas, mine and anyone else's. Within a week, Jamie's Hooch was the most popular spot on Neal among grunts and artillery guys.

It was late May, and the days grew even hotter. The ice leftovers weren't keeping up with demand. So I hung out on the helipad, looking to hitch a ride on a chopper headed to Song Be and back. I needed a whole block of ice. Eventually, I found a crew that agreed to take me. I was excited. Also a little scared. Technically, I didn't have orders to fly back to Vietnam, let alone to procure a block of ice. But I figured I wasn't under orders to do anything else either so why the hell not. It was a worthy cause and a public service. So off I went.

As always, the breeze felt good as we headed for Song Be (or really Firebase Buttons). The place was still bustling, choppers constantly landing and taking off. The crew told me I had to be back aboard in forty-five minutes and not a second more. Following directions, I made my way to the place where the ice was kept. A huge pile of neatly stacked blocks occupied the center of a tent building.

I found a Spec-4 and said, "Who I should I talk to about getting some ice?"

He gave me a strange look, but pointed to a heavyset E-6 on the other side of the ice mountain.

I approached the sergeant, who was busily directing the men loading pallets with blocks of ice and forklifts that ferried them to their destinations.

"I'd like to get a block of ice," I said.

"Okay, give me your requisition." He stuck out a hand.

"I don't have one," I said.

"Then I can't help you." He turned back to his men and equipment.

"Let me explain, Sergeant," I said. "I hitched a ride from Firebase Neal in Cambodia. We grunts don't have enough ice up there to keep our soda and beer cool. I'm trying to fix that. I'm on profile for a couple weeks, and I'm trying to make things a hair better for my fellow grunts when they come in from the field. Is there anything you can do for us?"

It was common knowledge that things were tough in Cambodia, especially for the grunts operating out of Neal. He paused. "Look, I wanna help you, but I can't do anything myself. But there's an informal forward HQ for the chopper pilots about a hundred meters that way," he said, pointing. "They can order as much ice as they want, so you might be able to strike a deal with them. That's the best I can do."

It took some trial and error, but I finally located the pilots' lounge and approached a Spec-4. I explained my situation, and he motioned me out of the hearing of a few pilots. "I can do that, but it'll cost you ten bucks MPC."

This was less than I expected, so I said, "Can I get two blocks? And transport to the helipad?"

He bent his head down and fingered his chin for a second. "Yeah, I can do that for twenty-five."

"Deal!" I said. "But we gotta go now. My ride won't wait."

They made quick work of loading the two blocks, and we were off. I pointed toward my waiting chopper.

"So you did it, huh?" the door gunner said with a smile. "Gotta admit, I'm surprised!"

"Hey, it's clean living!" I answered with an even bigger smile.

The PFCs quickly slid the ice blocks onto the floor of the chopper to where the door-gunner specified, and less than five minutes later we were airborne again. I noted that we were also carrying numerous crates of M16 ammo, several crates of grenades and a couple of resupply bags full of Cs, LRRPs, cartons of cigarettes, cans of soda and beer, etc.

"Looks like you're gonna be busy the rest of the day," I yelled.

"Yeah. As soon as we drop you, the crates of grenades and the ice off at Neal we're headed out to resupply a company of grunts in the boonies," he yelled back.

I looked at him very seriously and said, "I hope you know how much all of us grunts appreciate what you guys do for us," I yelled.

"Thanks. We don't get to talk to grunts much and that's damn good to hear," he said.

I stuck out my hand and we shook.

Ten minutes later we were on the ground at Neal. We shoved the ice blocks out the door and I quickly followed. The grenades were unloaded a bit more carefully.

I grabbed a plastic sheet from my hooch and returned to drag my prizes into the firebase. When I got near the berm, a couple of grunts lent a hand. I manhandled one block into my field expedient ice chest and dragged it into the shade. I had no choice but to leave the other on the plastic sheet, with many layers folded over the ice to insulate it as best I could.

I had no problem scrounging sodas and nearly as many beers. With the presence of ice, my hooch became even more popular. There were spades games from dusk until 2300 and lots of great conversation. Sometimes we just talked and didn't bother to play cards at all. There was something about my set up that gave people a taste of home and an escape. It was a welcome break for everyone who stopped by.

Jerry Pickering peeking through the window of Jamie's Hooch, FSB Neal May 1970.
(photo 23-1)

Chapter 24 – The Flood; The Body Bag

I wasn't completely without supervision during this time; I checked in with the HQ during my time there. Jerry Pickering, my fellow shake 'n bake, continued to work in Operations and Intelligence, so I had someone I knew on Neal.

One afternoon I looked up from my latest efforts to make my hooch more watertight to see Steve Warner approaching.

"Hey! How the hell are ya?" I said.

"Pretty fair. Pretty fair. At least I'm still here to tell the tale," he said.

"Yeah, I know it's been bad," I said, guilt written all over me.

"Well, yes and no. Your platoon hasn't been in much contact in the past few days, but the risks are still damned high, as witness what happened with Bravo Company." Our sister company had discovered a huge cache of enemy weapons and supplies at a place they named Shakey's Hill, but not before they went through hell to take it.

"Yeah, I know. I also haven't seen my friend Kurt for weeks and haven't heard much about what's been going on with Alpha Company."

That night, as we sat around the makeshift card table in my hooch, the talk turned to the Kent State incident.

Raúl, an Echo Company grunt, said, "That was WRONG, man! To shoot those kids. Jesus, what were they thinkin'?"

"I don't think they were THINKING at all," I said. "I think they were scared shitless."

The heads of everyone in the group nodded in agreement. "I can tell you one thing," I continued, "if they'd pulled a line company out of the boonies over here and sent 'em back without a change of clothes to put down the student unrest, nobody would've fired a shot. For one thing, we know what bullets can do and those poor National Guard fucks don't, so no shots would've been fired. And for another, one look at us, our uniforms and our faces, and the unrest would have melted away."

"That's the damn truth!" said Eric, a medic with Delta Company who was just back from the rear where he'd recovered from wounds suffered in the attack on Firebase Wood. "But the Army'd never do something like that. It's too damn logical!" At this everybody laughed in agreement and took more swigs of their beers or sodas.

Steve sometimes participated in the general banter, but mostly he just observed and listened. Being based in the ultimate rear area of Long Binh, just outside of Saigon, his perspective was unique. He had a much broader view of the war than any of us, but also in a strange way, a more complete one. Steve understood that to know the essence of the Vietnam War required being in the fighting, and to be in the fighting required being with us, the grunts of either the Marines or the Army infantry.

That night, we made a sleeping platform of artillery boxes on the outside of the hooch for Steve so we could still shoot the breeze through a window in the wall as we drifted off. He tied his poncho to the top edge of the outside wall and slanted it down over his bunk to a couple of stakes in the ground. We talked about girls at home, but that was such an unreal thing to us that we soon just fell asleep.

There was a Mad Minute around 0130, but I fell asleep again within minutes. Three hours later something disturbed my sleep. My unconscious brain thought it might be an unscheduled Mad Minute, but when I realized it was a thunderstorm in the distance, I drifted into peaceful slumber once again. Half an hour before dawn, I couldn't ignore the sound and intensity of the storm any longer, partly because my sleeping platform of empty artillery boxes was doing its darnedest to float.

"Hey! You awake in there?" Steve yelled over the storm's roar.

"It's impossible not to be," I answered with disgust.

"Jeez, man, I'm about to be washed away here."

"Yeah, me, too. But I think I know what we can do about it."

"I'm all ears!"

"Can you see at all out there?" Inside the hooch, it was still pitch black.

"Yeah, a little. I can make out shapes."

"Good. Can you see my entrenching tool leaning against the hooch at the end of your bed?"

"Um ... yeah, I see it."

"Great. Grab that and make your way to the top of the berm. Be careful to stay to the left as you go; the water should be shallower there. When you're on top of the berm work your way north to the lowest point and scratch a little trench across the top. Once you've done that, get the hell away as fast as you can. That should do the trick."

"You really think that'll work?"

"I'm pretty sure it will."

By now the lightning and thunder had let up, but it was still raining steadily. I heard Steve slosh his way toward the berm. A few minutes later I heard a muffled curse and then nothing. I leaned out the flap and called to him. "How's it going?"

"I'm just about through, but it's not much of a trench."

"Is the water on our side in the bottom of it?"

"Yes, but just barely."

"That's okay. Once you cut all the way through, just scrape the tool along the bottom to get a little water running and get the hell away from it, fast."

"Okay, there's a trickle running through it now," he said.

"Back away! Fast!"

"Okay, I'm moving." There was brief pause. "Holy shit! You gotta come out and see this."

I stepped outside and watched as a twelve-foot wide gap was torn through the berm in less than two minutes. Tens of thousands of gallons of water that had been dammed up inside the firebase rushed out. The flow spread out across the helipad and on down the mountainside and away.

Steve and I laughed our asses off until I suggested we get back to the hooch to avoid notoriety, although telling the flood story entertained a lot of grunts—including Steve and me—for a long time.

It's hard to understand why no one provided drainage through the berm in the first place. But hey, grunts are expected to come up with field expedients, and that's just what we did, thereby saving Jamie's Hooch and the whole west side of Neal.

The next day a pump to drain the weapons cache and a dozer to repair the berm were flown in. The berm repair was loud, but only took half a day, and this time they added drainpipes through it. Beginning in mid-morning on the day after the flood, the gas-powered pump began draining the cache; it was close, loud and ran non-stop twenty-four hours a day for three days. Sleeping was damn hard. Steve stuck around through this time working on firebase stories for *Stars and Stripes Pacific* and working on getting a ride to rejoin my company in the field. He got a little more sleep than I did having the whole hooch between his bunk and the pump, but not much more.

On the third day, Pickering came by. "Hey, guys. Thought you might like to know that an Arc Light is scheduled for 1520 this afternoon about ten klicks west-northwest of us. You might be able to see it hit if you stand on top of the *reconstructed* berm. He emphasized 'reconstructed' and smiled knowingly at us. It was an open secret that we were responsible for the breech, but it was understood that it had to be done to prevent even worse damage. It enhanced our images!

"Cool, man! We'll watch for sure. Thanks for telling us."

"Any time, said Pickering," as he headed back to the HQ.

The pumps finally finished draining the weapons cache just after noon. What a relief that was! Steve and I were in high spirits when we positioned ourselves atop the berm. "It was damn nice of the engineers to knock over the trees on the far side of the helipad for us," I said. "We can see for miles out over the jungle to the west now."

"True," said Steve, "but they didn't do it for us."

"I know it was to deny close cover to the enemy and improve our fields of fire, but I'll take it anyway," I said with enthusiasm. I asked Steve what time it was because my "water-proof" Omega watch had developed green mold inside the case and stopped working after my first week in the boonies; I'd sent it to the battalion rear to be stashed with some other stuff. It was sad, because my parents gave it to me as a high school graduation present.

"1515," he answered.

"Thanks." I moved a little to the south along the berm to get a better vantage point to the west-northwest and gazed absently in that direction. As far as the eye could see, the land to the west was mostly flat or very gently rolling beneath an unbroken canopy of dense jungle. It felt hotter than usual because the humidity had been near a hundred per cent since the heavy rain. Steve and I wiped sweat from our foreheads with our sleeves and gazed out waiting for the supposed Arc Light.

"You suppose they cancelled it?" Steve asked. "What time is it now?" I asked. "1522," said Steve. "Hey. Who knows?" I said. "Could be. It is the military after all."

"There is that!" Steve said with a chuckle. But just then, at 1523, with no sight or sound of an aircraft anywhere in the broad, blue sky, a strip of jungle exploded into gray clouds of billowing dirt, dust and what had been vegetation and other living things. The rip in the Earth began in the SSW and extended like someone pulling a zipper to the NNE. Automatically, I counted from the first puff of dust: "One Mississippi, two Mississippi, three Mississippi…" When I reached thirty-four Mississippi, a deep, thunderous roar reached us that persisted for several seconds with a very slight break in the middle. We could also feel a shimmering in the ground beneath our feet.

"Near as I can figure it, that was about seven miles or a bit over ten klicks away," I volunteered.

"It's awesome," Steve said, "but awful, too."

"Yeah," I agreed. "What a waste. Do you suppose there were any enemy troops or materiel under that?"

"It's possible, but doubtful," he answered softly.

"My thoughts exactly," I responded. "Oh, well, let's grab some cold beers and play some spades!"

"Sounds good!" said Steve, and back to the hooch we went.

Later that evening our card game continued in the hooch; Steve and I were partnered against Pickering and a fellow shake 'n bake from Delta Company. The main topic of conversation was the Arc Light. The Delta Company guy asked, "Can you imagine what it'd be like to be hit by one of those?"

"Well, actually, I can," I said, and then told them about walking through the tangled destruction left from the arc light west of Firebase Wood. "There's not a lot left, so on the bright side it's unlikely you'd be aware of anything. Just here today and gone today, if you get my drift."

"Yeah, but if you *do* survive somehow, I've heard horror stories, about guys wandering aimlessly with eyeballs hanging down on their cheeks, making animal sounds," said Steve.

"Yeah, me, too," I said, "so it's likely true. Damage from the concussive force of the blast, you know."

"Makes sense," said Pickering. He scanned the group and said, "Listen guys, I can't tell you anything specific, but I can say that there was a good reason for calling in that Arc Light."

We all nodded, as Steve pulled in another trick.

The next morning Steve left to rejoin Charlie Company, and the Delta Company guy, whose name was Dan, took over his sleeping platform. I was in the last few days of my profile and my heel was feeling much better. Because of that, I often went out to the pad and helped unload the choppers and carry stuff inside the berm. Around 1000 hours, while Dan and I were out there, a slick came in and unloaded a body bag onto the ground. I looked at the crewmen doing the job and they explained that they had to make a quick turnaround to the field and the body would be transported back to Nam by a different bird.

"What unit did he come from?" I yelled over the sound of the rotor blades.

"Charlie Company, 5th of the 7th," he answered quickly. "Hey, keep an eye on him 'til the other bird gets here, will ya?"

My blood ran cold as I answered, "You can count on it!" I said. "Do you know what happened to him?"

"Yeah. They've been finding a lot of enemy equipment cached in bunkers, stuff like saw blades, nails, screws, and tools. We've been flying in there for a coupl'a days hauling the stuff back to the rear. The area was hit with our artillery just before they walked in there and some of the rounds exploded in the treetops. This morning, one of our choppers blew the broken top of one of those trees loose and it fell on the trail where he and some other guys were hauling stuff from the caches to the pad for pickup. No one else was hurt, but it fell right on him and killed him instantly."

I was as tight as a guitar string as I looked at that body bag. I walked over to it and bent down at the end I dearly hoped was where the feet were. "What are you doing?" asked Dan as he walked over.

"This guy is from my Company. I have to know who it is," I explained.

"I understand, but God man are you sure you want to do this?" asked Dan.

"I don't want to do it at all, but I have to," I said with a sigh. I slowly unzipped the end of the bag and carefully bent back the flap. To my great relief, I saw a pair of mud-stained jungle boots. I folded the flap back a little more and could see the dog tags tied on with a bootlace. I twisted the tag until I could read it. A cold, hard wave permeated my chest as I read, "BERNING, ROBERT R.", his RA Number, Blood Type, and Religion." I let go of the dog tags, gently folded the flap back down and zipped the bag shut.

"Did you know him?" Dan asked.

"Yes. He was my Platoon RTO. A good kid, from Kentucky, named Bob Berning."

"Jesus man, I'm sorry."

"Yeah, me, too. Let's carry in the last of the supplies we came out here to get. Then I'm gonna just sit on the berm and keep an eye on Bob 'til his ride comes."

"Would you mind some company?" asked Dan.

"No, I don't mind, but I'm pretty sure I won't be very talkative for a while."

We moved the last of the supplies into the firebase. I found a place on the berm where it wasn't too uncomfortable to sit and lit a cigarette. It was stiflingly hot under a cloudless sky. Pretty soon, Dan came out and sat down near me. I looked over at him with a blank look, and said, "Thanks man. I appreciate the company."

"Any time," he said with a somber nod.

It was an hour and a half before a shithook landed and Bob was loaded aboard. As it left and the sound of its large twin rotors began to fade into the distance to the south, I said, "C'mon Dan, let's grab a couple of cold beers."

That night, I wasn't the life of the party I usually was, but I played spades for a few hours. We listened for a while to a portable cassette tape player someone had, and I paid special attention to Buffalo Springfield's *"For What It's Worth."* After the line, *"Nobody's right if everybody's wrong"* I said, "Truer words were never spoken." This was met with muttered "Amens," and other affirmations from the group.

This reminded me again of the different mindsets of juicers and dopers. While it's true that we were all drinking beer, as usual all the grunts in my hooch were dopers in the sense that they saw nothing wrong or dangerous about smoking pot, physically, mentally or morally. It struck me that the vast majority of dopers had never bought into the underlying arguments for fighting the Vietnam War, while the majority of juicers had. This had everything to do with people's sober mindsets before their first toke or swig and nothing to do with the effects of either intoxicant. It was just a fact that dopers tended to be free thinkers and juicers tended not to be. In a general sense, there was no difference at all in either's personal courage or fighting ability except that someone who was drunk couldn't instantly sober up and someone who was high could. But in the field, intoxication was unthinkable, so that was a nearly moot point. Firebases like Neal, though, were considered rear areas by grunts, so intoxication within reason was fine.

It was May 28, 1970.

A couple of days later, a commotion outside my hooch woke me earlier than I intended to wake up. Near the southwest opening in the berm, quite close to my hooch, I saw several Montagnard men and an elephant approaching. It had a bamboo-frame carrying rack on its back with high sides. I watched in fascination as the elephant was instructed to squat forward on its belly while a half-dozen fifty-kilogram bags of the rice we'd stockpiled were loaded into the rack. The small, wiry Montagnards had little trouble hefting these 110-pound bags onto their elephant.

I saw Pickering nearby and walked over to him. "So that's how they're getting the rice to the village," I said.

"Yeah, they're planning to make the trip up here as often as needed 'til we leave," he said.

"I didn't know they had an elephant."

"Yeah, I guess they keep it well hidden, 'cause we have no idea where."

"I have a very good idea," I offered.

"Really?"

"Yes. A few days after we walked into Neal, I took a patrol two and a half klicks north of the pad and we heard an elephant less than 500 meters to our front where we turned back. So I'd say they keep it about three klicks to the north, just inside the entrance to a deep, forested ravine that drops down from here to there. Or they did then," I explained.

"Thanks, I'll pass that along, so we don't fire the arty up there. It would be bad karma to kill their village elephant!" he said with a grin.

"That it would."

I saw several Montagnard women nearby and noticed they were wearing tied cloth tops. "What gives with the women's tops?" I asked.

"It seems too many of our guys leered at them and did some whistling and cat calling. The Montagnard men didn't like that one bit, so this is the result. I guess it's the same down in the village, too" he said.

"Jesus, Jerry," I exclaimed, "what's gonna happen to these people when we leave?"

"I don't know," he said somberly.

One night after the spades game, I said, "Say, does anyone know the date?"

A visiting grunt looked at his Seiko watch. "It's the second of June. Why? Dates don't mean nothin'."

"Usually, I'd agree, but as it turns out, it happens to be my birthday," I said.

"Happy thirty-fifth, old man," he grinned.

"Thanks a lot. Though you're not far off. I managed to make it to twenty-six." I raised my can of soda in a toast to the group.

"And we forgot to get you anything," another grunt offered with mock sorrow.

"Don't worry about it. I've got what I want most."

"What's that, an all-expenses-paid trip to Cambodia?"

"There is that," I said, "but no, just to still be around to turn twenty-six."

"Amen, man," said another player.

"You know, it's weird how I didn't even remember my birthday," I said. "I mean I've never been big on celebrating it, but I've always remembered it before."

"You have a few other things on your mind, man," said the first grunt.

"Yeah, I guess."

The next day, around noon, I saw a sight that really upset me. A helicopter landed on the pad and disembarked a Green Beret and a prisoner. The Green Beret was at least six-foot-five and built like a fire hydrant. Over his shoulder he held one end of a bamboo pole about eight feet long, a loop at the other end was around the neck of his prisoner. He pulled the prisoner, whose hands were tied behind his back, along behind him quite roughly. The prisoner, who fell several times, was a typical local, perhaps five-feet-two, wearing a loin cloth, and skinny as a rail. The guy looked like one of the Montagnards to me.

"God, that looks bad!" I said to no one in particular. I meant that literally, the scene itself, the imagery, was just awful. My mind immediately went to the title of the well-known book, "The Ugly American," about United States diplomatic ignorance of and missteps toward Southeast Asia.

"What's going on?" I asked the gate guard. "The prisoner's being taken to Battalion HQ for questioning," he said.

About forty-five minutes later I saw the Green Beret leading the prisoner back out through the opening in the berm, shaking hands with him and letting him walk away. Later, I asked Pickering what happened. He told me it didn't take Ellis more than a few minutes to discover that the so-called prisoner was, in fact, a member of the Montagnard tribe from our village, one who'd refused to move into the town. "This experience changed his mind," said Pickering with a raised eyebrow, "so the guy decided to walk down to the village and stay there till we leave."

"I would have had the same change of heart given the circumstances," I said.

"Yeah, me too. Say, doesn't your profile end soon?"

"Tomorrow," I said.

"That's too bad," he said.

"I'm okay with it. It's time to get back to business."

The next morning, I didn't even think about seeing a doctor again. I just loaded my pack with what I needed for the field and waited for transport to Charlie Company. It turned out that wasn't gonna happen 'til the next day when they were due for resupply, so that afternoon I decided to visit the well down in the swale and maybe take another cold bucket shower. It was the first time in weeks that I'd been there. When I came within sight of it, I was surprised there were no grunts around. The ground was strewn with trash, a few C cans, crumpled cigarette packs, a couple of LRRP bags, some ragged GI towels and boxer shorts, and several whole and partial bars of soap. I went to the edge of the well and looked down. It was hard to see the water in the deep shadow, but I feared the worst. I picked up the bucket that was lying on its side beside the well, retied it securely to the rope that was dangling down into the well, and dropped it in. I heard it splash, waited a few seconds and hauled it back up. The water was a brackish gray color and there was a torn OD T-shirt hanging half out of the bucket. I felt angry and ashamed at the uncaring destruction we'd caused to this magical water source in the Cambodian foothills. "How many years will it take to recover from this," I wondered… "can it ever recover?"

That night Pickering, and half the grunts on Neal stopped by my hooch for a farewell get together. About an hour into it, Pickering gestured around at the twelve to fifteen grunts gathered inside and outside the hooch at the time and whispered in my ear: "It makes no sense, but it almost looks like you're going to be missed around here."

I'd been lost in thought, but hearing that, I laughed, looked up and glanced around. "You're right on both counts; it does kinda look like I'll be missed, and it makes no damn sense at all! Any port in a storm, I guess."

Pickering patted me on the shoulder and then we began talking to everybody else about the news of the day. "Alpha hit some shit this morning. Two guys wounded and one killed," said one grunt.

"Yeah, I heard that. I guess Alpha's had contact off and on for a week, though I don't know about other casualties."

I scrunched up my face a bit hearing about Kurt's Alpha Company. Pickering said, "Kurt's all right, Jamie." I thanked him for that, but the truth was there was nothing any of us could do but keep on keeping on, so I kept my thoughts to myself. "What about Charlie? Anybody heard anything about them?"

"Not for a few days," one guy volunteered. "I haven't heard anything since your friend was killed."

"Well, here's hoping no news is good news," I said with a half-hearted smile, raising my beer can in a group toast.

"Right on man," said my friend Castro, who had recovered from his wound at Wood and rejoined Echo Company a few days earlier.

"How ya doin' man?" I asked Castro.

"I'm still a little sore, but considering the alternative I'm good to go," he said nervously, but that was his style and I knew he wasn't nearly as nervous as he looked.

"How 'bout you, man?" he asked me.

"My heel is never going to be a hundred percent, but like you, I'm okay for the field. Besides, crazy as it may be, I want to be with my guys. It's been almost two weeks since I've seen any of 'em. Well, except for one," I said distantly, "and I feel like I'm shirking a responsibility, you know?"

"I understand, man. There's somethin' about this shit that sucks you in, chews you up, but won't spit you out!" he declared loudly with a huge grin.

"Hey man, can we quote you on that?" asked a grunt on the far side of the group.

"You bet, just make sure that whenever you do, you attribute it to Gordon J. Castro, Sergeant E-5, Echo Company, fifth of the seventh!" he answered.

"You got it man, maybe it'll become the new motto of the infantry. You know, replacing that tired old standby, 'Follow me.'" The other grunt responded.

At that, everybody laughed heartily and several of us slipped away to the berm to smoke some weed. I still had about ten of the twenty marijuana cigarettes I'd bought from the ARVNs in Tay Ninh. That had only been six or seven weeks ago, but it felt like a hundred years had passed.

I found a guard position with a frequent hooch visitor manning it and asked if he minded if I shared a joint with him.

"Sounds like a fine idea to me," he said. "'Specially since my stash ran out last night!"

It was good that he let me share the position with him because it wasn't as if we could climb up on the berm to enjoy the breeze and take in the view, not at night anyway. "You know," he said under his breath between holding smoke in his lungs, "this shit gets old in a hurry."

"Tell me about it!" I said with feeling. "But it's where we are and we gotta deal with it 'til it's over, one way or another."

"Yeah, it's that 'another' I try not to think on much," he offered.

"I hear ya, man," I said, "but the truth is if we stay focused and careful all we're doin' is improving our odds a little. There's a hell of a lot o' luck involved in if or how we come outta this."

"I know. I just wish I didn't," he sighed.

We sat in silence for a while, occasionally looking up at a few stars that were barely visible through the thick, humid air. When the filter began to burn, I policed it by separating the fibers and flipping the paper ball out into the night.

"Take care, man," I said as I rose to leave.

"You, too, friend," he said with a small wave from the waist.

When I got back to my hooch, I said to the group, "Okay, here's the deal. As you know, I'm headin' back to the boonies tomorrow. When I leave I'm packing up my ponchos, so whoever takes charge of this place will need to use their own for a door flap and roof. You can't use the artillery's plastic sheets alone for that 'cause they're so clear the sun would cook you alive in here! I just wanna say it's been a real pleasure spending time with all of you. I'm gonna remember all of this. And I hope someone does keep Jamie's Hooch going for a while longer. God knows, we grunts need it, or something very much like it, to help us get through this shit."

"Right on, Sarge" a drunk private yelled across the group. This was followed by a rousing chorus of "For he's a jolly good fellow." I was so embarrassed I wanted to hide, but it really touched me. Pickering caught my eye and smiled.

Montagnard Village Elephant arriving at FSB Neal for rice, May 1970.
(photo 24-1)

Captured NVA rice is loaded for transport to Montagnard village.
(photo 24-3)

Elephant waits patiently while villagers prepare to load it with rice.
(photo 24-2)

Montagnards watch as elephant takes rice to their village.
(photo 24-4)

Chapter 25 – Footfalls in the Jungle; Magic Forest

My slick landed in a swirl of leaves in a small LZ hacked out of the jungle with machetes. I exited along with all the resupply items.

As I walked through the debris, Superman shouted, "How they hangin' Sarge?"

"They *are* still hanging, and that's all that matters," I said.

"True enough. Follow me and I'll take you to the new LT," he said.

I hadn't thought about meeting a new LT. We walked to the tree line at the west edge of the makeshift LZ and approached a group of three or four men seated on their packs eating. As I got closer, I made out the blackened, combat version of a first lieutenant's bars on the lapels of one man's jungle fatigue shirt.

"Lieutenant James Griffith, this is the long-lost Sergeant Jamie Thompson."

Griffith stood up and extended his hand. He was tall, probably six foot four. He wore glasses and had a studious demeanor. "Glad you're back with us, Sergeant. Are you ready to take over First Squad again?"

"Yes, sir, I'm fit for duty and glad to be back."

"Your timing's good, Sergeant. Dread's tour is up in two weeks. Rejoin your squad, and I'll fill you in later on what's going on."

Once we were out of earshot, Superman said, "Well, wha'd'ya think of our new LT?"

"Geez, I just met the guy."

"So?"

"Well, he seems a little too civilized for this line of work. But that might be unfair," I answered.

"No, I'd say you're a pretty good judge of character. He's been with us for nine days and basically just acts as a conduit from higher HQ to the sergeants. He lets them run the show," Superman said.

"He seems a little older than most line LTs, and he's already a first lieutenant, which means he's done his six months in the boonies ... or he's been doing something else for longer than that," I said.

"Word is he was a line officer for a month and was pulled back to the rear because he wasn't suited for the field. I haven't heard he did anything unforgiveable, but the powers-that-be must've felt he could better serve behind a desk than out here in the real war. I guess Cambodia's been chewin' up infantry officers pretty bad." Superman paused and we looked at each other. "Anyway, they've sent him as an interim platoon leader 'til they send out someone permanently."

"Did Griffith tell you this?" I asked with concern.

"Only the part about being here temporarily, not the rest. We got some of that from your friend Steve Warner and some from the rumor mill."

"Well, as long as he really does defer to the sergeants, we should be okay. Course, I'm biased about that," I said with a laugh.

When we walked up to my squad, Dread said, "'Bout damn time. What the hell you been doin' back there?"

"Not much. Playing spades, drinking beer, and smoking pot," I said offhandedly. "Oh, and healing up so I could come back and keep your sorry ass outta trouble."

"Well, set up your hooch and I'll fill you in," he said.

"You mean we're staying here tonight?" I asked.

"That's what the LT said." Dread had a look of unhappy resignation.

It was unusual to set up an NDP in the same place where we got resupplied. It was dangerous to stay near a spot where helicopters had been landing and taking off for an hour or more. The only exception was when it was so late that darkness fell before we could move out. I realized Lieutenant Griffith was going to need help.

Superman and I set up a hooch together that night. Then I headed over to meet with the LT; Sergeant Crippen, Dread, and Second Squad's new leader were already there.

"Okay, men. First of all, Sergeant Thompson is officially squad leader of First Squad again. Corporal Dread, you've done a good job in the sergeant's absence, and I appreciate it."

"Thanks, LT," said Dread, rather unenthusiastically.

"Well, tomorrow," the LT continued, "We're to head on an azimuth of two hundred fifty degrees for two klicks, then turn south on an azimuth of one-ninety for one and a half klicks." He pulled out a topo map that indicated the terrain was flat, dense jungle all the way. "Based on the map, we might need to use our machetes to cut through about half of the route tomorrow so be aware. There are no villages or roads indicated, so let's hope it's just another day of humping and nothing more. Any questions?"

"Who's got the point?" I asked.

Griffith turned to Crippen. "Sergeant, can you answer that?"

"Yes, sir," said Crippen. "Second Squad."

The next morning, I grabbed my entrenching tool and some toilet paper. It felt like I'd never left as I walked outside the NDP, keeping my M16 inches from my fingertips, on high alert to danger. It was amazing how fast one could evacuate and move on, as it were. Within a couple of minutes, I was back at my hooch washing my hands and brushing my teeth. Then I pulled out a C.

"Hey, the date on the box says, July 1958. We must be doing something right to move up the priority list for fresher chow," I said.

"Could be. Lately, I've noticed a lot of Cs that are less than fifteen years old," Superman answered, shoveling in a spoonful of oatmeal.

The truth was we grunts thrived on making do with the worst of everything, within reason. The harder and worse things were for us, the better we liked it. It was a pride thing. There was one exception, though. We never wanted to lack for firepower. We had all the weapons and fresh ammo we could carry, and we had a lot of support when we needed it. That was as it should be, because it was grunts, after all, who were actually fighting the damn war. We were the point of the American spear and we knew it, but we seldom spoke of such things. We just carried on.

When we were ready to saddle up, I said to Dread, "Albert, I know I don't need to tell you this, but I want you to stay in the middle of the platoon today and tomorrow. You're too damn short to take unnecessary risks."

"I was planning to do that anyway, but I appreciate you saying it," he replied.

The terrain that day was what we expected, flat ground and thick bush most of the way. As always, it was like being in a steam bath. By 0900 hours I'd pushed Firebase Neal and Jamie's Hooch into the deepest recesses of my mind.

Long lines of ants crossed our path here and there, and sometimes as I brushed against low branches, little clouds of mosquitos rose from the undersides of the leaves. At first, they were just unhappy at having their rest disturbed, but they became energized when they sensed fresh blood.

When we broke for lunch, Superman said, "You hangin' in there all right?"

"Yes!" I was surprised to realize I didn't feel tired or out of condition, despite ten days of drinking beer and shooting the bull in the rear. "My heel doesn't even hurt," I added.

I finished my beans and franks, and lit a cigarette, thinking, *"Oh, my God, this seems normal to me, now."* I looked around at my platoon mates. So far, we'd had four men killed and Lieutenant Bowen and Nathan Ardmore wounded in our first month in Cambodia, and three others were lost to bees back in Vietnam. Ardmore was shot in the arm while I was on Neal and replaced by Charles Riddle from the 173rd Airborne. Over a third of the men who'd been in the platoon when I joined it were gone. Soon enough we were making our way through thick brush again and my mind focused solely on the present.

The next day, since we were in a platoon size element, I took the point. As we started out, I checked my compass and made sure I was on the correct azimuth. We would move nearly four klicks for the day. This would be a short distance back in the World, but was a typical day's humping for us. The combination of the heat, the weight we carried, the terrain, the fact that we stayed off trails, and the ever-present danger of enemy contact made traveling faster and farther extremely difficult and highly inadvisable. We also had to remain within range of our artillery.

As I stepped out, I began counting every step. When I first got to the boonies, I found it difficult to keep an accurate running total in my head while remaining totally focused on everything around me. But after a while, it became natural—an added autonomic function, like breathing. I chose Emory Blaine as my cover man, and I knew he was also counting steps in his head.

The length of a marching step is identical for all soldiers; they're trained that way. But each man has a different natural stride. Moving through natural terrain in a combat situation requires care and stealth, not speed. It was essential that every man in the infantry know how many of his natural steps in such conditions equaled 100 meters. In my case, it was eighty-three. So after every eighty-third step, I made a mental notch for 100 meters and added these up as the day progressed.

Every couple of hundred meters, the cover man and I compared counts to make sure we agreed. The importance of this cannot be overstated. If we needed a medevac, resupply, an air strike, or artillery fire, we had to know where we were. The only way was to know exactly how far we had moved on what azimuths from the time the unit left a known position—in our case a firebase or an LZ. Often this involved dozens of azimuths and pace counts covering weeks. The platoon leader or company commander would note on topo maps our exact route of travel every day, to track as closely as possible where we were.

In country with many roads, power lines, bridges, and buildings, such precision wasn't required; it was relatively easy to ascertain one's location. The same can be said of country where there are easily identifiable natural features like rivers, distinctive rock formations, or distant mountains. But in a wilderness covered by dense forest, where the field of view was almost never over fifty meters and usually much less, and there were few distinctive features even when you could see farther, only pace counts and compass azimuths could be relied upon.

Every third day—when we needed resupply, or at unpredictable times when wounded men needed to be medevacked—the map coordinates we radioed to indicate our location were based on azimuths and counted steps. When we heard the approaching choppers, we could send up a flare or pop smoke to guide them over the last few hundred meters. But to get them close enough for us to hear them and for them to see our smoke, everything depended on the silent, never-ending counts of footfalls in the jungle.

Lieutenant Griffith had reminded me it was uncommon for squad leaders to take the point, and asked me if I was sure I didn't want to pick someone else.

I explained my reasons and added, "Sir, I could never order anyone to do something I wouldn't do myself. Besides, I'm good at it, probably better than anyone else in the platoon or the company." We all like doing things we're good at, and I liked walking point.

"All right, Sergeant," he said reluctantly.

There was one less admirable reason I didn't mention. For me at least, walking point was highly addictive. I'd never been so alert and focused or felt so alive. It kept my mind off anything not within range of my eyes and ears.

The day was uneventful; we saw nothing to indicate that another human had ever been in the area. Other than insects, most wildlife was nowhere to be seen or heard. Had I been a monkey or a tiger, I would have headed far away from the noise and danger of war, too. Thinking about it that evening as I ate next to Superman, I said, "Ya know, I bet northern Burma is overcrowded with wildlife now."

"Huh? Why do you think that?"

"Because there's no wildlife anywhere in the war zone anymore. I'm guessing they got the hell outta Dodge."

The next day, Dread finally left the field with only seven days left on his tour. It was overdue in the opinion of every man in the platoon. When he climbed on the resupply slick, I waved and smiled, and he did the same.

The next few days were pretty much the same: no sign of enemy activity or evidence of the hand of man. We humped on and on, slowly and circuitously working our way southward and westward, then coming back to the north and again reversing course to the south.

President Nixon had announced in advance that the Cambodian Incursion would end on June 30. So in theory we would return to Vietnam in less than a month. None of us believed it. The First Cavalry Division had found enormous quantities of enemy weapons and materiel and had effectively driven the North Vietnamese out of a thirty-mile wide corridor along Cambodia's border with Vietnam. It was obvious, whatever you thought of the war, that the Cambodia operation was a major military success, one of the biggest of the entire war and certainly the most important since the aftermath of Tet of 1968.

On a resupply day, we gathered into a company-size element again. Woody slipped off the chopper with the mail bags and I greeted him. With some trepidation, I asked, "How's your father doing?"

"It was a close thing, but he's stronger'n way-back-holler moonshine. He pulled through and appears to be on the mend. At least fer now."

"I'm glad to hear it. Welcome back, man!"

"Can't say I'm glad ta be back, but the sentiment's appreciated," he answered with a smile.

A few days later, in late afternoon, we found ourselves in an area where the vegetation began to gradually thin out around us. Soon, we were surrounded by clumps of brush with a few vines in them interspersed with grass about six inches to a foot high. The brush gave way to scattered bushes, and then the most wonderful sight opened before us. Suddenly there was no brush, no vines and no bushes, only thigh-high grass interspersed with large, long-stemmed wildflowers, all in the shade of enormous jungle trees separated from one another by at least twenty-five meters. I'd estimate each tree at 100 to 150 feet in height. This created a very high, technically single canopy jungle, though from about thirty feet above the ground to the treetops many layers of leafy limbs spread out broadly from every tree.

No one spoke as we silently moved through this Alice in Wonderland setting; it was beautiful beyond words. The tall grass parted as we passed and swayed closed behind us, as though no one had ever passed this way. The area was completely shaded, but it was not as dark as most of the jungle we traversed. The giant trees had fluted bases looking almost like the fins on a rocket. Ten to twenty feet above the ground, these flutes slanted outward from the tree trunks until the far ends sank below ground level from twelve to twenty feet away from the trunks.

We set up our NDP in this magical place, but instead of digging guard holes we used several of the pockets created by these flutes as our guard positions. Most of the men chose to sleep in the protected enclaves as close as they could get to the main tree trunks. I chose to set up my hooch near the outer end of a notch between two high flutes rather than next to the trunk, because it occurred to me that if we were hit, a person could get trapped in there with no way to safely get out.

That evening at the spades game I said, "This place is beautiful. I've never seen anything like it, even in pictures or movies."

"Yeah," muttered Riddle, "we've stumbled into our very own Magic Forest!" We all nodded and chuckled.

After the game I stood up and said, "Hey, I'm gonna hit the hay early. Same guard shifts as last night, guys. I'll take the point in the morning and Woody—big surprise—you'll be my cover."

The next morning, we moved south. The first 500 meters was an easy walk, but then it gave way to dense jungle. I hacked my way through fifty meters of brush before it cleared out to the normal density. After another 200 meters the terrain dropped off precipitously into a ravine about seventy meters deep. The slope was covered in brush and small saplings with occasional larger trees. I sent word back that the LT and CO should come to the point and see the situation for themselves.

When they arrived, I addressed the CO saying, "Sir, it's clear the aerial photos mistook the treetops—which touch each other above the ravine—as indicating level ground underneath. This is going to be a rough go. The far side is as steep as this side, which will slow us down for sure. I might be able to find an easier place to cross, or even a way around it altogether, but that would take time, too, and there's no guarantee I'll find a better spot."

Captain Osgood said, "What do you recommend, Sergeant?"

"Much as I hate to say this, sir, I think we should go across, but do it carefully. I'm guessing it'll take us a good two hours, but it would take a hell of a lot longer to search out another route."

The slope was sixty degrees or more, so we slid down on our butts and packs, grabbing saplings along the way to keep from crashing to the bottom. The slope faced south, so even the shaded sunlight cooked us, making our hands slippery with muddy sweat. The other side, while cooler, was damned difficult to climb. The eighty-pound packs could pull a man backwards if he didn't lean into the slope. There were close calls, but everyone made it.

When the last of the company climbed over the far edge, Captain Osgood said, "Break for chow—for an hour!"

That was longer than usual, but we were grateful for the added rest. We needed it.

Chapter 26 – Ho Chi Minh Trail; Rice and Blood

Two days later, we were resupplied. Master Sergeant Winter came out on the first chopper. He sometimes did that and stayed with us until the next resupply. But this time he only planned to stay a few hours to consult with the officers and senior NCOs and to handle any special circumstances that might have arisen. During chow, I sought him out.

"Hello, Sergeant Thompson, how's it going?" he asked.

"Fair to middling, Top. I've got a question for you," I said.

"What's that?"

"I was wondering if it's possible to get someone out of the field."

I saw a flicker on Top's face and realized he thought I was asking for myself. It bothered me that he'd think that, but I went on as though I hadn't noticed.

"I'm asking because the FNG, Merton Krolicki is completely unsuited for the field."

Relief flooded Top's face. "What do you mean?"

I told him how Krolicki left his pack at the bottom of the hill, how he was always scared to the point of not thinking clearly, how I couldn't assign any responsibility to him, and how none of the other men trusted him to have their backs. "Top, I've never been surer of anything. If he stays out here, he'll get himself or one of us killed. So if there's any way to transfer him to a rear desk job, it would be best for everybody, and I'd be grateful."

"Sergeant, if I can arrange this, don't let anyone know about it. The last goddamn thing I need is a shitload of grunts asking me to get them out of the field."

"Understood, Top. And thanks."

The next few days were humping as usual, with nothing memorable occurring, which was a good thing. During resupply on the sixth day, Krolicki came over to me all excited.

"Sergeant, I've got orders," he said. "Lieutenant Griffith just told me I'm being transferred to the rear to be a clerk typist."

I looked up from my hot lunch of chicken and mashed potatoes. "That's great, Merton. When do you report?"

"I leave on the last bird today."

"You better get your pack set up then. Oh, and leave your C-4, Claymore, and M60 ammo belts with us. We might need 'em."

"Yes, Sergeant!" he said, as crisply as he had the day I first saw him.

José and Superman were eating on either side of me.

"That's damn strange," said Superman.

"Si," said José, "I was thinking the same thing."

"I agree, but it's probably for the best, don't ya think?" I said, raising an eyebrow.

Twenty minutes later, I walked with Krolicki to the chopper and shook his hand. "I wish you the best of luck, man." *"I hope you live a long and decent life, Merton,"* I thought as the roar of rotors and wind swept over me.

* * *

In a ten-day stretch, I only lost two hands of spades and no games. I was getting good at it. After one particularly successful run, I said to Riddle, who'd been my partner, "It's amazing how this game can take our minds off the shit we're in."

"Yeah, and I'm glad it does," he said.

"Oh, me, too," I said. "You know, I never heard of spades, let alone played it, before I got here."

"Me neither," said Riddle, "but then I've never done most of the things we do over here."

For several days, we moved in a hilly area of dense jungle on the Ho Chi Minh Trail proper. It was unlike any trail I'd ever seen. There was no single pathway. Instead, it consisted of dozens—maybe hundreds—of narrow paths that twisted across each other over a width of hundreds if not thousands of meters. The most efficient way to construct a trail in such a rugged place would have been to create a single broad path. But that would have been easier to detect from the air and would also concentrate the people and materiel passing along it, which meant more would be lost in a single ambush, artillery bombardment, air strike, or Arc Light. Building it this way, individuals and groups using the trail could pick random paths and switch around among them, greatly reducing the risk of discovery.

The attention to detail was impressive. Every root that would normally be an obstacle was hewn flat to the ground. When paths climbed or descended hills, the hewn roots became stair steps. For this reason, the going was not hard for us, but it was tense. It was evident that every trail had been heavily used for many years.

I had point and Woody walked cover. He was still my preferred cover man, because he had great eyes and didn't talk much. I was so focused when on point that I didn't like to be even a hair distracted. Woody instinctively understood that and besides, he was just as focused as I was.

About ten meters upslope from the trail we were on, I spotted a bamboo platform about half a meter above ground. On it were placed fifty-kilogram bags of rice in three layers of about forty bags each. We set up a perimeter around the cache and broke for chow.

Captain Osgood checked to see if the rice could be airlifted out, but no choppers were available, and we already had more captured rice stockpiled at Neal than we or the Montagnards could use. So we had to come up with a way to destroy 13,200 pounds of rice. Not wishing to call attention to ourselves by burning, we resorted to slashing the bags with our machetes, scattering it as best we could and taking turns pissing on it. As the operation was finishing up, I turned to Superman.

"I know we had to do this, but I don't like destroying what other men work hard to produce. It feels wrong," I said.

"I feel the same, but as you said, it had to be done."

"Yeah, but I don't have to feel good about it, though. Besides, I'm not so sure the gooks won't just wait 'til after it rains and eat the stuff anyway."

When we formed up again, I continued along the trail for another klick, mainly because it paralleled our assigned azimuth. At that point, the trail descended into a narrow valley. This is where we changed azimuth, turning south, and began to move up a steep hill.

About thirty meters up, Woody urgently whispered, "Hooch!"

I stopped moving. "Where? I don't see anything."

Woody stepped to my side and pointed. "See up there? The crossed bamboo poles of a hooch frame."

I looked hard, finally spotting the peak of a roof under construction. "I see it! Go back and call up the gun and the chunker."

A minute later, Superman came up silently on my left and Ferde Salazar with his assistant gunner, Bauman, appeared to my right. I pointed to the crossbars, barely visible through the jungle.

"I see it," said Salazar.

"Okay, take these," I said, as Woody, Superman and I handed over our loops of M60 ammo. "Since we're in a free-fire zone, find a spot where you can get good fire on the crest of the hill. When you're ready to go, open up. Got it?"

"Got it, Sarge." Salazar and Bauman bent low and made their way to a fallen tree ten meters to our right and five meters farther up the slope.

I wasn't comfortable using reconnaissance by fire, but given that we were on the Ho Chi Minh Trail in Cambodia, it was the prudent thing to do. Salazar set up the machine gun and got in position. Bauman placed a belt of ammo over the top, and Salazar slammed the ammo cover down, securing the belt in place. He pulled the cocking mechanism twice. Then he glanced over at me and I gave him a thumbs-up.

When Salazar pulled the trigger, the M60 fired a single round and jammed. The two worked furiously to restart the gun, but within a few seconds of that one round firing, all hell broke loose with automatic weapons fire from the hilltop.

Salazar screamed and rolled onto his back, but once Bauman succeeded in clearing the gun, he kept firing up the hill by pulling the trigger with his thumb.

"C'mon!" I yelled at Woody.

"Are you crazy?" he yelled back.

"Somebody's gotta do it!" I took off up the hill. All I knew was I had to get to where I could protect Salazar and Bauman, meaning at least as high up the hill as they were to provide supporting fire on the hilltop. I took a position behind a tree trunk and fired across the lip of the hill, sweeping the front of the hooch frame on full auto. Woody was a little behind me and just to my right, as I knew he would be! I was peripherally aware that grenades were going off around me.

In close small-unit combat, whoever holds the higher ground has a tremendous advantage, especially when it comes to throwing grenades. But a chunker, which fired 40mm grenades, could counter that advantage.

Superman was behind a tree three meters to my left and a few feet higher upslope. He was trying to fire his chunker to drop its grenades on the hilltop, but bullets were splintering the trees he and I were sheltering behind so he couldn't point the chunker as well he needed to. Some of his rounds were bouncing off trees between us and the hooch and others were impacting the slope below the top. To protect the soldier firing it and other nearby friendly troops, chunker rounds would not explode closer than twenty-five feet from where they were fired, so the rounds hitting the intervening trees were dropping harmlessly to the ground, but they weren't doing us any damn good!

"All right," I said to Superman, "I'm going to tell you before I open up so you can poke around and aim that thing while I'm keeping their heads down."

He nodded. "Go! I'm ready!"

"Okay here we go ... now!"

I leaned out and fired, still on full automatic. Superman leaned out, pointed his chunker, and fired. The round exploded right at the lip of the hill. It was working. We continued this pattern for what seemed an eternity, but was certainly no more than a few minutes. I'd emptied half of my magazines, so I flipped the selector switch to fire and fired bursts of three to five rounds for the remainder of the firefight.

Eventually, the return fire faded, so I moved up the hill firing all the way and motioning the squad—which by now had moved up just behind me—to follow me. At the top, we sprayed automatic fire across the area. I could see that the hooch was still under construction and was just a bamboo frame all the way to the ground, but with a bunker dug under its center. I told José to drop a frag in it as we passed.

"Damn!" he yelled, when it didn't explode. "I forgot to take off the safety clip."

"Don't worry about it. Just throw in another one," I shouted.

After it exploded, the bunker was no longer a concern. We swept past it and completely across the hilltop, crouching along the far lip and firing down into the surrounding jungle. I don't think we received any enemy fire there, but in the cacophony of firing and yelling it was impossible to tell for sure. A minute later, as I continued to fire, I grabbed the inside of my right thigh and sat down hard.

José, to my immediate left, yelled, "Are you hit?"

I removed my hand and saw blood. "I guess so," I said, popping another magazine into my M16 and continuing to fire down into the jungle.

"Hey, man! You're hit; you need to get back. Get in the center!" said José.

"I suppose you're right," I said, slipping back and moving to the other side of the hooch. I felt fine, but as I lit a cigarette I was fascinated by the shaking of my hands; they were vibrating as though I were holding live wires. I felt like I was seeing myself in a movie. Meantime, blood was turning my pant leg red.

The men moved Salazar up the hill, placing him near me in the center of our new perimeter. He winced and cried out. Jacobs quickly cut off his right pantleg, but couldn't see the problem. Then Bauman helped remove Salazar's pants completely. An AK round had hit Salazar on the top of his right thigh, torn upward through muscles, tendons, and maybe bones, and was protruding straight out to the side halfway through the skin at the point of his right hip. There was a lot of blood at the entry point, but the skin was so tight around the bullet that there was no blood at the exit point. The bullet was shiny, as if it hadn't even been fired.

"Ferde," said Jacobs, "I'm going to clean the wounds, dress the lower one, and put a loose dressing on the upper one. I'm also giving you morphine to help with the pain. Do you understand?"

"Yes," Ferde grunted through clenched teeth.

After a couple of minutes, Jacobs came over to me. "Let's see what we've got," he said, cutting off my blood-stained pants leg above the wound.

"It's not bad," I said. "In fact, it doesn't hurt at all."

He glanced up from examining the wound to look me in the eye. "Not now, it doesn't, but that will change," he said.

"Maybe, but it could have been a lot worse."

"That's for sure," Jacobs said. "But this is a puncture wound. It has an entry point and no exit, and it's in a bad place. Whatever hit you is still in there. You're going in."

"Whatever you say," I said with a smile.

"Listen, you might have a million-dollar wound, but don't smile when you're on the medevac bird. Those guys hate that," he said, cleaning the wound and tying a dressing over it.

As Jacobs finished, three Cobra gunships arrived and flew in circles around our position, firing rockets into the surrounding jungle. They started close in and gradually worked farther out. One of our men shouted in pain and reached over his back. I looked over and saw Cal Singleton, our new squad RTO, standing where I'd been hit. A twisted jagged piece of steel about seven inches long was sticking edgewise out of his upper back near his right shoulder, possibly a piece of casing from one of the Cobra rockets.

Jacobs was there in a heartbeat. He carefully cut away and removed Singleton's shirt and T-shirt, examined the wound, and said, "Look, I think I can pull this out so bear with me."

Cal nodded.

"Okay, face away from me, intertwine the fingers of your hands, and push your elbows forward."

Singleton did this, stretching the skin across his upper back.

"I'm gonna try to work it out now so don't move," said Jacobs.

"All right, Doc, pull away," said Singleton as he steeled himself.

Jacobs worked the metal back and forth until he was sure it wasn't more than an inch deep, then pulled sharply, straight back. The shrapnel came out cleanly, but the wound began to bleed freely.

"Okay, it's out," said Jacobs. "Now bend over and put your hands on that log."

Jacobs cleaned the area and sprinkled some of his magic medical powder over the wound. The bleeding stopped and he taped a dressing over it.

"You're going in, too," he said.

"Sure, Doc." Cal smiled broadly.

"Like I told Sergeant Thompson, don't smile on the medevac. It's bad karma."

A few minutes later, Lieutenant Griffith saw me leaning against the tree. "Sergeant Thompson, you got wounded, too?"

I thought that was a strange question and wondered where the hell the LT had been during the firefight, but I said, "Yes, sir. By the way, don't let anybody go down in the bunker under the hooch. The first grenade we threw in didn't explode, and there's no way to be sure the second grenade set it off."

"All right. Thank you, Sergeant. You take care." He turned toward the hooch.

When we heard the medevac chopper, we radioed the crew that we were popping yellow smoke so they could find us. The cloud of bright yellow smoke slowly dispersed through the trees. The chopper crew radioed that they couldn't see any smoke and asked us to try again.

The jungle canopy was so thick that no smoke was making it through. I suggested taping a smoke grenade to the end of a bamboo pole and holding it as high as we could. That smoke didn't make it out either. Eventually, we taped three poles together and a few wisps of smoke managed to exit. The pilot positioned himself and dropped the jungle penetrator through a gap in the treetops seventy-five feet above us.

Jacobs came over and said, "You're going up first, then Salazar. Singleton last. Leave your pack and weapon; we'll send that stuff later. Be sure to let the cable touch the ground to discharge any static electricity before you touch it. And remember, no smiling!"

As soon as the cable touched, I flipped one of the three arms down and off to the side to form a narrow L-shaped seat and fastened a safety belt around my waist. Then I was pulled up through a three-by-five-foot gap in the foliage without touching a leaf. I was amazed at how the pilot kept that chopper from moving. I was even more impressed when I looked around and realized that the treetops were whipping wildly in the throes of a major windstorm. When I was opposite the open door, a medic leaned out, grabbed me around the hip and swung me into the helicopter.

As the cable went back down, I yelled over the noise at the medic. "The next man up has an AK round sticking out of his right hip, so don't grab him there."

In a few minutes, Salazar rose, and my worst fears were realized. The medic reached around and grabbed Salazar by his hip, causing him to twist in pain and scream.

The shocked medic gently positioned Ferde on his left side, lifted the loose dressing, and saw that shiny bullet stuck tight in his skin. "Jesus. I never saw anything like that before!"

"Me either," I said. "I tried to warn you."

He nodded apologetically, as he sent the cable down for Cal.

The medevac chopper hovered as though nailed in place, even as treetops as far as the eye could see whipped and waved in gusty forty-mile-an-hour winds. The Cobra gunships kept the medevac bird in the center as they continued to fly in circles, firing missiles and miniguns into the hostile jungle.

I felt like a child after a fall, when his mother comforts him by kissing and bandaging a cut. For the first time since I'd arrived in the war, I felt that somebody gave a damn; that my country cared about us, about me; that it cared about what we were doing here. It was a powerful feeling. It occurred to me that once in a while the little parts are greater than the whole.

Half an hour later, we landed at the aid station at Firebase Buttons near the village of Song Be, Vietnam, where I'd gotten the ice. Cal and I were escorted inside a large tent that served as the operating theater and told to lie on operating tables. Many of the tables were occupied. Doctors hustled here and there, examining and operating as quickly as they could.

When it was my turn, my field dressing was removed. The docs had me roll onto my stomach so they could inject a huge shot of penicillin into my right buttocks. They also injected a local pain killer at the site of my wound and waited a few minutes.

"All right, Sergeant," said my surgeon, "I'm going to probe the wound now. Let me know if you feel anything."

I turned my head to look at the unmoving man on the next table. He was a bloody mess. A team of three surgeons engaged in rapid-fire discourse as they worked furiously on his abdominal area.

"How are you doing, Sergeant?" my surgeon asked.

"Fine, sir. Have you started yet?"

"Oh, yes. Again, let me know if you feel anything," he said.

"I will," I said, continuing to watch the team of doctors next to me.

After several minutes, I felt a tug.

"Hey, I think you've got it," I said.

"No, that's a tendon. I'm going to leave that shrapnel right where it is."

"Whatever you think, sir," I said.

"I think that's best. I don't want to do any more damage than has already been done. You're lucky, Sergeant. The shrapnel is no more than an inch from the femoral artery. If it had cut that artery, you and I likely wouldn't be talking right now. Your wound needs to drain, so I'm going to put a loose dressing on it but not stitch the wound."

At the table next to me, the efforts of the three doctors slowed, and they stepped back. "He's gone," one of them said. "Do you agree?"

The other two nodded. "Do we know what happened?"

"He threw himself on a grenade to save his buddies," said the one who appeared to be most senior.

"My God," said one of the others, "do people really do that?"

"A few do," said the leader softly. Then they pulled a sheet over the man and moved to the next wounded man.

I stared at the form under the sheet as my surgeon said, "All right, Sergeant, wait here while I get you a crutch."

"Yes, Sir," I said dully.

In a moment, the doctor returned and asked me to try standing. I did that with little difficulty. Then he handed me the crutch and adjusted it to fit comfortably under my right armpit.

"Take a few steps for me," he said. "You'll be on a profile for thirty days. Take it easy. We don't want that shrapnel moving around. No heavy lifting, no bending or running, and only limited walking. Got it?"

"Yes, sir," I answered.

The corporal at the exit table weighed me and then got me antibiotics, pain pills, and an instruction sheet.

"Out of curiosity, how much do I weigh?" I asked.

"One thirty-seven, Sergeant."

"Are you sure?" I asked incredulously.

"Absolutely sure," he said.

I'd weighed 176 when I got drafted and 154 when I left the States almost three months before.

It was June 22, 1970.

Medic beside slick demonstrating a Jungle Penetrator — How author was medevacked. (photo 26-1)

Chapter 27 – Respite

I found our HQ, walked in, and reported to Top. "Hello, Sergeant Thompson. How're you feeling?"

"I've been better, Top, but it could've been a hell of a lot worse."

"That's for certain," he said. "Well, you can take it easy for the next thirty days and we'll re-evaluate things. For now, let's get you settled. Corporal Simmons show Sergeant Thompson his bunk. He'll be with us for at least a month."

Simmons checked a logbook and recorded my bunk location. He headed out to the adjacent barracks tent, and I followed unsteadily.

When we were out of Top's earshot, Simmons said, "What the hell happened?"

"I had the point and we spotted a hooch. We used the gun to recon by fire, but it jammed after firing a round or two and we received return fire. Sometime between that and when we swept over the hilltop, I was hit with grenade shrapnel."

"Uh, huh. Well, here's your bunk." He pointed to a lower bunk.

"Thanks." I gingerly sat myself down on the bed.

"When your pack and weapon come in, I'll let you know," he said.

"Can I get something to read, in the meantime?" I asked.

"Yeah, we have a box of paperbacks in my office. You can take anything you want."

"Good. I think I'll just lie down for a while first. You probably already know Cal Singleton and Ferde Salazar were hit, too. Salazar got it pretty bad, so I doubt we'll be seeing him for a long time."

I dozed off and slept until I heard someone say it was chow time. I was starving. I asked a nearby grunt where the nearest piss tube was and made my way out the back door.

Pissing leaning on a crutch takes some getting used to, but I managed it. I stared at the lone mountain very close by to the east. I hadn't noticed it on my other trips here.

"Geez!" I blurted. When I'd turned from the piss tube, a sharp stabbing pain had shot through my leg.

Mountains always raise my spirits, so despite the physical pain I felt a little better as I walked to the mess hall. More cautious in my movements now, I got a tray of tuna casserole. I hardly looked at anyone while I ate, just stared into space. Later, at Simmons's office, I dug a sci-fi book out of the box and shoved it into the left side pocket of my jungle fatigue pants. I didn't have a lower right pantleg. *"Gotta do something about that tomorrow,"* I thought absently. Back at the barracks, I tried to read, but my eyes kept closing, and I fell asleep.

For the first few days at Firebase Buttons, Cal Singleton and I hung out together. Ferde Salazar had been flown to a military hospital in the Philippines, and we had no idea if or when we'd see him again. I spent most of my time in my bunk or wandering around to familiarize myself with the place.

Superficially, Buttons was just a smaller version of the Bien Hoa-Long Binh complex. It had a fixed wing airstrip, a high berm with large bunkers dug into it, and a well-oiled logistics operation that kept the line troops supplied with whatever they needed—including ice, as I well knew. Buttons also had a large contingent of cooks who did double duty feeding the soldiers on the firebase as well as the field units. It was a beehive of olive drab activity.

Since I had no duties, I got to know some of the cooks. They were good guys who, largely by luck, cooked in the rear instead of humping in the boonies. But they were conscious of their luck and didn't flaunt it or make derogatory remarks about grunts.

One afternoon Seth, a Spec-4 cook, pulled me aside. "Hey, man, meet me after chow tonight. I have someone I want you to meet."

That evening he introduced me to Sam Dodge, a truck driver who was their pot supplier. I liked Sam, but wasn't sure I wanted to be identified as one of his close associates.

He offered me some good advice, though. "It isn't cool to keep a stash when you live in the barracks here—sometimes they pull surprise inspections—but when you know you're leaving, find me and I'll fix you up."

The next day, I reported to the aid station for my one-week evaluation. The doctor removed the dressing and examined my leg. It appeared to have healed over, but looked odd to me, kind of like flesh-colored plastic stretched across the entry point.

"How does it feel, Sergeant?" the doctor asked.

"Better, sir," I said, "but there's a dull ache most of the time and sometimes stabbing pain."

"It may look better, but it's certainly not healed yet," he said. "The reason we worry about puncture wounds is that they have difficulty draining. And in this damn climate they're prone to infection. For now, I'm pleased with how the wound looks. I want you to clean it and replace the dressing at least once a day. Can you do that, Sergeant?"

"I'll certainly do my best, sir."

The doctor cleaned and redressed the wound. "Off you go, until I see you in three weeks."

The next day, June 30, much to my surprise—and everyone else's—all U.S. troops were out of Cambodia and back in Vietnam, just as President Nixon had promised. That same day Top told me the commander of the First Cavalry Division, Major General George W. Casey, had ordered the entire 5/7 to stand down for a five-day, in-country R&R. Even those of us who were the walking wounded, would be flown from Buttons to Bien Hoa. I was to join my platoon right after morning chow on July 2.

By sundown on July 1, the whole battalion was camped inside the berm. I had a chance to see Kurt for the first time in a month.

Right after morning chow the next day, I ditched my crutch at the aid station, deciding I would just limp wherever I needed to go. The flight to Bien Hoa was less than an hour, and we landed at the airport where new troops arrived fresh from the World—the same place where Kurt and I had landed. There were fifty-some of us in Charlie Company; we'd gone into Cambodia two months before with close to ninety.

As we walked through that terminal, which was wide open inside, with high ceilings and relatively cool air, we were bent forward under the weight of our rucksacks, camouflaged helmets pulled low over our eyes, M16 rifles carried by their top handles at our sides, with two bandoliers of M16 magazines and two loops of M60 machine gun ammunition crossed over our chests. Most of us were filthy. Our jungle fatigues were soiled and tattered, some with shredded holes at the knees. As always, despite the oppressive heat and humidity, we wore long-sleeved fatigue shirts with sleeves rolled back to mid-forearm. Our jungle boots were stained red from the jungle soil, the deep-treaded soles were worn, and the black leather was cracked over the toes and at the backs of the heels. Many of us had small plastic squeeze bottles of bug repellent stuck under elastic bands on our helmets and some had grenades snapped onto rucksack straps. Beneath every rucksack was the tightly strapped M16 or M60 ammo can containing our letters and photos from home, our writing materials and maybe a dog-eared paperback book ... all the stuff we wanted to keep dry. And our skin was dark reddish brown from the sun and the mud and the sweat.

As we trudged single file across that terminal toward the front doors, we passed directly in front of rows of chairs filled with several hundred very clean young men sporting new haircuts and a few regulation mustaches. At the time, the handlebars on mine reached my eyes when I pulled 'em straight. Apparently, in the months since we'd arrived, it had been decided that newly arriving troops would no longer wear jungle fatigues, because these men were wearing starched stateside uniforms and OD baseball caps. These were men who had just arrived in-country from the States, who had just stepped off a Pan Am jet airliner into the furnace heat of a typical day in the Nam. They were scared ... and after they saw us filing across their front, they were much more scared.

No one said a word in that terminal. Over the hushed sounds of rubber soles on concrete, you could have heard a pin drop. For us, at the time, it was just another hump, albeit on smoother ground than we were used to, but we were aware of the sight we must have presented both to those silently sitting Newbies and to the American and Vietnamese military and civilian terminal employees silently watching from behind the long ticket counter. We were combat veterans ... and we were damn proud of it!

At the First Cav R&R Center, we were assigned bunks in timber frame barracks. Towels, soap, and clean uniforms were issued. In a heartbeat, everyone was lined up to use the showers and scrape off at least a few layers of accumulated grime. When the entire unit was cleaned up, we assembled in battalion formation on the parade ground.

A colonel stepped up to the center of a raised platform. "Ten-HUT!" he said.

We snapped to attention like Pavlov's dogs.

"Major General George Casey, Commander of the First Cavalry Division, has a few words to say to you," the colonel said.

A trim man of average height, wearing starched fatigues and spit-shined boots, stepped to the center of the stage.

"At ease, men," he said. In unison, we spread our feet slightly apart. "I'm sure most of you are wondering what the hell you're doing here," General Casey said. Small chuckles erupted here and there among us. "Well, I'll tell you. What you did in Cambodia was important. Your battalion, the Fifth of the Seventh, found more weapons and ammunition, more food and supplies, and more miscellaneous equipment and materiel than any other unit involved in the Incursion. And ... you suffered more casualties accomplishing that than any other battalion—about fifty percent. What you did was extraordinary and exemplary, and in the finest tradition of the United States military. You should be proud of what you've done to help bring this war to an end. I'm certainly proud of you, and that's why you're here on the first In-Country R&R

following the Incursion. Now that's enough from me. You men are here to rest and recuperate, not to listen to me. So try to unwind and have some fun. Dis-missed!"

I was dumbstruck. I had no idea what we'd done or how badly we'd been hurt. That evening in the NCO-EM Club, Kurt and I drank beer and watched our fellow grunts.

"It's fascinating how the guys who acquitted themselves well in combat separate from those who didn't," I said. "It's like watching globs of oil in a lava lamp. They mix with one another and yet they don't."

"Yeah," said Kurt, "but it feels natural, doesn't it?"

"There is that. But somehow, we have to get past that, because the people who most need to be around us grizzled combat vets are exactly the ones we tend not to want to be around."

"Good point. Hey, how's the leg?" Kurt asked.

"I think it'll be fine, but the doctor says a puncture wound is prone to infection, so I have to keep it clean and be careful not to injure it further."

"What happened exactly?" he asked.

I told him and then said, "Want another beer?"

"Does a grunt shit in the boonies?" he said.

I limped to the bar to get a couple more beers.

When I returned, Kurt said, "Say, do you remember Hal, my bunkmate at the Oakland Army Base?"

"Yeah, and I still feel bad about getting him drunk," I said.

"Me, too, but he obviously got back to his strait-laced, no-nonsense ways," continued Kurt.

"Glad to hear it, but what makes you say that?"

"He got a battlefield commission. He's a second lieutenant now."

"Man, that's rare. Good for him."

We toasted Hal's achievement, which he might have found ironic, but I suspected would have appreciated anyway.

A day or so later, browsing the shops operated by Vietnamese civilians I noticed several embroidered boonie hats hanging on pegs. I pointed to one and asked, "Do you make these?" The shopkeeper said, "Yes," and pointed to the far end of the shop. I walked down there and was greeted by an old man at a stitching machine. I asked, "Can you make me one of these boonie hats?"

"Yes," he said, "what you want, GI?"

I thought about it, then motioned for a pencil and paper to draw on. He produced that and I sketched a Playboy bunny head with the pointed ears, a peace symbol, and pointed to the crossed rifle patch of the infantry, the Combat Infantryman Badge (CIB) patch, and I drew an "Airmobile" patch shaped like a gentle arch and asked if he could embroider that. He said he could make the things I wanted. I indicated on my sketch that the Peace Symbol should be large enough to fill most of the round top of the hat, the CIB should be centered at the top front just below the top of the hat, the bunny should be just below that, "Airmobile" below that, the crossed rifles centered below that where a hatband would go on a Stetson, and Cambodia and Vietnam in large caps along the brim on opposite sides of the crossed rifles. When I was sure he understood, we picked out a camouflage boonie hat that fit me, and he went to work. I was worried that it might be too busy, but I really wanted all those things on it! The only decoration I had some misgivings about was the crossed rifles patch because I thought it might be only for officers. It turns out, I needn't have been concerned because crossed rifles are a symbol that applies to everyone in the infantry regardless of rank. I told the old man I'd be back in half an hour and he said, "Numba One." I browsed a few other shops, and the PX where I bought a Seiko watch for less than $10 MPC. When I returned the job was done! I paid the old man $5 MPC and had myself a functional boonie hat and a life-long souvenir!

The next night, we were joined by our NCO School buddy, Gordon Castro, and Staff Sergeant Terry Harris, the platoon sergeant of Charlie Company's Second Platoon. We were quite the group. Castro was a Cuban American. Terry was black. Kurt was of German stock. And I was mostly

Scottish and English with some French, German, and Iroquois in the mix. But in the Nam, we all had the same job, ground-pounding and search-and-destroy.

"Now that we're all 'combat hardened' as they say, what do you think of this damn war?" I asked the table.

Terry said, "To quote William Bendix from *The Life of Riley*, 'What a revoltin' development this is.'"

We laughed and raised our glasses.

"Amen, bros," said Castro. "Hey, how 'bout another toast? To breathin'!"

We raised our glasses again. You'd think such a toast would be sobering, but for us it wasn't. It was merely an acknowledgment of the simple truth that we were lucky to still be around.

"Have you guys concluded the same thing I have, that we're fighting here for each other rather than for any higher cause?" asked Terry.

"Yes," said Kurt.

"Absolutely, man," I agreed.

"No doubt about it," Castro added.

"All right, then. To each other." Terry raised his glass.

"To each other!" we echoed.

The remaining nights at the R&R Center were much the same, with lots of beer drinking and way too much war talk, though most of it was truthful. Kurt and I made grandiose plans to develop a total immersion sound room for homes when we got back to the World. Kurt was a sound engineer and I was a listener. Before we knew it, our five days were over.

Our time had been a rest, but not an escape. You could take the grunt out of the boonies, but you couldn't take the boonies out of the grunt.

After a night at Buttons, all the companies were sent back out into the field.

I was left behind on the firebase.

Leaving Cambodia, Firebase Neal evacuates, late June 1970.
(photo 27-1)

Chapter 28 – Danger Is a Relative Thing

The next afternoon someone mentioned that it might be possible to make a phone call back to the World. It could be done using something called MARS, the Military Affiliate Radio System. It had belatedly occurred to me that the Army must have notified my parents that I'd been wounded, and they might be very worried about me. I asked Jay about it and he told me to head over to near where I'd picked up the ice and look for a tent that said M.A.R.S. on a sign hanging over the door. The system used volunteer civilian ham radio operators to patch together radio-telephone calls to and from the most distant parts of the world and a soldier, sailor or airman's home country. Jay said they only allowed MARS calls to be made from 2000 to 2200 hours and the calls were restricted to just three minutes because of the high demand and limited capabilities of the system. There was no charge for it.

I found the right tent, got in line and waited over half an hour until it was finally my turn. I filled out a short form that said who I was, my rank and unit, who I wanted to talk to and why, and their address and telephone number in the States. I handed this to a Spec-4 Signal Corps guy who began to work his magic. It took several minutes to get through a number of ham radio operators and get connected to my parents' phone, but eventually he did it! I pressed the radio-telephone receiver tightly to my ear as my mother answered the phone. I quickly told her it was me and explained that I had only three minutes to talk.

To say she was surprised is an understatement, but she quickly recovered and sounded so normal that it was a bit shocking to me. She sounded just as she would have if I'd seen her just a few minutes earlier, but she was very glad to hear from me. Then I explained that I'd called because I didn't want them to worry when they heard I'd been wounded.

She said, "What! You've been wounded?"

"Yes," I said, "but don't worry. I've got some shrapnel in my right leg, but I'm fine. I'll be all right." Then added, "I take it the Army has not notified you that I was wounded, then?"

"Egads, no! This is the first we've heard about it. Let me get your father for you. Hold on!" Luckily it was a Saturday, so my father was at home. A moment passed and he came on the line.

"Hello? Are you there, son?" he asked.

"Yes, I'm here," I answered.

"What's this about you being wounded?"

I told him the same thing I'd told my mother and then added, "I'm going to be fine. I just didn't want you to worry, but I guess since the Army never told you I was wounded, I've probably done just the opposite!"

"Nonsense, son. We're very glad to hear from you. Where are you now?"

"I'm not allowed to tell you exactly where I am, but I'm back in Vietnam, which, strange to say, is a safer place to be than Cambodia was. Say, what time is it there… and what day?" The Spec-4 tapped his watch with a forefinger. I nodded at him.

"It's eleven o'clock Saturday morning."

"That's fascinating. I can never keep the times and days straight, but it's eleven o'clock Saturday night here! So, in a way, I'm talking to you twelve hours ago, or is it twelve hours from now? But listen, I've got to end the call, we're limited to three minutes. But I'm fine and I love you both, and Julie and Mimi."

Apparently, my parents were on different extensions, because they said together, "I love you, too. Write to us!"

"I will," I promised. "Goodbye, I love you!" and that was that. I handed the receiver to the Signal Corps guy, thanked him, and left the tent.

"What a strange-ass world!" I thought to myself as I walked back to my bunk through another hot, steamy night.

* * *

The next evening, I ate chow with our battalion clerk, Jay Simmons.

"Did you hear about General Casey?" he asked.

"You mean the Division CO? The guy that talked to us at Bien Hoa?"

"The same."

"No. What about him?"

"He was killed today."

"Jesus, man. How'd it happen?" I asked.

"Things are a bit sketchy, but it seems he was flying to Cam Ranh Bay to visit wounded grunts when his slick hit a mountain in a storm. There were no survivors."

"I liked him," I said sadly. "He was a different kind of general. I think he cared about us and was even proud of us."

"Yeah, I feel that way, too," said Jay.

"Of course, you know what the other generals will learn from this, don't you?"

"No, what?"

"That it's a bad idea to go out to the field. Shit, man. It's a damn shame about General Casey." We ate mostly in silence after that.

It was July 7, 1970.

Simmons and I often partnered up for spades games with anyone foolish enough to try their luck against us. When Jay wasn't available, Cal Singleton was just as good. And when I wasn't playing, Cal and Jay beat all comers.

After one of these games, Jay said, "I know how you're feeling."

"Well, I wish you'd tell me, because I haven't got a clue," I said.

"I'll do that, but first I want you to know that I spent my first three months in the Nam as a grunt, just like you. I was a rifleman in Third Platoon, Alpha Company, until I took an AK round in the arm. When you and I first met, I'd only had my arm out of a sling for two weeks."

"I didn't realize that."

"I know. I don't talk about it much, kinda like you." He chuckled.

"I guess you're right," I said.

"That's normal, but not to worry. We all know what happened to you because word about damn near everything that happens on the line gets to us faster than most medevac birds."

"I'm not sure how comforting that is," I said.

"Sometimes it isn't, but in your case it's all good. But my point is I know you're bored out of your mind here. Top knows it, too," he said with a nod and raised eyebrow. "We're working on that and if all goes well, you'll have better times ahead. Just wanted you to know."

"Thanks, man. I know I can't go back to the field yet, but I hate just lying around all day."

"We get it."

That night, against my better judgment, I went to a USO-sponsored bingo night in the mess hall. The place was filled. At some point, I won a game and went to the front to pick a prize from a table full of trinkets, which is where I saw three Red Cross Doughnut Dollies. To me they seemed the most beautiful girls I'd ever laid eyes on. I had trouble sleeping that night.

The next morning, Top said, "Sergeant, I've got an assignment that you can do even on your profile."

"That's good, Top. I'm going stir crazy."

"I know. Anyway, I think you might like this assignment," he said with a wink. "Have you noticed the mountain that's close to us?"

"It's pretty hard to miss," I said.

"That it is. It's called Nui Ba Ra—White Virgin Mountain. It rises two thousand feet damn near straight up. We have a base up there with fifty to seventy-five guys. It's an important relay point for military communications, so most of the personnel are commo and commissary types who don't know one end of a weapon from the other," Top said.

"So who's keeping them safe?"

"Exactly. Somebody has to protect them and their equipment, so there are always grunts up there for perimeter guard. There's no organized infantry unit, though. Grunts rotate in and out on TDY (Temporary Duty assignments), mostly guys getting discharged for medical reasons or getting booted out on Section Eights. And there're a few on profiles, like you. Think you can handle it?"

"I think so, Top. When do I leave?"

"Report here tomorrow morning after chow, and Corporal Simmons will give you the details on when a helo can ferry you up there. There's no road; the only way up or down is by helicopter or on foot through dense bush. Got it, Sergeant?"

"Yes, Top," I said rather cheerfully. "Can I ask you about something else?"

"Sure, but make it quick."

I told him about the bingo game and asked him why I'd never seen a Doughnut Dolly before or even known there were any in Nam.

"They don't stray far from 'officer country,'" he said.

I took his meaning and instinctively understood that line officers would fare little better with them than ordinary grunts. Who could blame them, really? But just glimpsing them was a morale booster—a reminder of what we were fighting for so to speak. The military was such a totally male world that I'd hardly had a thought about a woman since I'd set foot in-country. In the circumstances, it was just as well.

As I passed by Jay's desk, I smiled and gave him a thumbs-up. I was excited to be doing something. A little later, I remembered Sam Dodge's offer and headed to the mess hall to ask if Seth had seen him lately.

"As a matter of fact, you're in luck," Seth said. "He's due in tonight. Come back around 2130 hours and I'll put you guys together. Oh, and bring your pack with you."

"But, I just wanna buy some pot from the guy. Do I really need my pack for that?"

"Trust me," said Seth, "Sam doesn't fool around. Besides, he's got a soft spot for grunts. Something about an infantry squad pulling his sorry butt out of a VC ambush last spring."

At the appointed time, I met Seth and Sam Dodge appeared. "I hear you're leavin' this fair firebase and headin' up the hill," he said.

"That's right. I'm joining the TDY infantry guards up there 'til my profile runs out."

"I've never been up there myself," said Sam. "But I know it's kind of a catch-all for troubled grunts. There might be some hard cases up there, so you'll need a variety of pot that really mellows you out."

"You mean you have a selection?"

"Hell, yeah." He looked over at Seth and said, "It might be better to adjourn to the berm. Wha'd'ya think?"

"Sounds like a good idea," Seth said. "Jorge Calderon is on guard in one of those big-ass bunkers. I'm sure he wouldn't mind some company."

Ten minutes later we found Jorge's bunker and Sam whispered loudly, "Is this the home of WHORE–HAY Cauldron?"

"Close enough, Gringo, come on into *mi casa!*"

We filed into the bunker and found places to sit or lean.

Sam opened the festivities. "If everyone's comfy, let's get this show on the road. Sergeant Thompson, here, needs a pot supply to last him—and all those who'll be bumming joints off him—for a whole month. But being as how he's a grunt and unsophisticated about such things, I've brought a selection of my personal favorites for him to sample. With our help and guidance, of course."

"Of course," said Jorge.

"Someone's got to do it," added Seth.

I watched with great interest as Sam removed three plastic bags from his fatigue pants; each bag contained several joints. He spread the bags out on a sandbag and removed a number from the first bag.

"This," he explained, "is Cambodian Red, so named because its seeds have a reddish tint. We'll start with this and work our way through the others."

He handed me the number along with his Zippo lighter. I bent below the opening in the front of the bunker and used his lighter behind my cupped hands. When the joint was lit, I took a deep drag and held my breath, passing it to the others. To his credit, Jorge kept his focus out over the wire as we talked. When the joint was reduced to the size of a pencil eraser, Sam rubbed it in the dirt, dressed it, and blew the remnants out into the night.

"Well, what do you think?" he asked.

After a pause I said, "Oh. Are you asking me?"

"Who else would I be asking?"

"I'm sorry; I'm a little high, ya know? This stuff hits fast, man!"

"Yep, that's its claim to fame."

"Shee-it, man. That don't seem right," said a half-serious Jorge, nervously grinning.

"Hey, not to worry, man. It wears off just as quick. I promise," Sam said. "Anyway, let's shoot the breeze for a few minutes and then give the Cambodian Pale a taste, shall we?"

"Sounds good to me." I smiled. "And, Jorge, not to worry. Danger is a relative thing."

"What do you mean?"

"Look at it this way. If you were to tell your mama you were in a bunker on a perimeter berm in the Nam with concertina wire, fougasse barrels, and Claymore mines set out in front of you, and carrying an M16 and bandoliers, she'd probably consider that pretty dangerous, don't ya think?"

"You bet your ass she would. She loves her little Jorge."

"But if you're a grunt who's spent months in the boonies walking point, you'd feel pretty safe in this big-ass bunker. Am I right?"

"I don't know ... maybe," he said.

"Take it from me, you'd feel damn safe. So lighten up and let's light another joint," I said, patting Jorge on the shoulder.

"Okay," said Sam. "Now for the Cambodian Pale."

"Don't tell me," I said, "It's called that because its seeds are pale, right?"

"Kinda white, actually, but yes." He lit the number and passed it around.

The effects of the Cambodian Red had worn off as fast as they came on. I took a toke and passed the joint to Seth.

"This feels milder on the mouth and throat," I said hoarsely while trying to hold my breath.

"Yeah, that's one of its benefits," said Sam.

It took us a few minutes to polish off that number and Sam again asked what I thought.

"It's mellow, and the high feels like it'll last a while, too."

"You got it, man. Pale is for when you've got plenty of time to enjoy it and maybe some snacks and music."

"What's next?" I asked.

"Tay Ninh O, but let's give ourselves a half hour before we try it. That's the only way to give it a fair test."

"Okay," I said, "and in the meantime, I think I'll just lie back and contemplate the meaning of existence."

"I don't plan on waiting long enough for you to figure that shit out," Sam said with a chuckle. "But go ahead. I'll roust you when I light up again."

I spent the next half hour in a completely relaxed state of mind. I had random thoughts of home and family—my parents and my sisters and our home on the lake with its mowed lawn and cool night breezes. It was so different from this existence it might as well have been on another planet.

I sat up straight when Sam lit the third and last joint. "Tell me about Tay Ninh O," I said.

"Well, obviously, it comes from down near Tay Ninh, but the O comes from its being laced with opium."

"What?" I said with a start.

"Oh, don't worry, there's so little opium in it that I've never known anyone to get addicted. But there's enough to make its effects last longer than pot alone. For what it's worth,

I like it," he said, as though this was the equivalent of a Good Housekeeping Seal of Approval.

We smoked that joint to the bitter end, and I said, "Sam, I like this, too. It has some strength to it, but it's almost as mellow as the Cambodian Pale."

"That's right," he said. "It feels damn near the same, but I can tell you the seeds aren't white, and it's not as mellow or long-lasting when it's not laced with opium."

"Interesting," I said lazily.

"Have you made a choice?" Sam asked me.

"I think so. I'd like a little each of the Cambodian Red and the Tay Ninh O, but a larger amount of the Cambodian Pale. I really like how mellow it makes me feel."

"Okay. I see you brought your pack, so let's make a stop at my truck and I'll fix you up."

At the deuce-and-a-half, Seth removed a trap door under the driver's seat and reached into a customized steel box he'd rigged up.

"That's ingenious, man!" I said.

"Thanks. Believe me, it wasn't easy to do."

"I do believe you."

"Listen, if you have twenty-five dollars MPC, I can sell you two packs each of the Red and the O, and ten pounds of Cambodian Pale. Will that work for you?"

"Good God, how big is ten pounds of pot?"

"About this big," he said, pulling out a clear plastic sack a third the size of a typical kitchen trash bag. "Stuff this in the bottom of your pack and put your clothes on top. And take these, too," he added as he handed me four packs of 'cigarettes'. "The 'Winstons' are Tay Ninh O, and the 'Belairs' are Cambodian Red. With luck, this might be enough to last you for the rest of your tour."

"You're right about that, since I don't smoke weed in the field."

"That's smart, man. Listen, you take care, all right?"

"I'll do my damnedest."

Chapter 29 – A Mountain Climb

In the morning, Cal Singleton and I went to breakfast together. I was leaving Buttons and he was staying, so we weren't sure when we'd see each other again.

"Cal, are you gonna keep Top and Jay in line while I'm gone?"

"Absolutely," he said. "Are you looking forward to the mountain?"

"Yeah. It makes little sense, but I love mountains. Always have."

"In a way, I envy you," said Cal. "I mean, we've been treated really well here, but it's so damn boring."

"Tell me about it. Who knew the war would turn us into adventurous types?"

"Exactly!"

We walked back to the barracks and I hung my pack over one shoulder, picked up my M16 and bandoliers, and headed for Top's office.

When I walked in, Jay said, "Now, there's the Sergeant Thompson we all know and love. Top's out of the office, but I'll let him know you're headin' out."

"So that's it?"

"Well, except for this." He handed me a couple of slips of paper. "It's your orders to go to the base on Nui Ba Ra. Just give a copy to the guys at the airstrip, and they'll set you up with a helicopter. When you get up there, give copies to the CO. I think it's an LT at the moment. Oh, and be damn sure to give him a copy of your profile."

"Thanks, Jay."

"No problem, man. Take care of yourself."

"I always do my best," I said, hitching the pack strap higher on my shoulder and heading out the door. It was a walk of about five hundred meters to the airfield.

One rule that seemed to always hold true in Nam was that airfields were hot as hell, dusty as hell, and noisy as hell.

Partly this was due to there being no trees nearby, which meant there was almost no shade.

I showed my orders to the guys in the terminal building. The Spec-4 in charge said, "Hang around nearby and I'll let you know when your ride's ready to go."

I glanced around looking for shade and said, "I'll likely be near the north end of your building."

"That's the smart choice!" he replied. "I'll find you."

"Thanks," I said moving to the sliver of shade off the northwest corner of the building. I put down my pack, sat on it, leaned my M16 against the siding and began watching the activity at the Buttons Airfield. Over the next several hours, a couple of C-123s and a larger C-130 landed and quickly unloaded supplies. Later, a CH-54 Sky Crane, came in. It didn't land, but hovered over the south end of the airfield until the large Caterpillar dozer suspended beneath it touched the ground. As soon as several soldiers unhooked the cables, it rose and moved away. A little later another Sky Crane arrived, or maybe the same one on a second lift, which did land. This one was carrying an entire conex, one of the roughly six feet wide by eight feet long by seven feet high, corrugated steel boxes developed as containers for export (hence the name) during the Korean War. They come in two sizes and are mostly seen stacked on large cargo ships or on flat-bed railroad cars. These versatile containers were used by the military for hauling or storage and for use as secure buildings for offices and equipment in the field. To carry one, the Sky Crane's stick-like frame was positioned directly over the conex, which was then secured tightly to the chopper. The Sky Crane was designed to fit snugly over a conex making it the belly of the beast. Again, the conex was quickly detached from the helicopter by skilled GI's and left in place. Within minutes, a small dozer appeared and dragged the conex, which was built on skids, away from the landing area.

Late in the morning, a formation of five slicks approached from the north. I guessed that they'd been engaged in a CA and were returning to base, or just to the nearest airfield. I heard the formation before I saw it because the sound was off and drew my attention. The formation was low, so I couldn't see it well 'til it was very close. The first four helicopters were fine, but the fifth was clearly damaged, whether by enemy fire or not, I didn't know, but as it approached its tail kept dipping down to point toward the ground at a thirty-degree angle and then the pilot would rev it and the tail would lift for a bit, only to drop again. He kept this up all the way to the extreme north end of the airfield, but the tail rotor finally touched the ground before the rest of the chopper. There was a sound like a car crash, as pieces of the tail rotor and blades flew into the air and a thick dust cloud rose over the scene. When it cleared, the chopper was upright on its skids as it should be, and it appeared that no one had been seriously injured. But even so I had no doubt it was a thrill ride they'd not soon forget.

A bit later, as I sat there with nothing to do but observe and think, I became aware of an ache in my lower left jaw that I'd first noticed a few days earlier. I figured I'd bitten down on something the wrong way or gotten something stuck between a molar and the gum. It was annoying, but I expected it to go away and ignored it. Finally, around 1130 hours, the Terminal Spec-4 came out and got me. "See that slick over there?" he said, pointing to a helicopter about 200 meters to the south on the same side of the field.

"Yes," I answered.

"They're gonna hook onto a blivet and take it up to the Nui Ba Ra base. You can ride with them."

"Thanks," I said, heading over there.

When I arrived, the Spec-4 Crew Chief said, "Headin' up the mountain?"

"Yep," I nodded.

"Well, hop aboard," he said. "We'll be ready to leave in a few more minutes."

"Thanks," I answered, sliding my pack in and gingerly climbing aboard.

As promised, within five minutes, we slowly rose until the blivet was directly under the helicopter and the cables were stretched taut. Then the pilot stepped on the gas and the noise increased as the chopper applied enough power to lift the 500-gallon blivet and the five of us. When we'd risen about forty feet or so, with the blivet well above the ground, we moved off to the south, then turned east toward the mountain.

"Ever been up there before?" the crew chief yelled above the roar.

"No," I said shaking my head.

"I think you'll like it," he smiled. "It's a lot cooler up there!"

"That's good news!"

The helicopter blades made a harder, louder chopping or thwacking sound than in a usual CA due to the weight of the blivet and the fact that we were in a constant climb from the airfield until we reached an altitude of about 2500', or about a hundred feet higher than the top of the mountain. I yelled to the crew chief, "I'm surprised we can lift a 500-gallon blivet." He shouted back, "Oh, we can't. The blivet's only about two-thirds full. It's the best we can do!" he shrugged.

With the load we were carrying, to climb so high to a destination so close to the airfield the pilot flew a 'J' shaped route, first aiming for the south flank of the mountain and circling around the far, or eastern side, before approaching the base from the northeast.

The base itself was a tiny circle of sandbags and bunkers only about seventy-five meters across. Inside it were sandbagged conexs, and wood and canvas structures, and lots of tall antennas. About eighty meters north of the perimeter and a hundred feet below it was what passed for a helipad; a rectangular area about twenty meters by sixty meters covered with PSP. Our pilot hovered over the west end of the pad and lowered the blivet to the ground. Two grunts from the base ran out, quickly detached the straps and gave the crew chief a thumbs up, which he passed along to the pilot using his hard-wired headset and mike. At that point, the pilot gently lifted up a bit, drifted to the east end of the pad, and landed with nary a noticeable bump.

"Okay, off you go, man" yelled the crew chief.

"Thanks, for the ride!" I shouted back as I slid out the door with my weapon and pack. As always, I bent low until I was beyond the reach of the blades. Then I headed for the grunts at the blivet as my ride took off and literally shot down the mountain to the northwest.

"Hi," I said as I reached them and the noise rapidly faded.

"You been assigned here?" one of the grunts there asked.

"Yep," I answered.

"Well, head on up the trail there. Ask for Top. He's also our mess sergeant." This made me realize these were commissary guys, not grunts.

The trail was steep but only about a hundred meters long, so I managed it. But I definitely felt my wound. Halfway up, I passed half a dozen guys that I was pretty sure really were grunts. They didn't look happy.

Reaching the perimeter, I saw that the berm was constructed solely of sandbags, because there was no extra dirt to push up. It would have slid down the mountainside anyway. So the field expedient was to level a footing and build a tightly packed sandbag wall on it. It was only thigh-high, but given that the terrain dropped off at a forty-five-degree angle, it was plenty good enough. I decided to inspect the berm in detail as soon as I got settled.

At the HQ, a private reading a magazine at a makeshift desk looked up and said, "Can I help you?"

"Yes. I'm Sergeant Jamie Thompson reporting in from Buttons." I handed him copies of my orders and profile, which he took through the office door in the back.

In a few minutes a voice called out from the back room. "Sergeant Thompson, come on back."

Top was a lean black man named Aaron Gilbert. I sized him up as a lifer. He looked up from behind his desk and said, "Welcome to the mountain, Sergeant."

"Thank you, Top. Happy to be here," I said.

"You have more time in grade than any other sergeant E-5 up here, so you're in command of the infantry guards. Private Smith, get Sergeant Thompson settled in Bunker One, and then introduce him to Sergeant Kratz."

"Yes, Top," came the reply.

"Sergeant Kratz is running the guards, but he'll be leaving soon. If he has any questions about relinquishing command, tell him to see me. And have him show you the ropes," said Top.

Private Smith walked me to a large bunker, the outer side of which created a high point in the berm overlooking the helipad, rather like a turret on a castle wall. Against a side wall, sandbag steps led to the top, which served as one of the perimeter guard positions. We went inside, where it was quite dark and noticeably cooler. I heaved my pack and M16 onto an unoccupied bunk and hung my bandoliers on the bedpost.

"We can find Sergeant Kratz in Bunker Two," Smith said.

"Are there only four perimeter bunkers?"

"Yes. It's a small base so there's one at roughly the northeast, southeast, northwest, and southwest compass points. Sergeant Kratz can fill you in on all that."

We reached Bunker Two and entered.

"Sergeant Kratz? Top asked me to introduce you to Sergeant Thompson, here, who'll be taking command of the infantry guards," said Smith.

"Okay," said Kratz, standing up. "Let's go outside where we can see each other better."

We stepped out and Private Smith left.

"Well, Sergeant Thompson, I can't say I'm bothered by you taking command of the guards," Kratz said.

I stuck out my hand and we shook. "Call me Jamie," I said.

"My name's Irvin. Glad to meet ya."

"Can you fill me in on what I've gotten myself into up here?"

"Sure. Let's walk the perimeter while we talk," he said. "It's such a small base that four bunkers are enough to provide good fields of fire to cover the entire area. And it's so steep outside the perimeter that we get issued Willie Petes to use during our Mad Minutes."

"Jesus," I said. "They never give those to line units."

The Army had found out in a hurry that the average guy couldn't throw the white phosphorus grenades far enough to avoid the splash-back when they exploded.

"Up here it's pretty safe. By the time they explode they're so far below you that there's no problem," Irvin said. "But to get back to the tour—as you can see, the entire berm is constructed of hard-packed sandbags, two bags wide and at least six high. It's probably the best they could do because of the terrain, and so far it's been adequate."

"Has the base ever been attacked?" I asked.

"Keeping in mind that I've only been up here for two weeks, I haven't heard of any attacks. But you should ask around to confirm that."

We stopped at the next bunker. "This is Bunker Three. As you can see, all four bunkers are identical. They're strong, and since the actual guard positions are on top, they provide wide, deep, and unobstructed fields of fire."

As we walked, I said, "Tell me about yourself, Irvin. How long have you been in Nam?"

"About a month. I graduated NCO school in February, had OJT at Fort Leonard Wood, and arrived in Bien Hoa last month. I guess the Cambodia thing and the units being sent back to the States has caused some disruption, because they didn't know what to do with a lot of us. We got temporary assignments 'til they could determine our permanent assignments. I just got word I'm going to Echo Company, Fifth of the Seventh. I'll be joining them when they come in from the field, whenever that is."

"Fifth of the Seventh is my battalion. I'm in Charlie Company. But when you get to Echo, say hi to Gordon Castro for me. It's a good unit and Gordon's a good man. He and I graduated NCO school together last December."

"If you don't mind my asking, why did they send you up here?" Irvin asked.

"I picked up some shrapnel in Cambodia so I'm on limited duty. The Top on Buttons got tired of having me hanging around, so he sent me up here to get me out of his hair," I said with a grin.

"I've met him, so I doubt he did it for that reason. But let's move on. The terrain is a little less steep directly to the front of each bunker, which I think is why they were positioned where they are. But anyway, it's good that there are only four bunkers, because we're so short of infantry guards. The number varies, depending on who's available and for how long."

"What kind of grunts are they?" I asked.

"None of 'em seem to care much for taking orders from a shake 'n bake FNG."

"I can imagine. But hey, there's a right way, a wrong way…"

"And the Army way," we finished in unison.

"Yeah. There's that," agreed Irvin. "So far, the guys have sucked it up and done as they've been told. But as to what kind of grunts they are, it depends."

"What do you mean?"

"Some are terrific, just up here to convalesce like you. Some are waiting for permanent assignments like me. And some were sent here in hopes they'd get their heads screwed on straight after either cracking up or fucking up. But we also get some Section Eights. It can take thirty days to process a Section Eight, probably because the Army doesn't want to admit it failed to make a man out of anybody. There are a couple of guys here now in that category, but they've been fairly reasonable. I mean, they bitch and moan, but in the end, they do their duty."

"All right, I get the picture. Anything else I should know?" I asked as we approached Bunker Four.

"I'm sure there's a lot, including stuff I don't even know about. But for now, all I can think of is that we have a formation at 0900 every morning to show the flag, tell the guys what orders we have for the day—if there are any—and assign guard duty. I inherited the system from the guy before me," Irvin added.

"Not that I mind, but why is the morning formation so late?"

"Because the morning staff meeting is at 0800 in the HQ building, and that's when I get my orders for the day."

"Makes sense," I said.

"Let me give an example. I'm sure you don't remember, but I was leading a group of grunts down the trail when you were on your way up. In our formation this morning, I picked five guys to accompany me when the water blivet came in to roll the damn thing up the trail."

"No wonder they looked unhappy. That sucker is heavy."

"Yeah, over three thousand pounds heavy even though it was less than full so the slick could lift it, and it's awkward to roll," he said with a frown. "We don't always have to do that. They usually send up the smaller plastic balloons which are bad enough to hump up the trail, but they were short of balloons. So you saw what we got today."

"I'm amazed you could get it up here at all."

"We wouldn't have, if I hadn't requisitioned half a dozen guys from the commissary to help," said Irvin. "Top won't care for that when he finds out, but I had no choice if we wanted water."

"You did what had to be done."

"Yeah, but it wore me out. That's why I was lying down when you came. We got back about five minutes before you showed up."

"You should've said something; this tour could've waited."

"Maybe, but this is important, too. I do want to point out that just below us here, straight west of the perimeter, is the dump. The commissary guys burn it every Wednesday. If they didn't, this place would be uninhabitable. But even doing that doesn't keep us from having a rat problem."

"Great," I said.

"Yeah, but even with its drawbacks, being up here is pretty damn nice compared to being down there I bet." He nodded toward Buttons and the endless jungle stretching away over the horizon.

"So far, I agree," I said. "I doubt it's more than ninety degrees up here right now."

"There you go!" said Irvin as we both smiled. "Listen, I'll take care of tonight's guard detail. Show up at the 0800 staff meeting tomorrow and I'll introduce you as my replacement at our 0900 formation. Since the CO is down at Buttons, you might not see him before the staff meeting, anyway."

"Who is the CO?"

"A second lieutenant named Carmichael, Larry Carmichael."

"A *second* lieutenant!" I exclaimed, "That's unusual."

"He's signal corps, so this is his six months in the field," Irvin explained. "He's a go-by-the-book type, but doesn't have the personality to make it work. He's also away half the time. I think he's an all right guy, but the jury's still out on how good an officer he is."

"I'll reserve judgment, I guess, but I appreciate the information and insight."

"My pleasure. See you at chow this evening, which is right there, by the way." He pointed to a wood frame mess hall about fifty feet from the HQ.

"What time do they serve chow here?"

"Between 1800 and 1900. And don't be late," Irvin cautioned. "Top runs a tight ship—at least as far as the mess hall is concerned."

I went to my bunker and unpacked, spreading everything out on a wood shelf fastened into the sandbag wall. It was dark, even during the day, and although there was a bare lightbulb hanging from the ceiling, I made a mental note to get a light that would fit on the shelf so I could read in my bunk.

I'd managed to miss lunch again, so I pulled a C-rat chocolate bar out of my pack. I absently realized I had adjusted to the Nam because I found the candy palatable.

"Wonders never cease," I said aloud.

Chapter 30 – Nui Ba Ra

I needed to give my leg a rest, so I lay on my bunk thinking about nothing. Somehow, I dozed off, but my aching jaw woke me up. I found the latrine, a true four-holer, wood frame construction with screened windows and door, and un-sandbagged corrugated steel roof and sides. After that, I began a detailed reconnaissance of the perimeter and the rest of the base.

I started at Bunker Four which was closest to the privy. I gingerly took the steps to the roof. The entire top, about fifteen by fifteen feet, was covered with three layers of sandbags. In the middle, a galvanized corrugated half-culvert pipe was aligned with its open side buried securely in the sandbagged roof. The culvert pipe enclosure was covered with two layers of sandbags up its sides and over its top. On both ends, ponchos were attached to the sandbags, but folded open. They could be repositioned to keep out wind and rain. I crawled in and found that it was about four feet high, so sitting on the sandbags inside was not at all cramped. A semicircle of clackers was positioned just inside the outer end. Obviously, the range of vision and field of fire was better outside the culvert pipe than in it, but it wasn't bad inside and provided good protection from hostile fire. I imagined it was also a good shelter in bad weather.

I crawled out onto the roof and surveyed the ground beyond the perimeter. There were the usual rings of concertina wire, barrels of fougasse, trip flares, and Claymores. The dump was to the left front, about fifty feet below the perimeter. But the view beyond was incredible. I could make out only the far fringes of Firebase Buttons, the rest was so close to the base of the mountain it was concealed from view by the dense jungle on the slope. Other than that small hint of human activity, the entire panorama was deep green jungle stretching to the horizon.

Maybe because it was a monadnock, an isolated lone mountain, it felt like it was much higher than 2,000 feet above the jungle floor. The air was noticeably less humid and hot than anywhere I'd been for the past three months. It smelled fresher, too.

Reluctantly, I climbed down the steps and continued to Bunker Three. It was set up exactly the same way; the only real difference was the view. The terrain dropped away more gradually, but there were no visible signs of civilization. Poking up from the far horizon the peak of another lone mountain could just be made out in the clear air. I realized it had to be Nui Ba Den, the mountain just east of our old Battalion HQ in Tay Ninh. Both mountains are extinct volcanoes.

There are several Vietnamese legends involving the sister mountains of Nui Ba Den and Nui Ba Ra. In Vietnamese, the names translate roughly as Black Lady Mountain and White Lady Mountain respectively, or sometimes Black Virgin and White Virgin. Some legends say the mountains were formed from grief-stricken lovers of fallen Vietnamese soldiers. The one I heard said that upon their deaths two ancient princes who had sworn to protect their lovers and Vietnam itself from enemies, were turned to stone by the gods to protect Vietnam for as long as they stood. I liked that legend.

Bunker Two sat above the steepest slope of the mountain. It, too, surveyed a green expanse that seemed endless.

Finally, I returned to my bunker. From its roof, I could see the helipad to the left front, a hundred feet below. Beyond that, nothing but the endless green ocean that was Southeast Asia. The Song Be River (really the Be River, since song in Vietnamese means river) was closest to the base of the mountain to the right front, the water visible here and there.

I washed up and headed to the mess hall. The chow looked good: fried chicken and mashed potatoes, with a choice of cherry or apple pie, even *a la mode* if you wanted a scoop of ice cream, which I did. I saw Irvin and joined him.

"Have you had a chance to look around?" he asked.

"As a matter of fact, yes," I said. "I can see why the base hasn't been attacked. I looked at the guard bunkers' fields of fire, which overlap except for really close to the perimeter where we're well covered by fougasse and Claymores. Not to mention that the terrain is brutal."

"That's the truth," Irvin agreed. "There's never a guarantee that a determined enemy won't attack on even the steepest slope, but it's damned unlikely."

"True," I said. "Soldiers—like snakes—don't like to take high ground unless it absolutely has to be done."

"What do you mean?" he asked.

"You may not have thought about it, but you see damn few snakes on mountain tops."

"Isn't that because it's colder?" he asked.

"Partly, but the main reason is that slithering *up* a mountain takes a tremendous amount of energy. And the farther up you go, the less ground is above you to support the critters you depend on for food. In other words, the higher you go, the greater the cost and the risk and the smaller the reward. So unless it becomes critical for the NVA to destroy the communications relays up here, it's unlikely they'll waste the energy, equipment, and manpower to try. In short, this is about as safe a place as anywhere in Vietnam," I said.

"I like your reasoning, and don't disagree," Irvin said, shoving a fork full of chicken into his mouth.

As I took a swallow of coffee toward the end of our meal, I asked, "Do you run Mad Minutes up here?"

"At morning formation, I tell the guys when to let loose that night. Usually, it's just the infantry guards, but a few times a week I coordinate with Top, and the commissary guys get in on it."

"What about the commo guys?" I asked.

"No, not them. Their function is always to protect, maintain, and operate the commo gear."

"And we have no artillery?" I asked.

"Right, but from what I hear, if intel is picked up justifying it, a couple of howitzers or a mortar platoon are sent up 'til the threat evaporates."

"Good to know," I said. "Say, is there any place to get a beer up here?"

"For now, Top rotates guys to sell beer in the mess hall from 1930 to 2300," said Irvin. "But there are rumors we might get some kind of personnel-wide club one of these days."

"Sounds like a project everyone could get behind," I speculated.

"It is, but the trick is doing it without any official sanction or funding," Irvin said. "Say, I don't suppose you play poker?"

"I'm fair at it, why?"

"Because there's a poker game on Monday, Wednesday, and Friday nights at 2000 in the HQ conference room. Top's almost always there, and at least one or two commissary guys. And me, of course," he said with a smile.

"Hmm, a challenge I can't refuse. See you there tomorrow night."

"Sounds like a plan," said Irvin, "By the way, I'm pulling first shift on Bunker Four tonight, if you want to join me up top to watch the sunset."

"I'll be there, man."

Back at my bunker I removed a pack of 'Belairs' from the bottom of my rucksack, grabbed my M16 and bandoliers and went outside to enjoy the evening. It was fascinating watching the mountain's pointed shadow advancing eastward across the jungle as the sun lowered. *"I'm stationed on a giant sundial,"* I thought.

Irvin walked over on his way to Bunker Four. "You ready?"

"Yep, let's go."

We took the stairs and sat down outside the culvert pipe.

"How do you feel about pot, man?" I asked.

"Just fine."

"Is it cool to smoke it up here?"

"Most of the time, yes. Top never comes up, and the CO is seldom seen after dark."

"Is Lieutenant Carmichael a problem?" I asked.

"So far, no. But he's a bit of a stickler at unpredictable times. As far as I know, no one's ever smoked in front of him, so it's probably best not to test him. Why do you ask?"

"Because I have some really good weed that might enhance the sunset," I said.

"Sounds good. But let's wait 'til it's darker."

By 1945, the sun was well below the western horizon, so I pulled out the pack and opened the cellophane.

"Jeez, man. I thought you were gonna light up a number."

"Irvin, one thing you'll learn in a hurry is that things are often not what they seem in Nam."

A grin spread across my face as I shook out one of the "cigarettes." I turned back toward the closed end of the culvert pipe, cupped my hands to conceal the light even more, and lit it. Irvin accepted it without a word and inhaled deeply.

"Holy crap, man! What is this shit?" asked a slightly hoarse Irvin.

"It's called Cambodian Red, because the seeds are reddish. It hits you like a runaway freight train, but it wears off within a half hour or so," I said as if I'd possessed this knowledge from birth.

We leaned back against the sandbagged front edges of the culvert pipe, silently soaking in the time and place until the first stars appeared in an unusually clear sky. I slid a joint from the pack and handed it to Irvin.

"I'll leave this with you for later," I said. "I'm dog tired and need to rest my leg."

No one woke me for the Mad Minute, and I slept like a baby that night. Apparently, I needed it. Besides, the Cambodian Red eased the dull pain in my jaw.

After chow the next morning, Irvin and I went to the staff meeting together. Top called the meeting to order. He introduced me to Spec-4 Denton Donelson—a commissary guy who was often in charge of breakfast shift—and head cook, Corporal Harold Strasser. I'd already met the base clerk, Private Chad Smith. Chad was also the CO's clerk. So the staff consisted of just six of us.

"First off," said Top, "Lieutenant Carmichael will be returning by Chinook this afternoon. Sergeant Thompson, you'll need to get your men to help unload the chopper and work with our commissary people to haul the supplies up from the pad. It's mostly food, but there will be some ammo, too. Sergeant Kratz can show you where to store it. When that's done, I'd like you to report to HQ to meet Lieutenant Carmichael."

I nodded.

"Since the only other items on the agenda deal with commissary and commo matters, Sergeants Thompson and Kratz can go now. Again, it's good to have you here, Sergeant Thompson."

Irvin and I went outside and smoked cigarettes and shot the breeze until the grunts showed up for our morning formation. Within a few minutes everyone appeared to have arrived.

He called the group of fifteen men to attention, then had them stand at ease as he called the roll. All were present and accounted for. Then he introduced me.

"Men, this Sergeant Jamie Thompson, who's taking over for me, starting now. I'll be leaving in a few days to join my field unit. Sergeant Thompson is on a medical profile due to wounds received in Cambodia and will likely be here until that profile ends. Sergeant Thompson?"

"Thank you, Sergeant Kratz. It'll take me a few days to familiarize myself, so Sergeant Kratz will be involved in supervisory duties during the transition. I don't plan to do anything differently. I'm a believer in the 'if it ain't broke, don't fix it' philosophy. I know Sergeant Kratz has made guard assignments through the next five days and scheduled a patrol outside the wire in two days, so we'll leave those as they are. I'll make the rounds of the guard bunkers at various times at least once every night.

"Today, we're expecting a resupply shithook, so we'll help the cooks unload the supplies and haul them up. Aside from that, your time is your own. If you have any questions, feel free to ask me any time. I think you'll find that I'm fair. But when the need arises, I will be firm. Any questions now?" I paused. "All right, men. I'll notify you when the shithook comes in. Until then, dismissed!"

"Good job," Irvin said after the men had dispersed.

"Hey, you've been doing the job just fine, so I can't see any reason to change things."

He laughed. "I suspect we can thank some poor forgotten E-5 from years ago. Though from what I understand, most of the time there were entire line platoons rotated up here, kind of a poor man's R&R."

"That makes sense," I said. "During the incursion it was all hands on deck, or to be precise, all grunts in Cambodia. Then our entire battalion was sent to Bien Hoa for an in-country R&R, so there was no need to send anyone up here for a break. And there's an abundance of grunts on profiles to send up here instead."

"Wait. That sounds too logical. I mean, you and I and the whole damn world knows 'there's the right way, the wrong way…'"

"And the Army way,'" we finished in unison.

"It's more likely that a screw-up ended up looking logical by pure chance," I said.

"I can buy that," said Irvin as we strolled into the mess hall and grabbed some coffee.

"Listen, Irvin," I said suddenly. "When you get to the field, stay focused, put people where their abilities can be best used, and don't do anything stupid. Beyond that, you have to trust to luck."

"Well, that was certainly serious."

"I meant it to be. Advice is plentiful and cheap. But in the end, all you can do here is improve your odds. I kinda like you, and want you to make it through this shit."

"I'll take it to heart," he promised.

"For me, as a squad leader, all that matters is protecting my men. That's my focus and my purpose; I'm not gung-ho or a super patriot. I didn't know shit when I got here, but I paid attention to everything the guys who were here before me said and did. It works ... or it has so far. The most important thing is keeping your men alive. And to do that *you* have to stay alive. I'm sure you've heard us say, 'Fuck it; it don't mean nothin',' right?"

"A time or two."

"If there's any single saying that describes the situation here, that's it. Literally *nothing* matters here except staying alive. You got that?"

"Yes, Sergeant!" he said formally with a grin.

Half-culvert perimeter guard position on a berm; similar to those atop bunkers on Nui Ba Ra. (photo 30-1)

Chapter 31 – Rats

The Chinook came in around 1330. It was impossible to miss, not just because of the noise, but because it took up the majority of the helipad when it landed. They were nice enough to orient the chopper so its rear ramp opened close to the trail. Irvin and I and our fifteen guards—along with an equal number of commissary guys—hurried down the trail to help the crew unload. About half-way down, we passed a second lieutenant carrying a duffel bag. It had to be Carmichael, my new CO.

It took ten minutes to unload, but thirty more to haul the crates and boxes up to the base and put them away. Among the goodies were eight cases of M34 Willie Pete hand grenades. We put one case inside each guard position on the perimeter and the other four in the armory. We also put the ten cases of fragmentation grenades, ten cases of M16 ammo, ten cases of M60 ammo, and four cases of M79 grenade-launcher rounds there.

"Jesus, you'd think there was a war or something," a sweating Irvin said.

"You would, wouldn't you?" I said. "But from the looks of the stock in the armory, we needed it."

"Yeah, we go through our share during Mad Minutes."

"Speaking of that, there's good reason for them." I told him about the night the Mad Minute blunted the NVA attack on Firebase Wood. "Well, I guess I better get cleaned up and head to the HQ to meet the CO."

Twenty minutes later, I entered the HQ. "Hello, Chad. If it's convenient, I thought I should report to the CO."

"I'll check. Give me a moment," he said, knocking on the CO's office door and being ushered inside.

"He needs a few minutes," he said, returning.

I sat down and began reading a handy *Stars and Stripes*. A few minutes later, I looked up. "Good news, Chad. According to this, we've damn near won the war."

Chad smiled and said just above a whisper, "Don't believe everything you read."

Eventually, the CO called out. "Send Sergeant Thompson in, Chad."

Chad turned to me and with a sweep of his arm said, "You heard the man."

I went in and stood at attention in front of the CO's desk. "Sergeant Thompson, reporting for duty, sir."

"At ease, Sergeant, and welcome to Nui Ba Ra. I know you've been here since yesterday, so I assume you've familiarized yourself with the base and the guard situation," he said.

"Yes, sir, but I'm sure there's more to learn. Sergeant Kratz has been a great help."

"Well, I won't keep you. I expect you to set a good example, attend staff meetings, and help Top whenever he asks. This place is an excellent defensive position, but that doesn't mean we can let our guard down."

"Yes, sir," I responded. "Sir, you should be aware I'm due for evaluation of my wound on the twenty-second."

"Be sure to remind Top a few days in advance, so he can make sure we get you down to Buttons. That'll be all, Sergeant. You're dismissed."

Outside, Irvin caught up with me. "What did you think?"

"I'm not sure," I said. "I think he's competent, but my overall impression was that he's kind of cold. I also found it a bit strange when he said he expected me to *help out* when asked. I mean, this is the Army for chrissake. He and Top outrank me, so there's no question I'll do what they ask, tell, or order me to do. I don't know. Maybe he's unsure of himself, or maybe he's just preoccupied."

"Maybe," Irvin said skeptically, "but unless he's always preoccupied, I'm going with the unsure thing."

"Well, he's what we've got, so we'll make the best of it. Say, is the poker game still on tonight?"

"Absolutely."

"Can you switch guard shifts with someone and make it to the game?"

Irvin smiled. "I have the second shift every Monday, Wednesday, and Friday."

"Smart thinking, Sergeant Kratz," I said, patting him on the shoulder.

Right after sundown, Irvin and I visited every bunker and made sure all was in order. Then we entered the HQ conference room and took seats at the table. I noted that Top had cold beer and sodas in the room. Everyone put two dollars in the middle of the table for the drinks.

At 2000 hours sharp, Top introduced me to the players. In addition to Irvin, Top, and Chad, there was Donelson, Strasser, and me.

"Okay," said Top, "since this is Sergeant Thompson's first time, I'll go over the house rules. We play five card stud and seven card stud, only. It's okay to announce wildcards, but only one kind per game, like deuces or one-eyed jacks—but never more than one kind. The stakes are a minimum ten-dollar buy-in, quarter ante, minimum bets of a nickel and maximum of two dollars, with a maximum of three raises. The deal starts with whoever cuts the highest card and moves clockwise."

I wanted to get a feel for the players, so I stayed out of most of the hands at first. When I was comfortable, I began playing in earnest. That night I ended up almost breaking even and really enjoyed myself. The military formalities were absent, which was a pleasant change.

Afterward, I said to Irvin, "It seems like Top fancies himself a better poker player than he really is. What do you think?"

Irvin had won close to ten dollars, about half from Top.

"That agrees with my sense of things."

"Well, this could be profitable and a bit interesting, too. Though not always in a good way," I said.

"Yes, some restraint might be called for from time to time."

"I'll keep that in mind. By the way, I think I'll keep you company tonight on your guard shift, but starting tomorrow I should really be assigned a shift, so let's figure that out before the formation tomorrow."

That night, the cool silence atop Bunker Four lent itself to deep conversation.

"What do you think about this?" Irvin asked

"You mean about the war?"

"Yeah, what do you think about the war."

"To be honest, I don't think about it much. I mean, what the hell good does it do? I've spent a quarter of my life knowing I'd end up over here. Don't ask me how, but I was as sure of it as that the sun would rise in the morning. The clincher was watching the evening news during the Tet Offensive a couple years ago. Maybe you remember the reporter hunched down behind a stone wall in Hue with a squad of Marine grunts. The grunts would fire over the wall, then hunker down and answer the reporter's questions. Somehow, I knew I'd end up over here, just like them."

"I remember that," said Irvin. "I was struck by how normal the guys sounded. One of 'em answered the reporter's question about what they were fighting for, with something about how they were fighting just to survive and get home. That stayed with me."

"Me, too. All this stuff about democracy versus communism, freedom versus authoritarianism, right versus wrong sounds good, but at our level none of that matters. All that matters is keeping your men and yourself alive. Period. I'll tell you something else, too. This goddamn war has a life of its own. It almost doesn't matter what the politicians say or do; nothing changes for us. Every day we get up, break camp, hump through the boonies, unpack, set up our NDP, go to bed, and get a night of uncomfortable sleep broken up by guard shifts, Mad Minutes, or attacks. Wake up the next morning and do it all again. And oh, by the way, try not to get shot or blown up."

"Geez, I can hardly wait to join my unit."

"Oh, it gets better. I haven't gotten to the mosquitoes, scorpions, centipedes, and snakes yet. Or the balmy tropical weather. Sorry, Irvin, but you asked what I thought." I smiled into the darkness of our half-culvert. "Let's smoke a doobie before the Mad Minute."

"Now you're talking," Irvin replied.

"Listen, I didn't mean to sound like such a downer before. There are fun times, too, and you make friends that you literally trust with your life. But the bottom line is there's nothing highfalutin, noble, or heroic about this shit, except for the way we conduct ourselves and protect our fellow grunts and innocent civilians." I lit the joint. "You need to cherish the times you're relatively safe and have some good weed to take your mind off the shit you're in. One other thing," I added. "Never smoke pot in the boonies. The gooks can smell it two klicks away. And don't let any of your men smoke it out there either."

He nodded and took a deep toke. Neither of us spoke for a few minutes, then Irvin and I looked at each other. Grins spread across our faces as we did our best to suppress spontaneous laughs. "That's some good shit, man!" Irvin said through a snicker.

"Yep!" I blurted through pursed lips still holding in my last toke.

At precisely 0129, Irvin and I sprayed bursts from our M16s into the jungle, signaling the rest of the guards to do the same for the next sixty seconds. Then we threw some fragmentation grenades.

After more bursts of M16 fire, Irvin said, "Okay, now it's time for the real fireworks. Grab one of those Willie Petes and hand me one. You throw to the right and I'll throw to the left. Ready?"

"Yep," I said as I removed the safety clip.

"All right pull the pin and throw on three. One, two, three!"

Both grenades ended up a hundred feet below us before they exploded, sending up fountains of white-hot globs trailing streamers of pure white smoke. It lit the landscape nearly as bright as day but quickly faded, leaving smoking white spots across the jungle.

"That was awesome, man," I said, "though not quite as impressive as I imagined it would be."

"Yeah, that's what I thought the first time I threw one, too. But remember, if we ever do get hit up here, those little glowing spots are burning at 5,000 degrees and nothing can put them out."

"Oh, I remember all right. And it's good to throw them for practice like this, 'cause I have to admit to feeling a bit of trepidation about it. I mean there's a damn good reason these aren't issued to troops in the bush."

"Yep."

"See, this is the kind of distraction you need," I said. "A little pot and blowing shit up helps keep your head screwed on straight."

"You know, that sounds nuts, but it's so goddamn true! You're a philosopher, man."

"I try," I said with false modesty.

That night I felt rats scurrying over me a couple of times, but slept soundly.

The next morning I said, "Irvin, something's gotta be done about the damn rats."

"Hey, you'll get no argument from me. But aside from burning the dump once a week, I'm not sure what more we can do."

"I have a feeling the dump burning is just providing them with a hot meal," I said.

"You could be right. Have you got any other ideas?"

"Well, we could shoot the damn things. I mean it's not as if they try hard to hide."

"True, but how can we do it safely?"

"Remove the slug from an M16 round and push the open end of the casing into a bar of soap to create a sort of lethal blank—at least lethal for rats."

"It just might work." Irvin grinned.

"Oh, it'll work. A neighbor of mine back in Illinois raised geese. But the damn rats had trenched trails under the wire floor of the coop and were constantly eating the grain and sometimes the goose eggs. Every so often we'd shoot 'em with pellet guns as they ran through their trails. I figure M16 soap rounds should be a slight improvement."

"You know, I could get into this idea," said Irvin.

"Well, we'll never eliminate them, but we might force them to stay away from us. If nothing else, it'll be good for morale," I said.

When I explained my idea at the staff meeting there was some concern, but I assured Top and the LT that base security would not be compromised, and safety would be maintained at all times. The idea was approved.

At guard formation, I explained the proposal and required that soap rounds only be loaded one round at a time and weapons always be pointed at rats with either the ground or sandbags behind them. The men were excited, and I thought it might hone their skills, sort of like the Quick Kill course in Basic. Later I saw most of the men carefully bending, twisting, and pulling the slugs out of some of their M16 rounds. I almost felt sorry for the rats.

The best time to hunt rats is just before dark as they emerge to forage, but while there's still enough light to see them. It's a window of less than half an hour. That first night there were only two kills, but it was a start, and enthusiasm ran high. The second night there were three kills.

Later, at the poker game, I reported on the success which was met with universal approval. But the big news was that I won twenty-three dollars, mostly from Top. That night, I pulled guard alone at Bunker Four. I spent the first hour sitting on the roof just outside the open end of the culvert pipe, but then it got chilly. It was strange to feel chilly when it was seventy degrees, but my body had adjusted to the incessant tropical heat.

Few situations lend themselves to introspection as much as being on guard duty. But it's an introspection tempered by the need for constant vigilance—even at Nui Ba Ra, probably the safest base in Vietnam. That night was the beginning of a journey into feelings and thoughts that had all but disappeared during the previous two and half months. Even though my eyes searched for movement and my ears listened for the slightest unnatural sound, images of Julie and Kara appeared in my mind. With those images came jolts of longing, desire, regret, and resignation. Then my mind moved on to other things. I thought of the men in my squad, especially José and Superman, and hoped they were all safe.

At last my four hours were up, so I woke my replacement. When he arrived to relieve me, I made my way to Bunker One and crawled into my bunk. If there were rats that night, I didn't feel or hear them.

Chapter 32 – Kinship across Time; Section Eights

The next morning Irvin got his orders to join his unit in the field; he'd be leaving that afternoon. I couldn't keep the concern off my face.

"Irvin, I'll miss you. And if there's anything I can do or any question I can answer, let me know."

"You've already been a bigger help than you know. You've been in the shit and still have your shit together, and you've shared lots of important things that I'll remember. I don't think there's anything more you can do for me, other than wish me well."

"You know I wish you well. Believe me, not all shake 'n bakes are created equal. Some are scared shitless and just want to disappear in their units like overpaid privates. Some are capable of leading men and willing to do it. There's no doubt in my mind that you're both capable and willing. You earned the respect of the men up here. And you earned my respect." I paused. "I see I've embarrassed you, but it's the goddamn truth."

At our guard formation, I rearranged the shift assignments to account for the loss of Irvin. The next night, I won twenty-six dollars, again mostly from Top. I considered myself a slightly better than average poker player, but among the players on Nui Ba Ra, it seemed I was a wolf among sheep.

A few days later, I reminded Top I had to go to Buttons to get my wound evaluated and asked if I could see a dentist for my jaw. At the guard formation, I assigned a grunt the job of commanding the infantry guards. The fact that he didn't balk at the job boded well.

"I'll only be gone one night," I told him. "You'll have to do the head count at the morning formation, but everything else is in place."

"I think I can do that," he answered, "but can I ask you a question?"

"Sure."

"Why the hell do we do head counts up here? I mean, look around. Where would anyone go?"

I laughed. "I'm tempted to say, there's the right way…"

He joined me, saying, "…the wrong way, and the Army way."

"But the truth is we do it to make sure they're fit for duty and present to receive the morning orders."

The following day, I checked in at HQ with Jay Simmons and was surprised to see Cal Singleton sitting at a nearby desk.

"What's this? Have you been demoted from grunt?"

"What? Nah, I'm just helping our overworked battalion clerk with some paperwork. It keeps me busy. How do you like the mountain?"

"I like it a lot. It's cooler up there, the views are fantastic, and it's probably the safest place in the whole country outside of Long Binh."

The next morning, I saw my surgeon. He cleaned and examined the wound. "Sergeant," he said, "Do you see that crack across the surface of the entry point? That crack indicates there's a lot of fluid that needs to drain. I'm extending your profile another thirty days."

A bit later the dentist examined me and gave me the bad news. "Sergeant, you have a badly impacted wisdom tooth. It has to be extracted." He picked up a syringe and vial from a nearby tray. "Lean back and open wide."

Twenty minutes later, my lower left wisdom tooth was out, and the hole was packed with what seemed like twenty feet of dental gauze. "I want to see you back here in a month," said the dentist, handing me a slip of paper.

The clerk gave me a bottle of codeine tablets, a bottle of Tylenol, and an appointment for August 21, 1970.

Two hours later I was back on the mountain, settling in as though I'd never left—except for the growing pain in my jaw. I gave Top my extended profile along with my next dental appointment.

The next morning, I told the men we were expecting four more grunts. "That should shorten our guard shifts by an hour, which I assume will be all right with you."

"Does a grunt shit in the jungle, Sergeant? You're damn straight it's okay!" said one.

"Oh, one other thing," I said. "I've been keeping track, and whoever shoots the most rats by August first will get a six-pack of beer on me. Dis-missed!"

The men wandered off, talking among themselves. My jaw hurt, my leg was having one of its sharp pain episodes, and I missed Irvin. *"I'm going to hell in a hand basket,"* I thought. Then I remembered where I was, shrugged, and crawled into my bunk in hopes of getting a nap.

The next day, the supply chopper dropped off four new infantry grunts. One was another shake 'n bake who'd just arrived in Nam, Sergeant Tim Calvert. The other three were privates who'd spent quite a bit of time in the boonies: Elroy Jervis, James Leland, and Homer Ellington.

Calvert seemed scared—I'd help him with that—while Jervis, Leland, and Ellington looked angry. I wondered how three guys with months of field duty under their belts were still privates. I took the three to my bunker and told them which bunks were available. Then I excused myself and waited at the HQ for Chad, who was escorting Calvert to Irvin's old bunk.

"Okay, Chad, what's up with Jervis, Leland, and Ellington?"

"Funny you should ask. They're waiting for their Section Eight Dishonorable Discharges to come through."

"What'd they do?"

"As I understand it, the three of 'em beat the living shit outta their platoon sergeant."

"Do we know why?"

"Not for sure, but word is they felt he was always giving them the worst, most dangerous jobs. This time, they refused. When he threatened them with discipline, they got physical."

"Being as how they're black, Chad, my gut is telling me this platoon sergeant is a white guy from the South with some baggage. I'll see what I can do. How long will they be up here?"

"I'm guessing your gut is right, but don't know for sure. As to how long they'll be here, it takes two to four weeks for the paperwork to process."

I went back to my bunker and told the new privates where and when the morning formation was, where the mess hall and latrines were located, and also that our main duties were to pull perimeter guard, help haul supplies, and police the base.

"Tonight, your time is your own," I said. "I won't assign guard shifts until tomorrow. Evening chow is 1800 to 1900 and the hours are firm, so if you're late you'll go hungry. Oh, by the way, this is my bunk," I said, pointing to it.

Next, I met with Sergeant Calvert. "How long have you been in Nam?" I asked him.

"Ten days. I'm supposed to join Alpha Company, Fifth of the Seventh, in a few days, but in the meantime, I've been sent up here."

"Where are you from?" I asked.

"I was born and raised in Pennsylvania, near Pittsburgh, graduated high school last summer, and got drafted a month later. I graduated from NCO school in March, and did my OJT at Fort Ord."

"I took AIT at Ord and graduated from NCO school last December. I joined my field unit, Charlie Company, Fifth of the Seventh, in April, became squad leader two weeks later, went into Cambodia in May, and was hit with shrapnel in June. I've been on a profile while the wound heals, so here I am." I added, "Look, I know you're nervous. If you weren't, I'd be worried. But I'll teach you whatever I can. First, let me give you a tour of the base."

I took him up on all the bunkers, so he could see the terrain from the guard positions. I also told him about the intermittent patrols run outside the wire every seven to ten days, which he'd have to go on and eventually lead until I was fit to do it. Afterwards, I said, "If for any reason, I'm not here, you'll be in charge. I don't foresee that happening, but just in case, pay attention to how this setup operates, especially at the morning formation."

"Yes, Sergeant," he said.

"Hey," I said, "when we're alone, just call me Jamie, okay?"

"Okay, and you can call me Tim."

Like the privates, I didn't assign Tim a guard shift on his first night, but I asked him to join me for an hour of my shift. Shortly after he left me alone, a steady west wind began to blow. I pulled a poncho liner around my shoulders and hunkered down. It was moonless, dark, and soundless, except for the whisper of the wind as it rustled the poncho entry flap. I thought about how lonely guard duty was, and how the lack of external stimuli inevitably turned one's thoughts inward.

It occurred to me that, two thousand years before, a Roman soldier guarding an alpine pass against the barbarians felt the chill of the night just as I was doing now and experienced feelings virtually identical to mine. I could see him in my mind's eye as clearly as a photograph, huddled under a rock overhang high on a mountainside, staring into the black silence, guarding the very edge of his civilization against any who dared challenge or threaten it. I knew the analogy wasn't 100% correct, but it was astonishingly similar, at least from my perspective as an American guarding the ragged edge of my country's power and influence. I felt as close a kinship with that nameless Roman soldier so distant in time and place, as I did to anyone on Nui Ba Ra. At the core, all wars and all soldiers who fight them are alike.

The next morning, I assigned the four new men guard shifts. This made it possible to reduce the shift length to three hours, which was welcome news for most of us. The three new privates were clearly not happy. I had decided to assign them the first three shifts in sequence on Bunker One, and myself the last shift, even though this wasn't my preferred location or shift. I hoped this would cut down on the number of interactions they had with other people.

For a few days, everything went smoothly. But then one morning, Sergeant Calvert led half the guards on a police call while I led the other half.

A few minutes into this routine detail, Tim came up to me. "Jervis, Leland, and Ellington refused and walked away, despite my ordering them back. I wasn't sure what to do, so I thought I'd come to you."

"Okay, you did the right thing. Go back to your detail and finish the job. I'll handle it."

After I completed my police call, I walked into our bunker.

"Homer?" I called into the darkened interior.

"Yeah. What you want?"

All three privates were tall, but Homer Ellington, nicknamed Home, was a little taller and had been a sergeant before all three were busted to private. He was the clear leader.

"I need to talk to you, all three of you," I said in what I hoped was a firm but unthreatening way. "I hear you refused to take part in the police call."

"You damn right!" bellowed Home. "Why the fuck should we take any goddamn orders from a shake 'n bake who ain't done shit and don't know shit? Fuck him!"

"Let me ask you something," I said.

"Go ahead," said Home in a way that sounded like a dare.

"All you want is to get the hell outta the Army and back to the World as fast as possible, right?"

"That's right!" all three said in unison.

"Well, first, let me remind you that *all* of us would rather be back in the World than here." At this, all three gave me looks that could kill. They clearly didn't think I had a clue how badly they wanted to be home.

"You probably feel like if you've gotta fight for something, you'd rather be doing it in Detroit or Chicago than here." Now they were listening. "And you've found a way to get home faster that works for you, namely the Section Eight Dishonorable Discharge, right?"

"Right," said Home.

"Okay, first off, is it true you beat the shit outta your platoon sergeant?"

"Fuckin' A, we did," said Home.

"You damn right," echoed Jervis.

"His redneck ass deserved what he got and more," Leland added.

"That tells me you must've had cause. And the Army thought so, too, or you'd be in Long Binh Jail instead of lounging around up here, waiting for discharge." They calmed down at that. "If you get written up for some new violation, it could change the Army's mind. It could mean spending another damn thirty days here in the Nam and spending it in the LBJ. Is that what you want?"

"Aw, hell, no," said Home.

"All right, here's the deal. If you can hold it together for another couple of weeks, your Section Eights will come through, and you'll be home in less than a month. I won't write you up for refusing Sergeant Calvert's lawful order today, and you won't be asked to do anything that Sergeant Calvert and I don't do ourselves. I'll make it as easy as I can, but you've got to help each other toe the line and do what little we ask of you in the meantime. And if you ever feel anyone here is treating you unfairly, you come to me! Is it a deal?"

They looked at each other and nodded. "It's a deal."

"All right, get some rest and I'll see you this afternoon when we unload the damn supply chopper."

"Okay, Sergeant," said Home.

I related the gist of my conversation to Tim, adding that we wouldn't be including them on the patrols. Telling him with a grin, "I think we're good, but there's no reason to tempt fate."

Over the next few days, my jaw felt progressively worse, until I could no longer avoid doing something about it. I pulled out the dental gauze and stuck the tip of my little finger in the hole. Feeling something hard in the bottom, I thought it might be a broken fragment of the extracted tooth. Then I was afraid it might be the jawbone itself, which couldn't be good. Top arranged for me to go to Buttons.

"Jesus, you've got a dry socket," the medic at Buttons said. "I'm surprised you can stand it. I'm recommending you be flown to Bien Hoa to see the dentist. You need to get that fixed ASAP."

This was unexpected. I went back to Battalion HQ and asked Top if he could keep Sergeant Calvert on the mountain base until I got back. "And ask him to buy six beers for Private Slade for shooting the most rats this month. I'll reimburse him when I get back."

"We'll do that, Sergeant," said Top with a barely concealed grin. "Now get some rest and we'll get your paperwork done so you can get that damn tooth problem taken care of!"

The next morning, I arrived in Bien Hoa and got directions to the dentist. As I limped along the road, a jeep with two MPs approached me from the rear. It made me uneasy because of my experience at Fort Sill. The jeep pulled up alongside and stopped.

"Where you headed, Sergeant?"

"To the dentist," I said.

"Hop in. We'll give you a lift."

Along the way, the MP's asked me what unit I was with. I told them, still suspecting that I was being interrogated.

"Say," said the driver, "I don't suppose you smoke pot, do you?"

I said nothing, wondering how I should answer. Then the MP in the passenger seat lit a number, took a drag, and passed it back to me. I took a toke and handed it to the driver.

"Thanks," I said. "I've got a dry socket from a tooth extraction. This'll help."

Noticing a cluster of widely separated houses, landscaped yards, and palm trees, down a driveway at least a quarter mile long, I said, "What's that?"

"Oh, that's the generals' compound," said the driver.

"You mean the generals live there?"

"Yep. The highest-ranking ones have houses to themselves, with air conditioning and TV. And the compound has a nine-hole golf course."

I looked more closely and saw that the grassy area around the cluster of homes was indeed a manicured golf course with fairways, greens, and flags. I was speechless.

"Yeah, and they're in the center of the complex, too. If a mortar was fired from the perimeter it couldn't reach them," volunteered the passenger.

"Jesus!" I was appalled by how profoundly out of touch with the real war much of our leadership was.

"You said it, man," said the driver. "This next building on the right is the dentist's office; we'll drop you off here, Sergeant."

A few minutes later, the same dentist who pulled my tooth was examining me. "You have a classic dry socket, Sergeant. How much pain are you in?"

"It's pretty bad, but I ignored it as long as I could."

"I'm surprised you stood it this long." He rinsed the socket and packed the hole full of some kind of gel and more gauze. "I need to see you day after tomorrow. Can you come back then?" he asked.

"If you can notify my unit, I think so," I answered.

Before I left, I asked the clerk if there was a way I could call someone at USARV HQ. He said, "Sure, who do you want to reach?"

"Steve Warner," I said. "He's an Army Reporter there." A few seconds later I was talking to Steve. He was amazed and happy to hear from me, and said I could stay with him in his barracks while I was there. He gave me walking directions and off I went. It wasn't too terribly far to Steve's barracks, and when I arrived he was there to meet me.

Chapter 33 – Numba One

It was great to see Steve, but very weird. His barracks were wood frame construction like houses back in the World. It had a kitchen at the north end, then a rec room with bookshelves, lounge chairs and a TV mounted up in a corner. There were half a dozen guys in there watching a sitcom of some kind with a pretty girl in it; I'd never seen the show or the girl before. It was beyond odd to both hear and see a TV for the first time in three-and-a-half months, and to be in an air-conditioned building! The whole scene gave me a strong feeling of unreality. I was uncomfortable, but tried not to show it as Steve introduced me to his barracks mates.

"This is my friend, Jamie Thompson, the grunt I wrote the story about," he said.

"Oh, yeah. That was a great story, man."

I was dumbfounded. "What story, Steve?"

"Sorry about that. I didn't get a chance to tell you, but I wrote a story about your setup at Neal: 'The Hooch that Jamie Built.'"

"Should I be worried about going to Leavenworth?" I asked, mostly joking.

"No. I mentioned beer and booze, but not weed, so you should be fine," he said, grinning. "It'll be submitted to *Stars and Stripes* and syndicated in newspapers across the States. You'll be famous, sort of."

"You've got to be kidding!"

"It's a good story, Jamie. It might help people understand what the guys actually fighting this damn war are like."

"That has to be a good thing, I guess."

"Say, listen" he said. "You're gonna be here 'til Monday, right?"

"Yeah."

"Good. Do you have any money?"

"Sure, I like having money in my pocket, even when I have no place to spend it," I said. "I've got well over five hundred MPC on me."

"Great. Here's what I'm thinking. If I can swing it, we'll head into Saigon tomorrow and get rooms and women."

"Holy shit, man. We can do that?"

"Well, not legally. Saigon is off limits for grunts."

"Really! We're good enough to fight and die, but can't be trusted in civilized society. Is that it?"

"Not to put too fine a point on it, yes. But I think I can arrange for you to use a pass issued to a Spec-4 here. If so, you can wear one of his shirts with his name tag and rank insignia and off we go."

"What the hell, I'm game," I said.

"Okay! Tonight, we'll eat at the Chinese restaurant on the base and get a good night's sleep."

"A Chinese restaurant? Here on the base?"

"Yep. You can shower, and I'll see you back here in an hour." Steve pointed out the window to the bathrooms in the next building.

"Okay, I can take a hint."

There was nothing special about the bathrooms, unless you considered hot water, electric lights, and mirrors special, which I did. I got back to Steve's room about 1630.

"In case you're wondering," he said," I got off early today, mainly because I told my captain I was meeting the grunt I wrote the story about."

I smiled. "Well, I'm glad my fame can accomplish some good."

"Me, too," said Steve. "Our reservation's for 1930, so we've got some time to kill. Let's take a walk."

We took a dirt path on higher ground, skirting the head of a grassy swale that sloped away to the south. A low wooden fence paralleled the path and we leaned on it, gazing out over the swale. It was pretty and tranquil.

"I'm betting you come here often."

"Yes," said Steve. "I can relax and think here."

"I can see why," I said. "It's quiet and you can see far without worrying about getting shot."

"True, but it also reminds me a tiny bit of home, the part of New Jersey that's green and rolling. I went to Gettysburg College and think of that as home, too. I miss it. In fact, I'm thinking of making the college the beneficiary of my GI insurance with the caveat that it be used to set up a chair in Southeast Asian Studies."

"Well, I hope the chair never gets funded—at least not that way," I said.

"Oh, I'm with you on that. But just in case, I'd like something decent to come out of this clusterfuck."

"For now, my insurance goes to my parents if I die. God knows I can never repay them for the money they've spent trying to get me educated, but it would be a start."

When we got to the restaurant, it looked like any other Chinese restaurant. A well-dressed Chinese greeter ushered us to a table.

"Steve, is it just me or is this weird?" I said in a whisper.

"It's not just you. This restaurant only exists because the generals wanted a place to entertain visiting dignitaries. But to make it viable, they have to allow other paying guests. Plus, I'm pretty sure the military guarantees it an income if the paying clientele doesn't come through in great enough numbers."

"What a deal," I said. "Frankly, the generals' compound seems ill-advised and inappropriate enough all by itself, without adding this anomaly."

The next day, I spent time watching TV and talking to Steve's barracks mates. They were nice enough, but there was a distance between us that was unbridgeable. The real war was only a rumor to them, but I'd experienced it and would be going back to it. I answered their questions, but felt they were asked more to make conversation with the strange creature among them than to really get the answers. When Steve showed up, I was glad.

"I spent the day feeling like an exotic zoo animal being examined by passing tourists," I told him.

"Well, let's get the hell outta here and have some fun, then." He handed me a shirt and a pass to Saigon.

"Wow, you did it!"

"Natch, man. Now get changed. I made reservations at the Rex Hotel. We each have a room and we can get a bottle of bourbon and a girl for the night."

"What? I thought you were kidding about the girl."

Twenty minutes later we crammed ourselves into the back of a jeep with half a dozen other guys. At the checkpoint, I handed my pass to the MP. He glanced at it and moved on to the next guy.

As we got close to the city the traffic got heavy. We worked our way through the seething mass of motorbikes with various military and civilian vehicles mixed in and hordes of pedestrians milling about. I felt besieged by all the movement and the cacophony of engines, honks, sirens, and the singsong words of people within earshot. The fumes from tens of thousands of motorbike engines produced a choking fog that made breathing unpleasant as well as unhealthy.

"How can people live in this smog?" I asked.

"They don't have any choice," said Steve, "but not to worry. Our rooms are on the third floor, so we should be above it."

"Thank God!"

It was about 1800 when we approached the hotel. Avoiding collisions with motorbikes in the bumper-to-bumper traffic caused us to stop and go and gave me time to observe the old French architecture of the downtown buildings and the stone walls and fences that surrounded many of them. I also saw several Australian and ROK (Republic of Korea) military vehicles moving along the main drag. I guessed that they were heading for some recreation just as we were. This was the only time I'd ever seen any Australian or ROK presence in the country. "It's easy to forget that we have any allies in this war," I yelled to Steve over the din, nodding at an Aussie Land Rover, packed with men with broad-brimmed hats tied up on one side.

"That's true," he said, "Especially where you are. But you know, Australia has one Brigade here, and that's a bigger national commitment, population wise, than we have!"

"I didn't realize that," I said.

"It's almost twice the percentage of their population compared to ours, something to keep in mind."

"Yes, it is."

In a few more minutes, we were dropped off in front of a four-story, light beige building that said Rex Hotel on it. We checked in and took the elevator to the third floor. I went into my room and looked out the window. I could see that Steve was right; a thick layer of fumes hugged the ground but didn't reach this high.

It was a simple room and large at about fifteen feet wide east-west by twenty-five feet long north-south. Immediately inside on the right was a large cupboard with a hanger bar at the top and two drawers at the bottom. There was a king size bed with a brass headboard against the west wall with bedside tables on both sides, a desk and chair in the northeast corner, and a small table near the window with an armchair on either side of it. The floor was a dark wood. The bathroom was immediately inside the door to the left or west. It was large with small black and white tiles on the floor, a simple porcelain sink on a pedestal, and a toilet with a reservoir mounted on the wall high above it with a pull-chain to flush it. The shower was enclosed with a shower curtain on a curved pipe across the far end of the bathroom. The shower had lever-type hot and cold porcelain water handles, there was no tub. The accommodations seemed even larger than they really were because the ceilings were quite high, twelve feet I think.

I rinsed my face, combed my hair, and set off to get Steve.

"All right!" he said. "Let's get some dinner."

We took the elevator past the fourth floor to the roof, where a mostly open-air restaurant was located. After being seated, we ordered a bottle of French wine. Neither of us knew anything about wine, so we didn't know whether we'd bought the French equivalent of Boone's Farm or not, but it tasted wonderful to our uneducated palates. I ordered filet mignon and escargot, because that was all the French I knew. After dinner, we enjoyed excellent coffee and finished our wine.

"Boy, being a REMF has its moments," I said, licking my lips.

"That it does.

"I didn't know Australia has a greater national commitment to Vietnam than we do."

"Yep," said Steve, "but if you buy the 'domino theory', you can understand why. Australia's a lot closer to Vietnam than the States."

"That's for sure."

"Well, anyway, at the peaks of our troop deployments, the United States had 550,000 men here, roughly a quarter of a percent of our population, and Australia had 60,000, roughly half a percent of theirs."

"How 'bout the ROK?"

"South Korea keeps just under 50,000 troops here, which is about 0.15% of its population," Steve rattled off without missing a beat.

"How do you know this stuff?" I asked.

"I've tried to memorize as much factual data as possible so when I write a story I have my background facts in perspective. There's a lot I don't know, but things like this, I do!"

"Well, I'm duly impressed."

Hey, drain the last drops from that wine glass and let's get our girls lined up."

"I have to tell you I'm not sure about this," I said. "I haven't even thought about being with a woman for months."

"Don't worry, man. Nature will take its course."

From Steve's room we called room service. Steve explained what we wanted and settled on a price of thirty-five dollars MPC each for bourbon, ginger ale, ice, and a prostitute for the entire night. Fifteen dollars of this would be billed to our rooms for the refreshments, but the remaining twenty dollars was to be paid directly to the girls.

"That seems awfully cheap for a whole night," I said.

"You can bet the girls only get a fraction of that, too. But you can always tip her afterward if she makes you feel better," Steve said.

I went to my room and waited. I was nervous. Despite having a philandering bent, I have a great respect and liking for women. I wasn't sure how I'd handle this kind of situation, being sober despite the wine. I hoped I wouldn't make a fool of myself. *"It's not like you do this kind of thing every night, or even often, especially lately!"* I thought.

There was a knock at the door. I opened it and was relieved that it was the bourbon, ginger ale, and ice. I thanked the server and tipped him a five-dollar MPC note. I'd barely placed these items on the table when there was a second knock on the door. With great trepidation, I opened it.

A pretty Vietnamese girl stood there in a black, skin-tight silk dress with a colorful flower design. The cut in front was low between her diminutive but shapely breasts, and it was slit to mid-thigh on one side. She wore strappy black shoes with broad high heels and had a flower in her shining, coal black, medium-length hair.

"Hi, GI," she said in a melodic singsong voice. "You want girl?"

I may have hesitated a bit longer than she was used to, because she added, "GI, no like?"

I turned red and quickly said, "No, no. GI like," I stammered, "You're Number One. Very pretty. Please come in."

"GI pay now," she said before even sitting down.

I handed her a twenty-dollar MPC note, and she put the bill into her pocketbook.

"Would you like a drink?" I asked, gesturing toward the bottle.

She nodded so I fixed two glasses. She smiled and we slowly sipped our drinks.

"GI from Bien Hoa?" she asked.

"No," I said. "Cambodia, Song Be, Nui Ba Ra, then here." I accompanied the words with movements of my index finger in the air. Watching her eyes as I spoke, I think she got the gist of it, but I'm not sure. I continued to talk about whatever was on my mind for several hours. Through it all, she smiled and nodded a lot. Sometimes she'd say, "Numba one" or "Numba ten" to signify that she agreed or disagreed. Around midnight, I sensed she was growing a bit impatient with me. I reminded myself that for me this was therapeutic, but for her it was a job.

"GI want go to bed?" she asked.

I was embarrassed but said, "Yes."

She slowly undressed. When this performance was completed, she sat on the edge of the bed, waiting for me. I mixed two fresh drinks and placed them on a bedside table. Then I unceremoniously removed my clothes, leaving them in a heap on an armchair. I went to the bed and sat on the opposite side. Nearly simultaneously, we swung our legs onto the bed and lay down beside each other.

I rolled over and looked into her eyes. "What is your name?"

"May," she said.

As I looked more closely at her face and felt her flawless skin, I was struck by how very young she looked. This put me off a bit. Finally, I asked, "How old are you, May?"

She immediately answered, "Ay-teen."

"Eight-teen?" I enunciated clearly.

"Yes."

The age of Vietnamese people was far from obvious to U.S. servicemen. Sometimes it seemed that the Vietnamese, especially the women, were either teenagers or septuagenarians, with nothing in between. May's answer was so quick that I had no doubt she'd heard the question many times and rehearsed an acceptable answer.

I leaned close and kissed her. Her lips were as soft as a newborn's cheek and her teeth were white and straight. Her tongue darted into my mouth and began squirming around, massaging my tongue. She wrapped her arms around me, though they could barely reach around my chest. I felt her open her legs to me and didn't hesitate to accept the invitation. For the next five minutes, I thrust into her with all I had, but wasn't able to reach a climax. Drenched in sweat, I withdrew and rolled over onto my back. May propped herself up on an elbow and looked me in the eye. She looked devastated.

"GI no like May?" she said with deep and genuine concern.

"No, no," I said gently stroking her silky black hair. "I like May a lot. It's just ... I don't know. I feel sad."

"Sad?" said May.

"Yes," I said, "Sad about the war. Sad about the people who are hurt and killed in the war."

"Tell May about war."

So I did. I told her about my friends who'd been wounded—Gordon Castro, Lieutenant Bowen, Ferde Salazar, and Cal Singleton—and about the three sergeants and Bob Berning who'd been killed. I talked about the Montagnard village in Cambodia. But I didn't talk about my wound.

Whenever I mentioned Cambodia and Montagnards, she looked angry and said, "Combodja numba ten!" or "Montagnard numba ten!"

I tried explaining that Cambodians and Montagnards were our allies, but this fell on deaf ears. She made it clear that the hatred she felt was ancient and deep and would far outlast the current war, which was but a flicker in the timeless flame of Vietnamese history and culture.

May's values, beliefs, and thoughts were very different from mine. Whether those differences were based on ignorance or deeper knowledge of Southeast Asia by one or the other or both of us, was an open question ... and ultimately irrelevant in the moment. The point was that May had become a person to me, no longer an object. I looked at her differently. She recognized that and responded to it.

I kissed her again, but more deeply than before. Soon we were deep in the throes of passionate lovemaking, only this time I exploded inside her. I lay atop her for several minutes, breathing in the aroma of her beautiful hair and kissing her cheeks and ears and lips and eyes. Eventually, I withdrew and looked at May. She was smiling. I smiled back and said softly, "Thank you, May."

She leaned over, kissed me on the cheek and got up to go to the bathroom. She smiled at me over her shoulder and softly said, "Numba one." I lay there, more relaxed than I'd felt in a very long time. May hadn't closed the bathroom door so I heard the shower come on. *"Not a bad idea,"* I thought.

A few seconds later, an excited May called out "GI come!"

Thinking May might have slipped in the shower and hurt herself, I crushed out my cigarette in the ashtray and hurried into the bathroom. May was standing in the shower with the curtain pulled aside pointing down toward the white fluid streaming down her inner thighs. With a huge smile, she said excitedly, "GI numba one! GI numba one!"

Two thoughts went through my mind: *"She's proud of a job well done"* and *"I wonder if May is really eighteen!"*

My random thoughts evaporated when she once again said, quite excitedly, "NUMBA ONE!"

I joined May in the shower, and afterward we went back to bed and fell asleep in each other's arms. In the morning she dressed and prepared to leave, but before she did, I hugged her, kissed her cheek and handed her fifty dollars MPC.

"May number one. This is for *you*," I said with narrowed eyes and an emphatic nod.

At breakfast on the roof, Steve asked, "So how was it?"

"Her name was May, or so she said. And she was very pretty."

"Well how did it go?" he pressed.

"I'm not a kiss and tell type of guy, but I will say that I obviously needed this. She was sweet and while young and ignorant, smart in her way."

"So are you glad we did this?"

"Without a doubt. To be honest, I had no idea how badly I needed this. I'm more relaxed after last night than I've been since I got to the Nam. So thank you Steve ... from the bottom of my heart."

"It was my pleasure, Jamie. You welcomed me into your world in the bush and gave me entre into a line unit. I'm very grateful for that. This is the least I could do in return."

"You're a good friend, Steve. You didn't need to do anything."

"Thanks." He was a little embarrassed, I think.

Chapter 34 – Awful News

After breakfast, we got a ride back to Steve's barracks and spent the rest of the day, relaxing and talking. It was a wonderful break for me. The next morning I made it to the dentist's office for my examination. Things appeared to be on the mend. The dentist added a little more gel, gave me some aspirin and an antibiotic, and sent me on my way. I began walking to the terminal, but this time I didn't get a ride, so it was a long hot trudge. My shrapnel wound felt like someone was twisting red hot rebar in my leg.

Around 1530 I caught a ride to Buttons, and because of the time of day spent the night there. I had evening chow with Cal, and he told me he was being made the Battalion Awards and Decorations clerk.

"That's great, Cal. Don't take this the wrong way, but I didn't even know we gave out awards and decorations, let alone that we needed a clerk to do it."

"I know what you mean, but it turns out we do give out a few here and there. My job is not to give 'em out, as you put it, but to process the requests and make sure everything is in order."

"Well, I'm glad for you, man. Say, how is your back?"

"It's pretty much healed, but there's a hell of a scar. How's your leg?"

"If you asked me a few days ago, I'd have said pretty darn good. But this morning I walked two klicks on hard ground, and it's been killing me ever since. It's oozing fluid again, too."

"I wondered, because you were limping when you walked into the office," he said.

In the morning, I ate breakfast with Jay.

"You heard Kent Shepard took over your job as squad leader, right?" he asked.

"No, he was in Third Platoon last I heard."

"Well, they moved him to First Squad, First Platoon two weeks after you were hit, right after the in-country R&R. Griffith didn't think anyone in First Platoon could do the job."

"I suppose that's a compliment," I said.

"Oh, it is. Especially since it was Top who put the bug in the LT's ear."

"Based on what I know of Kent from NCO school, he can certainly do the job, but I don't know anything about how he is in the field."

"There's more," Jay went on. "Two days ago, when you were down in Bien Hoa, Kent was walking point, following your example, I guess."

"Just as I followed Roger Campbell's ... and?" I asked.

"Well, he kept Woody as his cover man, and they walked right into an ambush."

"Jesus. How are they?"

"AK rounds hit a tree within inches of Woody and a couple of feet from Kent. They both got hit in the face by wood splinters," Jay said. "There was eye damage, so they're down at the 93rd Evac Hospital. Looks like they're gonna be fine, but we won't know for sure for a few days."

"I wish I'd known. I could've visited."

"I know, but we didn't have a way to contact you. Anyway, for now, Corporal Charlie Riddle is acting squad leader."

"Charlie's a good man. He'll do well. But Christ, man. Woody's had two close calls in six weeks. I hope he comes outta this all right."

"Me, too. He's a likable cuss! By the way, your ride will be a slick taking ammo up the mountain. It's due to leave at about 1000 hours."

By 1030 I was back on the mountain and felt like I'd come home. Tim Calvert met me as I walked through the berm.

"Welcome back, Sergeant!"

"Glad to be back. How did it go?"

"All's well. No problems, I'm happy to say."

"Where do you need me to pull guard?" I asked.

"I didn't schedule you for tonight. We got a couple new grunts yesterday so you can get some rest and start in the morning," he said.

"That's damn nice of you, man. Listen, here's five bucks for Slade's beer. I'm gonna put my stuff away, and take a nap. I'll fill you in on my adventures later."

The next day, I plugged myself into the guard duty roster and led a detail down to the pad to bring up supplies. A little after that, at mail call, I got a letter from my mother.

Dear Cam,

I have some terrible news to tell you. Last week, your good friend Gary was killed in a car crash in North Barrington.

Apparently, his girlfriend broke up with him and he reacted by getting drunk and driving to her house. He took his father's Jaguar, missed a turn at about a hundred miles an hour, and hit a tree. He was killed instantly.

I went to the funeral because I knew you would want me to. It was awful. In the midst of the service, Gary's mother began wailing and screaming and literally threw herself on the coffin. It was simply horrible. Gary's father and brother had to pull her off and take her out of the church.

I hated to have to write you about this, but I knew you would want to know.

I Love You, Didi
XXOO

Shocked doesn't do justice to the devastation I felt. There were very few people I considered best friends, Gary was one of them. I hadn't thought a lot about Gary because he'd finished his stint in the Army as an MP in Germany and was back in the World and safe. I folded the letter, put it back in the envelope and just lay there. I was frozen. I didn't move for an hour.

One of the ways we coped with the fragility of our lives in Vietnam was to think of it as temporary. Over the horizon was the World, where the sun always shone, no one shot at you, and people died of old age. Gary's death caused a fundamental shift in my view of the world.

I went to chow and picked at my food. I didn't go to the poker game that night. Tim knew something was wrong, but didn't intrude. I walked slowly around the perimeter several times, finally lingering to watch the sunset.

Later that night on guard in the culvert pipe atop Bunker One, I used my lighter to read parts of the letter again. I could see Gary as clearly as if he were there with me. He was one of the kindest and gentlest people I'd ever known. All the girls liked him, but he was childlike in ways that tended to end his relationships earlier than he liked. He fell fast and hard. Several times in high school he'd come perilously close to doing things very much like what killed him. But he'd called me, and I was there for him. I never left him alone at such times. It was a burden I was happy to bear because he was my friend.

Tears welled in my eyes. I stared into the night, feeling the cool breeze against my face, and began to sob. I couldn't help it. I'd never felt grief so viscerally. I was angry because the fucking war and the Army had made it impossible for me to be there for Gary.

"If I'd been there, this never would have happened," I whispered aloud.

It was two days before I mentioned Gary's death to Tim, and I didn't elaborate. It was several more days before the press of daily responsibilities and the passage of time began to return me to a state of external normalcy. Pretending everything is all right, and acting as though it is, gradually changes the pretender into the normal person he or she has been portraying. It happens slowly, without fanfare or notice of any kind. But one day you realize that somewhere along the way you weathered the storm, and the seas calmed.

A week later, the Section Eight paperwork for Privates Ellington, Leland, and Jervis came through. After they packed their gear, they came to me.

Homer said, "Sergeant Thompson, we want to thank you. You're a good man who treated us fair and helped us. I wish there were more like you in the Army."

I was embarrassed. "Homer, James, Elroy, you're all good men. I'm sorry you had to take the route you did, but I know you felt you had no choice. I wish you the best."

At our poker game that night, a visiting supply sergeant who'd joined us lost over fifty dollars. He asked if anyone could break a hundred-dollar greenback. I gave him four twenties and two tens MPC for it. He then said real greenbacks could fetch five times their face value in MPC if sold on the black market. I said, "First of all, I wouldn't know where to find the 'Black Market' and second, is there any doubt that those greenbacks would be used to provide supplies and aid to the enemy? I don't think so!" So that ended the discussion.

That night I put the hundred-dollar bill in the ammo can under my backpack. A few days later, I discovered it had been stolen. The visiting supply sergeant had left the day before, so I had no doubt who'd taken it.

I couldn't understand how anyone's personal greed could trump the safety of U.S. troops, but for some people it clearly did.

Chapter 35 – Doc's Place

The signal corps guys on the mountain were an unknown quantity to me, because there was little contact between grunts and commo guys. We saw each other at chow, but really at no other time. This changed when Top and Lieutenant Carmichael proposed constructing a recreation building. It would require a non-military effort by as many people on the base as possible. The materials would be surplus military, because there simply were no other materials there. The LT made an announcement that laid out the location and size of the proposed structure and emphasized that while he and Top would scrounge materials, the labor was strictly voluntary on our off-duty time. He encouraged everyone to participate, but told us there would be no repercussions for those who opted not to. It may have been his finest hour.

Within a few days, the location was cleared and leveled entirely by hand, using entrenching tools. Corner stakes were pounded in, lines were laid out, and doorways were marked. Materials were gathered from various spots around the base. Sooner than anyone thought possible, construction began under Top's direction. The basic design was a modified mess hall, which made perfect sense. Over the years enough extra screening, two-by-fours, hinges, and fasteners (nails, screws and staples) had accumulated, so there were very few last-minute needs to be met by dog-robbing.

Ten days later, we had our club. It had been a base-wide project, but Top and the commissary guys did ninety percent of the work, with some of the grunt work being done by, well, the grunts. A bar across the far end sold snacks, beer, and soda. Hard liquor was tougher, since there wasn't much on the mountain and no quick way to get it up there, but gradually the beer money paid for enough bottles from the official club on Buttons to meet our meager needs. Someone donated a tape player and half a dozen tapes, so we had music. It was darn nice and greatly improved morale on our little base in the sky. An unexpected bonus was that the sandbagged roof was large, flat, and solid. It soon became the preferred place to go at night to get above it all. It was also a terrific observation deck at sunset.

* * *

Because Nui Ba Ra was considered relatively safe and had a great view, we often had visitors from among the brass who worked in USARV or MACV or other higher headquarters. Some of these visits were unscheduled landings, when colonels or generals en route to other places saw the mountain and thought, why not?

One day, a full bird colonel and his aides landed beside our supply chopper. I was leading several infantry guards down the trail to unload as we passed the colonel's group coming up. We moved as close to the right edge as we could to give them room to pass and walked on by. I glimpsed the colonel's eyes as I moved past and had a premonition of trouble.

"Did you forget something?" an arrogant voice called out from behind me. I ignored it because I hadn't forgotten anything and figured the words were directed to someone else.

"Sergeant! I'm talking to you!" said the colonel.

I turned and walked back. "Yes, sir, what can I do for you?"

"You failed to salute me just now," he shouted in my face.

I saw that he was in the Signal Corps and realized he might not have any experience in the field. I said, "Sir, in the field we don't salute officers. It's for their own protection. We don't want to identify officers to the enemy."

"That's an inexcusable breach of military discipline," he blustered. "I'll speak to your commanding officer about this."

"That's your privilege, sir," I said. "But if you'll excuse me, I have to unload ammo from the supply chopper."

"Go ahead." He waved dismissively.

Lieutenant Carmichael summoned me to his office that evening. "Sergeant, I know you were right not to salute the colonel, but in the future try to defuse the situation a little better than you did today. All right?"

"Sir," I said, "I explained why it was in his best interest that I not salute him in the field. I suppose I could have seemed more cowed, but it would have been hard."

"I understand, but do your best from now on."

At chow, Tim asked me how it went with the LT. "He was fine, but that colonel is a fucking idiot. Who does he think he is telling *me* how to act in the field? He doesn't know shit from Shinola, or a mortar tube from a piss tube."

Tim glanced around the mess hall. "Take it easy, man. I've never seen you like this."

I took a deep breath. "I'm slow to anger, usually. But sometimes, if someone does something *really* stupid, or if something is really wrong, I just explode."

At the poker game that night, Tim won seventeen dollars and I won thirty-two. "Beer is on me tomorrow night," I said.

"I'll be there!" said Tim.

The next evening, Tim and I went to the club and I bought us each a beer. There were some new faces, including one fellow I'd seen around, but never met. We went over and introduced ourselves.

"When you two are ready for more beer, it's on me," I said.

"Thanks, we'll take you up on that. Everyone calls me Doc. And this is Lamar Jenkins."

"Glad to meet, ya," I said. "Is that a Kentucky accent?"

"Sure as hell is," said Doc. "I'll tell you what, gents, why don't you come on over to Doc's place later tonight?"

"We're on guard until 2330 hours. Is that too late?" I asked.

"Oh, hell no! I've got some good tunes and some other stuff I think you'll like. Stop on by."

"Where is your place?" I asked.

"That's right, you grunts hardly mix with us Commo types. We'll have to remedy that. Just head over to Bunker Two, then face the center of the base and walk ten meters. There's a bunch of conexes there," he said. "When you come to the one that's welded to another one with a sign over the door that says Restricted Area – Authorized Personnel Only, knock and I'll let you in."

"It's a deal! We'll see you there!"

On guard, a little later, I decided to tape record a message to my parents. It was warm, so I squatted on the northeast corner of the bunker's roof holding my M16, turned on the recorder and began to talk. I described where I was and what I could see.

"I can see a few tiny lights at the far edge of Firebase Buttons about half a mile below and a few miles to the west, but other than that, the jungle all around is black on this moonless night as far as the eye can see. Oh, just now, out of the darkness far to the northwest, a line of red light, like a laser with a definite beginning and end, is streaming in a shallow arc from the black sky into the jungle below. It's tracer rounds from a minigun or an M60 machine gun on an American aircraft, either a helicopter or a fixed wing of some kind. It's amazing!"

I continued to talk off and on about whatever thoughts crossed my mind. Among them was the comparison that had occurred to me earlier between my situation and that of a Roman soldier guarding an alpine pass thousands of years ago. The streams of red continued intermittently for about twenty minutes, then disappeared. I described that in the tape as well, adding just before I closed, "It's so far away that there's no sound at all, which adds to the awful wonder of it."

At the end of my shift, I went looking for Doc's place. The door was concealed from the circular pathway around the base, but when you passed through the conexes it was plain as day under a small hooded lamp that barely put out enough light to navigate the route. I knocked.

"Who is it?"

"It's Jamie, Sergeant Thompson"

"Welcome, man!" Doc said in that smooth, mild Southern accent unique to people of the Bluegrass State. Doc was a lanky guy about six feet tall who was probably twenty-two but had the demeanor of someone older and more mature. He had a personality that was naturally friendly, humorous, and welcoming—the kind of guy people gravitated to and wanted to be around.

What immediately struck me was that Doc's Place was air-conditioned. "I cannot believe this place has AC!" I said, looking around.

"It's required. All this electronic gear puts out a lotta heat," Doc said. "Without the AC, it would fry in no time."

Counting me, there were six people present: Doc, Tim, Lamar, and two others who looked familiar.

"This is Joe Biggs and Daryl Harding," Doc said. "They're two of the best damn cooks in the Army and usually bring munchies. But with or without the snacks, they're great guys who're always welcome."

Doc's conex was crammed full of top-secret radio gear on racks and shelves. I asked him what it was for and he said some of it was USARV's eyes and ears, and the rest was radio gear that relayed routine comm traffic between the northern half of Vietnam and higher headquarters near Saigon.

"When it works like it's supposed to," he said, "it relays radio traffic automatically. When it fails, I do it manually. So my job is to keep it all running right and step in when it fails."

Over time I learned more, but that night I was more interested in listening to music, which was the Mamas and Papas' *California Dreamin'* album. It wasn't too loud, but it sure wasn't too soft either.

"Well, let's play some spades," said Doc. "Since there are six of us tonight, we'll form three sets of partners. If you win a game, you keep playing. If you lose, you step aside for the team that wasn't playing. Whatever team wins three games first is tonight's grand champ and gets to take two rolled joints of any variety of weed when they leave."

"How many varieties do you have?" I asked.

"Funny you should ask."

Doc reached behind a stack of electronic gear and slid out a small suitcase. Inside, the case was divided into twenty-four compartments filled with either pill bottles or baggies—labeled and tagged.

"Holy shit, man. No wonder they call you Doc."

"You got it," he said with pride.

"Is every compartment a different kind of pot?"

"For the most part, yeah. Right now, I have about eighteen varieties."

"How in the world did you amass this collection?"

"Well, I've always been a friendly cuss, and lots of guys who've had a good time at Doc's Place have left samples. You'd be surprised how many come back the next time they're up here and bring me exotic stuff from wherever they've been. It adds up. But for now, let's crack open some beers and start the game. Lamar, can you do the honors?"

"Sure thing," said Lamar opening a makeshift beer cooler a lot like the one I'd concocted at Neal.

"Okay, well, Lamar and I usually team up, and Joe and Daryl do, too. So I'm assuming you two can partner up."

"We can," I said, "but I don't know if Tim's ever played spades. Have you, Tim?"

"Nope, but how hard can it be?"

"Okay, that makes the starting teams easy to pick," said Doc. "Jamie and Tim can watch the first game. Tim, feel free to ask any questions, but only after the hand is played out."

I said, "Learning spades is a survival skill you'll need in the bush, Tim. We play it every night unless we set up the NDP after dark or it's raining."

Doc dealt the first hand. I spent much of the game whispering the ins and outs of spades in Tim's ear. By the time Doc and Lamar claimed victory, Tim felt he would at least not make a complete fool of himself. When we played Doc and Lamar he did a credible job, but we lost by 173 points. As we watched the next game, Tim and I discussed what we'd done right and wrong during our game. I was confident that if Joe and Daryl managed to win, Tim and I would be a good match for them in the next game.

Joe and Daryl pulled it off by a thirteen-point margin. Tim and I were so determined to do better that beads of sweat appeared on our foreheads during the game. Somehow, we won by 254 points.

Next was our second game against Doc and Lamar. It was amazing how into it we were. That was the virtue of spades. It was easy enough that damn near anyone could learn to play, but required a level of thinking, planning, and strategizing that completely focused the mind to the exclusion of all else. On Nui Ba Ra, "all else" was mostly routine and boredom, but in the boonies it was danger, death, and despair in varying degrees.

Tim and I played well but lost. This was the third win for Doc and Lamar, so they claimed victory for the night.

"Does this mean you leave your two joints in the case?" I asked Doc.

"Hell, no. It means Lamar and I smoke two more than usual."

"Of course, it does. Why did I even ask?" I said with a laugh.

Doc lit a rolled number from one of the compartments, took a toke, and passed it to me.

"Hey, I hear you had a bit of a run in with Colonel Adamson a few days ago," Doc said.

"I didn't know his name, but if you're referring to the colonel we passed on the trail to the pad the other day, then yes," I said, suddenly very serious.

"Good for you. The guy's a roaring asshole. This was his first time up here even though he's been nominally in charge of all this commo stuff for months. He spends his time sending bullshit memos to the field units like the need for alertness at all times, and how important personal hygiene is to maintaining a sharp mind."

"Good God! You've got to be kidding," I exclaimed.

"Nope," Lamar chimed in, "Like Doc said, he's a roaring asshole."

"What exactly was he upset with you about?" asked Doc.

"He chewed me out in front of my men for not saluting him as we passed him on the trail. Or, let me rephrase that, he tried to chew me out. Of course, I pointed out that not saluting officers in the field was SOP to keep them from standing out to enemies who might be watching."

"How did he react to that news?" Doc asked.

"He filed a formal complaint with the CO stating that I failed to follow proper military protocols."

"What did the LT say?"

"He said he understood, but asked me to try to handle similar situations a bit more diplomatically in the future. I told him I supposed I could try to do that."

"Like I said, Colonel Adamson is an asshole!" Doc said again, sucking in another deep drag on the joint and passing it to me.

When I exhaled my next drag, I said, "You know those sidewalk signs you see people wearing over their shoulders? You know, two panels, one over the chest and one over the back of some poor soul that say something like "Like Italian? Eat at Vito's!"

"Yeah," said Tim, "what about 'em?"

I think we should make one up for Colonel Adamson to wear that simply says, "Salute when in the field!"

There was silence for about five seconds. But when this scene was envisioned in each person's head and its implications had sunk in, everyone burst into uncontrolled laughter. "That would be perfect!" said Doc. "It's so understated, but EVERYONE would know what it was really saying was 'Here walks an asshole!'" At this, everyone laughed even harder, in fact so hard that people were having trouble catching their breath! It was great!

"I almost hate to ask, but what kind of variety or mix is in this number, man?" I asked. "It's some good shit!"

"It's a mixture of Mekong Madness and Danang Dynamite," he said proudly.

"Jesus, man. I think you're onto something here! You can call it MD Squared, patent it, and advertise it as 'Doc's special blend.'"

"Wow! You're right man! I hadn't thought about the MM DD aspect before. In a perfect world, I'd do just what you suggest, but in this one, it'll have to be part of our secret stash!"

"Whatever, man. It's some really good shit!" put in Tim. At that, five other heads nodded in agreement.

At breakfast the next day, I said to Tim, "You know those decompression chambers deep divers use to readjust to normal air pressure?"

"Yeah," said Tim.

"I think Doc's Place is kinda like that. I mean, I feel so much better today than I usually do, and that's the only explanation I can think of."

"Now that you mention it, I feel better today, too."

Two days later Tim got his orders to join Alpha Company. I spent most of his last day with him.

"When you get to Alpha, stay close to Kurt Stephan," I said. "He's smart as hell and doesn't do anything stupid. If you learn from him, you'll be learning from the best."

Tim nodded.

"I probably don't need to tell you this, but I will anyway," I said. "Getting high is okay in the rear, which includes firebases, but it's never okay in the field. Never. Got it?"

"Got it."

I went to Doc's almost every night after that. We were playing spades in a thick cloud of smoke to a cranked-up *Break on Through* by the Doors one night when loud knocking permeated our pot-soaked brains. It was damned annoying.

Without moving from the table or turning down the music, Doc turned toward the door and shouted, "Yeah, what can I do for you?"

"It's Top. Open up."

"No can do, Top!"

I looked at Doc in disbelief, but he remained unflappable.

"God dammit, open the door! That's an order!" shouted Top.

"Can't do it, Top. Sorry."

"Open the damn door, right now!" shouted an increasingly frustrated and angry Top.

"I can't do that," shouted Doc.

"God dammit, I know what you're doing in there. Now open the damn door."

"I can't, Top. I'm relaying top secret transmissions, and you don't have the clearance to be in here." Doc raised his eyebrow with a grin only we could see.

"Jesus Christ!" shouted Top. "You'll regret this, Specialist."

"I'm truly sorry you feel that way, but regulations are regulations. My hands are tied."

We heard a mumbled "Goddamn son of a bitch" that trailed off as Top left the area.

The whole group's muffled snickering then burst out in howls of laughter that took several minutes to die down.

"Is that business about the clearance true?" I asked.

"Yep!" said Doc, "There are only two of us up here with clearances high enough to be authorized inside here, and that's me and another Spec-4 you haven't met because he's sleeping when I'm on duty. We pull twelve-hour shifts. And as to the top-secret transmissions, that's true, too. The communications that go through the equipment in here are the most sensitive and most secret in the war zone."

"If it's not forbidden, can you give me some idea of what kind of communications do go through here?" I asked.

"I can tell you this," he said. "Remote monitoring equipment and human observers are scattered all over Vietnam, Cambodia, and Laos. Damn near every bit of that information, raw intelligence really, is relayed through this equipment."

"I remember reading that we have detectors with bed bugs in them, and that when a VC or NVA passes within something like fifty feet they get excited and start squealing or something and it gets amplified and triggers a signal. Is that what you're relaying?" I asked.

Doc laughed. "There are some of those, but mostly we use electronic sensors that detect movement, body heat, and ground vibrations. They're dropped from the air and work for ninety days or so. The bed bug sensors, not so long," he said with a sad look. "Of course, no matter what kind of sensor is used, it can't tell the difference between people, deer, tigers, monkeys, and water buffalo. The raw data is filtered by human experts who analyze it and try to make those distinctions, but it's an inexact science."

"What a deal," I muttered.

"Yeah, but there it is. Say, are you gonna pass that number or not?" Doc asked Joe, who'd frozen while listening to Doc.

"Oh. Yeah, man. Sorry."

Chapter 36 – Spit Shined

A few nights later, I was on guard duty—listening to the Moody Blues' *Nights in White Satin* through earphones, slowly smoking a Cambodian Pale joint, and contemplating the meaning of life—when a hand lightly touched my left shoulder. I was startled because no one ever lifted the poncho flap at the inside end of the culvert pipe. I turned my head and saw the CO. A jolt of anxiety shot through me. I was holding a joint in my right hand and the space was permeated with pot smoke. My stomach tightened. I was caught red-handed smoking pot on guard duty. There was no question that it was *verboten*, and the fact that it was perfectly safe in the circumstances made no difference at all by the book.

In a nanosecond that seemed like an eternity, I calmly said, "Hello, sir."

Lieutenant Carmichael said, "Sergeant, put that out."

"Yes, sir."

"I expect you to report to my office in a few days to discuss this. Is that clear, Sergeant?"

"Yes, sir. I'll be there when you want me, sir."

"Carry on," he said and left as quietly as he'd come.

I was worried, but not overly so. I mean, what could they do, send me to Nam? I told Doc about it after chow the next evening.

"Aw, don't worry about it. The LT's a wimp," he said.

"Maybe so, but he's an officer, and I'm still concerned," I said. "It bothers me that he was able to sneak in behind me like that."

Earlier that afternoon some brass had arrived at the base and it soon became clear this was a surprise inspection tour. It was highly unusual because it apparently *really was* a complete and total surprise to the CO and Top. A brigadier general and two aides walked the entire perimeter and through every building, including our new club building. The general pointed to things on the ground and the aides took notes, occasionally digging a shell casing or cigarette butt out of a crack in the sandbagged wall and placing it in a small plastic bag. After two hours, the general entered the HQ. Twenty minutes later he and his entourage left.

At the staff meeting the next morning, Lieutenant Carmichael barely said a word until the end, when he announced a change of command. "I'll be leaving in the next couple of days, and I don't know yet who the new CO will be."

After the LT left the meeting, Top told us Carmichael had been reassigned. None of us had ever seen an officer relieved of command. I felt a twinge of pity, but the change gave me a temporary reprieve.

Two days later, as I led my detail down the trail to the pad, we passed a first lieutenant whose fatigues were actually starched and whose boots were spit shined—things we never saw in the field. *"Uh, oh,"* I thought. *"Long Binh Jail, here I come."*

Lieutenant Carmichael made it down the trail with his gear in less than twenty minutes and left unceremoniously on the supply chopper. He held his head up, but it was plain to see he was hurting. We watched the helicopter dip out of sight over the edge of the mountain and finished hauling the boxes up the hill.

The next morning at the staff meeting, the new LT introduced himself.

"I'm Lieutenant Harding Chesterton," he said with a cultured, Deep South accent. The first thing I noticed about him—other than the starched fatigues and spit shined boots—was that instead of the crossed flags of the Signal Corps, his uniform bore the crossed rifles of the Infantry. "As you've probably figured out, I've been sent here to get this place shipshape. And that's exactly what I'm going to do. But for now, let's continue operations as you have been until I get the lay of the land. Understood?"

"Understood, sir!" we said in unison.

"That's it then. Dismissed until tomorrow."

This LT was different. He didn't raise his voice, act intimidating, or defer overly much; he just led. I liked him immediately, though given my current situation I didn't know how he'd feel about me. I think all of us were wondering if our lives were going to get more difficult.

The transition was smooth. Lieutenant Chesterton was crystal clear in his orders. This was a change from Lieutenant Carmichael, who tended to give orders that were less than precise, almost as though they were requests or suggestions, which is not how the U.S. Army operates.

Several days into his tenure, Lieutenant Chesterton told me he'd like a tour of the guard bunkers. I took him around the perimeter and showed him the inside and outside of every bunker and where the ammo was stored and what we currently had in inventory. He was as surprised as I had been about the Willie Pete grenades until I explained how the terrain made it safe to throw them.

"We use them regularly during Mad Minutes, sir. I think they're a pretty effective deterrent."

"I'm sure they are," he agreed with a chuckle. "By the way, Sergeant, in case you've wondered, I did my six months in the field with the Twenty-Fifth and spent the last three months in MACV HQ, so I understand what the real war here is about."

"Yes, sir. That's good to know. Lieutenant Carmichael was a good man, but he didn't seem well versed in combat or base defense. That wasn't critical, because the system up here has been working for years. As far as I can tell, no CO has changed it for quite a while," I said. "The most important things are to staff the bunkers with grunts during all hours of darkness and make sure we have more than enough ammo on hand."

"I agree to a point, but you should be aware that this place was hit by the NVA and VC on thirty August last year. I'm not sure what our casualties were, but ten enemy bodies were found on the slopes just below the base the next morning, so we can never take perimeter security for granted. I believe since that time the only substantive change was the switch from sending line platoons up for a few weeks at a time to sending infantry soldiers who were between assignments or otherwise available."

"I didn't know about that attack, but can confirm that some of my guards are awaiting dishonorable discharge, but I've had no problems."

"So I understand from the reports," he replied.

The mention of reports about the infantry guards made me wince. As we neared the HQ, the LT turned to me.

"Do you have any marijuana, Sergeant?"

I froze in my tracks. Clearly, he'd read about Carmichael catching me. Or maybe Carmichael told him before he left. I didn't know how to answer. If I said no, the LT would know I was lying. But if I said yes, he could bring me up on charges. In the end, I opted for the truth, regardless of the potential consequences.

"Yes, sir. I do."

"When and where is your guard shift tonight?" he asked.

"This is poker night, so my shift is 2330 to 0330 hours. I'll be on Bunker Four."

"Good. I'll be joining you for a while tonight. Bring some pot, Sergeant," he said.

"Yes, sir," I said, still unsure of his intentions.

I was nervous for the rest of the day and into the evening, winning only twelve dollars at the poker game, an off night. At 2330 I relieved my predecessor on guard duty. About fifteen minutes later, I heard the LT climbing up the steps.

"Sergeant Thompson are you in there?" he asked in a whisper.

"Yes, sir," I said, sounding much more normal than I felt.

"Did you bring the pot?" he asked.

"Yes, sir, but I have to tell you that I'm nervous about this. Do you plan to confiscate it?"

"Hell no! I plan to help you destroy it by burning it, one joint at a time."

"Thank God," I blurted out. "Lieutenant Carmichael caught me, and I've been worried sick ever since."

"Not to worry, Sergeant. I had my own rock band in Atlanta and hope to start it up again when I get out of the Army. In other words, I'm a normal guy. And you talk about nervous. Do you have any idea how hard it is to procure weed as an officer without risking Leavenworth? If you ask the wrong person or even the right person in the wrong way, your life could be ruined," he said.

"I never thought about that," I said. "In fact, I don't think the words 'pot' and 'officer' have ever once been associated in my thoughts."

"Hah! Well consider yourself educated. Now, let's light up a number and listen to some tunes."

First, I put in a Crosby, Stills and Nash tape, turning the sound up just enough for us to hear it bouncing around inside our culvert pipe but not enough for it to carry more than a few feet outside it. I'd brought an open pack of Tay Ninh O, so I pulled one out. As *Marrakesh Express* began to play, I lit it behind cupped hands in the cramped culvert pipe.

Thus, began a wonderful friendship.

A day later, Chesterton asked if there was someplace a little less cramped where we could smoke privately. The only place I could think of was the roof of the club, so that evening we went up there. We gravitated to the extreme northwest corner. Since I was with the CO, we were given a lot of space. But there were always four or five guys up there and more wandering up and down all the time. There was no way we could light up in such a place.

"I have a better idea," said the LT. "Follow me."

We went down into the HQ. I figured he needed to get something there and we'd be on our way. I was wrong. We went down the hall past the offices, conference room, and radio room. This was deeper than I'd ventured before.

"In here," he said opening a door on the right. "These are my quarters. I have an idea that might work."

"If you say so," I said doubtfully.

"It's a risk, but an acceptable one I think. First, let's pack this bowl with some of your Cambodian Pale."

"That's a beautiful pipe," I said. "Where did you get it?"

"Japan. I was on R&R last month. Cost me over a hundred dollars, but it's hand-carved ivory, and I think it was worth it," he said, admiring it as he stuffed it with Cambodian Pale.

As he finished tamping, he asked me to turn on a small oscillating fan. "Better put it on medium," he suggested.

Next, he produced some incense sticks, set them up in an open soda can, and lit them. They produced a pleasant aroma of sandalwood and cloves—not overpowering, but certainly strong enough to mask most other odors.

The LT lit the bowl and we were soon lost in the sounds of Steppenwolf's *Born to be Wild*, which was turned up loud enough to drown out our words and laughter. When we were halfway through a second bowl of Pale, we realized the room was foggy with pot smoke, so the LT pulled out a can of bug spray and squirted it into the back of the fan. It didn't eliminate the fog but did thin it, and in combination with the incense it confused the odors to the point that no one could say with certainty what they smelled.

Over the next weeks, Hardy and I talked about everything that came to our minds. Strangely, that didn't include the war. Mostly he talked about life in Atlanta, and I talked about life in Tucson. We talked about old girlfriends and our hopes for the future in terms of careers and women.

"The truth is," I told him one night, "I still have no idea what I want to do when I grow up, if I ever manage to do that."

"Don't stress out about it," he said. "You're a bright guy, and things have a way of working out, as long as you don't do anything too damn stupid."

"I appreciate that. But to be honest, I can't get too excited about a future that might never materialize."

"Well, that's a fast way to kill a high. There's a fair chance you won't go back to the field. You have to think positively, Jamie."

"Maybe I should, but for some reason I can't. It's not as though I'm wallowing in self-pity or feeling depressed. But I am being realistic, or at least I think I am."

"I respect that," said the LT, "but try to be at least a bit more optimistic about things."

Chapter 37 – Another Month; The Leech

The next day I went down to Buttons for my second profile evaluation. The doctor could see that the wound was red and tender. It continued to shorten my stride and send sporadic shooting pains into my leg.

"I'm happy with the way it's healing, but you're not fit for duty yet," he said. I'm writing you another thirty-day profile, but with fewer physical restrictions. You can perform light duties to include occasional lifting of up to fifty pounds. I don't think you need anything for pain other than Tylenol now. In a pinch, you can take aspirin, but since that can cause bleeding—and the shrapnel has sharp edges—you really should stick with Tylenol."

That night I ate with Cal Singleton.

"I know Jay told you about Kent Shepard and Woody getting hit," he said.

"Yeah. How are they?"

"Kent's back in the field, but Woody's a different story. When he went back out, he kinda froze up. The LT sent him back three days later.

"Two close calls in such a short time. Who can blame him?" I said. "Shit, where is he now?"

"That's the good news. Top arranged a job in the rear. He's a mail clerk at Bien Hoa. That's where he'll stay 'til his tour ends." I was happy for him.

The next day I was back on the mountain. The LT saw me as I came up the trail and asked how it went.

"Another thirty-day profile," I said with a smile that I didn't feel good about, for some reason.

"See? You need to be optimistic. I'm just glad you'll continue to be with us."

That night, I won thirty-four dollars at poker and hit the sack right after my guard shift. I needed the sleep. Unfortunately, I was awakened twice during the night by large rats running over me. The next day, I made it my mission to do more about the damn rats.

As I sipped my coffee at breakfast a plan began to form in my mind for a kind of Alpha-Alpha for rats. By afternoon, I thought I had the bugs worked out of it and set to work. I got an empty C-rat can from the mess hall and used my P38 to cut a small hole in the side of the can below the rim of the open end. Then I cut a small triangular hole in the closed bottom of the can. I then twisted the bare end of a discarded clacker wire to the rim below the open end and tied a horsehair from a sandbag to a small chunk of Spam. I passed the horsehair through the hole in the closed end of the can and tied it to a loop of bare wire positioned loosely about half an inch from the outside of the can's bottom. I was careful to position the Spam about two-thirds of the way toward the closed bottom of the can. I reasoned that this would put the bait within reach of a rat, but the closed end of the can would make the rat leery and would cause him or her to grab the Spam and try to pull it out of the open end. I lightly buried a blasting cap from a Claymore about an inch outside the open end of the can, about where a rat's belly would be when trying to pull out the bait. One wire from the blasting cap was twisted onto the wire attached to the can's open-end rim and the other to one pole of a battery. The other pole of the battery was wired to the bare loop tied to the horsehair loosely positioned just outside the closed end of the can. I put the can on its side about eighteen inches from the door to Bunker One and the battery about five feet away up against the sandbagged wall of the bunker. I buried all the connecting wires. If a rat did try to pull that Spam out the open end of the can, it would close the circuit and the cap would blow. I hoped this would result in the demise of one of the damn rats that spent their evenings frolicking over me in my bunk!

About 0300 that night, I heard a loud thud which momentarily awakened me and brought a small smile to my lips. The next morning, I found a disemboweled rat several feet away from my exploded C-rat can. I deposited the carcass in the nearest trash can and headed to breakfast. At the staff meeting, I proudly shared the news that I really had invented a better mouse or rat trap. Unfortunately, I spoke too soon. Rats are very smart, so only one other rat went to its reward in this way, and that one was just two days later. However, I must have gotten the right rats because I was never again awakened by rats running over me in my sleep!

When the LT read my new profile, he told me he wanted me to lead patrols completely around the base at least once every four or five days, "To keep the gooks honest." I told him I'd do that starting the next morning right after formation.

At mail call that morning, I received a couple of tapes from my father along with a note telling me how much the whole family had hung on every word in the tape I'd sent them. He also told me to "Stay safe," and that he missed me. The tapes were the soundtrack from "Victory at Sea," the classic World War II TV series from the early 1950s. I smiled, and my eyes might have misted a little. *"He knows how much I love that music,"* I thought.

It was a bit odd the first time I led a patrol out, but combat patrolling in hostile territory is like riding a bike, I guess. Within minutes I felt like I'd never stopped doing it. I concentrated on the area inside and just beyond the wire, looking for enemy trip wires and booby traps, and checking our clackers and trip wires. I found several of our trip flares with their wires cut and wrapped around the handles. We repaired and reset them.

I informed the LT immediately upon reentering the base. "Sir, my guess is that this was a sort of test or probe or possibly an attempt to clear a way through to reach the dump for scavenging. In other words, I don't think we're under any kind of serious or imminent threat. But I do think it's very important that we continue the patrols, increase them to every couple of days and move some of them farther out beyond the wire. We need to show the gooks that we're alert and aware of their activity."

"I agree. Do that. Increase the frequency of the patrols to two or three a week, at different times of day and on different routes."

"Will do."

The next morning the LT asked me to report what I found to the rest of the staff, which I did, and then he told them that I'd be running more patrols from then on. Once in a while, more trip wires were cut and wrapped, but nothing beyond that materialized. I had the feeling that there were only a few VC on the mountain who were not inclined to risk a major assault on the base.

After returning to the base following one of these patrols, when I took off my sweat-soaked fatigue shirt and T-shirt, I found a large, swollen leech stuck firmly on my chest. In the jungle, leeches don't live just in water as they do back in the World, they also live on wet vegetation and are more than happy to latch onto any warm-blooded creature that happens to brush by them. When I saw the leech, I sent somebody to get Doc and ask him to bring his camera.

A few minutes later he arrived and said, "What's up?"

I pointed to his camera and said, "You got any film in that thing?"

"Yep, Why?"

"See this leech?"

"It's hard to miss!" smiled Doc. "You want me to take a picture of it?"

"No, not exactly, but here's the deal. I'm sweating like a Roman mule, so when I remove this thing the anticoagulant it's injected in the wound will spread blood all over my chest. I thought I'd lean back against these sandbags here and pretend I've been shot. Can you take a picture of that for me?"

"Sure!"

With that settled I pulled the little squeeze bottle of bug juice out of the elastic band on my steel pot and squirted bug repellant on and around the leech. Within seconds, as a trace of bug juice was sucked in by the leech, it lost its appetite, released its hold and dropped off. I picked it up and threw it into the trash dump down below. What looked like a lot of blood spread rapidly downward through the sweat from the leech's suction point. When it looked sufficiently serious, I leaned backward awkwardly against the sandbags and put a blank stare on my face. "How's this?"

"That's terrific! Do that again and don't move. I'll take three or four shots and at least one is bound to come out."

"Can you get these developed?"

"Leave that to me."

The next several weeks were occupied with patrols, guard duties, police calls, hauling supplies up from the pad, spending evenings at the club, in poker games, and in the LT's quarters, and, of course, at Doc's. I never mentioned a word to anyone about my friendship with the LT.

One of the good things about the mountain was that the commissary guys burned the shit, so we didn't have to. I guess that started because the infantry guards used to rotate in and out, often without overlaps, so there were days when it didn't get burned unless the cooks did it. For that reason, it became enshrined by tradition and who was I to suggest a change?

One afternoon, yet another chopper load of visiting dignitaries arrived. It included a lieutenant colonel, a major, a spec 4, and four doughnut dollies. They were there to look around and enjoy the sights, not to lift our morale or entertain us. While at this point, any round-eyed woman would have looked damn good to me, these girls were truly pretty, filled with energy and exuding the bloom of youth. They never ventured beyond arm's length from either the colonel or the major.

I may have overreacted, but I resented the visit and especially the doughnut dollies. On several occasions my duties caused me to walk right past them. At one point the girls were posing at the berm just east of my bunker, while the Spec-4 took photos of them with the two officers using the jungle spread out 2,000' below and behind them for a backdrop. I couldn't even muster a small smile for them as I passed. In fact, I might have sneered a bit. I knew it was probably unfair to the girls to feel as I did, but it was a gut reaction. It struck me as very wrong to sight-see in a war zone, especially when it was done in an Army helicopter. Besides, I didn't like being part of the scenery along their tour. It was one of those times when I was again reminded that for way too many people, grunts were non-entities, when in my opinion we were not just the point of the spear, but the blood and guts of our country, the personification of the real war. It hit me then, that a large reason why grunts were often maligned was because we reminded non-combatants that there was a real war being fought and that real people were fighting it. That night I won fifty-three dollars in the poker game—a record.

The next evening I went to Doc's after my guard shift and he gave me a copy of the developed photo of me bleeding while leaning back on the sandbags. It looked very real. "Thanks, Doc," I said. "How'd you get it developed?"

"I sent the film to my girlfriend back in the World and told her to put a rush on it. She also sent me a letter, telling me it was wrong to take pictures of people who'd been shot like that," he smiled crookedly.

"Shit, man! I hadn't thought about anybody seeing it without an explanation."

"Me, neither. That was a mistake, but I'll correct it in my next letter to her. It wasn't the only photo on the roll, and it just never occurred to me," he said rather lamely.

"Apologize to her for me, will ya?"

"You bet."

The next evening in the LT's quarters, as we lit a third bowl of Cambodian Pale, the LT said, "Your profile's up in a week, you know?"

"I'm well aware of it."

"What are you going to do?"

"Wha'd'ya mean?"

"I mean, when the doctor asks you how you're feeling, what are you going to say?"

"I'll tell him the wound has healed pretty well, but my stride's a bit shorter than it used to be and that once in a while I feel a sharp pain there."

"That's fine as far as it goes, but listen to me! You've done your time in hell! You should exaggerate the symptoms you're feeling and stay the hell out of the field."

"But there's more to it than that."

"What are you talking about?"

"I keep thinking about my platoon and the men in my squad. It doesn't feel right that they're out there and I'm not."

"I understand, but think about what I said. We'll talk about this again."

I didn't dwell on the profile coming to an end, but the subject lurked in the back of my mind. The sense of not doing my duty and feeling like I should be out there with my men was strong. It wasn't a new feeling. I'd felt that way for the past month, maybe longer. I knew that physically I could do the job of an infantryman in the field. What I wrestled with was whether knowing that I *could* meant that I *should*.

The last two days and nights before I headed down to Buttons to see the doctor were completely routine in every way but one. Whenever I was with the LT, he gently prodded me.

"Jamie, tell the doctor whatever's necessary to get that profile extended. I don't need to tell you what's at stake."

"Sir, Hardy, I appreciate everything you've said. And I know it comes from the right place for the right reasons. But I won't know what I'm going to say to the doctor 'til I'm saying it. One thing's for sure, though. I'll leave my gear up here, so no matter what happens I'll have to come back up for it."

After breakfast the next day, I went to the staff meeting and reminded everyone that I'd be going down to Buttons. "I'll let you know what happens as soon as I know," I said, directing the comment to Top and the LT.

At the guard formation, I told the men what was up, put the newest shake 'n bake in command, and took myself off guard duty. At around 1030 I hitched a ride down the mountain in a "Loach," what we called an L.O.H. or Light Observation Helicopter. These were very small choppers with essentially a clear glass bubble surrounding a cockpit that could seat two people side-by-side. As the name implied, Loaches were mostly used for observation purposes, like directing artillery fire and spotting enemy and friendly positions on the ground. Sometimes they were used for quick little jobs like delivering sealed orders or special personnel or equipment. On this day, some special piece of classified gear had been delivered through the CO to Doc and his compatriots in the Signal Corps, so it was available to transport me to Buttons.

The ride was a thrill! The pilot lifted off the ground heading northwest and within a hundred feet or so of the edge of the pad, he angled sharply downward and we skimmed the treetops at a sixty-degree angle all the way down to the valley below. Loaches have a distinctive high-pitched whirring sound, kind of like a bee. Riding in one felt like you were riding a bee, too! It was swift and sure and amazingly maneuverable. But it was also extremely vulnerable. All that stood between the pilot and passenger and hostile fire was a Plexiglas bubble, parts of the metal framework here and there and a metal skin directly beneath the seats. A skilled pilot could reduce the danger by rapidly zigzagging and darting up and down, meaning that it took carelessness on his part or luck on the enemy's part to bring down a Loach, but it did happen.

"Thanks!" I shouted to the pilot, as we touched down at Buttons all too soon. He touched two fingers to his forehead in a friendly gesture and then buzzed off to his next assignment.

I checked in at Battalion HQ. Jay knew why I was there, but formality required me to report in anyway. Then I walked to the aid station.

"How are you feeling, Sergeant?" the doctor asked as he examined my wound.

"That's the million-dollar question," I thought. "Well, I still can't extend my right leg fully and still have off-and-on sharp pain at the wound site. But all in all, I'm feeling pretty good."

"What duties have you performed over the past month?"

"I've had command responsibility over the infantry guards on Nui Ba Ra, helped carry supplies, and led a dozen combat patrols around the base outside the wire."

"Here's the thing," he said. "Your leg may never be a hundred percent again, but it won't prevent you from doing pretty much anything you could do before. Therefore, you're fit for full duty, Sergeant."

He scribbled a note, handed me the paper, and told me to give it to the clerk. "Be careful out there, Sergeant," he admonished me.

"You can count on that, sir. I know what I'm getting myself into."

As I checked out, the clerk took my weight again; it was 152. *"That's more like it,"* I thought. I took my "cleared for duty" form and headed to the HQ.

Chapter 38 – Back to the Bush

"Well," said Jay, "what's the verdict?"

"Jeez. I wish you hadn't put it quite like that, but to answer your question, I'm fit for full duties."

"I guess that's a good thing, right?"

"As far as it goes. I mean, I didn't want to be crippled for the rest of my life. But it'll be a transition going back to humping the boonies."

"Yeah, there is that. I'll figure out how to get you back, but tonight you're stuck with us."

A little later, I lay on my bunk and stared at the metal supports on the bottom of the bunk above mine. I napped for a couple of hours, then went back to see Jay.

"Okay, here's the deal," he said. "Tomorrow, you go back up on the resupply chopper and stay for two nights."

Later, at chow, Jay, Cal, and I reminisced about when we were FNGs, but the elephant in the tent was my going back to the boonies after a three-month break. I knew they were concerned for me, but nothing would change it.

Finally, Cal said, "So how do you feel about goin' back to the bush?"

"I wondered when one of you would ask," I said. "Truthfully, I'm not sure. I mean, on the one hand I'm glad my leg's healed up, but on the other…" I turned my palms up and raised my eyebrows. "I'm not scared, but I'm damn sure aware of the dangers in a way that I wasn't before. I guess I won't really know how I feel 'til I get there. One thing's sure, Kent's been leading the squad for the past three months, and it would be wrong to make an issue of that. As far as I'm concerned, he'll stay the squad leader. Beyond that, I have absolutely no idea how I'm gonna react or how I'm gonna feel. We'll just have to see."

After chow, I didn't feel like socializing. Besides, I was assigned perimeter guard duty from midnight to 0200, so I was given a temporary place to bed down nearer the bunker. As I slept, I gradually became aware that I was feeling hotter than usual. Then I realized I was sweating more than usual, too. I opened my eyes and lay there for a minute shivering, even though I felt hot. My uniform was drenched, and I couldn't stop vibrating.

I thought it might help to walk around outside for a few minutes, but when I tried to get up, I discovered I couldn't move at all, not even to turn my head. I should have been terrified—knowing I was paralyzed—but my brain was foggy. I vaguely realized I was delirious and found it merely curious. I gave up trying to get up and drifted back to sleep again. Two hours later, I was awakened for my guard shift. My uniform was stiff with drying sweat, but otherwise I felt fine.

The next day, I grabbed a ride up the mountain and reported to the LT.

"Well?" he asked when I entered his office.

"I couldn't lie," I said.

The LT looked down at the ground with a slight wince. "Dammit, Jamie."

"I know, but I am fit for duty, and I felt I should be out there with my men," I said a little defensively. "I'll be here 'til day after tomorrow."

"All right," he said. "Well, you know my feelings about it, but I understand and respect you for it."

"Thanks. That means a lot to me. I'll figure out what to do about transferring leadership of the guards and report at tomorrow's staff meeting."

"Okay, give your orders to Top. I'll see you later tonight."

I handed Chad my "fit for duty" orders. He read them and looked up. "So you're going back to the field, huh?"

"Well, somebody's gotta fight this damn war," I said with a grin.

"I s'pose you're right. I'll get these to Top and we'll see you at the staff meeting in the morning."

"Actually, you'll see me at two more staff meetings," I clarified.

That night the LT and I smoked pot, laughing harder and louder than usual. The clouds of marijuana smoke and bug spray were thicker than usual, too. I was determined not to be down about my situation. The bottom line was that I wanted to go back to the field. But I was also going to miss Hardy Chesterton, Doc, and several others, even Top Gilbert ... and, of course, the storied mountain of Nui Ba Ra.

The next morning, it felt cooler than it had in months. The peak of the mountain was bathed in sunlight beneath a cloudless sky, but a thick layer of clouds covered everything below from horizon to horizon. The two exceptions were a high ridge in the Central Highlands many miles to the east that had never been visible before, and the peak of Nui Ba Den about 100 kilometers south. It was a mesmerizing sight. The purity of the light was magnified in the clear air by the reflection from the white cloud tops below the peak.

At 0900 I told my infantry guards the news that I was going back to the field and spent most of the remaining day with my replacement, going over all the details of the job as best I could.

"Enjoy this while you can," I told him. He looked at me askance, and I added, "Believe me, this is the best job for an infantry sergeant in this whole damn war."

That night, I won twenty-four dollars at the poker game.

Top said, "Sergeant Thompson, I can't say I'm sorry to see you leave our games, but I will miss you up here."

"I'm going to miss all of you, too." I said with feeling.

I made a quick stop at my bunker and then went to Doc's. I donated a pound or so of Cambodian Pale and eight 'cigarettes' to his stash, we laughed a lot, and I said my goodbyes.

Then I went back to the HQ and knocked lightly on the LT's door. He opened it and asked me to come in.

"Listen up!" he said in a command voice, "You damn well better live through this. You hear me?"

"Yes, sir. I'll do my damnedest. Even if we never see each other again, I consider you a friend—a good friend. And I don't say that lightly."

"I feel the same, Jamie."

Neither of us felt like smoking so we talked for a while. Just before I left, I reached into one of the deep pockets of my jungle fatigue pants and pulled out a dark green plasticized canvas bag I'd saved from a LRRP.

"This is for you," I said. "I know it's not easy for you to acquire such things—especially up here. So here's a pound of Cambodian Pale and half-a-pack each of the special 'Belairs' and 'Winstons'. Use it wisely," I smiled.

The LT was nonplussed.

"I don't smoke the stuff in the field anyway. So just take it," I said.

The next morning, I packed and went to chow, the staff meeting, and guard formation. I felt nostalgic and sad, but thoughts about the near future were beginning to supplant such feelings. A few hours later, I was winging down the mountain to Buttons.

I made sure I had all fifteen M16 magazines filled with eighteen rounds each, a Claymore and clacker, a new bar of C-4, a new bottle of bug juice, a few Cs and LRRPs, and about four gallons of water. I'd top everything off in the field when the company resupplied, just like everyone else.

The next morning, I headed to the pad and waited for the right chopper. I got aboard and settled down with my feet dangling out the open door, holding my loaded M16 across my knees. So far, it was again like riding a bicycle.

Twenty minutes later the chopper's tail dropped as it slowed on approach to a small clearing in the jungle. I could make out a few grunts here and there, but most were invisible until we touched down, when more of them emerged from the bush. I slid off, bent low, and made my way toward the perimeter.

"Well, look what the slick dragged in," said a familiar voice.

"Superman! How the hell are ya?" I said excitedly.

"I'm fine, but how are you?"

"Good enough. We'll talk later, but where's Kent?"

"Right over there." Superman motioned to a small knot of men at the edge of the clearing.

"Thanks, I'd better get the formalities out of the way."

As I neared the tree line, I saw Kent sitting on his pack. "Hey, man. How goes it?" I called to him.

"Not bad. It's good to see you," he answered.

"Yeah, it's been a while, three months to be exact."

"The in-country R&R," he said.

"Listen, man," I said just above a whisper, "I have no idea what you or the new LT and CO have discussed about this, but you've been running this squad for three months. As far as I'm concerned, it's yours. I have no issues with that at all."

"You know, we haven't really discussed it, but I appreciate you saying that. For one thing, it's a new bunch of people except for two or three guys. And besides, they're used to me—or they damn well should be by now."

"Okay, well, where do you want me?" I asked.

"Settle in. We'll talk about it in a few days, but let's get you officially onboard with the LT and the CO."

Kent took me fifty feet down the perimeter and introduced me to Lieutenant Jonah Collins and Captain Phillip Reynolds. I handed the LT my orders. He was about my height and had a pleasant demeanor. I liked him. But Captain Reynolds, the company CO, was another kettle of fish entirely. He observed the niceties, but had the cold detached persona I associated with officers who were focused on advancing their careers above all other considerations. Knowing that first impressions could be mistaken—and that I was not the world's best judge of character—I smiled and greeted them formally and politely. I determined to bury my impressions until time and familiarity revealed what kind of people they were.

Lieutenant Collins said, "Welcome, Sergeant. It's good to have you back with us."

"Thank you, sir. I'm glad to be back," I said, realizing that I meant it.

"Yes, welcome back," said Captain Reynolds. "Is Sergeant Shepard getting you squared away?"

"Yes, sir."

"All right then. We'll talk later," he said in a manner that made clear that my audience was over.

I found a spot near Kent to drop my pack and headed back to the chopper to load up on Cs and LRRPs, socks, t-shirts, jungle fatigue pants, and towels. I put together two 100-round loops of M60 ammo and went back to fill all my canteens so that I had the eleven quarts I knew I'd need.

I felt strange and didn't like it. Everything was familiar and alien at the same time. On the one hand, it felt like I'd never left the boonies. But on the other, the only familiar faces in my squad were Superman, Blaine, Riddle, Stadler, and Bauman. And Kent, of course, but he was new in the squad—at least to me. Two-thirds of the men were guys I didn't know at all. I felt isolated and alone.

Within the hour, Kent said, "Saddle up!"

Chapter 39 – Fear

I suddenly realized I wouldn't be at the front of the platoon. I hadn't thought about it until just then and wasn't sure where I should position myself. Third Platoon led out, and we fell in behind them. It felt odd to be so buried in the line, but I'd been gone a long time and the pure physical demands—the pack straps digging into my shoulders and the quick thirst I felt—kept me from dwelling on it.

Since it was a resupply day, we only humped for four hours before setting up our NDP. I set up my hooch alone.

I wanted to be alone.

I felt alone.

Two FNGs set up near me. At least they were FNGs to me. *"Hell, maybe they've been humpin' the boonies for three goddamn months,"* I thought. Anyway, I ignored them. I grabbed a LRRP and sought out Superman. "Mind if I join you?"

"Hell, no!" he said. "Tell me what you've been up to."

As I boiled water in my canteen cup, I described some of the highlights. How the generals in the rear had their own little subdivision with a driving range and Chinese restaurant. And how the barracks at Bien Hoa had air conditioning and TV. And about my stay with Steve Warner and my night with May.

Superman, always able to cut through to the important stuff, said, "Holy crap! Air conditioning? You gotta be kidding!"

"Nope. That's the straight skinny. Oh, and every two barracks share an indoor bathroom with showers, flush toilets, and real sinks."

"Jesus!" said Superman. "That gives REMF a much deeper, or should I say lower, meaning."

"True, but in all fairness, 'There, but for the grace of God go we.' Believe me, they know how lucky they are not to be grunts. And while some might look down on us as the scum of the earth, I think many feel guilty about their good fortune."

"I'm glad to hear that," Superman said quite seriously.

"How are things going out here?" I asked.

"Well, as you probably know, Kent and Woody were wounded in an ambush a while back," he said.

"Yeah, Woody's a mail clerk back in Bien Hoa now."

"He was super jittery from the day you got hit. I don't know how he held it together as long as he did. It might've had something to do with Kent, though. They're from the same part of the country and had a kind of understanding that seemed to ground Woody."

"Makes sense," I said.

"Oh," added Superman, "Stadler's the gunner now, and Bauman is still the assistant."

"I'm surprised Bauman didn't take over after Ferde got hit," I said.

"Yeah, I was, too, but he didn't want the job, and the LT thought it best not to put him in a job he really didn't want."

"So how's Stadler working out?"

"So far, so good, but he's still got a fuckin' chip on his shoulder and an attitude to boot."

"Always did," I said.

After we ate, we headed over to watch the spades game. Kent and Charlie Riddle were taking on two FNGs I didn't know.

"Who are they?" I asked.

"The skinny one with the blond hair is Corporal Seth Underwood. He's from Nebraska," said Superman.

"Corporal, huh? That's unusual for an FNG,"

"Yeah, but he did a tour in Germany before he got here. He seems to have his head screwed on straight. And the red-haired stocky kid is Hector Gonzalez from Texas, a good-hearted kid who listens."

"If I had to pick the one character trait that's essential to an FNG, listening would be it," I said.

We watched the game for a while and then wandered back toward our hooches.

"Looks like we might have to start up a second game," I said to Superman.

"Yeah, we can work on that tomorrow. The two FNGS who set up next to you play. Maybe we can educate 'em a little."

"Sounds good. Can you introduce me in the morning?"

"Will do," he said, "Now get some sleep, okay?"

"I must look like I feel, huh?" I asked.

"If by that you mean you feel like a horse that's been rode hard and put away wet, then yes. It'll take a few days to get your grunt legs back."

Later, trying to get comfortable on my air mattress, I thought, *"Thank God Superman is still here. For some reason, I don't even want to talk to anyone I don't know."* I wondered why that was.

In the morning, Superman introduced me to Len Scribner and Frank Ness. "Men, this is Sergeant Jamie Thompson, and we have a proposition for you," said Superman.

Scribner and Ness thrust out their hands.

"Glad to meet you, Sergeant."

"Pleased to know you."

A bit overeager, they were wide-eyed and deferential.

"Good to know you both," I said. "We'd like to know if you're interested in playing spades tonight with us."

"Sure thing, Sarge," said Ness.

"Absolutely," echoed Scribner.

They both had broad smiles, which I found a bit awkward.

"They had Basic together at Fort Bliss and AIT at Fort Lewis. You might say they're joined at the hip," said Superman.

"How long have you been in the Nam?" I asked.

"Three and a half weeks," said Scribner.

"Yeah, but just two weeks in the boonies," added Ness.

"It takes some getting used to," I said. "Or let me rephrase that. You never get used to it, but eventually you realize you haven't bitched about the heat or the sweat or the bugs or the vines—or even the gooks—for weeks. When that happens, you know you've arrived."

That day we had the fourth position, behind the Mortar Platoon. I could have taken the last position in the line if I'd wanted to, but I knew that bringing up the rear was vulnerable, so I stayed near the front of our platoon, near Kent.

Humping through the jungle was a surprisingly personal thing. There was no talking, beyond a few essential whispers up and down the line, so most of the time was taken up with private thoughts. About an hour into the day's hump, I was noticing the heat and sweat more than I remembered. Then it dawned on me. *Shit. I'm bored.*

Each step I took—over branches, into small puddles, over logs, around tree trunks, through curtains of vines—was in the tracks of nearly eighty men who'd stepped there before me. I'd been bored much of the time before, but this was different. I felt anonymous, more like a spot of rust on an old iron wheel than a cog in a well-oiled machine. But I was content to keep my place, my *safe* place in the formation.

I knew what I was doing. I wanted to survive and did whatever would increase my odds. At chow, I sat alone. When I finished, I sat expressionless and lit my plastic spoon, dripping flaming plastic droplets on passing ants and termites. In my peripheral vision, I saw Scribner and Ness glance furtively at me.

As the afternoon wore on, I became more and more uneasy. *I don't like myself or respect myself. Why?*

We took a break in midafternoon and Superman sat next to me. "How you doin', man?"

"Oh, I'm fine. Once your body adjusts, the rest is just repetition. One foot in front of the other, again and again and again."

"I didn't mean physically," he said under his breath.

"Oh!" I said with genuine surprise. "In that case, I really don't know yet. Something is bothering me big time, but I don't know what it is."

"Maybe the spades game will help."

"Maybe," I answered doubtfully.

After another hour or two of humping and assuring myself I was in the safest place I could be on this particular day, which I knew was as close to two-thirds of the way back from the point as possible no matter the size of the unit, the truth hit me. *I'm afraid.* A shiver ran through me that made even my sweat-soaked hair stand up, or at least feel like it did. I was never afraid before, because I refused to let myself be afraid. *My God. I can't live like this, especially knowing I might feel this way for the rest of my life.*

That evening, I went to see Kent.

"What's up?" he asked.

"We've got the point tomorrow, right?" I asked.

"Right. Why?"

"I wanna walk it," I said.

He paused, staring at me. "Really?"

"Yes," I said. "It's what I do, and I'm damn good at it."

"All right. It's all yours."

"I could use your advice on a good cover man," I said.

"Well, we're mostly FNGs now, so even though I don't like asking the experienced guys to do it, I'd recommend Riddle for now," he said.

"He'd be fine," I agreed. "But if you let me walk point whenever it's our responsibility, I'll work some of the new guys into the job."

"You got yourself a deal," said Kent.

We shook on it, and I headed back to my hooch to grab some dinner.

"What was that about?" asked Superman.

"I just volunteered to walk point from now on," I said.

"Jesus, man. Are you sure you wanna do that?"

"It's not a matter of wanting to. I have to. Remember when I told you something was bothering me, but I didn't know what it was?"

"Yeah," he said with narrowed eyes.

"Well, I figured it out. I'm scared. That's why I've been burying myself deep in the formation."

"It's understandable under the circumstances, don't ya think?"

"Yeah, but if I continue to act on that fear, it will scar me the rest of my life—much worse than the scar from that damn shrapnel. I can't live like that, man. If I don't nip it in the bud right now, it'll cripple me. And I'm not gonna let that happen!" I said, perhaps louder than I meant to.

"Well, if you're sure you know what you're doing. Let's eat up and get to playing some spades."

I got the distinct impression that Ness and Scribner were uncomfortable playing against Superman and me. I couldn't tell whether they were afraid or in awe of us. They showed some promise, but we cleaned their clocks. When we split up to head back to our hooches, they followed me like chicks after a mother hen. I sat on a log near my hooch and they gravitated to me and sat on the ground. I realized it was hero worship, though that made no sense to me. I wondered what exaggerated stories had evolved about the incident when I was wounded. I figured the best way to defuse that would be to be as friendly and accessible to them as I could.

"Listen, you two," I said, "I know this whole crazy situation is confusing and scary. That's normal. So if you have any questions, don't hesitate to ask. I don't know everything by any means, but I do know more than you do."

"Thank you, Sergeant," said Scribner.

"Likewise," said Ness.

"Listen guys, when it's just us, call me Jamie. I mean, Sergeant is okay, too, but it's not necessary unless we're in a military situation, if you get my drift."

"Yes, Sergeant," they said in unison.

"Okay," I said with a friendly squint of my eyes. "Now, remind me what your first names are."

"I'm Frank," said Ness.

"And I'm Len," said Scribner.

"Okay, Len and Frank, I know you feel like you've been cast adrift in a leaky boat with no oars, and that nobody gives a shit whether you float or drown. Sadly, most of the FNGs over here are right to think that, but your situation is different for two reasons. First, you've been thrown into the boat together. That's damned unusual. So that will help you. And second, you've landed in a good squad. We have fun when we can, but when the shit hits the fan, we strike like a coiled rattler, and we do it as one unit. We look out for each other.

"So the bottom line is this, I might look like a mean son of a bitch. But you should always feel free to ask me anything—except when things are hot. That's not the time for orders to be questioned or explained. Quick action is all that matters. Now, before we turn in for the night, I want to tell you the single most important thing to help you survive and get back to the World: watch, listen, and learn everything you can from guys who've been here longer than you have. That sounds simple, but it can be hard, especially when the guy you're trying to learn from is a mean-spirited asshole who doesn't wanna be bothered. I don't know if you've noticed, but there are a few of those types out here," I said with a grin.

They both laughed.

"Okay, let's hit the sack. By the way, thanks for the game. You'll get better at that, too."

I slept better that night. In fact, it was damn hard pulling myself off the air mattress for my guard shift. But when I awoke in the morning, I felt rested and ready. After morning chow, I talked to Emory Blaine.

"Emory, how short are you?" I asked.

"I got two months to go," he said.

"Here's the deal," I said, "Just like before I got hit, I'm gonna walk point every day our squad has it, starting today. I'll work the FNGs in as cover men, but it'll take a little time, so I'd appreciate it if you'd walk cover for me today. If you don't want to do it, I understand."

Even though Kent had recommended Charlie Riddle, Blaine had been in the squad from the beginning. He'd been walking point when I first arrived in Nam and later was my cover man. I trusted him.

"I'd be proud to," Emory said without hesitation.

"Thanks, man. I won't ask you more than once or twice more, but it means a lot to me that you'll have my back today."

"No problem, Sarge."

When I took the point and Emory walked out behind me, Kent gave me a flinty look but didn't say anything. I wondered if it was because I'd ignored his suggestion or because Blaine was black. Either way, he couldn't change it now.

At first, I was nervous and a little spooked, but in short order I found myself so concentrated on the wild world around me that all the nonsense went out the proverbial window. I saw glints of dappled sunlight striking dense vegetation to my front, and disturbed occasional clouds of mosquitos from their slumber on the undersides of leaves. There was no sound as we slid and wove through the dense undergrowth. I found it easier to breathe, easier to think, easier to be. About two hours out, I knew I'd passed one of the hardest and most important tests I'd ever face in my life. It was liberating.

The irony was not lost on me. I knew most people couldn't imagine feeling better walking point in the Vietnam War than doing literally anything else. But I already knew danger was a relative thing and now I realized that danger came in different forms, some external and some internal. The truth was I didn't care whether it was crazy or not.

Chapter 40 – Trust

Several times during the day, Emory and I compared pace counts and adjusted our direction of movement at the proper locations. That evening, we found a nice little clearing near a stream for our NDP. I thanked Emory again and set up my hooch. Superman was setting his up to one side, Scribner and Ness on the other.

"How was it up there?" Superman asked.

"The fear is gone," I said. "Or, at least the visceral incapacitating aspects are gone. Since that's the best I can reasonably expect, I'd say it went well. Having Emory walk cover helped a lot."

That evening, Superman and I sat with Len and Frank as we ate chow. As I devoured spaghetti and meatballs, I said, "I know it's kind of a tradition to complain about Army chow, but I gotta say, I've eaten a lot worse than this. Of course, damn near any LRRP is better than any C, but even the Cs will keep you fit."

"Not only that," added Superman with a grin, "but they keep your digestive tract as clean as a whistle. Especially the older Cs."

"You know," I added, "we make fun of the Army, saying things like 'there's the right way, the wrong way, and the Army way,' but the Army's smart sometimes. At home, I hear some companies are starting to put 'Use By' and 'Best By' dates on food packaging to warn people when the stuff inside might've gone up the creek. The Army's not gonna put some made-up date on its food. They'll wait until they know exactly what it should be. In the distant future, when the first grunt croaks after eating a 1950s C of scrambled eggs, they'll start stamping them with 'Use By' dates. Smart, right?"

Scribner was laughing so hard, he almost choked.

"You gonna be all right, man?" asked a concerned Superman.

When he cleared his throat, Len chokingly said, "I think so. But before I opened this meal, I saw it said packed August 12, 1957."

"That's good news," I said, "The ones we ate in NCO school were packed in 1954. It means we're getting close to using the last C-rats manufactured in the fifties."

The next day I just humped and watched Frank and Len. They were scared in the right kind of way. They watched the guys who'd survived for months, asked questions, and listened whenever anyone explained anything. Learning from the survivors wasn't easy. Few of us volunteered much information. Partly, this was because we learned how to survive mostly on our own and expected others to do the same. But it was also because we just didn't want to talk about the details of what we'd been through. It was almost as if we felt we'd lose our luck if we shared our secrets.

Most guys developed a detachment after a few months in the boonies. Some called it the thousand-yard stare. It was a stone-faced look, not without feeling, but with strong feelings buried at the core of the soul. Grunts didn't care to acknowledge this to anyone, not even themselves. This happened to all combat veterans, regardless of branch of service, MOS, duties, or unique experiences. But it was stronger in grunts who'd seen death up close and who'd been perilously close to the end of their own lives.

I felt a responsibility to teach the new guys and tried not to be cold to them. But I often failed because I got lost in my memories. I was finding that, even though I played spades every night and was always approachable to just about everyone, I preferred to hooch alone and eat alone or break alone, too.

The evening spades game was our campfire, our town hall, and our corner bar. Everyone either played or watched or hung around nearby. There was constant banter among the players, which was joined in by anyone nearby who'd been with us long enough to be accepted as one of us.

Over the next several days, I talked to Len and Frank as much as I could. They still looked at me in a way that made me uncomfortable, though. I wanted to tell them that there was nothing special about me, that all I'd ever done was my job and what anyone else in the same situations wouldn't have done. But I didn't do that because I really didn't want to talk about any of that.

One of the things I did talk about was walking cover. I explained the importance of knowing your pace count—how many normal strides it took to cover 100 meters while humping. I talked about the need to cover at least 160 degrees in sweeping arcs with your eyes, and especially to look out and up because the point man was concentrating his views closer and lower. I told them how Woody had spotted the crossbars of the hooch on the hilltop the day I was wounded. Each day, I provided them with the distances we were supposed to cover between changes in direction and compared them with the distances their pace counts indicated. In this way, they could refine their pace counts to conform with reality on the ground.

After about two weeks, which included two more turns at the point for me, I told Len and Frank I thought they were ready. "Okay, listen up. When I take the point tomorrow, Frank will walk cover behind me, Superman will follow Frank, and Len will follow Superman. Got it?"

"Got it!" they answered together.

"Great. I'm gonna tell Emory his days of walking cover are over."

I found Emory and squatted down next to him. "Thought you'd like to know that Frank's walking cover for me tomorrow."

"You sure he's ready?" asked Emory.

"Pretty sure," I said, "I've been trying to educate him and Len for the past couple of weeks, and they're as ready as they'll ever be. Besides, you're down to six weeks. It's time to start easing you back from the worst of this shit. Of course, if you wanna volunteer…"

He raised a hand palm forward toward me. "Hold up, man! Nah, I'm fine with steppin' back."

"I thought you might be, but I want you to know how much I appreciate you having my back these last few times."

I stood and walked back to the others. "Okay, let's get the game started."

Superman pulled out a pad of paper and a pencil, Len spread a poncho on the ground, and we arranged our packs around it for seats. I pulled a deck of cards out of my ammo box and began to shuffle. Another day in the Nam was coming to a close.

In the morning, I took the point, with Frank, Superman, and Len separated by gaps of three meters behind me. The rest of the platoon and company followed. Even though the company moved without a sound, it felt even quieter at the point, deathly quiet you might say. Nothing distracted me from my immediate front and flanks. I trusted Frank to be looking higher and farther out and to the sides, but I'd also asked Superman to remind him if he seemed to lose focus.

We moved along the base of a low rise to our left, which caused me to climb up it a bit to stay on our starting azimuth. The ground was slick from recent rains. Much of the rain that fell on one day would keep dripping from one canopy to the next to the next until finally dropping to the ground many hours or even a full day later.

Most of the time we were wet with sweat from the inside out and wet with raindrops from the outside in. We weren't cold, though. In fact, quite the contrary. We were walking through a sauna with eighty-pound rucksacks. After a short time in the boonies, we were only vaguely aware of these things, because even though we seldom met the enemy, we never forgot that he was out there.

My senses were finely attuned to anything not natural. I listened for the sound of cloth, leather, plastic, and metal, and I looked for the glint of anything not rock or plant. I supposed that the enemy's point men did the same thing. I'd long ago realized that strange as it might seem, those who were most like us—of all the people in the world—were our enemies. They endured the same hardships, experienced the same weather, and felt the loss of fellow soldiers who were wounded or killed.

I crossed over our trajectory's highest point on the slope and continued down to flatter terrain ahead. A tangle of roots and vines made footing unsure and the going slow, but we continued on the correct azimuth. I thought about Julie Morse back in Tucson. I was glad I'd met her and wondered if I'd ever see her again. I skirted a thick stand of bamboo to the left and reestablished my track on the other side.

Bamboo stalks were occasionally seen, but stands of them weren't common in double and triple canopy jungle. A storm—or perhaps artillery bursts—had thinned the canopy enough here to allow sunlight to penetrate deep enough for bamboo clumps to flourish, at least briefly. Luckily for us, bamboo stands were almost always separated by gaps of five to ten feet, so we could usually serpentine through without having to move too far off our azimuth. Moving around the bamboo reminded me of Gary wrapping his car around a tree. A wave of sadness washed through me.

Then I put up my hand, stopped, and whispered, "Frank, what's your distance calculation?"

Frank pulled a pad and pencil out of his pocket and did some math. "Three hundred eighty-five paces. About five hundred thirteen meters."

"Not bad," I said, "I've got four hundred fifteen paces ... five hundred meters on the nose. We'll go with my count and make our first turn onto our new azimuth. Get out your compass and point me on a line of thirty degrees." He did that and I picked out a gnarly root as my first guidepost. "Tonight, we'll check over your pace counts for the whole day and see if you need to tweak it or if this first leg was an aberration."

"Okay, Sergeant."

"All right let's move out," I whispered, motioning with my raised left hand for the company to follow.

At 1140 hours, the CO sent word up the line to stop for chow at the first decent spot we found. Twenty minutes later we entered a slightly less vegetated area, and I moved across it to the far edge, motioning for Frank and Superman to move up to either side of me and signaling for the company to break. The rest of the day went much the same. There was a light shower around 1530 hours and then it got steamy hot, but we saw no sign of the enemy, which was good.

When Frank and I looked over his pace count that evening it turned out he'd overestimated the distance by about two meters per hundred.

"That means you're taking more steps to reach a hundred meters than you thought you were. Part of that is probably because you counted too many of the extra steps we took around obstacles as full steps, and part because you take slightly shorter steps when you're up front than when you're farther back tramping in other people's footsteps. Next time adjust your pace count to seventy-seven paces per hundred meters instead of the seventy-five you've been using. We'll see how that works. You walk cover next time I'm up and then we'll give Len two times in a row."

"It's really hard to keep track of your paces when you're looking so hard at everything around you," Frank said with a concerned look.

"At first it is, but believe me, in almost no time at all it'll be automatic. It becomes almost unconscious, like breathing."

"What if it doesn't?"

"Then you won't be walking cover or point. Don't worry about it," I said. "You did just fine today."

Chapter 41 – Night Visitor; Wait a Minute

That night I fell asleep to the sound of occasional raindrops dripping on the poncho roof of my hooch. It was soothing. I wondered how Kara was doing as I drifted off to sleep.

The next day we split up into platoon-size elements and moved out on different azimuths. This was fine with me because I hadn't been able to warm up to Captain Reynolds, and he would be staying with the Mortar Platoon. Kent and I hadn't been close since our trip to Tampa when we were in NCO school together, but we got along fine. He left me alone for the most part, which was how I liked it. I still felt bad about what I'd said on that trip, but what separated us was more than that. Kent and I saw the world in very different ways. But when it came to doing what was best to keep our men alive, we were very much alike. The difference was the manner in which we led, not so much the substance of it.

Being in a platoon-size element meant First Squad had point every other day instead of every sixth day. I was fine with that, even though a little voice was saying I shouldn't be. Since I'd had point the day before, Second Squad took the point. It was an entirely uneventful day, as most were. We set up that evening in a stand of large trees with bare ground beneath them. The ground was harder than usual so it took longer to dig the guard holes. Since it was early October, the guard holes would be manned twelve hours from dusk to dawn. With fifteen riflemen in the platoon, each pulled guard for two hours, and a couple wouldn't have to pull it at all. Kent worked it out so that the men getting the night off changed every night. Little things like that meant a lot, so we were in good spirits.

The following day I took the point and had Frank walk cover again. I thought he seemed a little more nervous, so during the lunch break I asked, "Is this the first time you've patrolled in a platoon-size element?"

"Yeah, we've always been in a full company 'til today."

"Actually, that's unusual. Most of our humping is done in smaller units. In Cambodia we operated mostly in companies, but back here in the Nam it's just platoons about half the time. It can seem a little hairy at first, but there are pluses. Thirty or fewer guys make a lot less noise, and we've still got a hell of a lot of firepower. And we have the support of the Mortar Platoon, which stays in the same place. So the risks are about the same. And HQ wouldn't split us into platoons if they thought there were any NVA units in the area."

Superman took me aside. "That little talk almost made *me* feel better."

"Under the circumstances, I thought it best not to mention what we think of the intelligence we get."

"Yeah, that probably was wise. I'll never get over humping across the fucking Grand Canyon in Cambodia when our maps showed it as flat ground."

"Me either," I said. "In a few more weeks, when Frank and Len are more used to this shit, we'll fill in the blanks ... if they haven't already done that on their own by then."

"All right, men, saddle up," Lieutenant Collins said in his understated way.

I was already leaning back against my pack, so I just slipped my arms through my two M16 bandoliers, put the towel around the back of my neck, then put my arms through the pack straps, rolled to one side a bit, got on one knee and pushed myself up with hands and feet. When I was standing upright, I slipped the two 100-round belts of M60 machine gun ammo over my head and opposite shoulders crossing them over my chest. Then I grabbed my M16, looked around to make sure the rest of the men were ready, and turned in the direction of our movement. When the LT, said, "Lead out, Sergeant." I stepped out following the same azimuth as before we broke for chow.

Not for the first time, I figured one reason it was so quiet was because there was almost no animal life. I think it's likely that animals flee wars just as they flee wildfires. *"Damn sensible of them,"* I thought as I stepped across a small, crystal clear stream, *"but also a damn shame."* There was the occasional animal, of course, like that incident near the DMZ a year or two earlier when a Marine grunt was pulled out of a foxhole by a tiger, dragged a dozen meters or so and then dropped. But the most common warm-blooded critters were the soldiers on both sides and rats.

About 1400 I saw what appeared to be disturbed ground about ten meters to my left front. I raised a hand to halt the platoon and told Frank to bring Kent and the LT to the point. When they arrived, I pointed to the disturbed area and whispered, "This isn't a free-fire zone, so we'll have to check this out the old-fashioned way." The LT agreed and told me to move back a bit, then up the hill to our left and approach the disturbed place from above. That's what I would have suggested, so I liked it.

We swept around the place in question, finding no enemy, but there was a hole cut in the hill that clearly served as a guard hole or observation post over the terrain below, but which was partly covered by a bamboo mat and leaf litter. We carefully checked out the mat and, once we were sure it hadn't been boobytrapped, folded it back. Inside we found several items wrapped in palm fronds and cloth. There was a compass, a small pair of binoculars, a couple of cans of food, and a wool OD GI long-sleeved shirt. But the most interesting thing was an M1 carbine. It was wrapped in an oiled cloth and mostly clean, but smears of cosmoline grease were still present here and there. A clip and fifteen rounds of ammunition was wrapped up with it. We wiped off the rifle a bit and found it to be in perfect working order. All of us really liked that carbine. It was compact and felt good in the hand. We decided based on the wool shirt and the M1 that this stuff had made its way here from Korea, but of course we couldn't know that for sure. If we hadn't been in a war zone, I'd have thought the place was a hunting blind, but that wasn't something we could assume. So following a thorough check of the surrounding area without finding anything else of interest, we packed up our find from the mini cache and returned to our azimuth.

That night we had a really good spades game. Frank and Len damn near beat Superman and me. It seemed the two FNGs who adopted me were going to be just fine. I fell asleep the minute my head hit the poncho liner and I didn't have guard 'til 0430, so I was looking forward to a good long rest.

A few hours later I woke with a start from a deep sleep when something stabbed me in the palm of my left hand. I fumbled for my lighter and lit it inside my hooch just in time to see a dark, medium-size scorpion slowly walking away. In my sleep, I'd inadvertently pushed my left hand outside under the mosquito net.

The pain was intense, worse than stepping on a rusty nail, something I'd done several times during childhood adventures. But this was different in an interesting way, the pain didn't subside quickly as it had when the nail was removed, instead it burned like a hot iron and intensified. I thought about waking the medic, but then decided to tough it out. I lit a cigarette to calm my nerves, cupping it even inside the hooch. Over the next ten minutes, the effects of the sting spread. The thumb half of my hand, from the gap between my index and middle fingers down to the crease between the two pads of my palm at the wrist was burning and yet insensitive to touch. I was getting pretty concerned about it but decided to wait a little longer. After another ten minutes the pain and numbness had lessened a bit and I felt that the rest would soon dissipate. Within a few minutes, I was asleep again. At 0430 when I went to the guard hole, my hand was perfectly fine.

At morning chow, I mentioned my midnight visitor to Superman and the FNGs who were a little creeped out about it, and ended by saying, "Fuck it! Just another night in the Nam, boys. It don't mean *nothin'*!" We all smiled and laughed.

The next day we kept moving in roughly the same direction we'd been going for the past week. It dawned on me that we were paralleling the Cambodian border. I suppose the idea was to keep the NVA honest by creating a blocking force between their supply routes in Cambodia and the interior of

South Vietnam. So far, it seemed that enemy activity had been significantly lessened by the Cambodian Incursion, but it was early days.

The important thing was we weren't finding signs of the enemy and weren't making contact. For grunts, that was what mattered. But for officers who wanted to make names for themselves in what might be their last chance at a combat tour, it was not good news. This became clear to me from the orders Captain Reynolds began sending. He wanted each platoon to send out a small patrol every day to scout areas up to a klick to one side or the other of our route of travel. This put men at added risk. It also took time, but we were expected to cover just as much distance as before. To do this we shortened our lunch break and cut out our other breaks. Morale suffered, but I doubt anyone was saying that to Captain Reynolds.

For the next week, we kept this up and did exactly what we were ordered to do. We muttered among ourselves, but no one made a big deal out of it. One day, however, I was ordered to take most of the squad, including the chunker and the gun, a thousand meters to the southwest. Our objective was to reach a stream and check for signs of enemy activity for a short distance along it. Our topo map showed normal vegetation and relatively flat terrain. It looked easy enough: dense jungle interspersed with patches of lighter vegetation.

All was well until we came to an area of wait-a-minute vines, so-named for their habit of stopping a walking man in his tracks when one or more of the catclaw-like thorns penetrated clothing, skin, and sometimes deeper layers of flesh. This forced a man to extricate the thorns before moving forward.

We had run into the vines before, but only in short stretches or clumps. What stretched across our azimuth now was completely different. In front of us was an impenetrable mat of tangled wait-a-minute vines. We had less than three hours remaining to reach the stream 600 meters ahead and return to the platoon. We searched for a way around the vines fifty meters to our left and fifty meters to the right. There was no edge in either direction.

"Okay, boys," I said, "What we have here is probably a streak where Agent Orange was sprayed. The goddamn wait-a-minute vines are sometimes the first thing to come back. Since there's no way around, we have to go through. How many of you have machetes?" I counted three.

"All right. Let's get cutting." I saw a place where the edge of the mat seemed a little thinner and said, "I'll go first."

I slid my machete out of its sheath and started hacking. It was early afternoon and the air was as hot as ever. The humidity and closeness of the unmoving air was nearly unbearable. I had expected to cut a path through the tangle, but the tangle of vines was fifteen feet high, so I was cutting a tunnel seven feet high. I couldn't cheat by cutting the vines only at ground level, because the cut vines were held up by others to the sides and above. It was necessary to cut from the top down in order to make progress. And then we were walking on a foot-thick mat of chopped vines. Luckily, our jungle boots were tough enough to prevent the thorns from penetrating except through the vent/drain holes, but even these kept the thorns far enough away that they couldn't hurt our feet. Our hands, arms, faces, chests, and backs weren't so fortunate. We were soon sliced, punctured and bloodied pretty thoroughly.

When I'd cut about seven meters, sweat was running down my body and I was gassed. At eight meters, I backed out and let the next man move to the front. Swinging a machete in such a confined space made it unsafe for more than one man to cut at the front. Two others, spaced two meters apart, cleaned up the roof and sides of the tunnel, but that was about all they could do. The farther in we got, the hotter and more unbearable the conditions became. An hour and a half after starting the tunnel, we'd cut our way thirty meters in. I called a halt and told everyone to turn around and get out.

"Here's the deal," I said. "It's still a good five hundred meters to the stream. There's no end to the vines that we can see, and we only have an hour and a half to reach our objective and make it back to the platoon. We're also making more noise than normal with all this hacking, and that puts us at higher risk. So we're not going to the stream. If anyone who outranks me asks specifically if we reached the stream, I'll tell them we didn't. But if no one asks, I won't volunteer the information. Do we understand each other?"

Four exhausted grunts looked at me and nodded (five, if I'd had a mirror). We were dripping with sweat and bleeding from countless cuts, tears and punctures.

"All right, follow me."

I moved ten meters southwest of the route we'd taken to get there and paralleled it to return. It was never smart to use the same path you'd gone out on. We rejoined the platoon a few minutes past our expected arrival time, looking as done in as we felt.

"What the hell happened to you?" asked Kent.

"We had a run-in with the briar patch from hell," I said.

"Any sign of enemy activity?" he asked.

"Not a one," I answered truthfully.

That night, after a shorter than usual game of spades, I slept the sleep of the righteous. Every man on that patrol did.

Chapter 42 – The Ears; The Vase; Dehydration

The next morning we got word that the Mortar Platoon had killed two VC. Our guys had no casualties, which was good. None of the other platoons made any contact, so we rejoined the Mortar Platoon to start operating as a company shortly thereafter.

I noted that Mortar Platoon Sergeant SFC Throckmorton was wearing two bloody human ears strung on a bootlace around his neck. Two of the other grunts each wore one ear in the same way. I've never had much of a poker face, except when actually playing poker, and couldn't keep the disgust from showing as I walked past.

Superman and I heard all about the incident while playing spades with the mortar grunts that night. Most of the mortar grunts were like us and had no use for weird macho shit. It seems that the two gooks hadn't had a clue our guys were there. The perimeter guards heard them carrying on a conversation well before they came into sight. When they appeared, our guys opened up, and the gooks were killed instantly. When the firing stopped, Captain Reynolds ran out and arrived in time to see Throckmorton cutting off the gooks' ears with his machete. Two other grunts kicked out some of the dead gooks' teeth, which were now being carried around in the pockets of half a dozen guys who accepted them as souvenirs.

"Jesus! What did the CO do?" I asked.

"Nothing!" said PFC Haskins, one of the grunts who'd been talking to us. "Some of our guys just went fuckin' nuts. It was scary."

Later we compared notes with Frank and Len, who had played spades against a couple of the other guys from Mortar Platoon.

"The mortar guys are pretty shook up," said Len.

"Yeah," added Frank, "but I think it's because of how berserk some of their guys went, not because of the contact itself."

"They're scared they might lose control themselves someday," I said. "But guys, it will never happen to us. Never!" I was adamant. I remembered how I'd gone over the edge during Survival, Escape and Evasion training at Fort Ord. The specifics of that incident I kept to myself, but not what I learned from it: namely, that when leadership is poor, men can let their worst instincts wash away the thin veneer that makes us decent civilized human beings. I was no longer willing to give Captain Reynolds any benefit of the doubt.

The next day we were resupplied. I was glad for more than the usual reasons. My fatigues were shredded, and I was quite low on water. As I finished my hot chow, I got word that the LT wanted to see me.

"You've been in Nam for over six months and you're eligible for R&R," he said, handing me a form. "Fill that out ASAP and I'll send it in with this chopper."

I hadn't even thought about R&R. The form had my name and serial number and a list of R&R destinations. The list included Honolulu, Sydney, Bangkok, Hong Kong, Manila, Tokyo, and a few other places in the Orient. I was half afraid if I went to Hawaii I'd grab a flight home and never come back, so I rejected that destination right away. That narrowed my preferences to Hong Kong, Bangkok, and Sydney. English was spoken in Australia and Hong Kong, and I'd heard that in Bangkok guys got laid every night. My first choice would be Sydney. If I couldn't go there, I'd rather just get laid every night, so I made Bangkok my second choice and gave the form back to the LT.

After that, I took one of my sodas to the block of ice the chopper had brought out and rolled the dickens out of it. Shortly after I savored the last cold sip, we saddled up and moved out. I felt better in clean fatigues and a bit cooler after the soda. But both those sensations went away after the first hundred meters.

Late that afternoon, as we slowly followed a short stretch of foot path, where the trail made a sharp turn to the right I noticed something two or three meters off the trail that was obscured by vegetation. I parted the branches and saw that it was a large pottery vase. It was a little over a meter tall and was about half a meter wide at the widest bulge. It had two handles on opposite sides positioned where the narrow neck joined the body. I don't know why, but I pulled it out onto the trail, turned it upside down to empty a small amount of leaf litter, water and mud out of it and slung it over my left shoulder as we continued to move. That evening I stood it up next to my hooch, scraped the bottom with a long stick and shook a little more crud out of it. It was just a plain reddish-yellowish-brown vase with a few squiggles on the upper part of the bulge, but it was elegant looking and in perfect shape, with no cracks or chips. It was different and pretty. I liked looking at it.

I wondered who'd made it, when and where. Was it old? How did it get way out here in the middle of the wilderness? Who had brought it here? What was it for? I hoped it didn't have any religious significance, because I didn't want to disrespect something like that. No one pressed me about the vase, which was good because I didn't really have an answer.

The vase weighed at least thirty pounds, but I didn't care. At that point, it didn't seem there was any longer an upper limit to how much I could carry. I carried it with me for three days, but when it was my turn to walk point, I had to leave it behind. I found a sheltered spot inside our NDP near the base of a large tree with level ground and some obscuring vegetation and stood it up there. I felt much as I had as a child when releasing a small captured animal back to nature; I felt some regret, but knew it was the right thing to do.

It was particularly hot over the next couple of days—so hot that we talked about it, and that was unusual. By the evening of the second day, we were all running low on water. It sometimes happened that a few FNGs would run low, and the rest of us shared our water with them. But this was different. We'd been so hot that everyone was down to the dregs. When I hit the sack that night, I had three-fourths of a quart left.

In the morning, no one made coffee or hydrated freeze-dried LRRPs. Most of us didn't even brush our teeth. There was little talking that morning. We all knew the water situation was critical; a lot of guys had no water left at all. Luckily, I had a can of peaches from a C. I extracted the wedges and ate them one at a time. Then I sipped the juice, very slowly.

Third Platoon had the point and we followed, setting off to a place that was supposed to be a good LZ about 1,600 meters away. When we reached it around noon, only twenty guys had any water. No one had more than a quart. I was down to a quarter of a canteen and feeling strange.

The so-called LZ was an area that had been defoliated a few years earlier. It was large, a rough oval about 150 meters long with absolutely no shade. But the worst thing was that broken tree trunks poked up everywhere. We had to cut down enough of these standing dead trees to allow a chopper to land. The CO and the LTs instructed the sergeants to use only those men who were in the best condition. The rest of the company pulled out ponchos and tried to tie them between standing dead trees and fallen logs to create patches of shade. When the clearing was completed—not our best work and barely adequate—we all tried to find shade.

It was a losing proposition. The ponchos created only tiny spots of shade large enough for one or two men, and even they weren't completely shaded. With a very slight breeze, the air was no cooler in the shade than in direct sun. As time dragged on, one man suddenly started ranting incoherently. Several friends held him down and tried to calm him, but he was delirious. Within twenty minutes, several others had similar reactions. A couple of them began wandering aimlessly, and two or three jumped up and started running. One guy stood up and said he was going to see his girlfriend.

It was frightening. The only other time I'd experienced dehydration was on the twelve-mile bivouac march in Basic, but this was different. In Basic over-exertion and single-digit humidity were large contributors to the problem, but now the problem was the result of more than 24 hours of little to no water and stifling humidity. Just as in Basic, concentrating became very difficult. My vision clouded. I didn't want to talk or swallow because I was afraid my throat was so dry it would stick shut and be impossible to open an airway. But maybe because I'd had that experience in New Mexico, I was able to handle this episode of dehydration better than that earlier one.

The heat was like a red-hot hammer beating on us. The chopper was late. There was nothing more we could do. I'm sure I wasn't the only man who wondered if this was it—the day we were going to die.

Then, in the distance, we heard a slick. I gathered as many canteens from my squad as I could carry and took the last sip from mine. Then I shut down. The chopper seemed to approach in slow motion, but eventually someone popped a smoke grenade and the chopper managed to find a place to land.

I don't know how we did it, but Superman and I were among the four or five who made it to the helicopter and pulled a clear water bladder off onto the ground. We cut a hole in the top and I took a long drink directly from the fountaining water before filling the canteens. Most of the men could no longer move, and we had to take water to them. I threw two canteens to my squad and then took four more to the medics, who had gathered the worst of the delirious guys together. I was reacting, not thinking.

As soon as men were able to drink and rehydrate, they came out to help. It took half an hour for most of us to feel fairly normal, at which time the resupply proceeded in a more standard manner. The CO requested a medevac bird, which landed in the LZ. Its medic and several from the company checked the worst cases of heat stroke and dehydration, handing out salt pills, the only ones I ever saw in the Nam, and cooling the men with wet packs of various kinds. In the end, three men were medevacked.

In the NDP that night, we didn't talk much about it, but I'd bet not one of us ever took water for granted again.

Chapter 43 – FSB Snuffy; The Fifty

Three days later we were pulled into Fire Support Base Snuffy to stand down. Aircraft of all types, transporting men and materiel, were constantly landing and taking off, making the firebase quite a busy place. Adding to the activity, flights of slicks—sometimes two or three abreast—often sprayed the surrounding jungle for mosquitoes, or at least we hoped they were spraying for mosquitoes, since the dangers of Agent Orange were already beginning to be talked about.

Snuffy had been the base of field operations for the battalion since its pullout from Cambodia. Jerry Pickering was there with the field HQ. I looked him up, and we shot the shit. I asked him if my impression was correct that things had cooled down considerably, thanks to Cambodia.

"As near as anyone can tell," he said, "we captured or destroyed at least a year's supply of food, weapons, and ammo. So yes."

"What happened to all the weapons and ammo?"

"Most of it is being transferred to the Cambodian military," he said.

"There's a Cambodian military?" I said with surprise. "I suppose that's good."

"Well, in theory it's good, but it's not clear how stable the government is," said Pickering.

"I hope it makes it. I feel bad about those Montagnards."

"Me, too. When the helicopters pulled out the last of the troops from Neal, the Montagnards sent a delegation and begged us to take the whole village with us, including the elephant. Of course, we couldn't do it. It was awful."

The next evening, I walked along the berm, just taking in the sights. I spotted a large machine gun in one of the guard positions and wandered over to take a closer look.

"What is that?" I asked the grunt who was cleaning it.

"It's a fifty-caliber machine gun," said the grunt.

"I've never seen one in a guard position. Can I take a look?"

"Sure. It is a bit unusual. The rumor is that it's against the Geneva Convention to deliberately use fifty cal armor-piercing rounds against personnel, but I can't vouch for the truth of that. I'm Tom Aiken by the way," he said extending his hand.

"Jamie Thompson," I replied. "First Platoon, Charlie Company."

"I'm with Bravo Company," he said. "Pleased to meet you."

"So how'd you get this gig?"

"I got wounded in Cambodia. They put me here while I'm healing up."

"Well then, we have something in common," I said. "I got wounded there, too. I've only been back in the field for about three weeks, after three months on profile."

"Hey, if you wanna fire this baby, show up for the first Mad Minute tonight and have at it."

The first Mad Minute was relatively early that night, at 2327 hours, so I went to Tom's guard position around 2300. We talked a few minutes about home; he was from a small town in Ohio.

Then he said, "Where'd you get hit, if you don't mind my asking?"

"I don't mind. I got hit with shrapnel on the inside of my right thigh. They tell me it was close to the femoral artery. I didn't even know I'd been hit 'til after we'd swept across the hilltop. It was weird. How about you?"

"I was hit in the right side by an AK round. It tore me up pretty bad and broke a rib, so I've got about three weeks to go on my fourth thirty-day profile. But I was lucky; the two guys with me were killed."

"Jesus, man. You were lucky."

"What was it like when you went back to the field?"

"It was different," I said, pausing for a few seconds. "You obviously know this shit is dangerous before you even get in-country, but it was kind of an intellectual knowing and not a visceral thing. You know what I mean?"

"I think so," he said.

"Well anyway, when I rejoined my squad, I felt different. It took me a day to figure it out, but then I realized I was scared. I knew if I couldn't get past it right away, I might feel like that the rest of my life. I couldn't stand the thought of that."

"What did you do?"

I told my squad leader I wanted to walk point every day we had it."

Tom looked at me strangely.

"See, when I was squad leader, I always walked it and got good at it. I figured I needed the focus and constant adrenaline rush to steady my nerves."

"What happened?"

"I won't lie to you. The first hour I was scared. But then it began to feel like I'd never left the field. And I just sort of settled down. I've been fine ever since. Or let me put that a different way, I *feel* fine. Sometimes I have flashes of wondering if I just don't give a shit anymore, but I push that out of my mind and just keep on goin'. I mean, fuck it; it don't mean nothin', right?"

"If that's what works for you, it's just fine," he said. "I have no idea how I'll feel. But I appreciate your honesty."

"No hay problema!" as they say along the border. "You ready to check out the treat I brought?"

"Sure, man! Let's fire it up." He said with a smile.

We smoked a filtered Cambodian Red 'Belair,' first. After a few tokes, Tom said, "Holy crap, man! That's some good shit!"

"That it is. It's Cambodian Red and it gives a strong high, but it'll be mostly worn off before the Mad Minute," I assured him.

"Let's hope it's not completely worn off 'cause this beast fires some wicked tracer rounds!" Tom said with a grin.

Before the Mad Minute started, Tom showed me the basics of how to load and fire the .50 cal. It was pretty straightforward. You loaded the belt into the top of the breech and shut a trap door down on it, then pulled a lever all the way back and released it to load the first round. Every fifth round was a red tracer. The rounds themselves were twice as wide and twice as long as M16 ammo. It truly was a beast.

When the Mad Minute started, Tom pushed down the lever at the back of the breech with both thumbs and a hellish red stream poured into the tree line. It was difficult to imagine anything withstanding that kind of force. I could hear the tree trunks shattering as the fire pounded into them.

"Here, you try it," said Tom. I positioned myself and lowered the barrel to point at the tree line. Pushing down with my thumbs, I made long slow sweeps back and forth until the Mad Minute ended.

"That was amazing, man! The power is unbelievable."

"I know," he said. "I figure this is the safest position on the perimeter."

"There's little doubt about that. I mean, even though this would obviously be a position the gooks would target, you'd tear 'em up before they could get the range."

"That's the plan," he said, smiling.

We spent the next hour laughing and talking. We had a lot in common and some similar experiences that we didn't care to share with many other people.

The next morning, First Platoon had the shit-burning detail. On a base like Snuffy, it took damn near the whole platoon about an hour and a half. Superman and I tried to stay upwind from the thick noxious smoke, using broom handles to stir burning diesel fuel, shit, piss, toilet paper, and whatever else had been thrown into the half-55-gallon drums under the shitters.

I said, "I know we're supposed to have an attitude of 'ours not to reason why, ours but to do or die' about whatever the Army asks us to do, but there are times—like now for instance—when I wonder what kind of message the Army is trying to send when it has the men who're actually doing the fighting burn the shit of the REMFs who aren't."

Superman was concentrating hard at using his broom handle to keep a large chunk of something solid at the surface so it would burn better. Eventually, he glanced over at me. "Hell, Jamie, the Army's not trying to send any message at all. It just wants its shit burned. And in fairness, we are burning our own shit, too."

"There is that!" I said with a laugh.

An hour after the last of the shit-smoke had wafted over the berm, Steve Warner showed up.

I was very glad to see him. We had lunch together and I told him about Tom Aiken and his .50 cal. He wanted to meet him, and I told him I'd arrange it for that night.

He also asked me if I knew about early outs to go back to college. I told him I'd heard something about 'em, but didn't know any details and doubted I'd qualify anyway. "Well, here's the deal," Steve explained, "if you had less than one year left on your active duty military commitment when you arrived in Nam, you can get discharged up to three months early to go back to college. I think you should look into it." I promised him I would.

Around 2330 hours, Steve and I walked over to Tom's bunker and I introduced them. As I thought they would, they hit it off right away. Steve figured he wouldn't be hitting any people if he fired the .50 during the Mad Minute, so he bent his no weapons rule this once. The Mad Minute was at 0019 hours, but it was 0030 before Steve could wipe the smile off his face.

"My God! This thing is awesome!" Steve exclaimed.

"That it is," said Tom. "An M16 slug weighs about a third of an ounce and leaves the barrel at a little over 3,000 feet per second. This baby fires slugs weighing about 1.2 ounces at a little under 3,000 feet per second. The bottom line is that what you hit with it goes down!"

"I believe that!" said Steve. "You can hear the wood shattering and exploding when the rounds hit. It's incredible!"

In the once-again quiet of the night, we shared another number, this time it was a rolled joint of Cambodian Pale, which was definitely my personal favorite. For a few moments, we were quiet and into our own thoughts.

"You know, it's strange how even here I can sometimes feel so at peace when I'm in the company of good people I like."

"I was thinking much the same thing myself," said Tom.

"I wasn't thinking at all," put in Steve.

At that, Tom and I laughed, and Steve joined in.

Charlie Company was on Snuffy for the next five days, during which Lieutenant Collins gave me an update on my R&R.

"Boy that was a quick turnaround," I said.

"Yeah, these do tend to get processed pretty fast for officers and NCOs. You've been approved for Bangkok from November first to the eighth."

"Not my first choice, but I'll take it. By the way, is there something I can look at to see if I'm eligible for an early out to go back to school?"

He told me there was, and a few minutes later he came back and handed me a flyer with the skinny on early outs for school. Thanks to the delay in processing through Oakland Army Base, I'd arrived in Vietnam exactly two days into the last year of my military commitment. I met the first requirement, but I also had to be accepted for admission—or readmission in good academic standing—at the college of my choice. This was a problem, since the whole reason I was here in the first place was my academic suspension by the University of Arizona. My sister Julie was attending the U. of A. now and might be able to look into the problem for me, which gave me a glimmer of hope.

Chapter 44 – River Crossing; Kit Carson Scout

When Charlie Company went back to the field, Steve came along even though Captain Reynolds made it clear he wasn't in favor of it. This made me wonder even more about the CO. It was good for morale to have someone along who could act as a conduit to the World, someone who would tell our story like it really was. I'm pretty sure this never dawned on Captain Reynolds, though I noted that the ears were no longer on open display.

When I had the point, Steve would sometimes take the fourth position in line. He didn't carry a weapon so that was as far forward as he was allowed. He had guts. After a few days in the field, I talked to him about it.

"Steve, we all appreciate the job you're doing; I appreciate it. But you're taking some huge risks. Are you sure you want to keep doing that?"

"It's not a matter of wanting to. My job is to report on the war and the men fighting it, and that's what I'm going to do. Besides, what you're doing is a hell of lot riskier than anything I'm doing."

"Maybe," I answered, "but this is my job, and like you I'm going to do it. It's just that my head's in a different place now. I'm not sure I can explain it, but on some level I've decided to let the chips fall where they may. It's not that I don't give a shit, but that I've resigned myself to doing whatever needs to be done and not worrying about it or over-thinking it. I do wonder sometimes if that means I've gone nuts, but whether it does or doesn't, that's how I feel."

Steve hesitated. "To a slightly lesser degree, I feel the same way. I don't mean this as false bravado, but it's almost as though inside my head, I'm saying to the jungle and its bugs and critters and heat and humidity and rain and gooks, 'Bring it on, motherfuckers!'"

"That's it!" I said. "Now that we've settled that, let's go play some spades."

"You got a deal… so to speak."

Two days later, just before Steve went in on the resupply chopper, I told him I'd do my best to see him in a few weeks when I passed through for R&R.

"What're the dates again?" he asked.

"November first to eighth, so add a few days on either side to be safe."

"Okay, I'll do my best to be there."

We exchanged waves and he was gone. I went back to the perimeter, saddled up, and took my place in line as the company moved out. I didn't have the point that day, so I'd just be plodding along like everyone else. *"I hate humpin' the boonies even more when I'm not on point,"* I thought with a mental grunt.

Maybe I grunted out loud, because Superman glanced over. "What's the matter?"

"What? Oh, nothing really, I'm just bored. Some days the endless humping feels worse than others, I guess."

"You mean the days when you're not walking point?"

"Am I that transparent?"

"Yep. When you're not playing cards."

We moved about ten meters beyond the LZ and the jungle closed in. We stopped talking, bent forward under our loads, and trudged on in silence.

Just before lunch the next day our azimuth brought us to the west bank of a jungle river. I believe it was the Song Dak Huyt (pronounced "soong doc wheat") or Dak Huyt River. The river drains the southwestern flank of Vietnam's Central Highlands and the southeastern slopes of Cambodia's Sankambeng Range. Much of the year it meanders rather benignly through dense jungle, with many turns and loops, in a generally southwesterly direction, eventually joining the Song Be about thirty kilometers or eighteen miles northwest of Nui Ba Ra. It forms the border between Cambodia and Vietnam for most of its length, but our location was nearly ten klicks inside Vietnam.

The Monsoon Season was beginning. Rainfall where we'd been operating, on the jungle floor, had been intermittent thus far, but when we reached the Dak Huyt we realized that the mountains must have been getting much more rain. What we faced was a raging torrent at least 150 meters wide and of unknown depth. Captain Reynolds decided that we could cross it by forming a human chain, linked arm-in-arm. The idea wasn't a bad one in concept. In fact, this was how Spencer Tracy as Major Robert Rogers led his men across a river in the 1940 classic movie "Northwest Passage." However, the river crossed in the movie was about 100 feet wide and, well, it was a movie.

The expressions on our faces when the plan was presented to us are difficult to describe. Generally, they ranged from abject disbelief and horror, through the classic deer-in-the-headlights-of-a-Peterbilt, to narrow-eyed skepticism, with a few fuck-it-it-don't-mean-nothin's thrown in. The CO decided that it was best to send the largest men out first, reasoning that their height and weight could anchor the center of the human chain while others pushed past them to the far side and began to pull the rest of us across.

It turned out—not surprisingly to the skeptics among us, including me—that even the biggest men couldn't stand upright in the current as they neared the center third of the river. I assumed they'd reached what was normally the riverbank, because the depth quickly dropped off there and exceeded their heights. Luckily, the men immediately behind them did not lose their grip and were able to pull the two or three who were swept off their feet to the relative safety of shallower water. Captain Reynolds ordered two more attempts before conceding we couldn't cross the river on foot.

We moved back into the trees and called for helicopters. It took until the following morning to get it organized, but that day we made what may have been the shortest combat assault of the Vietnam War, a distance of less than two klicks to the nearest suitable LZ across the river. No one complained, though.

On this operation, we had our favorite Kit Carson scout with us. We called him Sam, which was certainly not his name. He was rumored to be fifty-four years old, though no one knew for sure and you couldn't tell by looking at him whether he was forty-something or seventy-something. He had a wiry build, deeply wrinkled face, and thick fingers. But his feet were his most remarkable physical feature. Sam had never worn shoes of any kind. The bottoms of his feet, including his toes, were calloused to a thickness of about an inch and were as tough and impervious to punctures, cuts, and abrasions as any combat boot. There was something likable about Sam. He could only speak a few essential words of English and he never smiled. But he was always friendly, helpful when asked a specific question, and reliable when sent out alone. Sam could go home to his village whenever he wanted, which he did quite often. In fact, he was only with us about a third of the time. I wondered how strange it would be to live a normal life and fight a war within days or hours of each other, over and over again.

Two days after our river-crossing CA, I had the point and Sam was the second man behind me. Suddenly the normal underbrush thinned and almost disappeared. I knew we were entering a large camp, and it wasn't one of ours. I held up my hand and passed the word back to the LT and the CO. They decided we should move on through. When we had gone a ways, I turned to Sam and whispered, "VC or NVA?"

"NVA," he whispered back.

I made a low sweep of my hand to indicate the camp area. "How many?"

He looked at me and whispered earnestly, "Beaucoup, beaucoup."

This confirmed my thoughts. As we passed through the camp, I picked up a few empty cigarette packs—which appeared to be Chinese—and a C-ration can, passing them back to the LT. Finding such things was not normal. The NVA never left traces like that unburied. It meant they'd left in a hurry and not long before we arrived. We spent twenty minutes investigating the entire camp area. We saw no enemy and made no contact, but determined, based on its size and the number of guard positions, that an NVA force of four to five hundred men had used it within the last two days. Discarded items we found had not been rained on, and it had rained two nights earlier. I guessed that our CA had alerted them and they were ordered to avoid contact, which was fortunate for us.

We moved about two klicks farther along and set up our NDP in an area of large trees on uneven terrain.

The next day we were resupplied near the same location. This was notable for one reason. It was the only time I ever saw a chaplain in the field. I stayed away from the service providing perimeter security, but I could hear a little of what the chaplain said. It made me uncomfortable, as I found discussions about the need to make sacrifices for the greater good and accepting God's will to be counterproductive in a war zone. The chaplain's sermon almost instilled a feeling of impending doom. I wondered if our discovery of a large NVA camp had made the brass think we were about to hit some very bad shit and that it might be a good idea to send in a padre to prepare us for the great beyond.

Superman didn't attend the service, either.

That evening over chow, I said, "I know the chaplain is probably a good man, but I was glad to see him leave. I just don't see how religion has a damn thing to do with fighting a war."

"It's had a lot to do with starting a bunch of 'em," Superman said. "But I agree. Back in the World, religion has its place, but this ungodly shit-storm is a whole other deal."

The next two days were unremarkable and gave me the opportunity to write letters to Julie Morse and George Keahey in Tucson, and to my parents in Illinois. I also wrote a letter to my sister Julie, asking her to send me an application for readmission and a catalogue for the second semester. I briefly explained the situation regarding a possible early out.

At some point we came upon a small hamlet or more likely the abandoned homestead of a family of slash-and-burn subsistence farmers. Weeds and grass covered two or three acres that had been cleared of trees. The main hooch was in good repair and there were several smaller hooches nearby that had probably served as storage sheds. The remnants of several older hooches were moldering away and being reabsorbed by the jungle. There were no personal items in the hooches, which lent credence to my belief that the place had been abandoned, perhaps for a year or more.

However, since it could provide shelter to the enemy, the CO ordered us to burn the hooches. Like urinating on the rice cache four months earlier this felt wrong, though we understood the reasoning for doing it.

Burning proved much more difficult than we'd imagined. It was late October and the monsoon season was ramping up. The grass and palm fronds were wet from rain and couldn't dry out in the extreme humidity. Since we didn't carry gasoline or diesel fuel with us, a few guys sprinkled lighter fluid and pieces of C-4 on the roof of the main hooch. Eventually, we were able to partially burn the hooches and stomp over what remained. The smoke was thick and acrid.

I thought of the effort a struggling family had expended to build these structures. The utter destructiveness of war is sickening. In the moment, though, I sucked it up, thinking, *"Fuck it; it don't mean nothin'."*

Chaplain in the field.
(photo 44-1)

Chapter 45 – The Waiting Room

That evening, I gave myself an upper body sponge bath using a bar of soap and half a quart of my precious drinking water. In the process, I absently scratched a little itch on the outside of my left upper arm, near some vaccination scars. To my surprise, the flesh was so soft and gooey it came off under my fingernail. I figured it was a spot of jungle rot, so I soaped the spot a second time, dried it off, and gave it no more thought.

Two days later, when I scratched the same spot, a lot more gooey flesh came out of a neat round hole about the size of a soda straw and a quarter-inch deep. When I hit the sack that night, I opened my first aid kit and put some mercurochrome on it. The next evening it was a little deeper. That's when I went to Henry Jacobs.

"Doc, could you take a look at something for me?"

"Sure, what's up?" he asked.

"That's what I'm hoping you can tell me," I said, rolling up my sleeve.

"Hmm," he muttered. He squeezed the area gently and pus came out. "I'm gonna clean this out, sterilize and bandage it. We'll take another look at it tomorrow."

"What do you think it is, Doc?"

"It's infected for sure, but I've never seen anything like it," he said. "It could've started with a poke from a stick or something, or maybe an insect bite, or some damn jungle fungus. But I gotta be honest; I really don't know."

He removed a scalpel from a sterile packet and scraped down a good half inch, running the sharp edge of the blade around the interior periphery. I felt nothing at all beyond the touch of his hand on my arm and the blade turning in the hole.

"That's damn peculiar," Doc said mostly to himself. "There's no bleeding, and you aren't feeling any pain."

"It does feel a tiny bit numb, now that you mention it," I responded. "Say, while you're at it, could you take a look at my right elbow?"

"Jesus, what's wrong with that?"

"It's puffed up a little," I said.

Doc finished putting disinfectant and a bandage on my upper left arm and lifted up my right arm to look at the elbow.

"Shit, man. A little puffed up, my ass! How long has it been like this?" He touched the sack of fluid hanging from my elbow.

"I'm not sure. Maybe a week, but it wasn't so noticeable then," I said defensively.

"Okay, well, all I can do for this is wrap it tight and see if the swelling goes down. It's probably what they call tennis elbow. It happens when the lining that holds the fluid around the elbow joint gets a tear that causes the fluid to leak out. Usually, compression will allow it to heal, but out here, who the hell knows?"

"Thanks, Doc," I said.

"Is there anything *else* wrong with you?" He asked with a squint.

"Not as far as I know, and this stuff isn't much. I mean, fuck it; it don't mean nothin', right?"

"Right!" he said sarcastically. "I'll see you tomorrow evening."

Over the next four days, Doc Jacobs changed the wrap on my right elbow and cleaned and dressed the hole in my left arm every night. Neither showed any improvement, and the upper arm hole worried Doc.

"Look," he said, "I'm running out of sterile blades and I'm down to an inch deep now. But what really worries me is this." He pointed to the red lines radiating from the hole. It looked like those radiating streams of electrical current flowing out from a Tesla coil. "That likely indicates blood poisoning. If it reaches your heart, it won't be good. I might have to send you in."

I looked down. "It's still got at least two inches to go. Besides, I'm heading in for R&R in two days. I don't want you to do anything to jeopardize that."

"All right, but I'm not happy about it. I'm giving you a note. When you go in, you *will* report to the aid station at Buttons. You got that?"

"Yes, *Corporal*, I've got it."

My use of his rank didn't escape his notice. "Listen. When it comes to things medical, *Sergeant*, I outrank you. Have you got that?"

"Yes, I've got it, Doc."

"All right, just try not to fuck yourself up even more over the next couple of days, and we'll stick with this plan."

Two days later, I headed in on the resupply chopper and turned my gear in to Jay at 5/7 Battalion Headquarters.

"And now I understand you're to report to the aid station," he said with more gravity than he usually used in dealing with me.

"Jesus!" I said, "Doc Jacobs really doesn't trust me to get myself examined, does he?"

"I think we both know the answer to that," Jay said.

"Fine. I'll head over there right now."

When I got to the table inside the aid station, I handed the clerk my note from Doc Jacobs.

"Have a seat over there," he said, pointing to a make-shift bench. "Someone will be out to get you in a few minutes."

Half an hour later, I muttered, "Some things never change."

"What was that?" asked the clerk.

"Oh, sorry, I was just thinking about the fact that long waits in doctors' offices are normal everywhere."

"Hmm," he said without further comment.

A few minutes later a doctor I hadn't seen before came out to escort me deeper into the tent.

After a thorough exam, he said, "I'm giving you a penicillin shot for the shoulder injury, but I want you to stop off at the 93rd Evac Hospital in Long Binh on your way to Tan Son Nhut to have the fluid drained from that elbow. If these things haven't improved by the time you get back, stop here to see me again."

He wrote out an order and cautioned me to take my malaria pills while I was in Bangkok. I thanked him and returned to the HQ.

"How'd it go?" Jay asked.

"All right," I said, handing him the slip the doctor had given me.

"Okay, we'll modify your travel orders to include a visit to the 93rd Evac, and you'll be all set. Stop by first thing in the morning."

At chow that evening I told Jay, "Sorry I'm not being very sociable. For some reason, I just feel like I haven't got anything to say. Maybe it's too much alertness and staring into the bush or something."

"Hey, don't worry about it, man. I'm surprised it's taken you this long to revert."

"Revert?"

"Oh, it's just my own term for it, but I mean when a guy kinda loses the cloak of civilization and goes completely grunt."

"Jesus. You think I'm turning into a Neanderthal or something?"

"No, man, it's just natural. It happens to almost everybody who spends months on end in the boonies. Some guys go completely bonkers and begin to enjoy killing people; others just stop talking. Most are somewhere in between, which is where I'd put you. Hell, I'm no psychologist, but from what I've seen, the smarter a guy is and the more education he's got, the less likely he is to go totally over the edge. But damn near everybody gets closer to that edge than he ever thought possible before becoming a ground pounder in the Nam."

I stared through the screening of the mess hall into the dust of Buttons. "You're right. Somewhere along the line, sweating and straining under an eighty-pound pack from dawn to dusk, having every night's sleep interrupted by guard duty, carrying an automatic weapon everywhere, seeing people die, getting wounded—it all seems routine and normal."

"Yep, and what's more you hardly say more than a few words about it, even to each other. And when you're not in the field with others with the same experiences, you say even less. I mean, how could anyone who hasn't lived it possibly understand it, want to hear about it, or even care?"

"Jay, you're a philosopher. You should write a book when you get back to the World."

"Who knows, maybe I will. But I doubt it. I probably won't ever want to think about this shit again."

In the morning, I picked up my revised orders. An hour later, I gave them to a Spec-4 behind the counter at the Bien Hoa terminal. He tore off two sheets—one concerning the 93rd Evac and the other R&R—and returned the rest to me along with directions.

I found the right bus and after a short ride the driver announced the hospital. There were many single-story rectangular buildings with rounded roofs, but eventually I found the one I was looking for, OUTPATIENT AND EMERGENCY. I walked in and was told to go to the end of the hall and take a seat in the waiting room until my name was called. It was like clinics and small hospitals in the States except that it was in a long, narrow one-story frame building, though I suspected it was connected to lots of others.

I entered the waiting room and sat along the east wall of the small room. There were about twenty chairs arranged along the east, north and west walls. The entry door was located in the middle of the south wall. Across from me, sat a Vietnamese woman holding an infant with her five-year-old little boy seated on her left. To my right, at the back of the room, sat a young ARVN (Vietnamese Army) Lieutenant. No one smiled or spoke. For one thing we spoke different languages, but for another the small space we shared seemed to emphasize just how profoundly different our two cultures really were. There was a magazine rack with American magazines in it, but none of us took one. We simply sat there silently, trying not to make eye contact with one another. To my Western eye, the expressions on the faces of my Vietnamese fellow patients seemed dour.

A small oscillating fan on a low table near the door provided just enough air movement to prevent sweat from beading on us, but it was still stuffy and borderline claustrophobic in the waiting room. Other than the purr of the fan motor and a whisper as its blades sliced through the air, the silence in the entire building was profound. The minutes dragged on. I'm sure all of us were hot, bored, uncomfortable, and eager to get on with our days.

Suddenly, a hodgepodge of high-pitched voices pierced the silence. It seemed to be coming from the entrance at the far end of the hall, so we all ignored it at first. But the intensity and loudness increased dramatically as the source moved closer and closer to us. It became clear that it was overlapping Vietnamese voices, spoken insistently and fearfully. By now the Lieutenant and I were looking toward the open door of the waiting room. From my position, I couldn't see what was going on out there, but he could, and he also must have understood some of the words. He stood and walked into the hallway; I followed. The woman with the children looked concerned, but stayed put with them.

When I stepped into the hall, I saw a doctor and two nurses rolling a kind of canvas cot apparatus toward us. In it I could see small arms and legs flailing about. Then I saw it clearly. The rolling cot had two small children in it. By their small size, I guessed they were about six or seven. Their combined weight caused the canvas they were lying on to depress in the center forming a trough. The children were both covered in blood and bleeding so much that a puddle of blood had formed in the bottom of the gurney. As they continued to flail in abject terror, drops of blood splashed or were flung into the air, some of which landed on the arms and uniforms of the doctor and nurses. The doctor was trying to calm them, but they clearly couldn't understand him, which terrified them even more.

I could imagine the mindless fear they must be experiencing being badly hurt and then being shunted around by giants whose language they couldn't understand for reasons they couldn't imagine. The Lieutenant walked to the doctor and quickly told him in English, that he might be able to help calm them by talking to them. The doctor said, "Please, go ahead!"

The Lieutenant leaned over the gurney and spoke calmly and reassuringly to the children. I couldn't understand the Vietnamese words, but gradually the children stopped screaming and looked at him with wide, thankful eyes. The doctor explained what he needed the children to do and the Lieutenant translated. By this time, they had rolled the gurney into an X-ray room located in the east side of the building just outside the waiting room door. The door to the room was left open. The doctor thought quickly and told the nurses that the best way to X-ray the children was not to separate them and place them on the usual X-ray table, but because they were so small to leave them together in the pool of blood on the gurney and X-ray them both at the same time. He asked the Lieutenant to tell the children not to move for a short time. He did that and the children did their very best to comply. The gurney was positioned under the X-ray emitter, which could slide left, right, forward, back, and up and down. The doctor wasted no time in setting everything up and taking the X-rays.

From what I overheard it seems the children had been playing together in a field and were injured by an explosion. I don't believe it was due to a current attack, but rather to some unexploded ordnance, perhaps a land mine, an artillery round, a rocket, or a grenade. When things had calmed down a bit and the children understood that the American giants were helping them, I returned to my seat in the waiting room. Soon, the Vietnamese Lieutenant also retook his seat. I seethed inside about what had happened to these innocent children and wondered whether the explosive device was ours or the enemy's. Then, it hit me, *"It doesn't matter! The fucking war itself is the true enemy."*

I looked over at the Lieutenant and gave a slight nod. No words were spoken, but we understood each other. He'd done good. We were soldiers and expected to experience injury and death, but children should never experience it... *never*.

A few minutes later, the Lieutenant was called for his appointment and a little later the woman and her children were escorted to theirs. Shortly after that, I was called for mine.

A doctor briefly examined, cleaned and redressed the strange infection in my left upper arm and approved of the penicillin shot and how the infection looked. "We'll leave that alone. I suspect it'll heal up now without any more intervention. So let's look at that right elbow."

He removed the wrapping to see a bag of skin hanging below the elbow like a small water-filled balloon. He gently squeezed it. "You've definitely torn the sack covering your elbow joint. I'm going to drain it and wrap it tightly. If the fluid is clear, it should heal and be fine in a week or so, but if it's cloudy, you may need long-term antibiotic treatment as well."

After removing the fluid with a large syringe, he said, "It's clear so you should be good. Make sure you keep it clean, and rewrap it every few days. Understood, Sergeant?"

"Yes, Sir. I'll do it."

"All right, let me gather up what you need, and I'll send you on your way."

Within just a few minutes I was standing outside the building waiting for the bus. It felt good to have both of my little medical problems properly handled, at least for the moment.

I decided to stop by Steve's barracks and hope he was in, so when the bus neared what looked right, I got off and luckily found Steve's building. He was in and was glad to see me. I explained that I only had a few minutes and then had to head to Camp Alpha for R&R processing. He said, "Okay, let's take a walk, I've got some news to share."

The way he said it made me apprehensive. We walked to his favorite spot overlooking the swale and he said, "Have you heard about Tom Aiken?"

"No, not a thing."

"He's in the 93rd Evac in Intensive Care."

"Jesus! What happened?"

"A day after he rejoined his unit in the field, he was sent a little way down a trail as a flanker as his unit crossed it. For reasons known only to him, he turned his M16 around, used his thumb to press the trigger and fired a burst on full auto into his gut."

"Oh, my God!" I said.

"Yeah. I guess the stress of being sent back to the field after what he went through the last time was more than he could handle."

"Jesus, Steve. I mean who can blame him. Who knows why *all* of us don't go nuts out there? It's a mystery to me. I've often wondered how we continue to function at all in combat, let alone function well. So what happens next?"

"The Army, in its wisdom wants to court martial him and dishonorably discharge him."

"That would be wrong! Don't they know what he's been through?"

"I'm sure they do, but they don't seem to care. But believe me, I'm doing everything I can to stop that from happening. I know some of the brass and lots of their clerks. I won't leave a stone unturned or a favor unasked!"

"I know you won't Steve, and thanks." I glanced at my watch. "Damnit, I've got to get going. The next time you see Tom, please give him my best and tell him he's got friends!"

"I will."

After another short bus ride, I entered a rather nondescript building with signs that said 90TH REPLACEMENT BATTALION, 178TH REPLACEMENT COMPANY, R&R PROCESSING CENTER, CAMP ALPHA. I joined the short line and handed my orders to a clerk who told me where and how to purchase civilian clothing for the trip.

As I turned to leave, he said, "Sergeant, I mean no offense, but you have to get your hair cut. They won't let you on the plane with your hair and moustache that long. There's a good Vietnamese barbershop on the base."

I found the barbershop and went in to get my mandatory haircut. I wasn't happy because I'd been carefully nurturing my moustache and was quite proud of its length. One of the barbers motioned me to his chair, and the haircut proceeded normally until the last step.

The barber may have asked if I wanted it done, but if I answered yes, I either hadn't understood him or was unclear about the full implications. He tilted the chair back until it was nearly horizontal. Then he took the straight razor and slowly inserted the blade between individual hairs in my lower right eyelash, turning it with a minute flick of the wrist to scrape away any sand or sweat or other detritus lodged there. I was on my back with the sharp edge of a straight razor descending to within a few millimeters of my eyeballs. Suddenly, the barber's Asian features seemed more sinister than inscrutable. I was concerned.

The barber's expression never changed, but he knew I was completely at his mercy. Could the two of us complete this task safely on his part and unflinchingly on mine? It seemed to take a long time for both sets of eyelashes. Amazingly, when it was over, no blood leaked from my eyelids, and no urine or feces soaked my underwear. As I rose from the chair, the barber showed me the barest suggestion of a smile, which I returned along with a generous tip.

I browsed the civvies at the PX and purchased shirts, slacks, a light sweater, undershirts, jockey shorts, and a bundle of mixed-color socks. I also purchased two cartons of real Winston cigarettes for $1.70 each and a canvas carrying bag to put everything in. Back at the R&R center, I exchanged my jungle fatigues for khakis to wear on the plane.

Chapter 46 – Down Under

The terminal at Tan Son Nhut Air Base teemed with hundreds of milling GIs staring at the overhead boards with flight destinations and departure times. As I waited for the boarding of the Bangkok plane, I heard my name called out over the PA.

"Sergeant Jamie Thompson, please report to the ticket counter where you dropped off your orders. Sergeant Thompson report to the ticket counter."

I made my way through the crowd to the counter, sure that some screw-up was sending me back to the field. "I'm Sergeant Thompson. I was called to report here?"

"Yes, Sergeant, your R&R application had Sydney as your first choice, correct?"

"Yes," I responded with uncertainty.

"We have a no-show for the Sydney flight leaving in ten minutes. If you still want to go, you can fill that slot."

I hurried away with my revised orders and a lilt in my step. I really hadn't wanted to take R&R in an Asian country. I wanted a place that reminded me of home without being home.

The flight took off around 1930. Five and a half hours later, the plane refueled in Darwin, Australia. After that I dozed until sunrise, when I began staring out the window eager to see a place I might never see again.

Darwin is on the north coast on the Timor Sea and Sydney is on the east coast on the South Pacific Ocean, so we were crossing the Australian continent diagonally from northwest to southeast at about 30,000'. The flight from Darwin to Sydney was nearly 2,000 miles mostly over desert, only the first few hundred, which we overflew in the dark, and the last couple of hundred as we neared the Pacific coast were significantly vegetated. While it wouldn't be everyone's cup of tea, I found the view fascinating. It was what Australian's call the Outback, which is most of the country really. It's dry and very sparsely populated. Nearly all the people live in narrow bands along the better watered sections of coastline. I'd expected it to look a lot like the American Southwest, an area I knew well, but it didn't. It was certainly sandy, rocky, and rough in places, but it lacked high mountains. I saw lines and bands of minerals that were different in color from the predominant reddish hue. Of course, other places in the world have such features, but I'd never seen them run virtually unbroken for tens of miles. "It looks like the world below was just made!" I said to the Spec-4 seated next to me.

"What?" he said looking up from the Life magazine he'd been reading. "Oh! Yeah, I guess it does," he agreed as he craned over me to look for himself. But then he went back to his reading, and I went back to my staring out the window. I wouldn't want to live in most of the Outback because I'd miss water, trees and mountains too much, but I certainly appreciate the unique natural wonder it is.

As the four and a quarter hour transcontinental flight neared its end in Sydney, the land below gradually began to green up. It wasn't much at first, but as we neared the city, we crossed over a range of mountains similar in size and appearance to the Coast Ranges in California. We disembarked into pleasantly cool weather with a softness to the air that reminded me of the sea borne breezes of Monterey and Fort Ord. Sydney sits at the same position south of the equator that Manhattan Beach, California (basically L.A.), does north of it.

Waiting buses took us to the R&R Center in downtown Sydney. Other than the traffic driving on the wrong side of the road, the city looked like any modern city in the United States. That was what I'd hoped for, and I was happy about it.

It was after 9:00 a.m. when we arrived at the R&R Center, where a fellow in a suit gave us a brief orientation. And then I was on my own for a week, until I returned to the center and went back to the war. It was November 1, 1970, spring in the Southern Hemisphere.

I looked through brochures and decided the King's Cross Rex Hotel looked good, so I caught a cab and booked a nice room on the third floor. The first thing I did was fill the bathtub. After a thorough wash and a twenty-minute soak, I stepped from the tub. As the water drained, a red ring remained. I cleaned it off and took a second bath, leaving a second red ring. After the third bath, the ring was light pink, so I decided that would do for now.

Clean at last, or clean enough, I watched TV for a while and browsed the hotel's information. It was nearing dinner time before I knew it, so I was pleased to see there was a restaurant in the hotel. I called down and made a reservation for 6:30. I thought of calling my parents, but it would have been the middle of the night there. I figured it would be better to call long after dinner so it would be morning in Illinois.

I dressed in clothes I hoped would be appropriate—a white shirt with subtle blue stripes and some dark slacks. The hotel was almost a self-contained village and I had no problem finding some shops. I purchased some Cokes, then returned to my room and turned on the television again to watch the evening news. It was disorienting to see so many similarities to American life that were not American at all.

At 6:15 I headed for the restaurant. It was dimly lit, with a wood dance floor that was fringed on the outer edges by tables and then with cushioned booths against the walls. I was escorted to a table at the edge of the dance floor. I studied the menu and decided on filet mignon, again.

A few minutes after I arrived, two young couples were escorted to a table about eight feet from mine. The girls were quite attractive, especially the one who sat with her back to me. At first, they engaged in friendly light banter as they shared a bottle of chilled wine, but then the conversation became louder and uncivil. It was becoming an annoying distraction, when to my astonishment, the girl I'd admired most was backhanded on the cheek by her date or husband so hard that her chair tipped over and she fell onto the dancefloor. I was shocked. Never in my life had I seen a woman treated like that in the United States. The girl picked herself up, straightened her dress, picked up her chair, slid it back in place and sat in it again as if nothing had happened. Every face in the now crowded restaurant was turned toward them, but no one said a word. Then the two couples continued their conversation as though all was as it should be, which maybe it was from their point of view.

When I finished my steak, I ordered the Chocolate Mousse and a cup of coffee with cream. The waiter asked, "Are you sure you want cream, sir?"

I looked at him strangely, wondering why he would ask such a thing. "Yes, real cream, please."

A few minutes later, the items arrived. The cream was delivered in a white porcelain creamer with a silver spoon standing straight up in it. It was so thick it had the consistency of butter. I now understood why the waiter had asked me what he did, but I behaved as though this was precisely what I expected and added two heaping spoons full of cream. This made for one of the best cups of coffee I've ever had in my life.

I was about half-way through my first cup when there was a light tap on my shoulder. I turned to see, just inches in front of me, the face of a young Aborigine woman. I was taken aback by this because her appearance was so unusual. I'd never seen an Aborigine person in real life before this. To my American eye, her face looked as though you had taken a Black American woman's face and broadened it considerably. I hope my surprise didn't show on my face.

She addressed me in a very pleasant, typical Australian accent, "Would you like to dance?"

I politely declined, saying, "No, but thank you for asking, though."

She said, "Are you sure? It would be fun."

I told her, quite truthfully, "I'm not a good dancer. Never have been. I'm sorry. But again, I appreciate your asking me."

She smiled brightly, and said, "All right, then," and rejoined the three White Australians, two men and a woman, in her party.

As I finished my first cup of coffee and drank a second, I noted that she was a very good dancer. I would have embarrassed myself, and her, badly had I attempted to dance with her. But I was still internally embarrassed at my initial reaction.

I charged the meal to my room and retreated to watch TV, but I was so tired I couldn't keep my eyes open. It was my first night in Sydney, Australia, and I was asleep by 10:00 p.m.

Following the best uninterrupted sleep I'd had in seven months, I awoke the next morning, determined to see some of the countryside and the city.

When I went out the entrance of the hotel, there weren't any taxis visible, so I lit a cigarette and just watched the people as they passed on the sidewalk. It was moderately busy, and I was impressed by how attractive most of them were and how nice they seemed. After a few minutes one of the hotel bell captains stepped out for a smoke, too, and we chatted for a while. He was in his early twenties with black hair and a slim build and had some kind of European accent.

"Where are you from originally," I asked.

"Bulgaria," he answered. "I came here four years ago for better opportunities."

"How do you like it?"

"I love it," he said with a smile. "At first, I had trouble meeting girls, but then I had an idea. Shortly after I started working here, I was so desperate to be with a woman, that I felt I had nothing to lose. So one day I came out here, right where I'm standing now, and every time a pretty girl walked by, I asked, "'Do you want to fuck?' or, 'Would you like to fuck?"

"My God! You really said that?" I asked incredulously.

"Yes!"

"What happened?" He had my full attention now.

"Sometimes a girl would act like she hadn't heard me. Other times, they'd tell me to 'fuck off.' But about one out of every three to five, would say 'Yes,' or 'Sure,' and off we'd go to my room or hers.

I said, "You've got to be kidding!"

"No! It's the truth! I was surprised, too," he said. "I did this during lunch time when the girls had a bit of free time, and I guess many of them were as much in need of sex as I was."

"That's quite a story, my friend," I said. "Did you do that back in Bulgaria, too?"

"Oh, no, my mother would have killed me if she'd found out," he said. "Besides, I do not think Bulgarian girls would be so easy."

With that, we introduced ourselves, his name was Rumen Nedkov, finished our cigarettes and went our separate ways. He went back into the hotel and I grabbed a cab as it pulled into the taxi parking zone. I'm sure he was exaggerating about his success rate, but still I had to admire my Bulgarian friend's guts! I would never have considered such a thing. *"I guess you just never know until you try,"* I thought sliding onto the back seat of the cab.

"Where to, mate?" the driver asked.

"That's a good question. How about taking me to the Australian Museum? I'd like to learn as much as I can about your country in the few days I'm going to be here."

"I can do that," he said, pulling away from the curb.

"Say, if I wanted to go out to the mountains what would it cost?"

"Depends on where you want to go, mate, but you can hire a taxi for half a day for twenty-five dollars or a whole day for forty."

"So ... would you be interested in hiring out for the day to ferry me around the countryside and educate me about Australia?"

"Well, I can't do it today, but I could meet you at the Rex tomorrow at 9:00 a.m." He handed me his business card. "Call me if there's a change in plan."

I took a moment to read his card. "Thank you … Ronald Townsend. I'm Jamie Thompson."

In a few minutes we pulled up in front of an imposing marble building built in the classical Greek style, with columns adorning its main entrance. As I paid Ronald I said, "Can you come back and pick me up in about two hours?"

"Sure, mate. I'll meet you here as close to noon as I can manage." He nodded and touched his right eyebrow with his index finger before he drove away.

I found the museum impressive and enjoyed browsing around. There were groups of children everywhere, all of whom were wearing school uniforms. It struck me as quaint, but strangely all right.

There are no hummingbirds in Australia, something I didn't know before this, so there was a fair-sized area devoted to them as unfamiliar curiosities. It included numerous stuffed hummingbirds displayed in various states, from perched, to hover, of course, that being their claim to fame. A large map purporting to show their ranges was in error as it indicated that no hummingbirds were found north of roughly the Mason-Dixon line and Ohio River in the eastern half of the United States. Since hummingbirds were common in summer to and beyond the Canadian border, this struck me as an odd and rather inexcusable mistake. It would have been very easy to check but, obviously, no one had.

I walked past the disappointing map to the windows at the north end of the building. The view was over what appeared to be a series of parks, or perhaps one large park, to Sydney Harbour. At the water's edge was the architecturally distinctive Opera House, which was under construction.

Near noon, I made my way back to the entrance, where I stopped to mention the problem with the hummingbird map to an employee there. When I emerged from the rather dark museum into the bright spring day, Ronald was sitting on the marble steps waiting for me. He stood when he saw me and said, "Where to now, mate?"

"I think just back to the hotel. I'm still pretty tired, and an afternoon of lounging around and napping is probably a good idea."

"What about tonight?" Ron asked.

"I thought I'd check out some local night spots. Any suggestions?"

"Well, you have to visit Texas Tavern and Whisky A-Go-Go or none of your mates will believe you were really here. They're within walking distance of the hotel and you can get directions at the front desk."

At the hotel, I headed up to my room. As soon as I closed the door behind me, I stripped down to my underwear and sprawled on the couch. Then I remembered to call home. It was evening in Illinois.

At the end of the call my father said, "You be careful, son. We miss you." My father seldom expressed such feelings in spoken words, so these struck deep.

"I will," I promised. Then I got my sisters' phone numbers, saying I might try to call them, too.

Immediately after hanging up, I dialed my sister in Tucson. It was a dorm, so Julie had to come down to the front desk to take the call. When she picked up, she was happy to hear from me.

"Is it really you?" she asked.

"None other," I said.

"What's up? How are you?"

"I'm good. I wanted to touch base and to ask whether you got my letter about the early out."

"Yes, and I already mailed you the application and the catalog."

"Wow. That's wonderful. Can I ask another favor? I'm pretty sure I'm still on academic probation, so there's a fellow I'd like you to meet with, if you can—an assistant dean of liberal arts. I took an independent study course from him a few years ago and he might be able to look into the probation problem for me."

"Okay," she said.

"I'll send you my application and class choices along with a letter to Dean Howard, asking if he can get me off probation and placed back in good standing. I think if you could hand deliver them to him, it would help. You have a way with people, Julie; they like you."

"I'm glad you think so. I'm not always so sure about that."

"I'm sure. Listen, I know this is a big inconvenience for you, but I can't tell you how much I'd appreciate it. Can you do it?"

"Of course, I'll do it," she said with exasperation in her voice. "You're my brother and I love you."

I knew she meant that, which made my eyes water. "I love you, too, Julie."

We talked about her life in Tucson and what Sydney was like for a few minutes before hanging up. After a good nap, I took another tub bath, leaving a barely noticeable ring. I donned slacks and a black turtleneck. One last self-exam in front of the mirror and I was off to see the sights.

At the desk, I asked for directions to the Texas Tavern. It was only a few blocks away, and the night was pleasantly cool. The Texas Tavern had all the elements of an R&R hot spot: loud music, a dance floor, good bartenders, and lots of girls and GIs milling around. But somehow it missed, at least from my perspective. I had one scotch and water and left.

At the Whisky A-Go-Go, there was a long line waiting to get in, which I took to be a good sign. At the entrance, I was carded. I was likely one of the oldest GIs in the place, but I wasn't surprised; without my handlebar moustache I often had my ID checked. The place had go-go girls in caged platforms along the walls. I've never been that hip when it comes to things musical—especially when dance was added to the mix—but I was under the impression that go-go had shot its wad several years before. I knew it was still around, but I didn't think it was still the "in" thing it had been. Be that as it may, the place was swinging. I spent an hour or two drinking scotch and making small talk with some of the local gals.

After I got a buzz on, I even danced a few times. But I just wasn't into a club scene. Truth be told, I'd always preferred quieter bars where you could hear your date and yourself talk.

I gradually worked my way back toward the entrance and when I neared it, I approached the bouncer. "I'm curious, are you an American?"

"Yes, from Grand Rapids, Michigan."

"How'd you end up working here?"

"It was a mistake," he said without hesitation.

"Wha'd'ya mean?"

"I came here on R&R, fell for a local girl and loved the place. When I was discharged in the States, I came back, but things just weren't the same, either with the girl or the place. It's hard to find work here if you're not Australian and I'd go home if I could, but I can't afford it. So, I'm trapped here, and I really don't like that."

"I'm sorry to hear that," I said, feeling a bit down after listening to his story. "Eventually, you should be able to buy a ticket home though, right?"

"Maybe, but the pay isn't great here and the living expenses are pretty high, so it'll be a few years, if I can do it at all. I tell you, man, it's the worst mistake I ever made. So, take it from me, enjoy your R&R and put this place out of your mind after you leave."

"Thanks for the advice, and good luck!" I said, as I exited.

The night was still young, but I was done for the evening. I slowly walked back to the hotel. The night air was wonderful. It retained the softness that's found in proximity to an ocean or a large lake. It caressed the skin and imparted a sense of wellness and rightness that I hadn't felt much lately. I soaked it in as I meandered, trying not to look too long at the occasional couples sharing embraces and kisses. To my eye, Sydney was a beautiful and wonderful city, but it wasn't home.

I was back in my room before midnight.

* * *

Precisely at 9:00 a.m. the next morning, Ron pulled up to the hotel. "Since you've hired me for the day, you can sit up front if you like, mate. Have you thought about where you want to go?"

"If it's not too far, I'd like to see some unpopulated country, preferably with some mountain scenery. Is that possible?"

"Sure thing, mate. Leave it to me. We'll drive to the Blue Mountains. I think you'll like that."

It took a while to weave our way out of the center of town, but eventually we were on the main drag out of the city to the west. The city thinned and slipped out of view behind us. We began a curvy rather gentle climb into forested hills, studded with occasional small towns. As we drove through the towns, my eyes were drawn to the local young women more than to the scenery.

"Ronald, you have some beautiful women in your country, you know that?" I tried not to strain my neck as I kept my eyes on a curvaceous gal around twenty.

The towns reminded me of small towns in Utah: well kept, everything in good repair and freshly painted, lawns neatly mowed. I felt generalized nostalgia mixed with an aura of unreality, as though they were a façade created just for me.

The terrain changed from rolling hills to mountains reminiscent of the Appalachians, where you sometimes didn't realize you'd driven up a mountain until a break in the trees revealed a valley hundreds of feet below.

We parked in front of a small restaurant called The Lookout and Ronald said, "Follow me. I think you'll want to see this."

We walked about a hundred and fifty meters and the world dropped away. An interpretive sign said this was Echo Point Lookout and a brass plaque commemorated a visit there by Queen Elizabeth II and Prince Philip in February 1954. It was quite pretty, but my ability to appreciate such things was strangely jaded at the time. The canyon bore a superficial resemblance, on a much smaller scale, to a place where I'd deer hunted once just below the Mogollon Rim in Arizona; from before sunrise, I'd waited for hours for a buck to come into view, but none ever did. I drank in the natural surroundings, the first I'd seen in seven months that held no enemies.

"Ronald, is every tree in Australia some variety of Eucalyptus?" I asked, waving my arm to take in the vast expanse of forest spread out before us. "Because it sure looks like it."

He chuckled, "No, mate. Though I can see why you might think that. We have a few conifers in some spots near the coasts, and palms in the north and elsewhere near the ocean including here in Sydney, but eucalypts of various kinds definitely do dominate the continent."

"I mean that's fine, but I'm not used to looking over a natural forest like this and not seeing lots of different species of trees mixed together," I said. "Sometimes pine forests can look a little like a monoculture, but even most of them are interspersed with several varieties of conifers and smatterings of birch, aspen, and other deciduous trees. It's strange to me, but I'm sure I'd adjust if I had the time to do it."

After gazing at the view for about fifteen minutes, we walked back to the restaurant. There was nothing fancy about it, but it had a unique feature: the center of the floor, where most of the tables and chairs were located, slowly rotated in a clockwise direction! This afforded every table a view of the canyon's edge beyond the parking lot. Of course, I wanted to try this experience, so we took a table on the rotating floor. We were among less than a half dozen customers at the time. It was a Tuesday, so few people were free to take long country drives. We both ordered fish and chips and while we waited, I checked out the jukebox. To my surprise, it had "I Remember You" by Frank Ifield on it! I always loved that song but hadn't heard it in a long time. I played it three times in a row. The other customers didn't seem to notice... or didn't mind.

"I haven't heard this played for close to five years," I told Ronald.

"I'm surprised, mate," he said. "I hear it played on the radio fairly frequently. I like it, too!"

"Well, Ifield is English and maybe your connection to Britain being closer than ours explains it," I suggested.

"Maybe," said a very dubious Ronald, "but frankly, I don't think our 'connection' as you put it is all that much closer."

"I defer to you on that, I'm just glad it was on the jukebox!"

When we returned to Sydney, I asked Ron if he knew of a quieter watering hole than the Texas Tavern or Whisky A-Go-Go.

"You might try the Sydney RSL Club."

"What's an RSL club?" I asked.

"Returned Servicemen's League, where veterans can shoot the breeze in a friendly environment. There's a pretty nice bar I'm told, though I haven't seen it myself. If I take you there before nine tonight, it's included in your daily hire," he added.

"Okay, can you pick me up in front of the hotel at 7:00?"

"Sure mate."

After a snack and some freshening up, I was out front at 7:00 sharp and climbed into Ronald's taxi.

"I won't be able to pick you up later," Ron said, "but if you ask inside, they can call you a taxi when you're ready to leave."

Chapter 47 – The RSL

Just inside the door to the club, a man sat on a high stool behind a podium. "Hello, mate," he said, "Are you a member?"

"No," I said, "I'm an American on R&R from Vietnam. Am I eligible?"

"Of course, mate. Just let me check your ID."

"Right you are. Take the elevator to the fifth floor, turn to the right, and you'll be there," he said motioning to the elevator located across the lobby.

The barroom was pleasingly dim, and the whole place created an atmosphere of old elegance, which surprised me in a veterans' club.

I walked to the bar and an attractive brunette asked, "What's your pleasure, sir?" Her obvious British accent surprised me, too.

"Scotch and water, please," I said.

"Coming right up," she said with a wonderful smile. "I'll start a tab."

When the Scotch came, I ordered a burger and a salad. "If I move to a booth will someone bring it to me?"

"Of course!"

"And can I get one of your excellent Australian beers with that?"

"Certainly. We have Victoria Bitters on tap."

"That'll be fine," I said, having no idea whether it was fine or not.

I was beginning to relax a little and it felt good. Within a few minutes, I had my salad, burger, and Victoria Bitters. I enjoyed every morsel as it caressed my taste buds. I ordered a second beer, and finished that, too, before sidling back up to the bar.

Australian beer seemed to have a higher percentage of alcohol, but whether it did or didn't, it certainly hit me faster and harder than an equivalent volume of American beer.

When I again sat at the bar, I had a buzz on and was less inhibited than earlier.

A few minutes after I took my seat, a distinguished gentleman turned to me and said, "Henry Graves, and who might you be?"

"Jamie Thompson. Glad to meet you."

"If you don't mind my asking, are you here on R&R?"

"Yes."

"Well then, welcome to Australia. Have you had a chance to get out and about much?"

"Not a lot, but I hired a cab and went out to Echo Point in the Blue Mountains today."

Henry and I talked for several hours. "If you had more time, I'd have you out to my sheep station; what you would call a ranch. It's a few hundred miles northwest of here. I'm quite proud of it, you see."

"How big is it Henry?"

"About 40,000 hectares."

"What's that in acres?" I asked.

"Let's see… about a hundred thousand, I reckon."

"That's huge Henry!"

"Not by Australian standards, mate. And not when in average years it takes about twenty acres to support a single sheep for meat, though it takes less to support them for wool."

I was impressed and really liked Henry, but realized it was time for me to call it a night. I paid the bartender for my bill—which wasn't as large as it should have been because of Henry's kindness—and asked if she could call me a taxi.

"Certainly, sir," she said, "What's your name, so I can tell the driver?"

"It's Jamie Thompson, and thanks very much."

After breakfast the next day, I walked around the area near the hotel, wandering in and out of shops and checking out the El Alamein Fountain, which memorializes the contributions of the Australian Army in the two World War II battles of El Alamein. The second battle began the campaign that drove the Germans out of North Africa. I wondered if someday somewhere there'd be a memorial to those who fought in Vietnam. *"I doubt it,"* I thought, moving on to grab lunch at a café.

I bought a paper while I was there and saw that the new movie *M*A*S*H* was playing in a nearby theater, so I decided to go see it. MASH was a military acronym for Mobile Army Surgical Hospital, a kind of field hospital that stood alone during the Korean War. It was much like the battalion aid station I'd been in. Even though the movie was nominally set in Korea, it was an open secret that it was clearly meant to portray the Vietnam War without raising the ire of the U.S. government. The movie brought out a wide range of emotions in me, which needed to be felt; it was cathartic. Afterward, I retreated to my room, where I lounged around until 7:00 p.m., when Ronald picked me up to go back to the RSL.

When I got to the bar, I was pleased to see the same woman bartender there.

"Hello, again. How are you, Jamie?" she said with a beautiful smile and intoxicating accent.

"You remembered my name. I'm impressed."

"Thanks, but it is part of the job, you understand."

"What is your name, if I might ask?"

"You may," she said. "It's Eveline, Evie for short."

"Pleased to meet you, Evie. Can you rustle up another JB and water for me?"

"Sure thing."

I moved to a booth and ordered a bowl of hearty soup, some fries—or chips as they were called there—and a Victoria Bitters. For the next forty-five minutes I ate and gazed out the window, clandestinely observing Evie from the corner of my eye. My thoughts occasionally strayed to danger and deep jungle, but I blocked such things from my consciousness almost before they occurred. I finished the last of my beer and moved back to the bar.

"Evie, are you British?"

"Yes," she said. "I moved here two years ago."

"How do you like it?"

"The people are wonderful for the most part, and the climate is certainly an improvement over England, but sometimes I get a bit wistful for the old country."

"Obviously my perspective is different, having only been here for a few days and knowing I'll be gone in a few more, but while I agree that the people are very nice and would add that the country is beautiful, two things make me feel that I could probably never feel like this was home."

"Really, what are they?"

"The first is a strong impression based on my watching of the TV news and reading of the papers that life is much simpler here. Now, on its surface, you'd think that was a good thing, which I suppose it is in some ways, but I'm used to a country, a society that is extremely complex, with innumerable events occurring and issues arising twenty-four hours a day every day, and a sense of itself as being vital to and inextricable from the international community. Rather surprisingly, I find I miss that very much. Being in a country so similar in appearance to the United States that is only a small percentage as complex feels odd and gives Australia an aura of naïveté and unreality that is prominent in my thoroughly American brain. The second is my inner sense of geography which causes a constant feeling of being out at the far end of a limb that may be too long and too weak to hold without breaking. And, even if it does hold, this is a continent that is for the most part essentially uninhabitable. In other words, geographically Australia feels more vulnerable than almost anywhere else on Earth. I suspect my American mind set is unlikely to fade, so taken together, these things make it nearly impossible to imagine myself living in Australia permanently. Does that make any sense?"

"Yes, in fact, I feel much the same way, though it helps that I've relatives who have lived here for two generations. I think the biggest difference in our views of the place is that I see and feel what you do but think of it as giving Australia a sense of excitement and promise for the future. I see this country as having a chance to start over and do it better this time than we in Europe and even North America have done. I like that sense of newness and adventure."

I smiled at her and said, "I hadn't thought of it that way. I understand what you're saying, and you may be right. In fact, I hope you are!" I raised my glass, tipped it slightly toward her and took a sip.

"Excuse me," she said moving to the inside end of the bar where a patron was waggling his glass for a refill.

"Of course," I smiled.

Just then, Henry Graves walked in and sat next to me at the bar. "Can I join you, mate?"

"Certainly, I'm glad to see you again Henry," I said, smiling. "Busy day?"

"Busy and tiresome," he answered. "I'd rather do most anything than meet with bankers, but needs must!" he said motioning to Evie.

"I spent the entire day doing as close to nothing at all as I could," I offered.

"That's as it should be for an infantry sergeant on furlough."

"I suppose, but I'm nagged by a feeling that I should be doing more. Truthfully though, I don't have a clue what else I could do and don't really feel like doing much more than I am anyway."

Henry looked me in the eye and said, "No worries, mate. Whatever you decide will be all right."

"There is one thing I might like to do, though," I said.

"What might that be?"

"I'd like to take our bartender out on a date," I said shifting my eyes in her direction.

"Evie? She's a looker all right, but also a damn pommie!" he offered.

"What's a pommie," I asked.

"Prisoner of Mother England," he explained.

"Oh, of course!" I said. "Is that bad?"

"Yes. Most pommies look down their noses at Aussies, and they've damn little cause to be doing it," he added vehemently.

"I really don't think Evie feels that way at all," I said in her defense.

"Perhaps not, but my experience causes me to assume otherwise," he said.

"On a different subject Henry," I said, "What was your military job and where did you serve?"

"I was a corporal and later sergeant in the army engineers and served in New Guinea and a few other islands when I was just a lad in the last world war," he said blandly.

"That must have been hell," I said.

"I've had better days," he said, "but what you're going through now is worse."

"Why do you say that" I asked.

"Because in my war, we knew we had to win or our people would be speaking Jap or German. In yours it's a bit less clear just what's at stake," he said with sympathetic eyes.

"That's true, but whatever your war you just do your job. Maybe after I'm home again I'll think more deeply about such things, but for now what's important is to try to get all my men home safely. When you get down to it, wars throughout the ages have more similarities than differences I think."

"You're right about that, mate."

I told Henry about my thoughts on guard duty on the mountain, of sensing kinship with an unknown Roman soldier. He listened as I talked about the mountain and how beautiful it could be at times. He asked about the legend of the two monadnocks Nui Ba Den and Nui Bah Ra, so I told him what little I'd heard about it.

Before we knew it, it was midnight and time for me to head back to my hotel. As I pushed away from the bar, he said, "I could be wrong about Evie. Give it a go, mate."

I stopped at the bar near the other side of the 'U' and again paid my bill and left a tip with Evie. As she took the payment and smiled, I leaned nearer and said, "Evie, would you consider going out to dinner with me?"

"I don't date customers and especially not American soldiers here on R&R." She said this in the nicest way it could be said, but my face must have betrayed deep disappointment and sadness, because she added, "I'm sorry, Jamie. That's the way it is."

I stood straighter and said, "I understand. Good night, Evie."

At breakfast the next morning I thought about how badly Evie's rejection had affected me. Halfway through my second cup of coffee—with half-and-half instead of cream—I realized it was because she'd forced me to think about the terrible reality of my situation; something I almost never allowed myself to do. The truth was my odds of surviving the next few months were in serious doubt. Almost as soon as I had this thought, I pushed it from my mind and decided to spend the day walking around Kings Cross again.

When I returned to the hotel in the early afternoon, I told one of the bell captains, "I've walked all over this part of the city, I've visited the Blue Mountains, and I've been to the museum and to a movie. What's left?"

"Have you been to Bondi Beach?" he asked. I'd seen the name in one of the brochures and hadn't realized it was pronounced Bon-dye. "It's a famous surfing beach and you can catch sun there on nice days."

"Thanks, I'll seriously consider visiting it tomorrow."

When I got myself together for another evening at the RSL, I realized I was in a rut, but I didn't care. I was beginning to unwind, I think. My thoughts were on Evie and not on the damn war. I sighed and headed out.

That evening, I could tell Evie was feeling bad about the way she told me she wouldn't go out with me. I smiled and said, "I hope you'll reconsider dinner with me."

"Jamie, you're a nice fellow, but in my experience, the boys on R&R get too drunk and grabby. And I just don't want to deal with that. I hope you understand."

"I do understand, but I'm different. I'm not like that," I assured her. "So please think about it and I'll ask again later, if that's all right."

"There's no harm in asking," she said with a gentle smile.

Later, Henry suggested I mention Bondi Beach to a sandy-haired man in his thirties sitting near the opposite end of the bar. "I think he lives near there," he said.

I introduced myself to him and asked about Bondi. "As it happens, tomorrow's Friday and a group of us leave work at noon and meet up there for drinks. You'd be welcome to join us, if you like. Just tell the taxi driver the Astra at Bondi. I'm Mick, by the way."

"Thanks Mick, I'll do that."

About an hour later, I moved to an unoccupied stretch of bar.

When the opportunity presented itself to talk privately to Evie, I said, "Have you thought about that dinner with me?"

"It's briefly entered my thoughts."

"What's the verdict?"

"Against my better judgment, I'd be happy to dine with you tomorrow evening."

"That's wonderful. Can you give me your address and number?"

"Yes, I've written it on the bottom of the coaster under your drink. Just don't forget to take it when you leave."

I was so darn excited about my date with Evie that it took a while to fall asleep that night. The next day, I stayed in the hotel 'til half past noon, when Ron picked me up and took me to the Astra.

"Have you got things straight?" I asked when we arrived.

"Yes, mate," he said, slightly annoyed with me for asking again. "I pick you up here at five, take you back to the hotel, then pick you up there at six-thirty for your date with Evie."

"Thanks, Ron. I'll see you at five."

When we arrived, I surveyed the area for a moment before going inside. The beach itself was a semicircle of sand open to the south-southeast. I could understand how the shape of the shoreline encouraged good surfing waves, but today was overcast, very windy, and seemed foreboding. The Astra Hotel was an older building whose front matched the curve of the road that paralleled the bend of Bondi Beach, which was located right across the street.

I found the pub and walked in. It was just one o'clock and there weren't many people there yet, but to my relief I spotted Mick.

"Hello, Mick," I said, extending my hand.

"Hello to you! Let me buy you a beer. What's your pleasure?"

"The only kind I've tried is Victoria Bitters so that would be fine."

"Oh, let's get you something different, shall we?"

He raised his hand to get the bartender's attention. "A bottle of Coopers Best Stout for my American friend here, if you please."

"This is wonderful," I said after my first taste.

"Thought you might like it."

Within half an hour, three of Mick's coworkers had arrived, and I was in the midst of a crowd of increasingly loud Aussies.

At some point, Mick said, "Gents, let's drink to our American friend, Jamie. He's here on R&R from Vietnam."

This brought on a "Here, here!" from one fellow, and a "To Jamie," from another. From that point on I never had an empty bottle and never bought a beer. Even total strangers at the bar bought me beers.

"Gentlemen," I said, "Let's drink to Australia!" We all did. "Let's drink to Sydney," I said with the same result. "Let's drink to new friends," again everyone raised their glasses.

Hours later, a young woman entered through a side door. She walked up to Mick, but he wasn't happy to see her. "What do you want?" he asked her rather shortly.

"I wanted to remind you that we have guests coming at 5:00 and you're cooking on the barbie."

"So what? This is my time with my friends!" he shot back.

"I know," she said softly, "but we need to leave soon to get things ready."

"Right," he said disappointedly. "I'll come get you in a few minutes. Oh, Clarissa, this is the American I told you about. Jamie, this is Clarissa."

"Happy to meet you," I said, extending my hand.

"I hope you're enjoying your visit here?"

"I am. Thank you."

"Well, if you'll excuse me, I'll be going back to my friends," she said as she turned to leave through the side door.

"Nice to have met you," I said to her back.

Turning back to the group, I said, "I hadn't noticed 'til just now, but there aren't any women in here at all, are there?"

"No, mate," answered one of Mick's friends. "This is a pub and like in Merry Olde England, pubs are for men only. Through that door is the lounge where both men and women are allowed."

"That would take some getting used to for me!"

Numerous chuckles erupted here and there in the group. "We mostly like it this way, but suspect the pub system won't survive much longer. The ladies don't care for it at all, you see," said one of the group.

"I did get that impression," I smiled.

"Yes, well, as long as we have the pub system, it should be respected," said a pretty intoxicated Mick. "But I suppose I should be going. Are you going to be all right, Jamie? You're welcome to come to the Barbie at my place this evening."

"I appreciate the offer, Mick, but I have plans for tonight and a taxi is calling for me here in… twenty minutes," I said checking my watch.

"All right then, I'll leave you to it."

"Thank you for introducing me to Bondi and the Astra. I'm leaving in the morning and it's a good sendoff," I lied. Mick made his way into the lounge and was gone.

I now dawned on me that I was pretty well lit myself. I suppose I'd realized it earlier, but as often happens when imbibing, good judgment is the first thing to go.

"My friends, I'm switching to soda water right now," I announced.

"It may be too late for that, mate," offered a helpful group member. "You've had eight or ten of those since I've been here."

"God, I hope you're wrong," I said. But I knew he was close to the mark.

After my soda water and handshakes all around, I stepped outside to wait for Ronald. Like clockwork he showed up at five.

"I'm snockered, Ron," I said.

"That you are, mate," he said with a crooked smile.

"But this is really bad. I have that date with Evie in two hours and really need to be on my best behavior."

"Let's get you back to your hotel and you can order some snacks and coffee," he suggested.

I followed Ron's suggestions, eating a room service ham sandwich and drinking two cups of coffee, but the hour and a half passed all too quickly. When I emerged onto the street, I was hanging on by a thread.

We arrived at Evie's high-rise apartment building, and it took longer than it should have to locate her name among mailboxes and push the button beside it. When she arrived, she took my breath away. I immediately felt completely out of my league ... and still zonked.

"You look stunning!" I blurted like an enamored schoolboy.

"Why, thank you," she said, clearly knowing I'd stated the obvious.

I walked her to the cab, opened the door for her, and got in the opposite side.

Ron asked, "Where to, mate?"

I realized I had no idea where to take Evie to dinner. "Do you have a favorite restaurant?" I asked her.

"There's one I'd love to try, but it's expensive," she cautioned.

"Price is no object," I assured her with an expansive wave of an arm.

"Well, if you're sure. It's the Summit Restaurant at the top of the Australia Square Building. The views of the city and harbor are said to be amazing."

"Ronald, can you get us to the Summit Restaurant?"

"Sure thing."

At this point, Evie had realized that I was several sheets to the wind. "Are you sure you want to do this?"

"Of course!" I said a bit too loudly. "Why wouldn't I? You're a beautiful woman and I'm proud to be in your company."

"Yes. Well, you're clearly quite intoxicated, so it's a reasonable question."

Ronald pulled up in front of the Australia Square Building.

"You're right and I apologize. Do you remember me talking to Mick in the RSL last night?"

"Yes, I do."

"Well, I wanted to see Bondi Beach, so I met him and some of his friends at the Astra. They bought me beer all afternoon and before I knew it, I was quite drunk. It's no excuse, but I didn't realize Coopers had a high alcohol content. I'm sorry, Evie."

"It's all right, Jamie, but I think it's best if you just take me home."

On the drive back to Evie's apartment building, I tentatively put my arm around her shoulders and tried several times to kiss her, but she'd clearly had enough. When we arrived at her place, I walked her to the door.

"Evie, I feel awful about this. I turned out to be exactly the kind of drunken, groping American GI you feared I would be."

"Not *exactly*," she said. "I was looking forward to our dinner and I'm disappointed in you, yes, but you were still a gentleman at heart. I wish you the best, Jamie. Take care of yourself, won't you?"

"I will, Evie, and I apologize that I disappointed you... and myself tonight." I held her hand briefly and then let it go, as she smiled sadly and used her key to pass through the inside door. I've always regretted my behavior that night with Evie. She was a fine girl.

I walked slowly back to the taxi, and slid in on the passenger side of the front seat. "That could have gone better."

"That it could, mate."

"I'm not quite ready to call it a night, can we drive around a little?"

"Certainly. I'll give you a tour of the red-light district, if that's agreeable."

"There's a red-light district?"

"Indeed, there is. Would you like to see it?"

"Sure. Why not?" I said with a sigh.

I have no idea where Ronald took me in relation to my hotel, but about fifteen minutes after leaving Evie, we were driving through what looked to me like the business district of the city. Wide streets were flanked by tall buildings all around. There were very few people on the streets at 8:30 on a Friday night. I did see several pairs of attractive, well-dressed young women walking here and there along the sidewalks. I assumed they'd worked late in nearby offices.

"Let me know when we get to the red-light district."

"We're in it now, mate."

"Wait! You're telling me that these gals right here," I said gesturing to a nearby pair of 'office workers,' "are prostitutes?"

"Right you are, mate," he chuckled.

"My God, Ronald, Australian hookers are on a much higher plane than I expected!"

"They're a national treasure, mate. For those so inclined, you understand" he said with pride. "Would you like to meet one?"

"How would we do that?" I asked.

"All that's necessary is to pull over to the curb and give a 'come hither' motion with your hand."

"If you say so," I replied skeptically. "Let's try it."

Ron pulled to the curb, I did as he'd suggested, and sure enough, the closest pair of ladies walked right up to the cab and started talking. "You're an American," a very pretty blonde said, "Here on R&R?"

"Yes," I said, trying to seem cool and experienced.

"Looking to have some fun, soldier?" her sultry brunette friend interjected.

"Maybe," I answered.

"It'll be twenty dollars apiece, forty for the two of us, or eighty for both of us all night, then," said the blonde.

"That sounds reasonable," I said. "Let me think about it for a few minutes. We'll drive around the block and catch up with you in little while."

"We may not be here when you come back," cautioned the brunette.

"Understood," I said, motioning to Ron to pull away.

"Ron, maybe there's something terribly wrong with me, but when I compare those two with Evie, there is no comparison. I've enjoyed the tour, but I'm ready to head back to the hotel now."

"Right, mate."

As we approached the hotel, I paid Ronald and said, "I'm leaving tomorrow. Can you pick me up at 8:30 in the morning and get me to the R&R Center by 9:00 a.m.?"

"Yes, mate. I'll be here."

With that, I made my way to my room with head hung low. *"Sometimes I'm a real ass!"* I thought.

I took a couple of aspirin, ordered a snack from room service, watched TV for an hour or two and was sound asleep by 11:00.

Chapter 48 – Up Over and Back Out

I awoke at 6:00 a.m. showered and shaved, went down to a hearty breakfast, packed my duffel, put on my khaki uniform and headed out. I paid my bill at the desk and smoked a cigarette on the sidewalk waiting for Ronald.

When he pulled up, I slid in next to him and said, "Once more unto the breach."

He smiled and said, "I'll miss you, mate."

"And I, you," I assured him.

We didn't talk much on the short drive to the R&R Center. I got out, paid him and included a tip of twenty dollars, and said, "Thank you Ronald, for being a guide and a friend while I was here."

"You're more than welcome. It's been my pleasure, mate. Take care of yourself," he said, shaking my hand.

"You, too, my friend!" I said with a smile. As I turned, he drove away.

Once inside the center, I took a seat and surveyed the scene. It looked as though there were about as many guys here now as there had been when we arrived, which was good I supposed. Right at 9:00 a.m. the same guy who'd given us the welcome orientation stepped onto the stage and said, "Men, your return flight has been delayed. Rather than keep you penned up in here, we're allowing you to go wherever you like for the next two hours. But you must report back here by 1100. You can check your bags at the counter and pick them up when you get back."

This wasn't met with cheers because we'd all burned our bridges in a sense, checked out of our rooms and said our goodbyes. Now we had to find something to occupy our time for the next several hours! A couple of guys headed for the phones to arrange a last few hours with people they were close to in Sydney, but for me it turned out to mean window shopping in a close radius of the center and spending time in a little sidewalk café enjoying coffee and a sundae.

Everyone was dutifully back at the R&R Center once again at 1100 and by 1120 we were on buses heading for the airport. When we arrived, we checked our bags at the ticket counter, and then moved as a group to our gate.

We milled around for perhaps another half-hour before someone finally told us why the plane had been delayed. "Men," said the same PR guy from the center, "a bomb threat was called in for your plane early this morning. Since that time, every square inch of the plane has been checked for explosives and none have been found. We've also just opened and inspected all your checked baggage and found nothing there either. As soon as I finish talking, you'll be taken down the stairs here at this gate to the tarmac where all your carry-on luggage will also be inspected, and each of you will be asked a few questions. We are very sorry for the delay, but we want to be absolutely certain that your flight is safe. Now, if you'll follow me, please."

With that, he led us through a door to one side of the extendable walkway, down a flight of stairs and out onto the windy and rather warm tarmac. All our luggage was spread out on the pavement beside our plane. We were asked to find our luggage and stand beside it. This took a few minutes since the bags looked much alike, but we managed it. This confirmed that all luggage did indeed belong to one of the passengers and there were no unaccompanied bags. After that, all carry-ons were opened and examined in front of their owners, and each of us was asked if anyone we didn't know had had access to any of our luggage since we packed it.

Within half an hour this procedure was complete, and we were led around to the passenger loading stairs that had been rolled up to the far side of the aircraft. Soon enough, we were seated comfortably in an air-conditioned jet once again.

When I glanced out the right-side window, I saw that there was an observation deck on the second level of the main airport building where our concourse branched from it. There were about a hundred women and children standing there waving at us, many with small American flags and a few Australian ones.

Several of us waved back, though I doubt our waves could be seen by the people on the deck. I guessed that news of the bomb threat had been on the TV and radio in Sydney and these people had been spurred to come out and show that they wished us well. The image of those friendly Australians waving American flags was powerful. It imbued in me a life-long feeling of warmth toward Australia and its people.

On the flight down, I'd had a window seat on the left side of the plane; this time I had an aisle seat on the right, so even when I strained to see out, I was seeing the same landscapes. That's why I spent most of this flight reading. An hour or so after takeoff, I selected a *Time* from among the magazines offered by one of the stewardesses. Sometime later, while thumbing somewhere past the middle of it, I stopped short. There was a photo there of the scene I'd thought was such an awful image at the time: the huge Special Forces guy leading a tiny Montagnard man behind him like a dog on a leash. That had happened at Neal in Cambodia and once it was discovered that the man was indeed a local Montagnard, he'd been released in less than hour. I read the caption, which said that it was a VC "prisoner" being brought in for interrogation in Vietnam. I told the Spec-4 seated next to me about the problems with it and added, "Things are not always what they seem."

It was the 8th of November 1970.

Our stop in Darwin was less than an hour, so about an hour before sunset we left Australian air space headed northwest across the Timor Sea. The flight was smooth, uneventful, and all of us were lost in our private thoughts. It was eerily quiet.

We landed at Tan Son Nhut close to 2300, were escorted to Camp Alpha and assigned bunks for the night. The next morning, I turned in the khakis and put on my jungle fatigues. By 1100, I was back at Bien Hoa boarding a C-130 for a flight to Buttons. At noon, I checked in at Battalion HQ and saw both Jay and Bob. They asked how Bangkok was and I said, let's have lunch and I'll tell you all about it. They assigned me a bunk and then we walked together to the mess hall.

Once we'd all sat down at a table with our trays, I said, "Well, the first news is that I didn't go to Bangkok."

"What?" said Jay, "What the hell happened?"

"I went to Sydney instead!" I said with a broad smile.

Over lunch, I told Jay and Cal about my unexpected trip to Australia and my date with Evie.

"How did that go?" asked Cal.

"Not well," I said. "I was drunk as a skunk before I picked her up and she asked to go home early. I was an idiot! Evie was a very nice girl."

"Evie, huh?" said Jay.

"Yep. A beautiful girl who deserved a hell of a lot better than she got from me."

"So do you feel like you unwound at all?" asked Cal.

"Yes, I think so, but the whole R&R thing already seems like a dream."

"Well, you'll be heading out to Snuffy in the morning. Charlie Company will be there, so you can join your platoon on the firebase."

"That's convenient," I said, raising my cup of fruit punch Kool-Aid. "Here's to Australia... and to the 5th of the 7th."

"Here, here," echoed Jay and Bob.

That afternoon, I retrieved my pack and the rest of my gear from the battalion lock-up and spent the afternoon cleaning my M16, making sure all the magazines were full, and other basic stuff like that. That night, being assigned to perimeter guard from 2300 to 0100, I was again given a place close to the bunker where I could lie down for a few hours.

Right after chow, I went out to the berm near battalion HQ to have a cigarette and met an ARVN LT doing the same thing. We were curious about each other's situations and struck up a conversation sitting side by side on top of the berm. "What unit are you with?" he asked in perfect English.

"Charlie Company, 5th of the 7th," I said. "I just got back from R&R in Sydney, Australia. It's the first real break I've had in seven months, unless you count my three months up on the mountain," I said, glancing at Nui Ba Ra to our front.

"It's different for us," he said. "We get to go home for one week every month, unless something very unusual happens."

"I'd think that could be very hard to deal with. I mean going from combat to home life and back again so often."

He looked at me and hesitated as though what I'd said surprised him, but said, "Yes, it is. I love my wife and my parents, and they love me, but seeing each other so often, makes us worry about each other more than we might if we saw each other less."

"Were you drafted?" I asked.

"Yes. I was a third-year student studying world literature at the University of Saigon when I was drafted."

"I was drafted out of college, too. My tour will be up early next year. When does your service end?"

"We are drafted for the duration," he said.

"What? That could be for many years. Is there a maximum?"

"No. I've already served for nearly seven years and we serve 'til the war ends, if we survive. In the meantime, my life is not my own. I cannot finish my college or leave the country."

"That must be very difficult," I said. "I had no idea."

"Who knows, we may meet again, if they send you back here in ten or twenty years."

"They won't be doing that!" I said. "I'll be out of the Army completely in less than a year and besides, the war will be over, one way or the other, long before that."

"Don't be so sure."

I looked at the expression on his face and said, "You don't think we're like the French do you? You do understand that we'll leave Vietnam as soon as we can, right?"

"There seems little difference between America and France to us. Most of us do not believe you will leave. Like the French, you will seek to control our economy and our government."

I was very surprised to hear this, but it made perfect sense from the LT's point of view when I thought about it. "Let me assure you, we are nothing like the French or the British. In fact, we were a colony ourselves until we won our freedom in our Revolutionary War. After World War II, when France tried to reassert its colonial rule over Indochina, it was out of character and a mistake for us to back the French. But I can guarantee you that we will not be staying here any longer than necessary to win this war... or give it our best shot. The American People wouldn't stand for it."

"I can see that you believe that, and I want to believe you," said the LT, "but I doubt you or I will have anything to say about it."

"On that, we're in complete agreement," I said, with narrowed eyes.

The ARVN LT and I then spent several minutes quietly looking at Nui Ba Ra as the sun sank lower behind us. I think we shared a sense of sadness and resignation, but we both hoped that I was right. When I finished my cigarette, I slid down the berm, stood up, turned to face the LT and extended my hand. He took it and shook it warmly.

"I wish you very good luck, Lieutenant."

"And I, you, Sergeant," he said.

We nodded, gave each other suggestions of smiles and I walked away.

Later, alone in the pitch black in the perimeter bunker, my thoughts wandered to the sparkling clean city of Sydney in the spring, and the people I'd met there. I made sure all the clackers were properly aligned and easily reachable. Then I realized that the most wonderful and appealing thing about Sydney was the absence of war. This was among the very few thoughts I would have about anything other than my immediate surroundings and current situation for the next three months. R&R was over.

At breakfast with Jay, I said, "Aren't you getting short, man?"

"Yes and no. I extended my tour six months. When I go home, I'll have a shorter time left in the Army."

"Some people might think that's crazy, but I understand."

"You do?"

I told him about my experience policing cigarette butts with Vietnam vets at Fort Sill. "From a purely administrative point of view, having combat vets do stuff like that makes sense, but it's wrong from a human one. The Army is what it's always been, a huge olive drab machine, but the guys in it and in this war are different. When they've done their time in hell, it should be enough."

We finished our breakfast mostly in silence and walked back to the HQ. Cal said he needed to talk to me privately, so I gathered my gear and headed outside.

"It turns out being A&D clerk isn't all fun and games," he said.

"Okay," I said warily.

"Are you familiar with the contact that occurred with Charlie Company's Mortar Platoon when a couple of gooks were killed?"

"We were in platoon elements that day, but I talked with the mortar guys afterward. Why?"

"Throckmorton submitted paperwork recommending Captain Reynolds for the Silver Star."

"What? My God, what did he say happened?"

"He says that Captain Reynolds rushed to the point of attack under heavy enemy fire to provide leadership and to personally engage the enemy alongside his men. And that his actions materially led to the repulse of the attack and to two enemy KIAs."

"That's not at all what happened! Two gooks walked right into the perimeter and were killed by the men on guard before they could fire a single shot. Reynolds got there in time to see

Throckmorton cutting off the gooks' ears with his machete. A couple of other grunts kicked out their teeth for souvenirs, and Reynolds did nothing to stop it. I bet that's how he got Throckmorton to put him in for the medal. 'I won't write you up for the ears, if you put me in for the medal.'"

"I suspected as much. It just didn't sound right. If I confirm what you told me, I'll recommend disapproval of the award."

"If Reynolds raises a stink about this—and I'm betting he will—keep in mind that Throckmorton and the other guys carried those ears and teeth around for weeks. A lot of people saw them. Be sure to talk to Private Haskins. He's one of the mortar guys who told us about it."

Two hours later I stepped off a slick at Snuffy and rejoined my platoon.

"Anything interesting happen while I was gone?" I asked Frank.

"Not a thing, Sarge, I'm happy to say."

I spotted Kent and reported to him. Captain Reynolds acknowledged my return with a deadpan nod from some distance away.

"Did Bangkok live up its name?" Kent asked, spitting tobacco juice.

"I'll never know. I ended up going to Sydney instead."

Later I repeated the story to the rest of the squad.

The LT smiled and said, "Good for you. Something tells me you're glad it worked out that way."

That evening, Superman introduced me to two FNGs who joined the squad while I was on R&R, Private Alonzo Smith from Louisiana and Private Kevin Connelly from Boston. Smith was a tall, easygoing man who had to feel even weirder than the rest of us since he was the only black man left in the squad. Connelly was a freckle-faced redhead with an outgoing disposition and a ready smile. He also introduced an FNG in Second Squad they'd taken a liking to, Private Darrel Henderson, a slim soft-spoken kid from Lander, Wyoming. I told all of them that if there was anything I could do to help them get used to things, all they had to do was ask.

The next day we had orders to CA to the field, and my squad had the point. I led out. The silence of the jungle wrapped itself around me. There's something about being surrounded solely by nature that has always made me feel better. I was aware that this seemed to contradict the reality of walking point in enemy territory in a war zone, but nonetheless, it was true. The main difference between how I felt on point in Vietnam and how I felt in the woods back home was that I needed my weapon here to balance against the threat of the human enemy.

That night, Superman and I won the spades game and the previous week slipped through the neck of my internal hourglass.

A few days later, the company was sent to find the site of a helicopter that crashed the week before. After a difficult hump, we emerged through a dense area of tangled vines and thick immature trees, where the trunks were much closer together than they would be when the forest matured and thinned itself.

We came upon the slick, lying on its side at the edge of a hastily hacked LZ. It was too close to the wall of jungle to be safely lifted out, so the decision was made to destroy it in place to prevent the enemy from removing its sophisticated instruments and electronics.

Once we secured the site, a slick arrived and pushed out two cases of C-4, together with plenty of detcord and timers for the job. As always, NCOs were responsible for setting and detonating the charges. Kent and I, along with two other NCOs, crawled over the slick from tail to nose, pushing bars and chunks of C-4 into and onto every spot that contained instruments and electronics, as well as structural points that seemed critical to keeping the slick together. We then cut lengths of detcord to connect all the pieces of C-4. When all the connections were made, we cut the timer fuse to a length that should give us twelve minutes to get out of Dodge.

Someone had a cigar, which we lit and pressed to the end of the timer fuse. When it was well and truly lit, we left fast. We needed to be 500 meters from the explosion before it blew. The twelve minutes came and went. At fourteen, we were looking at each other, wondering who would be ordered to go back and set another timer fuse. For most things, we'd volunteer, but for this it didn't seem wise.

We had expected a tremendous blast, but when it came—at roughly fourteen and a half minutes—it was a hollow whump muffled by the intervening vegetation. I raised an eyebrow and glanced at Kent. He was perplexed, too. But a second later we heard the whoosh as fragments shot through the treetops. We waited a few minutes and then moved back to the crash site to inspect the results. Nothing larger than a clenched fist remained.

When Captain Reynolds arrived, Kent said, "Mission accomplished, sir."

Captain Reynolds just nodded.

A few days later, we split into platoon-size units. I really disliked the captain by now, so putting distance between us was fine with me. We slipped into the familiar routine of slogging through the bush all day, setting up our NDP, and playing spades, doing the same thing the next day and the next, over and over again.

As I set out my Claymore in front of the guard hole one evening, I saw a chunk of metal lying on the ground about ten feet farther out. I walked over to take a closer look and saw that it was an unexploded 155mm high explosive round. I moved back to the Claymores and repositioned a few so they wouldn't impact the round if they were set off.

I reported the unexploded round to Kent and the LT, and we decided we had to blow it, but not until we were ready to move out in the morning. This didn't turn out to be the most memorable thing that happened that day, though. During our card game, Kent and Riddle were playing against Superman and me when Kent turned to Alonzo and said, "Boy, get me my canteen."

He used the tone one might have expected from an overseer talking to slaves in the antebellum South. All of us were shocked. But Alonzo's reaction was just as shocking. He went to Kent's pack, grabbed a canteen, and brought it to him without a word. To my shame, I said nothing, nor did anyone else. Seeing this overtly racist exchange was educational and disturbing. Old ways die hard, if they die at all.

The next morning, after we'd packed up, I broke off a chunk of C-4 from the bar I carried in my pack and rolled it into a string about an inch thick and a foot long. I bent it into a U shape and carefully placed it on the ground around the unexploded ordnance without quite touching it. Then I stuck a blasting cap on a five-minute length of timer fuse into the curve and lit it. As I passed through the NDP, I grabbed my pack and rejoined the rest of the platoon. When we'd gone about 200 meters, the round went up. We didn't go back to check our handiwork because the size of the explosion told us all we needed to know.

Crashed slick we blew up with two cases of C-4 to deny technology to the enemy. (photo 48-1)

Chapter 49 – Monsoon; On the Same Wavelength

We reformed into a company-size element to CA into an area farther north a few days later. As usual, I chose to sit in the open door of the slick with my legs dangling over the edge. Normally, you can't hear anything over the sound of the helicopter's engine and its blades thumping through the air. But this time, as we crossed over a valley, I clearly heard the distinctive tap-tap-tap of an AK-47. An AK has a slower beat and somewhat deeper tone than an M16. To combat soldiers, the sound is unmistakable.

I turned to Superman and yelled, "Did you hear that?"
"I sure did."

The sounds repeated twice more. I searched the green ocean beneath us, but saw no movement, flashes, reflections, or other sign to reveal the location of the gook firing at us. He had to be pointing the muzzle damn near right at us or we'd never have heard the shots. There was nothing we could do about it, so I just continued enjoying the cool breeze and the view of the verdant landscape. Soon enough we passed over the next ridge, beyond the reach of the unseen enemy, and continued to our destination.

Our new patrol area was rugged terrain laced with foothills and ridges rising 200 meters above the valley floors. With the monsoon season in full swing, the air was more humid than usual and the terrain more slippery and treacherous. The going became more arduous, so the distance we could safely cover each day should have been reduced. However, Captain Reynolds wanted us to cover the same amount regardless of the weather or the terrain, and he did his damnedest to make that happen.

Every morning began under a cloudless sky in relentless heat. Even though we were in the shade of double-canopy jungle, the heat and humidity were nearly intolerable by midmorning, reaching their worst around 1600. Then the sharp leading edge of a thick, black, unbroken layer of cloud would appear on the eastern horizon and rapidly spread westward.

When the edge passed overhead, there was a delay of about five minutes before the air turned to water. It was as if you were standing below a cliff when a flash flood suddenly poured over it directly onto your head. This kind of precipitation can occur anywhere, but not for the length of time it does during the height of the monsoons, and not repeatedly, day after day for weeks or even months.

For five days, within one or two minutes of 1730 hours, the cloud shield would pass over us, and the deluge would begin. You could set your watch by it. We started calling it Old Faithful in homage to the famous Yellowstone geyser. Every day we hoped and expected Reynolds to tell us to set up our NDP at 1700 so we could stay a bit drier. And every day we kept on slogging until 1830, by which time everything not in an ammo box was drenched.

We didn't hate Captain Reynolds, but we had little respect for him. His behavior made it clear he didn't give a rat's ass about us, so the feeling was reciprocated. The man knew his stuff in a military operations sense, but leading men was a means to an end for him, not a calling or something at which he wanted to excel. We understood to a man that his priorities were kissing the asses of those above him in the chain of command, receiving awards and favorable reviews, and doing all he could to further his military career in what might be his only combat assignment before the war ended.

One late afternoon we were moving westward along a narrow ridge that ran almost straight east west. At 1700, I looked over my shoulder through a gap in the trees and saw the leading edge of the monsoon poking over the horizon. By 1715 it was almost upon us. We all knew what was coming. At 1730, like clockwork, the South China Sea dropped on our heads. But still we slogged on. I could barely see the man in front of me, and the footing was treacherous. Fortunately, the ridge top was only ten meters across, so it was impossible for more than an inch or two of water to stand on the ground before it ran down both sides into the valleys below.

After just fifteen minutes of this, even Captain Reynolds had apparently had enough, because he ordered us to halt and set up our NDP. It wasn't lost on any of us that for just fifteen minutes of humping and perhaps fifty meters of progress, we had to endure one more soaking wet night. This was yet another night when I dared not take off my boots for fear they might shrink. This required me to again sleep with my toes pointed straight down all night so most of the water would stay below their tips. And the next day, like the previous ten or so, was spent moving through thick jungle in steam bath heat, while a steady 'rain' of water dripped through the countless layers of leaves above our heads. This drizzle would sometimes cease an hour or so before the next deluge began... but not always.

The following day we were down in a valley and needed to cross a raging torrent a meter deep and five meters wide. I prided myself on my sure-footedness regardless of weather and terrain, so I stepped in and quickly strode across and up the steep muddy bank on the far side. Even though I hadn't turned to look, I knew Captain Reynolds was right behind me. When I was safely on the far bank, I turned around and offered my hand to help pull him up. He looked surprised, but he took my hand, and I hauled him up. No words were exchanged, but I felt better for helping the man, despite what I thought of him.

A week later, we were back on Snuffy for a little down time. We needed it.

Our first full day saw everyone empty his pack and spread the contents out on any available surface to dry. To avoid the next deluge care had to be taken to put it all under cover before roughly 1700, but we managed to dry out a bit. While we were there, the medic told me I needed to see the doctor at the base aid station. I dutifully reported, and the doctor examined the jungle rot that had formed a boil on my left cheek that needed to be drained. He lanced it, stitched a wick through it with both ends dangling down, and placed a loose dressing over it. I looked like hell, but it did its job and drained the damn thing.

While I was in the aid station, I saw Darrel Henderson there. He had the worst case of jungle rot I'd ever seen. His whole body was covered in slime.

"Jesus, man. I hadn't noticed how bad your jungle rot was. How're you doin'?"

"I've been better, but it doesn't feel quite as bad as it looks, thank God!"

"Glad to hear it," I said skeptically. "What're they doin' for it?"

"Well, naturally they gave me a penicillin shot. I'll be on a ten-day profile, taking showers every day, and then they'll reassess," he said.

The next morning, I sent my sister Julie the letter I'd written to the assistant dean, my admission application, and a personal cover letter. In the letter to Dean Howard, I explained the Army policy and asked if there was anything that could be done about my academic standing. I shamelessly added that I'd already been wounded once, and it might save my life. I had no expectation of success, but I mailed the stuff anyway. I mean, what the hell?

Later that day, I saw a grunt walk onto the firebase with a huge snake draped across his shoulders. "What is that thing, man?" I asked.

"A Reticulated Python," he answered, as though anyone should know that.

"The Army lets you keep it on a firebase?"

"Hell, yes. In fact, they encourage it—informally, of course."

"Of course," I said, "but why?"

"His favorite food is small rodents, like mice and rats."

"Ah, say no more," I said, as understanding dawned.

"Yeah, I've had Hiss with me on Brown, Neal, and Buttons. And now I'm bringing him to Snuffy. He really is a better mouse trap."

"I've heard that before. In fact, I've *said* that before, but in this case, I believe it!"

Jerry Pickering had found me a place to sleep in his bunker, so the evening deluges couldn't reach me. It was a huge relief, at least for a few days. That evening he introduced me to the other two residents.

"Jamie, this is Sergeant Luis Acosta, from Puerto Rico" said Jerry. "And I think you may have already met Corporal Alex Norris here." Pickering pointed at the snake charmer I'd met earlier.

"Not by name. Glad to meet you, Alex."

"Same here."

"Just out of curiosity, where is Hiss?"

"Your guess is as good as mine. I put him beside the bunker and let him crawl under to get out of the sun and feed, but his current whereabouts are unknown."

I think my eyes widened a bit, because Alex quickly added, "Not to worry, this is his normal M.O. He just goes where he wants but stays under the structures where it's cooler and where the rats live."

The next night the four of us played spades. Pickering and I took on Luis and Alex. Luis was damn good. We split the games, with Alex and Luis winning the first and Jerry and I winning the second. The next morning Charlie Company was CAed back to the boonies.

The terrain in our new AO was hilly, but not as rugged as our last, and the monsoon rains continued to make our lives a slimy hell. To shelter from the daily heavy rains, the lower sides of the leaves along our route of travel were now home to hordes of mosquitoes perched upside down beneath them and numerous leeches had slithered up higher than usual from the jungle floor.

A few nights out from Snuffy, as I sat in my guard hole in the dark, I heard a voice on my radio.

"Hey, GI, is anyone there?" The speaker had a slight accent. By itself that wouldn't have caused me concern. However, since we never made small talk on the radio and almost never referred to ourselves as GIs, the hair on the back of my neck rose up and stood at attention.

I hesitated a moment, then thought it best to play along to confirm my suspicion that it was a gook, likely NVA, on the other end.

"I hear you," I whispered.

"Lonely night tonight," said the voice.

"That it is," I replied.

"What you doing?"

"I'm on guard, just like you," I answered.

"You like baseball?"

"No, I'm a football fan. How about this year's Superbowl, huh? I was glad the Vikings pulled it out."

"Yes. Good one!"

"I have to sign off now. Maybe we can talk again later."

"Sounds, good. Talk to you later," said my new best friend.

I was spooked that the enemy was using our frequency. This incident reminded me of stories about World War II when spies had been foiled by questions they answered wrongly about the World Series. I hadn't asked who won the World Series, though, because I didn't know.

I moved silently to the CP and shook the Company RTO awake. I related the conversation to him and reminded him that Kansas City had won the Superbowl.

"I'm telling you, man. The guy's a gook, and they have our frequency. I have to get back to my guard hole now, but I'll try to get the guy back on the horn and I want you to listen in *silently* and see what you think. Okay?"

"Okay," he answered.

A few minutes later, I picked up the handset and said, "Hello friend. Are you there?"

"Yes. Still here GI."

"Sometimes it's hard to stay awake on guard, so it's nice to have someone to talk to."

"Yes. I agree."

"I wish we could talk more, but I have to get the next man for guard duty. So I'll sign off now. Good talking to you."

"Good night GI."

When the sun came up, I asked the Company RTO what he thought. "I agree the guy was a gook. I reported it up the chain," he said.

That evening, the RTO came by. "I thought you'd like to know. Because of your report, every military frequency in III Corps was changed at 1200 today."

Grunts taking lunch break in the boonies during Monsoon Season.
(photo 49-1)

Monsoon mud NDP.
(photo 49-2)

Chapter 50 – Trial by Bunker

For the next week we made no contact, so we split into platoon elements again. In the following weeks I gradually trained privates Underwood, Smith, and Connelly in the art of walking cover—and indirectly, point. They took to it rather well, especially Connelly. The kid was smart and likeable. He had that trademark Boston accent and the prototypical red-haired Irish look about him. He turned nineteen sometime in early December, so we celebrated by touching canteens and drinking a watery toast to continued success in his ground pounding career.

Henderson joined us for a few minutes, but he was miserable with jungle rot again. A few days later, he was so covered with it that the CO sent him in to Snuffy for another treatment.

I turned to Superman and said, "You'd think the Army would get the damn message. Henderson shouldn't be in the fucking jungle."

"Yeah. No argument here. But you know what they say…"

"Yep. There's the right way, the wrong way, and the Army way." About halfway through saying this, we were joined by Connelly, Ness, Scribner and Gonzalez. For some reason, that mantra always made us feel better. It was kind of like screaming at your jailers, "Fuck you and the horse you rode in on. We're still here!" It was cathartic.

I turned to Superman. "Jim, when's your DEROS?"

"December nineteenth, less than two weeks."

"I've been afraid to ask. Of all the people I've met over here, I'll miss you the most."

"I feel the same. But I will be leaving on the nineteenth just the same," he said with a laugh.

I laughed, too. "I think it's time for you to go in. I'll talk to Kent about it."

"Thanks. It's gonna be tough learning to walk without a chunker, but I think I can handle it."

We played spades that night and wiped the jungle floor with Kent and Hector. Afterward, I spoke to Kent about Superman and he agreed to talk to the LT about sending him in on the next resupply.

"Besides, I'd rather you found a new spades partner anyway," he said.

On resupply day, I walked to the chopper with Superman. We shook hands. "Have a good life, my friend."

"Thanks, I'll do my best."

I moved back beyond the ends of the rotor blades and waved as Superman left for the World. I felt a degree of loneliness I hadn't felt since I arrived eight months earlier. I fought it back and headed to my pack in time to hear my name called as the mail was distributed. I grabbed the letter and saw that it was from the University of Arizona, Tucson.

"Great," I muttered, "just what I need now, another disappointment."

I tore open the envelope.

Dear Mr. Thompson,
Congratulations. As a returning student in good
standing, your application for readmission to attend
classes at the University of Arizona for the spring
semester of 1971 has been accepted. Please report to
this office to begin your matriculation process on
January 25, 1971.
Sincerely,
Office of the Registrar

I was speechless. I sat on my pack staring into space for a minute, as inklings of a normal life began slowly trickling into my mind.

I found Lieutenant Collins, told him about my acceptance letter, and said, "LT, can you get me the forms to request an early out to return to school?"

"Absolutely. I'll try to get them here on the next resupply so you can turn it around ASAP."

That night, instead of playing spades I wrote letters to George Keahey, my parents, and both sisters, telling them I might be home before the end of January. I wrote a special thank you to Julie, who'd gone the extra mile to make this happen.

I spent the next day following azimuths, keeping pace counts, and sharing knowledge with the FNGs. That evening, Frank and I decisively beat Kent and Hector at spades. I looked at Kent with raised eyebrows and shrugged.

We rejoined the rest of the company a week later and moved in a northeasterly direction with the intention of walking into Snuffy in three days. I looked forward to showering, seeing the guys on the firebase, and maybe hearing from Steve.

At 0430 the next morning, I felt a slight nudge at my shoulder and heard a softly spoken, "Jamie?"

"Yeah. Okay, I'll be there in a minute."

I squirmed groggily out from under my poncho liner and felt around blindly for my boots. I turned them upside down and shook them out, pulled them on, and tied them in the dark. I found my steel pot, picked up my M16 and bandoliers, and moved off, crouched and crawling, toward the perimeter.

As I slipped into the guard hole, Hector said softly, "Here's the radio."

It was a night like countless others I'd experienced in the Nam. I reached for the radio and adjusted the position of the handset until I knew exactly where to find it in a hurry, laid out the bandoliers near my left side with the covers over the magazines flipped open, and felt the edge of the hole in front of me until I located and repositioned all seven clackers. Then I adjusted myself until I was almost comfortable and picked up the radio handset.

"Red One, this is Red Four, over." I released the button and waited a couple of seconds. Nothing. Once again I said, "Red One, this is Red Four, over."

"Red Four, this is Red One, over."

"Red One, this is Red Four, commo check, over."

"Red Four, I read you Lima Charlie, over."

"Thanks, Red One, everything's A-Okay. Out." I put down the handset and began to look around and listen. This was when I did my best thinking.

You could never see anything when you first went on guard duty. Even when the moon was up, it didn't shine through the double-canopy jungle. Almost everything was shadows and darkness. After a half hour of impenetrable blackness, iridescence seemed to emerge here and there, small blurry blotches of shimmering light, all of which appeared to move and some of which really did.

Once in a while, I reached out to grasp some glowing spot, careful to avoid the moving ones, and put it in my pocket to look at in the morning. That's how I discovered they were nothing but decaying vegetation or molding wood. It wasn't easy to find these spots because when I tried to focus on them, they disappeared. Only when looking straight ahead would the dark ground light up in the periphery. Sometimes it seemed so bright I felt I must be clearly silhouetted in a ghostly glow for any unseen enemy who cared to look.

It was eerie. My physical world ended at the limits of the circle of iridescence about five meters away in all directions, where the whites, pinks, and aquas merged into total darkness. I thought about going back to school and being normal again, but I found I didn't want to think about things like that. I'd just go with the flow, like I always did. Then my thoughts moved on to walking point the next day. Before I knew it, the jungle began to lighten, and men began to stir.

At full light, I climbed out of the hole and went to my hooch to warm up a breakfast of 1958 C-rat Ham 'n Eggs.

It was our second day in the company-size element and my squad had the point. In mid-morning, our azimuth obliquely intersected a broad, well beaten path. It was unusual to follow trails for obvious reasons. Trails were the enemy's routes. He knew them and the terrain through which they passed far better than we did, so they provided him with great opportunities to set up booby traps and to ambush Americans.

Naturally, I assumed we would follow our normal procedure and move across it and roughly parallel it. To my surprise, Captain Reynolds passed the word up to me to stay on the trail, apparently so we could make better time.

I warily moved ahead.

"This is no ordinary trail," I whispered to Len Scribner, who was my cover man that day. "Keep a sharp eye ... even sharper than normal."

An hour later, I slowed down and motioned to the right front. "See that area there? How the vegetation is thinning out?" Len nodded and I said, "Pass the word to keep an eagle eye out to the right flank. And suggest to the LT that we send flankers five meters to both sides."

The area was beginning to remind me of the unoccupied enemy bivouac site I'd walked through with Sam, our Kit Carson Scout. The trail had meandered slightly for the past three hundred meters, but now it straightened. In fifty more meters, I raised my left hand, signaling the company to halt.

"Pass the word for Kent and the LT to come up here," I whispered to Len. About ninety seconds later, they were beside me.

"LT, this is a large complex of some kind. See that bunker on the right edge of the trail about fifteen meters up ahead? How do you want to handle this, sir? I mean, we could call in artillery or an airstrike, spread out and walk through the whole damn place, or continue as we are and move straight past it on the trail. If we do move down the trail, every bunker will have to be checked."

"Halt right here, Sergeant. I'll bring the CO up, and we'll figure this thing out. Meantime, Kent, bring up the rest of First Squad and spread them out behind and to either side of Jamie and Len."

A few minutes later, Captain Reynolds came forward. I gave him the lay of the land and he said, "Sergeant, let's maintain the formation we have right now. Continue on the trail and check out the bunkers as you go."

"Yes, sir." As the CO and LT moved back to the main body, I turned to Len. "Listen up. I'll go in the damn bunkers; you stay behind me and to one side so you can't be seen, and be ready to blast the shit outta anything that moves."

Because of the thinned trees, we were in intermittent direct sunlight. It was nearing midday and very bright. As I approached the first bunker, I poked my M16 through the opening and waved it back and forth. When that didn't provoke a response, I stepped inside using the three steps cut into the earth at the opening. Due to the contrast with the brightness outside, I could barely make out the dimensions, let alone see any details. I stayed in the bunker for thirty seconds, not long enough to allow my eyes to completely adjust to the darkness but enough to confirm that it was empty. Then I stepped back out and did the same thing with the next bunker.

If we'd known how many bunkers we were dealing with, we might have done things differently. But as it was, we continued with the same procedure. It turned out there were twenty-three bunkers in a zigzag line at the edge of the trail and I entered every one of them.

Len and the rest of the squad operated like a well-oiled military machine alongside me all the way. Every man in Charlie Company was depending on me to do my job, so I did it. The day of the bunkers was a confirmation that I was well and truly an infantryman.

That evening, Len and I won the spades game against Kent and Seth. Afterwards, I gathered the FNGs around me and told them about the likelihood that I'd be getting an early out to go back to college.

"Well, that's no good!" said Len.

"Wha'd'ya mean?"

"Who are we gonna partner with for spades?" he answered, and all of us cracked up.

"Hey," I said, "I think I've trained up all of you well enough to do just fine without me!" I smiled.

"That you have, Sarge," said Kevin. Everyone nodded. I yawned, put out my cigarette, crawled into my hooch, and hit the sack.

Chapter 51 – Brothers in Arms

Late the next morning, we walked into Snuffy. I waved at Henderson, who was nearing the end of his latest jungle rot profile, and headed for the shower. There was a line, as usual, but it was worth the wait. Lukewarm water or not, few things in life feel as good as a first shower in weeks.

On Snuffy, chow was often served outside using a long line of tables with the same double-walled, insulated containers we used on resupply days in the field. Call it a grunt buffet. This day it was roast beef and mashed potatoes. I headed for the berm and ate with my squad, then went back for seconds.

It dawned on me that I hadn't been bothered much by the chain of command since returning to the platoon after my three months of profile. They always knew where I was, and I always did as I was ordered, but most of the time—in our NDPs, on firebases, and certainly on point—people just left me the hell alone. That was fine by me; in fact, I preferred it that way. But I liked being around the men in my squad and Lieutenant Collins.

We knew each other's strengths and weaknesses without talking about it, and truth be told, there were damn few weaknesses. For months we'd counted on each other to do our respective jobs. We'd shared hardships, frustrations, miseries, joys, sorrows, and fears in a way that I suspected would never be equaled in my life. The small talk, jokes, and complaints circled around a strong center—a core of shared experience—like electrons locked in orbit around an atom's nucleus.

After chow and a short briefing from Kent assigning guard shifts, Mad Minute times, and the next morning's shit-burning detail, I went to the bunker and took a nap.

Pickering showed up just before evening chow and told me he'd seen Steve and he wanted me to know that he'd convinced the brass not to dishonorably discharge Tom Aiken. "Steve argued that before sending him back into combat, the Army should have recognized and treated the severe mental trauma Tom suffered when two squad mates were killed when he was wounded. Apparently, that carried the day."

"As it should have," I said when Pickering finished.

"I agree," said Jerry, "but it's still amazing that Steve had the pull to get this done."

"He's an extraordinary guy, Jerry."

"I guess so," he nodded.

That night Jerry and I split the spades games with Alex and Luis.

The effects of outgoing artillery on fire bases is significant. When a modern howitzer fires, much of the recoil is absorbed by the weapon itself, but not all of it. The earth itself serves as the recoil pad for the weapon. Every round that's fired causes the ground to rapidly jerk a fraction of an inch in the opposite direction to where the weapon is aimed and instantly snap back to its starting point. This turns the ground surface to fine dust in a surprisingly short period of time. The longer artillery stays in one location and fires regularly, the deeper the layer of dust becomes. Eventually, the firing raises clouds of ambient dust that drift and settle over everything. When it rains, that layer becomes clayey mud. And the noise of the firing is a series of concussive explosions that lasts as long as the fire mission. This is difficult to adjust to at first, but once intellect overcomes instinct and one understands that these explosive sounds and violent shakes don't pose imminent danger and cannot be avoided, you just kind of go with the flow. But the effects of a major shelling operation are very hard to ignore, especially when you're trying to catch up on much needed sleep. On this night the big guns fired even more than usual, and since the bunker was dug into the ground none of us slept well.

In the morning, squirrely winds kept shifting as Kevin Connolly and I stirred burning shit. We moved around the barrels, trying to stay out of the clouds of clingy, oily smoke, but it was a losing battle.

"You know, Kev, I wouldn't be surprised if I could still smell, taste, and feel shit smoke in my nose and mouth twenty years from now."

"Me eithah," he said, his Boston accent still strong, even after being in the Army melting pot for a while. "Say, you might get to meet my little brothah Sean in a few weeks."

"Really?"

"Yeah, he should be here about now."

"Ever heard of the Sullivan rule?" I asked.

"I think I know what you're tahkin' about," he said.

"Maybe I've got the name wrong, but since the five Sullivan brothers were killed in combat together in World War II, the military hasn't allowed brothers to serve in combat at the same time."

"I think you're mostly right. Fact is, I told my brothah not to enlist. But if he did, I told him to notify the Ahmy that I was already here. It did no good. The kid wuhships me, ya see."

I laughed as I looked at Kevin's toothy grin and thought how much like a kid he looked himself. Less than he had when he first got to the Nam, but still damn young.

"Just outta curiosity, how old is your kid brothah, er ... brother?"

"He turns eighteen in a few months."

"That doesn't sound right either," I said. "If you really want to protect him, run the age and Sullivan stuff by the LT and let him look into it."

"I'll do that, Sahge."

At lunch, I asked Alex how Hiss was doing.

"Haven't seen him in two weeks," he said. "He must be eating good, though, 'cause when he isn't, he finds me, and I feed him half a dozen Cs."

"That explains why he's so highly motivated to find his own food," I said.

Alex laughed. "No doubt."

Two days later, Alpha Company came in and we went out. I saw Kurt for a few minutes, and he told me he'd also applied for an early out to go back to school. He would not be going back to the field again before he left Vietnam for good on December 21. Even though we had arrived in country on the same day, the Army had approved him to leave earlier than the required ninety days because the University of Minnesota started its semester sooner. I was happy for him. We shook hands and vowed to see each other back in the World.

Within an hour, I was back in the boonies, this time in foothill terrain. The monsoons were letting up, so we didn't get soaked every day, and the footing was a bit better on the steep slopes.

On guard duty that night, a twinge of despair flowed through me, knowing that Kurt would soon no longer be sharing my world. I stared straight ahead into the abyssal blackness, hoping to see more iridescence, more light. Soon, my thoughts returned to the elemental state that was normal in the Nam. Almost before I knew it, the predawn glow of another day in the bush swept away the darkness.

On resupply day, I got my approval for the early out. My DEROS would be January 20, 1971, about seventy-five days earlier than it otherwise would have been. I was happy about it but also felt a little lost. I was surprised that I felt any ambivalence, but I did. I've often thought that we humans have two brains directing our decisions. One is the logical brain that bases decisions on numbers, data, facts, and personal experience. The other is the emotional brain, the one that makes decisions based on sexual attraction, love, desires, and childish things like wanting to impress. This latter category includes that bugaboo of young males: the perceived demands of manliness, patriotism, duty, and honor.

Now faced with the opportunity to leave the constant stress and danger of a war zone—and the near total absence of personal freedom that exists in the military—I felt qualms. I knew I was good at my job here, maybe better than I'd ever be at anything else in my life. I took pride in that but also felt I was helping keep my men safe.

I shared the details of my early out with the squad that night, and they seemed happy for me. We also got news about

Ferde Salazar, my gunner who had been recuperating in Manila ever since the day we were both wounded. Ferde had fallen in love with one of his Filipino nurses. Since it would be difficult for her to get U.S. citizenship, Ferde dropped his application for citizenship and married her. Following a medical discharge, he would stay in the Philippines. What an irony. The reason he joined the Army in the first place was to become a U.S. citizen and move to the States. Fate dictated that he go to his homeland for treatment, and all his priorities changed.

We slogged on for another two weeks without making any contact with the enemy. By taking my time tying down my ponchos and securing an extra strip of poncho over the top seam every night, I made damn sure I stayed dry in my hooch. I lost two air mattresses to termite bites, but that was only slightly above the normal loss rate to those damnable bugs.

During this time, those interested in seeing Bob Hope's Christmas USO tour were asked to submit their names. Since only a handful of people from line units would be selected, I didn't bother. On December 22, we were back on Snuffy. The place was packed with grunts, including Henderson again, who was still covered with fungus.

The Army did its best to bring almost everyone into the firebase for the holidays. Instead of full companies maneuvering many klicks from the firebase, smaller units rotated in and out, so everyone got as much downtime as possible. Alpha Company was on the firebase, but Kurt was probably getting home about now.

The USO flew in a Vietnamese band, complete with a couple of cute dancers and a good lead singer on December 23. When they performed *American Woman* by The Guess Who, we went wild. They took a break after that and I grabbed a cold can of Pepsi from a plastic lined box set out for the occasion and popped it open. I'm very glad I didn't immediately take a sip because thick slime began to ooze out of the opening. I'd never seen anything like it. It just kept coming and it stuck together in an unbroken string about an inch in diameter. I kept lifting the can higher and higher until my arm was fully extended above my head, yet the string of slime kept coming even after the slime string reached the ground. By this time three or four grunts were standing around watching it in amazement.

"Holy shit, man. What the fuck *is* that?" asked one obviously stoned guy.

"Your guess is as good as mine, but I'd say it's nothing but Pepsi that spent too much time in the hot sun on a slow boat from the World!"

"Jesus, man. I might never drink Pepsi again."

Finally, I shook the can free of its slime string and tossed it into the nearest trash can.

Shortly after that, the band closed out with *We Gotta Get Outta This Place* by the Animals. If there was one hands-down favorite song of American forces in Vietnam, this was it. The entire crowd and eventually damn near everyone on the firebase, sang along. It was a really good time, though I'm sure I wasn't the only guy who felt more nostalgic than usual, thinking about *really* getting outta the place.

A little after that, I saw Kevin talking to a kid who looked an awful lot like him. I walked over and he introduced me. "Hey, Sean, I want you to meet Sahgeant Thompson. He's our point man and mentah."

I raised an eyebrow at the mentor part. "Glad to meet you, Sean. Where did they assign you?"

"Originally Alpha Company, but when they realized Kevin was already heah, they changed that to the HHC until they decide how to handle it."

"I'm glad you two have the chance to see each other, but you know you shouldn't be here, Sean. The risk is too great, and you've got your parents to think of."

"I know, Sahgeant, but it's hahd having Kevin here and worrying about him all the time. I feel bettah now, having seen him. Plus, it looks like we'll be togethah for Christmas."

Chapter 52 – Christmas in the Nam

On Christmas Eve, Second Platoon was out in the field, and my platoon was assigned QRF (quick reaction force) in case they hit the shit. It was unusual for a QRF to actually CA in support of a unit in contact, so I—and damn near everyone else—got stoned to the onion that night. At the stroke of midnight, nearly 500 grunts fired off hand flares, machine guns, and light weapons into the night sky. Nominally it was to celebrate Christmas, but really it was to celebrate being alive—and to enhance the pot high for some of us with a major light show.

As the light show began to fade, we were notified that something was going on with Second Platoon and we should prepare to CA. We waited along the berm for further orders. Around 0100 we received word that we would not be sent out because the incident had been friendly fire.

I turned to Frank Ness. "What the hell does that mean? How would somebody firing out of the NDP at night damn near launch a QRF operation?"

"Got me," said Frank.

A few minutes later, Lieutenant Collins came by. "We don't have the details yet, but it appears that two men in Second Platoon were killed by friendly fire."

Goose bumps rose over my upper body and I was instantly sober. "Do we know who it was?" I asked, not sure I wanted to know.

"Partly." The LT hesitated. "One was Staff Sergeant Terry Harris."

"Jesus fucking Christ!" I yelled. I knew Terry and liked him. Hell, we all liked him. The enormity of this hit me like a sledgehammer in the gut. Everyone was happy because it was Christmas, and this fucking war couldn't even take a fucking break. I wanted to scream. I wanted to cry. I was mad as hell. I was sad. I was bitter.

"Damn it, LT, Terry was a good man!"

There were no more fireworks or celebrations that night, no more smiles or laughter. We went to our bunks or air mattresses or guard holes and peered into the darkness, lost in private thoughts.

The next day I learned more from Jerry Pickering. It seems that a man who'd been relieved at a listening post outside the NDP lost his way in the dark. Harris had gone out to find him. But unfortunately, an FNG manning a guard hole didn't get the word, and when he heard movement to his front, he opened up with his M16. An experienced grunt, knowing there was an LP out, would have held fire and tried to find out who was out there. At first, confusion reigned. No one was sure who'd fired first, and other grunts began firing out into the night. When they realized there was no return fire, they put two and two together and sent out a patrol. It was a terrible, wasteful tragedy, and one I could envision all too well. The constant influx of new men increased the risk to everyone in a unit. FNGs often didn't quite grasp their situations or didn't get the word even though everyone else had, possibly because they weren't really hearing all that was said or didn't realize the importance of what they were hearing.

Late Christmas morning, I talked with the LT again. "Damn it, I know these things happen, but they shouldn't. It's such a goddamn waste." The incident in Cambodia when we lost Corporal Belon still grated on me and probably always would. "It's a nearly impossible job, leading men in a war we know will be over soon—not because we win or lose it, but because our government decides it's time to end it. And things like this just make it all the worse!"

"I know," he said with a sigh. "I know."

The chow line was longer than usual for Christmas dinner. Whole turkeys were being carved into slices, wings, and drumsticks. Stuffing, cranberries, and pie a la mode were shoveled onto the plates of passing grunts. But the thing that grabbed my attention was the two-star general standing beside the line. This was odd. We never saw generals in the field, not even on forward firebases. He was glad-handing the grunts as they approached the serving table. I saw it as a cheap PR stunt. I didn't want some unknown general out here in the war with me; he hadn't earned the right.

I wasn't sure what I wanted to say when my turn came, but in the end, I loudly said, "Merry Christmas, General," before he could, and firmly shook his hand.

He looked at me strangely for a second, but then he smiled. "Thank you, Sergeant. Merry Christmas to you."

And that was that. I have no idea who he was or what his place was in the chain of command. As a line grunt, he didn't matter to me. Harris's death had brought feelings I barely knew I had to a flash point. I realized I was too on edge and somehow tamped them down. I found a quiet spot to myself along the berm and sat on some sandbags. I knew not all generals were alike and it was unfair of me to automatically dislike this particular one. But rather than pursue that thought, I said, "Fuck it! It don't mean *nothin'*!" to the midday heat. I was referring to my feelings, not to Terry's death.

The next day, we were flown into a location near where we'd been the previous week. I wasn't talkative for a few days, but after taking the point I was back in the groove. I got word from the LT that I'd be going in for good on the resupply chopper in six days. I was glad, but not excited. It was strange. I suppose you get used to damn near anything—and God knows I was used to humping the boonies armed to the teeth.

At spades that night, Kevin and I beat the daylights out of Seth and Henderson, who was back again from his latest profile.

"How're ya doin', man?" I asked him.

"Truth is, it only takes a few days for that fungus to cover me head to toe, but so far I'm okay."

"I don't know how you stand it," I said.

"What's the alternative?"

"There is that little problem, isn't there?"

The last day before I was due to go in, I had the point. I didn't feel any sense of loss or nostalgia. That night on guard, though, my thoughts meandered through the good times and the bad. Some of the people I'd met I really liked, including some who'd been killed and wounded. Just for an instant I felt tears trying to well up, but I couldn't have that. I couldn't afford blurred vision on guard. I convinced myself that was the reason I banished my sadness, even though it was impossible to see more than a few feet in the blackness anyway.

The next day during resupply, I gave Kent my two loops of M60 ammo, the Claymore, and what was left of my bar of C-4. As I ate with my squad for the last time, I listened in vain for my name during mail call. Then I bid farewell to Kent, Lieutenant Collins, even Captain Reynolds, and then the men in my squad. I slipped on my pack, sat in the open door of the chopper, raised my M16 over my head, and was gone. It was January 10, 1971.

When I arrived at Snuffy, I snagged my previous spot in Jerry's bunker. Jerry told me Alpha Company had hit the shit on the seventh and had three KIAs. He didn't know how many wounded, but it was bad.

"Jesus. I'm glad Kurt's already home," I said.

"Me, too," said Jerry, "me, too."

I spent a week on Snuffy. Nominally, my job was to serve as a gate guard. Every morning after chow, I grabbed my M16 and bandoliers and headed for a guard hut at the main entrance. Immediately outside the berm was the helipad where flights of slicks landed and lifted off as they ferried infantry units to and from the field. Sometimes larger choppers landed there, too, and the south end of the fixed-wing runway was about fifty meters to my left. It was a busy place, with individuals and whole platoons and companies coming and going through the gate. My real job was giving directions to FNGs and other first-time visitors and keeping a logbook of interesting events.

Most of the time, I read books. The one I enjoyed most was *The Peter Principle*. It was hilariously funny, which I really needed, but it also made a serious point. I not only realized the truth of the principle—namely that people tend to be promoted to their level of incompetence and no further—but also that the Army was as good an example as any of a large organization plagued with the problem.

On my third day in the guard hut, a shithook landed around 1600 and a minute or two later a soldier ran by holding his right wrist in his left hand. A chunk of the soft and meaty underside of his right forearm had been torn out. There was a clean excision about two-inches wide and over an inch deep where the muscle was just gone. It must have happened very recently because there was as yet no discernible bleeding. Anyway, the guy was making a beeline to the aid station, as he should have been. Meantime, I stepped out and saw the shithook crew on the ground inspecting their chopper. As a grunt who'd been onboard walked past, I asked what happened.

"An AK round penetrated the chopper and hit the guy's arm. The round probably flattened a bit before it hit him, 'cause it took a hell of a chunk outta him."

"Yeah, so I noticed. When did it happen?"

"Just a minute or two before we set down. Couldn't have been more'n maybe two klicks out," he said as he continued on his way.

"Thanks!" I said and made an entry in the logbook. The shithook remained on the ground for over an hour as the crew carefully inspected every inch of it for damage. A little after 1700 it lifted off and headed back to Buttons for the night.

During our spades game two days later, Pickering said, "Did you hear about Henderson?"

"Don't tell me jungle rot dissolved the poor bastard out in the boonies."

"Nope. The company crossed a trail and he was sent out as a flanker. He spotted two gooks walking toward him, so he opened up, killing 'em both. They were NVA. Anyway, when he was sent in the next day for jungle rot again, he was told to report to the 93rd Evac and he'd be reassigned to a job in the rear, back at Bien Hoa, I guess."

"So the Army repeatedly sends the guy back to the boonies despite his jungle rot issue, basically treating him like he's a fuckin' goldbricker—as if a guy could fake jungle rot, but after he kills two gooks, they decide he's not faking it and reassign him?"

"That's about the size of it," said Jerry.

"Just goes to show you: there's the right way, the wrong way—" "And the Army way!" we finished in unison.

I awoke the next day and it really hit me: I was well and truly short. I still had five pounds of the pot Sam had sold me six months before, so I gave it to Alex because I knew he'd see that it got distributed to people who would appreciate it. I also donated my Cs and LRRPs to the bunker to help when the munchies struck or to feed Hiss if the need arose.

I went to morning chow, grabbed my M16 and a paperback, and headed to my guard hut for the last time. Nothing of interest happened that day except that I briefed the grunt who'd be replacing me on the guard hut duties, such as they were. He was a Spec-4 with six days left, so he wouldn't be on the job long.

That night Jerry and I won the spades games handily. Afterwards, we talked for an hour or so.

The next morning was like many others except my only responsibility was to board the first available chopper for Buttons. I grabbed my pack, made sure I had my orders, and headed to the helipad, sitting on my pack until a slick bound for Buttons came along. As we lifted off, the sight of the firebase in its jungle clearing reminded me of my arrival at Firebase Wood nine and a half months earlier. So much had happened and yet nothing had really changed.

Chapter 53 – The Freedom Bird

When I got to the HQ, Jay Simmons was there to greet me. "Well, it looks like you made it."

"I guess so," I replied. "What do I do now?"

"Go over to S-4 and turn in your weapon, pack, and other gear. Then pick up your duffel and personal stuff. When you come back, I'll assign you a bunk."

The process went quickly, but there was a surprise at the end.

"Sergeant Thompson, as a veteran of the Cambodian Incursion, you've been awarded a weapon captured during that operation," the clerk said. "It's a Russian SKS rifle." He handed me a registration certificate and asked me to look the weapon over.

I hefted the rifle, opened the bolt to confirm it was unloaded, noted that there was a bayonet folded back near the muzzle and a crack in the stock. "It's not perfect, but it seems fully functional," I said. "Does everybody get one of these?"

"Everybody who was in the Incursion gets a captured weapon of some kind. Most of the officers get nine-millimeter automatic NVA officer pistols."

"Of course," I said with a wink.

I was back at Jay's desk within twenty minutes and gave him copies of the forms, which he placed in my file. "You'll only be here for one night. In the morning, you'll fly to Bien Hoa and take the bus to the 90th Replacement Battalion at Long Binh, where they'll process you out of the Nam."

"Sounds straightforward enough," I said. "What else do I have to do?"

"Stow your duffel on your bunk. When you come back, Cal should be here. He's your next stop."

I spent ten minutes looking through the personal items I'd stored in my duffel in the Battalion rear as well as what I'd been carrying around in the ammo can on my pack frame. I tossed quite a few things and threw what was left into the duffel, which was practically empty.

When I got back to the HQ office, Cal Singleton said, "Hello there, short-timer. I have to give you the re-up talk now."

"What? You've got to be kidding!"

"Nope. It's required as part of your out-processing."

Cal read through a spiel that discussed the benefits of an Army career and added that if I chose to reenlist for a second term of service, I'd receive a promotion of one or two grades in rank.

I looked at Cal. "You know, re-upping crossed my mind, but promotions, pay increases, and career opportunities had nothing to do with it. Walking point is the most addictive thing I've ever done in my life. If I were making the decision based on my heart, there'd be a fifty-fifty chance. But I'm making it with my head, because I know it would be crazy to do this any longer. So the answer is no."

"I hear what you're saying, man, but there's a formal way I'm required to do this. Do you understand the benefits of re-enlistment as they've been explained to you? Please answer yes or no."

"Yes."

"Is it your decision to re-enlist?"

"No."

"Is it your decision not to re-enlist?"

"Yes."

"All right, then please check the appropriate boxes on this form, and sign and date it where indicated."

I did so and we were finished.

Later, at chow with Cal and Jay, Cal told me he confirmed what I'd told him about Captain Reynolds with three eyewitnesses from the Mortar Platoon, so he recommended disapproval and Captain Reynolds's Silver Star was not approved.

"You know, I have nothing against the man, other than the emphasis he places on his own career advancement above everything else," I said. "But it would be wrong for him to receive anything for that incident."

"Hey, you might wanna know that Sean Connelly, Kevin's little brother, has been sent back to Bien Hoa and will be returning to the World to do his time in a stateside unit. In fact, he's probably already there."

I was glad to hear it. The rest of our time together was pretty quiet. A distance was already building between me—a guy who was leaving Vietnam—and Cal and Jay, who were staying. It was sad, but inevitable.

After breakfast, I picked up my orders and Army Personnel File from Jay, and said my goodbyes. That afternoon, at the 90th Replacement Battalion, a clerk gave me a sheaf of papers and told me to follow the instructions in them to the letter. I read the instructions and headed to S-2 to get a tag for the SKS, which authorized me to carry it aboard commercial airliners.

Next, I went to S-4 to get a Class A uniform for travel. That seemed like a waste to me, since it would probably be the last time I'd ever wear it. *"There's the right way, the wrong way and the Army way,"* I thought with a grin.

The place was packed with troops processing out. It was a madhouse, but eventually I got everything I needed. I put it all on my bunk and headed to the next place on the list, Awards and Decorations. When I reached a free desk, the Spec-4 looked over my records.

"All right, because of your service in Vietnam and Cambodia you're entitled to the following: Combat Infantryman Badge First Award, Purple Heart Medal, Good Conduct Medal, National Defense Service Medal, Vietnam Service Medal with Bronze Star Attachment triple."

"If you say so," I said.

"Did you ever go into combat zones by air, either helicopter or fixed wing?"

"Yes, a few dozen times. Why?"

"Because that entitles you to an Air Medal. I'll add it to the list."

"Thanks," I said, slightly bewildered.

"Would you like a Bronze Star Medal?" he asked.

"What?" I was sure I'd misheard him.

"Would you like a Bronze Star?" he repeated. "You were in combat situations for nine months, Sergeant. You're entitled to one, if you want it."

"Well, if that's true, sure. It might mean something to somebody, someday."

Luckily, the collection of colorful ribbons, medals and shiny pins came with several sheets of paper showing exactly how to place them on the uniform. My sergeant stripes and the First Cav patch were already sewn onto the uniform jacket, but I spent half an hour lining up the ribbons and pinning everything in their proper places. Appropriately enough, the Combat Infantryman Badge was pinned above all other ribbons and devices. I liked that, because this was the most important award to me.

Next, I attended a health briefing, warning us to get any suspected sexually transmitted diseases treated before having sex with any nice American girls, and also emphasizing the importance of continuing to take our malaria pills for thirty days.

Last, I attended a briefing on veterans' benefits. This was something I hadn't thought about. In fact, it seemed wrong to consider myself a veteran. I guess I'd always thought of veterans as being World War II guys like my father and uncles and others in their generation. I didn't feel like I belonged in the same category. When I left that briefing, I vaguely remembered that there was some kind of educational benefit mentioned and also something about home loans. But beyond that the only thing that stuck in my mind was that if we needed dental work performed within one year of leaving the Army, we could have it done by any dentist of our choice and the VA would pay for it.

After breakfast the next day, I exchanged my MPC for U.S. cash and picked up my new orders—the ones that authorized me to leave the Republic of Vietnam and fly home. I put on my Class A uniform for the first time. The trousers were hugely oversized in the waist, something like forty-eight inches instead of the thirty-four they were supposed to be. This size problem extended all the way down the legs, so while I could bunch up the waist and conceal it somewhat under the suit jacket, there was no way to hide the elephantine pantlegs. It was too late to fix it, so I sighed, threw the duffel over my shoulder, and headed out.

At Tan Son Nhut, I handed my orders to one of the clerks. He kept his copies, stamped the top copy of mine, and handed me a ticket. I dutifully joined the line of men, all wearing Class A uniforms. Looking around, I realized that combat soldiers were scarce—Combat Infantryman Badges were few and far between, and Purple Hearts were even scarcer. I felt very alone, even though I was in the midst of a couple hundred soldiers.

I settled into a window seat on the plane and shortly afterward, the engines roared as they powered up and pushed us down the runway into the air. An Air Force fighter jet was just off our right wing. I heard some guys across the aisle saying a fighter was off the left wing, too. I hadn't let myself dwell on it, but the thought that I might be shot down while leaving the country right at the end of my tour had occurred to me. While they weren't a guarantee of safety, it felt good to have the fighters flying cover for us.

They stayed with us until we were well over the South China Sea and outside of Vietnamese air space and the war zone. When the fighters veered off, our plane turned slightly left to a more northeasterly direction, making a beeline for Japan. My return route was different from my arrival one. This flight was making just one stop at Yokota Air Base on the west edge of Tokyo.

About three hours into the flight I heard loud, angry words coming from some distance to the front. Pretty soon I could make out obscenities mixed into rambling tirades that made no sense. The two stewards quickly reached the offending passenger and told him in no uncertain terms that his behavior wouldn't be tolerated. This was reinforced by the soldiers on either side of him who just wanted to get home without any hassles. This quieted him down for the next couple of hours, but his erratic behavior flared up again near the end of the flight, so the stewards escorted him to the rear of the plane, where they kept him quiet somehow for the rest of our flight. This underlined why stewards needed to be on these flights.

The 2700-mile flight to Yokota took six hours and there was a two-hour time difference, so we arrived at about 1700 local time, just after dark. We were allowed to deplane while the aircraft was refueled and serviced. The terminal building was almost empty of people, but didn't look or feel like a military base at all. It was light and airy inside, with high ceilings and the ambience of a civilian airport in the United States. I was still feeling like the odd man out among the passengers on my plane, so I looked for someplace where I could be alone. I found a long, unoccupied bench on the west side of the terminal. There were some vending machines nearby, so I bought a Coke and settled in for the wait.

A few minutes later, a Japanese man of around fifty approached, he was sweeping the mostly deserted terminal for any litter he could find. He had a sack over one shoulder and a broom and one of those dust pans on a stick that tipped back when lifted off the floor. I sat almost motionless on the bench as he very slowly passed between me and the wall. He looked at the floor as he walked, but many times his eyes would dart quickly to glance at me. At first, I thought he was as appalled at the bagginess of my pants as I was, but I noticed that he was looking at my face and my medals and ribbons more than he was at my pants. It crossed my mind that it was likely he'd been in the Japanese Imperial Army during World War II and may have fought Americans who looked very much like me. I got the impression that he knew what at least some of my medals, badges and ribbons meant. It also dawned on me that if my guesses about him were correct, we probably had more in common with each other than with most other people in the terminal. Eventually, he retraced his steps and moved across the open area to my right.

As I sat there sipping my Coke, I realized I was more than tired. I was drained—of energy and purpose. A tremendous burden had been lifted from me, but I was so used to bearing it that I felt lost without it. It was a strange, vacant feeling.

A few minutes later, it was announced over the PA that my flight would begin boarding in ten minutes. I finished my Coke, tossed the can in the nearest waste bin and slowly made my way back toward my gate. The offending passenger was nowhere to be seen, but the rest of us took the same seats we'd had during the first leg and off we went. This final leg was 5,150 miles and nine-and-a-half hours non-stop to Travis Air Force Base north of San Francisco. It was about 1830 local time when we took off and with a seven-hour time difference that meant it would be a little before 1100 Pacific Standard Time when we arrived at Travis.

I read a paperback and various magazines off and on and dozed here and there during the interminable night flight across the Pacific, but mostly my mind was blank. When it began to get light outside, I and others began trying to spot the California coastline to the east. Of course, we started doing that much earlier than there was any hope of seeing it, but we were anxious. Very surprisingly, about 0915 we did see it! Shortly after that the captain came on and told us we'd caught a strong jet stream tail wind and would be landing at Travis in about twenty minutes. There weren't any cheers, but there was a lot of excited talking.

The landing was as light as a feather and we were filing off the plane by 0945. A few guys kissed the tarmac at the foot of the stairs, but most of us just looked around and inhaled deeply. Vietnam didn't smell bad, but it smelled quite different from most of the United States.

We had to go through customs inside the terminal where they asked many of the same inane questions Vietnamese customs had asked when we landed at Bien Hoa. But here we were also required to literally turn our duffels upside down and dump the contents onto a very long metal slide or counter where everything we owned was sifted through by the customs agents. I resented that. A couple of M16 rounds fell out of mine, which were immediately grabbed and tossed in a bin beneath the counter.

"Is there any more ammo in here Sergeant?" the agent asked.

"Not as far as I know, but to be honest, I didn't know those rounds were in there either," I answered truthfully.

After the inspection and being reunited with my war trophy SKS, I was finally passed through to join another line waiting to board one in a herd of busses outside. For about an hour and a half we rolled along through the brown, grass-covered hills and saltwater marshes north of San Francisco Bay. Finally, we reached the Oakland Army Base, where some of us would receive orders for our next duty assignments and others, like me, would be discharged from the Army.

It was 1300 when we arrived and about 1400 when we finished checking in. We were assigned lockers where we could secure our duffels and my rifle, told to go to chow, and instructed to report back for processing by 1500. Much of the rest of the day was a blur except for one interesting and coincidental event. As I stood in the line for our discharge medical check, exactly as had happened on the day I entered the Army the guy immediately in front of me in the line for the blood draws fainted at the sight of the needle or the blood and began dropping to the concrete floor. Another guy and I grabbed him and eased him down gently. I reminded myself that not everyone who was in Vietnam was actually in the war. During this check, I was asked if I had any pain or physical problems. I didn't say a word about the infection in my shoulder, the jungle rot boil on my cheek, the tennis elbow, the residual pains and aches where the shrapnel resided in my leg, or anything else. I didn't want anything to slow down the process of getting out of the Army as quickly as possible.

At around 1930, we were assigned bunks. This was a huge disappointment. I'm sure everyone felt as I did, that we could keep going if it would get us out any earlier. But we accepted the inevitable and took the proffered pile of bedding. Even though I was exhausted, I slept badly.

In the morning, I was able to trade my oversized Class A pants for proper ones and at around 1030 I signed a DD-214 Armed Forces of The United States Report of Transfer or Discharge. An hour later, I was walking through the San Francisco airport terminal, carrying a duffel and a rifle in a cloth case, feeling even more out of place and alone than I had on the flight home.

Chapter 54 – Back in the World

My orders booked me on three United Airlines flights. The first was non-stop to Denver, where I had a two-and-a-half-hour layover. The second was non-stop from Denver to Chicago's O'Hare Field. I called my mother and gave her my flight number and arrival time. She said she had to pick my father up at the train station at almost the same time, so she'd call Ernie to pick me up at O'Hare. "I'll pay him, so don't worry about that, not even the tip," she said. I told her thanks and that I loved her, and boarded the plane to Denver. The third flight was from Chicago O'Hare to Tucson on Sunday, January 24.

Being January 21, the height of ski season, the plane to Colorado was packed with skiers heading to the Rockies. I checked my duffel at the counter, and as I boarded the aircraft a stewardess took my rifle and stowed it in a compartment behind the first-class section.

I ended up sitting in an aisle seat next to an Infantry 2nd Lieutenant. At first, we just nodded to each other, but about half an hour into the flight, he said, "Sergeant, do you mind if I ask you something?"

"No, Sir, go right ahead."

"Are you just back from Vietnam?"

"Yes," I said, "I got back yesterday and was processed out of the Army today. I'm headed home to the Chicago area now."

"I just recently graduated from Infantry OCS and have orders to go to Germany, but I'm sure I'll be sent to Vietnam after that. Can I pick your brain a little?"

"Sure. What would you like to know?"

"Well, I know tactics and strategy from my OCS training, but can you tell me exactly how the infantry operates in Vietnam?"

"Yes," I answered and began what turned out to be a two-hour course in infantry operations in the Vietnam War. I told him about the Corps Areas and the battalion structure and the function of the four companies in each battalion. I talked about how our field operations were kept within range of the big guns on the firebases and how we'd spend weeks or a month or more in the field and come into a firebase to rest and burn shit and pull perimeter guard for a few days and then go out again. I talked about how bad it was in Cambodia and how it had generally been better after that back in Vietnam. I talked about the heat, the humidity, scorpions, leeches, mosquitoes, bees, centipedes, termites, wait-a-minute vines, and how the canopy was so thick that you seldom saw the sun, and the brush was so thick you usually couldn't see more than twenty to fifty feet in front of you. He soaked up every word like a man whose life could depend on it, which it might. It was the last thing I wanted to talk about, but I liked the young lieutenant and wanted to do what I could to prepare him for the reality of the jungle war.

When the plane landed in Denver, I got my SKS and we went our separate ways. "Good luck, LT," I said as he rushed to make his connecting flight. "Thanks, Sergeant. To you, too!"

I found a bar and ordered a Coors; the bartender checked my ID. I was feeling kind of numb before I started that beer, but I nursed it and two more over the next two hours. When boarding was announced for my next flight, I managed to find the gate and get on board. Unlike the first plane, this one was practically empty. A small grin appeared on my face as I thought, *"Who would've guessed that so few people wanted to go to Chicago on a Thursday in January?"*

I again handed my rifle to a stewardess for stowing and was seated about two-thirds of the way back on the right side of the plane, there was a businessman seated on my right, next to the window. I nodded, but didn't speak and neither did he. The sun was setting over the Rockies as we took off. As soon as the plane leveled off at altitude, we were offered snacks and sodas or coffee. I took a bag of peanuts and yet another ginger ale. Ten minutes later a stewardess came over and took my detritus.

I'm not sure if it was because I probably looked like hell or that she knew I'd just returned from Vietnam, I suppose my reservation probably revealed that information or maybe it was the rifle, but she came back a few minutes later and said softly, "Sergeant, would you like to get some sleep?"

"Thank you, but I've never been able to sleep well on planes," I said.

"I think we can arrange something for you that might help," she said. "Please follow me." She led me to very near the front of the coach section and asked me to wait a moment. Then she bent over a set of three seats on the left side of the aircraft and flipped the armrests completely out of the way creating a couch across all three of them.

"Wow. I didn't know they'd even do that." I exclaimed.

"We keep it a secret," she said under her breath as she gave me a wonderful smile. Then she used a hand gesture to indicate that I should sit down, and reached in the overhead bin to remove a pillow.

I looked up at her sheepishly and said, "Do you think I could get another pillow?"

"Certainly," she said and handed me two more!

There are some very special things you never forget. The simple kindness shown me by that United Airlines stewardess is one. She looked down at me and said, "Don't worry, I'll wake you just before we land."

"Thank you," I said. Within five minutes, I was deeply asleep on an airplane for the first time in my life.

True to her word, she woke me just before the "Fasten Seat Belts" sign lit up and the Captain announced that we'd be landing within ten minutes.

In Chicago, I thanked the stewardess as she handed me my rifle and then headed to baggage claim to retrieve my duffel bag. Just after 10:00 p.m., the taxi my parents had arranged made its way down the long gravel driveway of their home.

"Are you hungry?" my father asked.

"Maybe a little, but I'm mainly tired."

"Didi, make the boy a sandwich," he said to my mother. For some reason, my father felt that it was his duty as a husband, father, and host to keep all those in his charge well fed, even guests.

"Let me take my stuff to my room and I'll be right back."

When I returned a few minutes later, my mother placed a sandwich and Coke on the dining room table for me. I sat down and took a bite. They sat down and watched me eat. It was the safest I'd felt in a long time.

I told them about my out-processing. They told me what my sisters were up to. And then I realized I was completely worn out.

"I hope you can forgive me, but I think I might have to go to bed. I've been on planes for twenty-four of the last forty-eight hours, and I think it's caught up with me."

"Of course, son," said my father. "Get some rest and we'll talk tomorrow."

In the morning after breakfast, I put on a winter coat, left the house, and walked across patches of snow and frozen grass, down the hill to the lake. It was frozen, of course, but I didn't care. The temperature was in the teens and there was a steady breeze of five miles per hour. It was bracing. I could see three houses on the hill across the lake, none of which had been there when we moved into our house fourteen years before. Things had changed around Orchard Lake. Many of the places I'd hunted birds and trapped muskrats had been drained, filled in, graded, and turned into lawns. *"Everything changes,"* I thought, *"whether we like it or not."*

I walked along the foot of the hill to the north where the remnants of my duck blind were inexorably returning to nature amid a tangle of shore brush and twisted limbs of native trees. I knew it would be gone completely in another few years.

Then I walked up the hill to the west along the fence—a fence my father and I had built. It was in pretty good shape, but the strange twisted iron nails he'd insisted would hold better were still rusting through faster than I could believe. The ends of a few rails were loose, separating from the posts and even dropping to the ground here and there. I walked along the west edge of the property and into the oak and hickory woods. Even without leaves, the woods were a dark and mysterious place, but not as dark and mysterious now as they'd been before.

Then I came through the east edge of the woods into our driveway circle and made my way past the garage down to the house. I had to be careful in this last stretch, because it was a shaded north-facing slope with more snow and ice. When I went through the back door, I realized I'd been outside for an hour. The house felt hot.

My mother was at her desk in the den, working on her weekly society column for the local paper. I put my coat away and said, "The place looks pretty good for midwinter."

"Hmm, oh yes. So far this hasn't been too bad a winter, but there's still plenty of time." Then she bent back to her task, so I wandered into the living room.

I made a beeline for the high-backed, yellow chair on the right end of the picture window and settled into it. I'd spent many hours in that chair since the age of thirteen. As I sat there, I remembered being in the same position, looking out the window and wondering what it was like to be a man and if I'd ever be one; what the wide world beyond our secluded property was really like and how I'd find a way to "make it" out there. Some of those questions were still unanswered, but I did know I was a man, mostly. Beyond that, I just wanted to forget everything: Vietnam, goals, everything—at least for a while.

In an hour or so, I got up and headed for the kitchen to make myself a sandwich and grab a Coke. When that was done, I intended to watch some TV in the dining room. My grandmother, who'd been sleeping when I arrived the night before, was doing some crocheting. "Can you tell me about the medals you earned?" she asked. "I want to write the information down while it's still fresh in your memory."

I was irritated. I did not want to talk about that stuff right then. But I loved my grandmother and knew she was a very patriotic woman who'd joined the Army in her late forties during World War II and worked in Intelligence. From her point of view, she was making a very reasonable request.

I couldn't keep the irritation out of my voice as I curtly said, "I got the Combat Infantryman Badge for thirty days or more in a combat zone, the Purple Heart for a shrapnel wound from a grenade on the Ho Chi Minh Trail in Cambodia, the Air Medal because I made a lot of combat air assaults, and the Bronze Star medal because they give it to everybody."

"What do you mean they give it to everybody?" she asked with skeptical, narrowed eyes.

I told her about the clerk who'd simply added it to my list of awards because he said I'd earned it. "I guess, technically it's awarded for meritorious service in a combat zone. It's the ground combat equivalent of the Air Medal. Apparently, by earning a CIB and a Purple Heart, I was automatically eligible for the Bronze Star."

"That's more like it," she said with a small frown.

"I'm sorry Momso. I just don't feel like talking much about this stuff right now."

"I understand, Cam, but it's important, you know."

"I guess so, but I don't want to deal with it now."

"All right. Go ahead and turn on the TV," she said in resignation.

The next day I went to Lipofsky's, the local clothing store in Barrington. When I walked in, Mr. Lipofsky asked what I was looking for. "Everything," I said. "I just got back from Vietnam day before yesterday and I have no civilian clothes at all. I guess I need underwear, socks, slacks, shirts and a couple of sweaters."

Lipofsky's employed four people on the floor in those days, a young man and woman who were younger Lipofskys and two other young women. Within minutes, as he spread the word, I was surrounded by the four young people, under the loose supervision of Mr. Lipofsky. They bent over backward to find everything I needed in record time. It was a wonderful experience and made me feel welcome in my little hometown.

I was truly glad to be home, but I wouldn't be there long. It was already Saturday, and registration at the University of Arizona was Monday. I'd be flying to Tucson on a night flight the next day, on Sunday. I felt rushed, and I didn't like it.

I had some good talks with my parents, but the feeling I'd had the previous spring that things had fundamentally changed was stronger now. My father was one of the smartest and most knowledgeable people I'd ever met, but he'd never fought in a war, and I had. It was a profound experience that could only be understood by participating in it—if then, and one my father didn't have and couldn't ever fully comprehend. It imparted a kind of self-knowledge that few other experiences could and was the first area in which my experience and knowledge clearly exceeded my father's. We didn't speak about it, but it was understood. It opened the door, at least a crack, to his acceptance of me as a fellow adult.

On Sunday afternoon, my parents drove me to O'Hare and saw me off. Because I was still flying on Army orders, I had to wear my Class As one more time. I must have made quite a sight, carrying my SKS rifle in its cloth sleeve onto the plane. I'd pre-selected my seat of choice, the window seat over the front edge of the wing on the right side. It was my preferred location because it was the most stable place to sit, but this time it was a mistake because I hadn't realized that this United flight was a propeller aircraft. Let's just say that conversation is limited when you're in the middle of four internal combustion aircraft engines!

The flight was entirely in the dark, so the only thing to see out the window were lights on the ground when there were no clouds below us. There was no moon either, so it was even darker than usual. However, toward the end of the five-hour flight, I sensed that we were descending, looked out the window, and was able to see the reflection of starlight off snow fields as we passed close over the peaks of the Rincon Mountains. From there it was just a few minutes before we landed in Tucson.

As I stepped from the tarmac into the airport concourse holding my cased rifle, my sister Julie was there to greet me. We hugged each other tightly. No one in this world gives better hugs. The deep throated hum that accompanies them makes them much more than skin deep! I really needed that hug. We made our way through the sparsely peopled airport, grabbed my lone suitcase at baggage claim and headed outside where her friend had waited for us in her car. She was kind enough to drop me off at the Geronimo Hotel before they headed back to the dorm.

Contrary to popular belief, typical winter nights in Tucson get quite chilly, often into the twenties; this was a typical night. The Geronimo Hotel was built in the 1920s and had fallen on hard times. It consisted of a medium-size two-story main building and a courtyard immediately to its east featuring mature date palm trees and ancient twisted prickly pears of the type with edible 'pears', and cholla or 'jumping' cactus in beds surrounding it. There may have been a round fountain in the middle of the courtyard at one time, but during my several stays there from the mid-60s to the mid-70s this was simply a flower bed. The courtyard was lined on three sides by apartments and guest houses. Like nearly all buildings in Tucson from its era and earlier, the structures were built of adobe covered by tiled roofs. The thick adobe walls were marvelous insulators, keeping the temperature nearly constant inside, despite outside temperatures that ranged from 105+ in summer to as low as occasional single digits in winter.

The smaller buildings around the courtyard ranged from duplex-type homes, to apartments that varied from studios with kitchenettes and a bathroom to larger two-bedroom suites. I had arranged to rent a studio off the southeast corner of the courtyard, because it was all I needed and could afford. I entered the main building, rang the bell on the hotel desk and was eventually greeted by a bleary-eyed, elderly woman. I signed a month-to-month lease agreement, paid for the first month in advance, and was given a key and directions.

I opened the door to the tiny cave-like apartment that would be my home for the next several years. I got a drink of water, stripped off my uniform for the last time, and hit the sack. I slept better that night than I had since Sydney.

I was up early the next day and headed to the campus, just a block and a half east. Registration started at 9:00, and the place was already packed with students queuing up. It took three hours, but I got all the courses I wanted, though not all the times I would have preferred. I wanted to have no morning classes, but ended up with two, though neither was at the crack of dawn. It could have been worse.

I went to the Student Union to get some lunch and was mesmerized by the high percentage of stunningly beautiful girls. It was the height of the mini-skirt era, and the sights reminded me in no uncertain terms that I was still alive. Eventually, I pulled myself away and headed to the registrar's office. I wanted to see how Dean Howard managed to get me off of the academic probation that had led to my being drafted two years earlier. My official transcript was on several three-by-five cards dating back to my first enrollment in September of 1962. I was astounded at what I saw. Labels had been stuck over the official records dealing with my academic probation and re-typed to erase all record of it. None of my grades were altered though, so I still had to dig myself out of the hole I'd created in the fall of 1968.

I made my way across campus to the dean's office and personally thanked him. He insisted it was nothing, but we both knew better.

My next stop was the bookstore where I bought all the required books and materials I'd need for the coming semester. Then I made a short stop at my apartment to drop them off before heading to George Keahey's barbershop. The shop was at street level in the north end of the Geronimo's main building.

George looked up at me from behind the head of hair he was working on, smiled and said, "Well, if it ain't ol' Jim. Went to Veet-nom and got his ass shot off!"

My answering smile may have been the broadest of my life. I walked over and shook his hand. "It's good to see you George, and good to be home."

"Are you gonna get a haircut?" he asked.

"Not for quite a while. Call it a statement."

"Well, welcome home anyway!" he said with a broad grin.

My next stop was Meade Select Market, right next door in the northeast corner of the building. When I walked in, Mrs. Meade, who was behind the counter, said, "Welcome home stranger! When did you get back?"

"Last night," I said. "It's wonderful to see you."

"Thanks! Well, you know where everything is so have at it!" I loaded up on staples and headed back to my apartment to put them away.

Looking around, I realized that I had to get some kind of cheap TV or I'd go stir crazy, but in the meantime I fixed some rice and beans, opened a can of Coke and started looking over my course schedule. I knew I'd be getting some kind of GI educational benefit, but until the first check arrived, I had to get by on what I had and what I could earn. After a while, I took a walk around the area between the Geronimo and Speedway Boulevard looking for places I might be able to get a job. I noted down a couple and then visited Julie at her dorm. I thanked her again for seeing the Dean for me. We talked for an hour or so and then I headed home for another early night.

On Thursday, my third class was Contemporary Civilization. It dawned on me that name might be rather contradictory—an oxymoron—but it was in one of my two areas of specialization: political science and history. Most classes were dismissed early on the first day, but not this one.

With about ten minutes to go, the professor asked if there were any topics the students would like to discuss. A bright girl in the front row—I had positioned myself inconspicuously near the back—raised her hand. Because she'd contributed numerous times during the hour, she was already a familiar voice and personality. I knew the type. While bright, she was far more ignorant than she imagined and didn't consider the implications of her words before charging ahead. Our classmates likely gave her more credit than she deserved when she confidently continued to express her "insights."

I didn't care since—as I'd learned the hard way—it don't mean nothin'.

But in the last minutes of that class, she started talking about the Cambodian Incursion. She said it had been a terrible mistake, was a crime against humanity, had widened a war we should never have fought, had accomplished nothing, and was counterproductive in every way, et cetera, et cetera, et cetera.

I felt like someone had kicked me in the gut. Hard. I thought about the shrapnel in my leg, the friends I'd lost, the Montagnards whose future was so bleak, and the tons of weapons and ammunition that would be denied to the enemy, making it easier and faster for us to get out of the war.

I sat there with a blank expression and said nothing. I was positive I was the only person in the class who'd been there and who knew the story firsthand. But I understood where my classmate was coming from and didn't entirely disagree with her. That just made it worse.

When the bell rang, I sighed, picked up my books and walked out, thinking... *"I'm home."*

Epilogue

What happened with me – Did the military make me a better person? Yes. In fact, I've always told anyone who asked that the military is a very positive experience, but that I can't recommend it to anyone, because there's no guarantee they'll survive it.

One way that I changed was that before being in the Army, my college was funded almost entirely by my parents, but afterward I stopped taking any money at all from them. In short, I took more personal responsibility for my life.

But there were other changes. I had dreams before I went to Vietnam: some specific, like wanting to live in the open country of the West, and some vague and not completely formed, like wanting a good and beautiful wife I loved and who loved me, and a decent income and having the respect of my peers. When I returned to the States and civilian life, I felt something was missing inside of me that had always been there before. It was a hollow feeling. Within a few months, I realized that I no longer had any dreams: none specific and none vague, just none at all. The existential anxiety I acquired in Vietnam, that sense that I and anyone I knew could be dead in a heartbeat, had become a part of me. I was adrift. I wanted to regain my dreams—or any dreams, even just one. I thought I'd never be able to dream again.

After returning to civilian life, I spent the next six years in Tucson drinking too much, occasionally trying various mind-altering drugs (no injectable or opioid ones, thank heaven), sleeping with too many different women (another kind of intoxicant), and playing at getting an education. The next two years, in Illinois and back in Tucson, I all but quit drinking, drugs and women, and fell into a funk that seemed bottomless and hopeless. Then by some miracle, I met Nancy Susan Wolff, a wonderful, old-fashioned girl with old-fashioned values like eternal, unconditional love, which for some reason she felt for me. We met in the workplace, a printing company in Tucson, Arizona. I thought of myself as irreparably damaged goods, but she absolutely would not give up on me, wouldn't tolerate any self-pity or self-deprecation from me, and gradually made it possible for me to heal and to dream again. We were married for 36 years until she died at the age of 63 of metastatic breast cancer in 2015. Because of her, I've remained a survivor and have a wonderful daughter and two beautiful granddaughters (who are five and two as I write this). During our marriage, I worked as a department manager at a Kmart and then in a career in federal service with the U.S. Forest Service and Bureau of Land Management, and in 2000, during a break from the career, I became the oldest male graduate of the University of South Dakota School of Law. I passed the bar on my first try and remain a member of the bar. Though I've never practiced law, the degree broke me through the ceiling I'd hit in federal service and enabled me to retire with financial independence and dignity.

Parents and Siblings – In March 1986, at age 69, my father dropped dead of a heart attack at home in Barrington Hills, Illinois. My mother first moved to Rapid City, South Dakota, to be near me and my family when I worked for the Forest Service in the Black Hills. Later she moved to Naples, Florida, and lived with her life-long friend and noted artist Phyllis Hollands-Robinson, then to Dallas, Texas, near my sister Langley (Mimi) and her family, and finally to Reno-Sparks, Nevada, to be near me and my family again. She died a month short of her 91st birthday in Reno in January 2009. My sisters are both well, one in Kentucky and the other in Arizona.

Shortly after I returned from Vietnam my father told me that, as a doctor, he could have gotten another MD to write me a medical diagnosis that would have exempted me from military service. This had never occurred to me. The reason he didn't pull those strings had nothing to do with his belief that the Army might "straighten me out" and everything to do with what was the "right thing to do." I completely agree with his decision.

The risks to which I would be exposed were fully understood by him. As an Army psychiatrist during the Korean War he clinically treated former prisoners of war and several Congressional Medal of Honor recipients who'd been deeply traumatized by their experiences. Many of his closest friends were killed in World War II. One brother was profoundly affected by his service as a medic in the Battle of the Bulge and the other suffered his entire life from bouts with malaria contracted during the Pacific island-hopping campaign. He knew about the dangers of war and he loved me, but he did the right thing, because that's the kind of man he was.

My father had strong convictions, but never arbitrary or unconsidered ones. He knew how an adult man should behave and held himself to that standard no matter the personal consequences. While I suspect that similar characteristics were in my DNA from birth, this sense of right and duty was something he reinforced in me. As a result, the character trait I value in myself and others above all is personal integrity. I believe in doing what I know to be right and fair regardless of potential negative consequences to me. It may sound unrealistic, dated or a bit corny, but my word is my bond—as it was for my father.

My mother was a very social person who got along well with almost everyone. She was also a gifted writer who wrote society columns and general interest articles in several suburban newspapers in the Chicago area for three decades. When she moved to Rapid City, she wrote similar columns and articles for the Rapid City Journal, and when she moved to Florida, she did the same for the Naples Daily News. Her easy ability to communicate with people of diverse backgrounds greatly influenced me. My instinct is to like and respect everyone I meet until they prove they don't deserve it. For that I can never thank her enough.

I have often wondered how my parents stood the strain when I was in Vietnam. In those days, communications between the war zone and home were not materially better than they'd been in previous wars. Many months went by with no more than a few letters sporadically being exchanged. But they did it.

More than anything else though, I always knew my parents loved me, and I loved them every bit as much. The rock-solid foundation that creates in my life makes dealing with the difficulties and unfairness that life throws at all of us much easier to handle. I am forever grateful to my parents.

George Keahey – George continued to work in his barber shop in the Geronimo Hotel until he just couldn't do it any longer. He remains one of the finest people I've ever known.

Kurt Stephan – Kurt married his wonderful wife Lin in his beloved Minnesota shortly after his return from Vietnam, and has worked in the sound design business ever since. We went on two canoe trips together in the Boundary Waters wilderness in the 1970s and remain close today. He provided valuable help to me in the writing of this book.

Steve Warner – In 1980, I belatedly sent Steve a letter to his home in New Jersey. A week or so later, I received a reply from his mother, telling me that Steve had been killed on Valentine's Day, 1971, about three weeks after I left Vietnam. He was riding on or in an APC with ARVN troops during their invasion of Laos when an RPG hit the vehicle. Steve's parents used the proceeds of his GI life insurance to establish the Stephen H. Warner Collection, in Special Collections and Archives, Musselman Library, at Gettysburg College. Later, this was expanded to include books related to peace studies and conflict resolution generally. Steve would have loved that.

Superman – While his nickname really was "Superman" because of his resemblance to Clark Kent, I cannot remember his real name. He was a wonderful squad mate. I've portrayed him in every way as closely as I can to the man I knew. He was a kindred spirit and if we were ever to meet again, I'm sure we still would be!

Jerry Pickering – I don't know anything about Jerry other than that he returned to Oklahoma and kept his word by sending me photos of Firebase Neal and the Montagnard village in Cambodia and other places, some of which I've included in this memoir.

Gordon Castro – I never saw or heard from Gordon after I left Vietnam, but I know he survived because somehow everyone in Echo Company did. He was a good man with a great sense of humor. I hope he's hale and hearty.

Woody Myrick – I heard nothing more about Woody after he got a rear job, but his keen eye spotting that hooch frame probably saved us both. Thank you my friend!

Drill Sergeants – I never saw my drill sergeants after training, but owe them a great deal. Drill Sergeant Jose Longoria in Basic was an excellent leader and guide, and I suspect a fine man. I'm very grateful to him for helping me make the difficult transition from soft civilian to hard soldier.

My Head Drill Sergeant in Infantry AIT, whom I've called Robert Harper in this memoir, was a special person. He kneaded the dough that Jose Longoria had allowed to rise and baked me into a man who had a far better chance to survive the Vietnam War than I would have had otherwise. It was an honor to know him.

Others – After returning to civilian life, I didn't stay in touch with anyone I served with in Vietnam or Cambodia other than Kurt. It wasn't a conscious decision, but I suspect it was a consequence of my strong desire to move on from the experience. That may have been necessary to a successful return to "civilization" at first, but I regret it now. I wish every one of them well.

Afterword

After the experience of Vietnam what questions are uppermost in my mind? One is obvious, was it worth it? The other is personal, did I do anything worth writing home about, let alone worthy of a book?

By roughly mid-1968, following a few years of heavy military involvement and increasing casualties, most Americans had heard of Vietnam and some could find it on a map. The U.S. public then began to realize that the truth was far more complicated than first impressions. But there were rational arguments that American involvement was the right thing to do from a national defense point of view. The "Domino Theory" postulated that non-communist countries adjacent to communist ones would be converted to communism by whatever means necessary. Then, like dominos, as soon as the first one fell others would fall one after another. This had some weight because of what had happened in Eastern Europe and East Asia following World War II, when nearly every country touching the Soviet Union and many of the next tier countries had become communist, among them North Korea and North Vietnam adjacent to Communist China.

I believed then and still believe that American intentions were good when we sent troops to Vietnam. I can't speak to all that was known and discussed in the halls of American power, but to the average American, defending South Vietnam made sense. Besides, in the 1960s, Americans saw their government as 'us' not 'them' and trusted its word and motivations. After all, it had only been twenty years since the United States and its allies had won World War II.

But for those of us who went to Vietnam, it became clear that the South Vietnamese government was hopelessly corrupt and profoundly distrusted by most people in the country. For the average citizen living in rural Vietnam, the Saigon government provided nothing and took much. Contact with the government tended to involve tax collection and compulsory military service, not schools, road building, power grids or communication networks. In short, there was an irreparable disconnect between the Saigon government and most of its people.

Complicating matters further was the legacy of French colonial rule. I have no doubt that to many ordinary Vietnamese, American soldiers were understood to be the instruments of another Western colonial power invited back by a Saigon government incapable of ruling without such interference. While some Vietnamese did appreciate the commitment of American materiel and blood in their defense, I think many others saw us as foreign mercenaries in the service of a corrupt and incompetent government.

There were many good people in South Vietnam who deserved protection and who certainly believed in democracy over communism, but the Vietnam War was a civil war. It is never a good idea for outside nations to directly involve themselves militarily in another nation's civil war. The problems Vietnam faced were its own and could only be solved by the Vietnamese people.

On the personal side, as alluded to earlier, I was reluctant to write about my experiences because I felt that I'd just done my job and how interesting would that be to anybody? Over time though, it began to seem important to attempt to describe what the American soldiers who fought the Vietnam War were really like, to provide a sense of our daily lives and to honor the decency and courage of the vast majority of us in the American infantry of 1970. I hope I've managed to do that to some extent, and that it will help future generations to remember and feel what it was like as well.

Americans must never forget that our combat troops are us—in trying times.

Appendix 1 – Terms and Definitions

AIT = Advanced Individual Training (the first training following Basic).

Alpha-Alpha = Automatic Ambush. A Claymore mine set to detonate when a wire stretched across a likely route of foot travel is tripped. Alpha-Alphas were often set out on approaches to NDPs as an added measure of protection.

AO = Area of Operations. The area within which an infantry unit operates. This varies in size depending on the size of the unit, but for an infantry battalion it included areas within the reach of its big guns, normally a radius of eighteen miles around the battalion rear and any forward firebases. Typically, a battalion only has one rear and one forward base, each of which can provide artillery support over approximately 325 square miles. But it must be remembered that in addition to this primary 650-square-mile area within which the four rifle companies normally operated, Echo Company often sent its long range reconnaissance patrols to areas beyond that, and of course our air support could and did cover everywhere else in the war zone.

APC = M113 Armored Personnel Carrier. A tracked vehicle designed to protect troops from small arms and medium machine-gun fire while transporting up to eleven infantrymen in combat areas. It usually employed a single .50 caliber machine gun in a top turret, but sometimes also employed two M60 machine guns and other offensive weapons depending on its specific role.

APO = Army Post Office code, what was used in lieu of a zip code for overseas military unit addresses.

Arc Light = B-52 bomb strike, devastating strip or carpet bombing by flights of three-aircraft dropping 54,000 pounds of bombs per plane.

Article 15 = An administrative punishment meted out on the authority of unit commanders, without the need to go through higher authorities or military courts.

ARVN = Army of the Republic of Vietnam, the South Vietnamese Army, pronounced 'arvin.'

Australian Field Shower = A five-gallon canvas bucket with a flat metal shower head beneath it that served as the turn-on/turn-off valve. Water was poured into the hanging bucket and controlled by turning the shower head. It was possible to wet-down and lather-up, turn off the water to wash, then turn the water back on and rinse off using a single bucket of water. I assume its name derives from its being originated in Australia, but don't know that for a fact.

Azimuth = The direction of movement as expressed in degrees on a magnetic compass. For instance, directly south is an azimuth of 180, directly west is an azimuth of 270, etc.

Bangalore Torpedo = Long hollow metal tube filled with explosive. They can be fastened together and pushed under obstructions, usually barbed wire but also downed trees and other heavy debris. Often, they are attached to empty sections of pipe to enable engineers to push them under obstacles from a safe distance. When in place they are remotely detonated.

Basic = Basic Training (the first generalized military training received by all recruits)

Beehive Round = Artillery round that spreads flechettes (nails with fins).

Blivet = Any container designed to hold liquid; usually large bladders of hard black rubber or smaller and softer clear rubber bladders. Most often used to transport water, but occasionally fuel.

C = C-Rations, a small box of rations in cans.

CA = Combat Assault; transport by air, usually by helicopter, into, out of, or over hostile territory.

Chi-Com = Sometimes also 'Chicom'; anything produced by Communist China, such as weapons, tools and foodstuffs.

Chinook = CH47 heavy-lift helicopter, called Shithooks by the grunts. These iconic two overhead rotor helicopters could carry up to 55 fully equipped combat troops or a little over 20,000 pounds of cargo. (See also Shithook.)

Chunker = M79 grenade launcher; a hand-carried, breech-loading, single-shot weapon firing 40mm grenades; one to each infantry squad. It fired 40mm grenades a good distance and was excellent for close combat in dense and steep terrain because rounds were designed not to explode within twenty-five feet of the end of the barrel making it safer to use than hand-thrown grenades. Some other divisions called it by different names, like "Thumper."

CIB = Combat Infantryman Badge; long rectangular badge with silver musket over an infantry blue background, encircled by a silver wreath, awarded only to infantrymen assigned to an infantry unit during times when the unit was engaged in active ground combat, who have actively engaged the enemy in ground combat.

Civvies = Civilian clothes.

Cobra = Bell AH-1G Huey Cobra attack helicopter; slim, tandem-seated chopper used for attacking ground targets, in support of ground combat operations, and to protect slicks engaged in troop and equipment transport and in medevacs; employed machineguns and/or miniguns, 40mm grenade launchers, and 70mm rockets.

Concertina Wire = A variety of barbed wire that has sharp blades instead of points. It comes in rolls that can be pulled open to form long open coils. These coils are then staked in place in rings around the defended perimeters of firebases and other large defended areas. Getting through them greatly slows an attacking enemy.

Conex = Corrugated steel boxes, roughly eight-by-eight-by-twenty feet in size; originally designed as containers for export, hence the name; used for hauling equipment and supplies, for storage, and as secure buildings for offices and equipment.

Cover and Cover Man = The second position from the front in a moving formation. The Cover Man has the job of eyeballing areas higher and wider than those focused upon by the Point Man, and provides cover for the Point Man. He also keeps an accurate pace count and assures that the unit moves along predesignated azimuths throughout each day. Works in cooperation with the Point Man to assure that the location of the unit in relation to its starting point is known at all times.

CQ = Charge of Quarters, the NCO tasked with performing the routine duties of a commanding officer during the absence of both the CO and his Executive Officer, normally on weekends and at night.

DEROS = Date Estimated Return from Overseas (end date of tours in Vietnam).

Detcord = Hollow flexible plastic tubing filled with an explosive called pentrite that explodes along its length at 6,400 meters per second. If a line of detcord were stretched between San Diego and Boston, the far end would explode less than eleven seconds after the near end was lit. In practical effect, the lengths normally used explode simultaneously, along with any larger explosive charges connected along the line.

Deuce-and-a-half = M35 2½-ton cargo truck, six-wheel-drive, cargo and troop transport truck. This was the basic truck used by the U.S. Army from World War II to the 1980s. Variants were produced from 1944 to 1999. It could carry up to 5,000 pounds of cargo or twenty-four troops.

Dog Robbing = In the military, dog robbing is an honorable avocation involving cleverly acquiring whatever is needed to achieve a goal, complete a task or satisfy a superior, that is not available through normal, officially authorized means. Stealth, scrounging and foraging abilities are required and the only unwritten rule is that it can put no one at serious risk of harm. An extensive and clandestine form of "Field Expedient."

DX = Direct Exchange; term applied to anything and anyone needing to be replaced due to wear or other unsuitability.

Entrenching Tool = The name goes back to the trench warfare of World War I. The M1951 folding shovel with pick was carried by all grunts in an M1956 Carrier (canvas sheath) and used to dig guard holes, chop roots, and level ground.

Field Expedient = Any ingenious fix for problems/situations accomplished without the usual equipment or means; clever solutions often made in the field to meet necessities.

Fifth of the Seventh or 5/7 = This was the battalion Charlie Company was in. It was a battalion within the 2nd Brigade of the 1st Cavalry Division (Air Mobile). The 5/7 signifies the 5th Battalion, 7th Regiment. By the time of the Vietnam War, regiments no longer existed as organizational units in the U.S. Army; they were used only as historical identifiers of the units from which current units were descended. Hence, it was known to all that the 5/7 and all other cavalry battalions with a 7 regimental identifier had their roots in the Seventh Cavalry Regiment of frontier fame or infamy.

Firebase = A forward base where artillery was positioned to provide offensive fire and defensive cover fire for infantry units operating roughly within a twenty-mile radius. Also known as Fire Support Base or FSB.

Flechette = Nail-like projectiles with fins; ballistic when fired in Beehive rounds by artillery, recoilless rifles or shotguns; a similar kinetic weapon could be dropped from aircraft in a Lazy Dog bomb.

FNG = Fucking New Guy; term applied to inexperienced men assigned to existing combat units.

Fougasse = Mixture of gasoline and powdered laundry detergent stirred into a napalm-like gel. Fifty-five-gallon oil drums filled with this were placed in the wire surrounding firebases and other permanent and semi-permanent U.S. bases. The closed ends of the barrels were partly dug into the ground to point the open ends outward and slightly upward. The explosive mixture could be set off electrically from perimeter bunkers projecting swaths of long-lasting flame.

Fourragère = Braided cord worn over the right shoulder of dress uniform jackets, pronounced foor-a-zhair. Robin's egg blue signifies infantry. Also called the Infantry Blue Cord. Infantry is the only branch in the U.S. Army always authorized to wear its fourragère with dress uniforms.

Frag = A fragmentation hand grenade. Carrying them in the field was voluntary and only a few grunts chose to do so. The secondary meaning is the killing of someone with a hand grenade, including the murder of unpopular officers and NCOs by their own men, which was an exceedingly rare event.

Free Fire Zone = Area considered so dangerous that U.S. troops were authorized to shoot first and perform conventional reconnaissance later, known as recon by fire.

Freedom Bird = Commercial flights that took service people from Vietnam home to the United States at the end of their tours of duty.

FSB = Fire Support Base or simply firebase. A forward base where artillery was positioned to provide offensive fire and defensive cover fire for infantry units operating roughly within a twenty-mile radius.

Gook = In the Vietnam War this was a generic term used by American service people to describe Vietnamese people. It may have been considered a racial slur by the Vietnamese, but to Americans it depended on who was being discussed, and on intonation and context. It was very negative and synonymous with "enemy" when applied to the VC or NVA, innocuous when used to describe ordinary Vietnamese, and negative again when applied to lowlifes, criminals or cheats. Most of us referred to local populations other than the Vietnamese as whatever they were: Montagnard, Cambodian, Laotian, etc.

Grunt = Most common term for an infantryman, Army and Marine; descriptive of the lot of the infantry soldier, it may have begun as a derogatory term, but rapidly became a term of respect and esteem, especially among grunts themselves.

Guidon = Small, swallow-tailed flags atop hand-carried wooden staffs displaying unit designations, pronounced guide-on. Both the flag and the person carrying it were called the guidon.

HHC = Headquarters & Headquarters Company, a unit's command and administrative group.

Hooch = Any structure (especially those used for sleeping) built either crudely or as a field expedient, or out of native materials. This includes the sleeping shelters built by grunts every night in NDPs using ponchos, mosquito nets, and ropes. It did not generally apply to sandbagged bunkers, masonry or frame structures, or tents.

KC = Kit Carson Scout, native Vietnamese scouts who patrolled with U.S. infantry units providing valuable insights and scouting reports in areas where they had personal knowledge.

KIA = Killed in Action.

LBJ = Long Binh Jail, where U.S. troops were incarcerated for serious infractions.

Lifer = A person who was career military.

Loach = Hughes & later Bell OH-6 Light Observation Helicopter (LOH). A single-engine helicopter that could seat a pilot and one other person. It was versatile and used to great effect, but was lightly armed and vulnerable to enemy fire; about 60% were destroyed in Vietnam.

LRRP = Pronounced 'lurp,' it is an acronym for Long Range Reconnaissance Patrol, also the name for freeze dried meals used in the field. Each infantry battalion had one recon company, Echo Company, tasked with these reconnaissance patrols. Such patrols varied in size from squads to the full company and in time and distance depending on the needs of the moment; they often penetrated well beyond the reach of our artillery.

LT = Pronounced 'El-Tee.' Generic term for lieutenants (both 1st and 2nd).

LZ = Landing Zone; any area where helicopters could land and take off; most often used to describe small areas in the boonies cleared of vegetation by grunts for use by helicopters.

MACV = Military Assistance Command Vietnam, Joint-service command under Department of Defense.

Medevac = Contraction of Medical Evacuation; also the extraction, usually by helicopter, of wounded or ill personnel from the field to the rear where they could receive medical treatment.

MIA = Missing in Action.

Minigun = M134 rotating-six-barrel, electric operated machine gun; firing up to 6,000 rounds per minute of the same .30 caliber ammo used by the M60 machine gun. Since electricity is required to fire it, it was employed on helicopters and other aircraft.

MP = Military Police.

MOS = Military Occupational Specialty; jobs in the military, each of which has a unique alphanumeric designation.

MPC = Military Payment Certificate, paper money solely for use in war zones.

NCO = Non-Commissioned Officer, sergeants and corporals.

NDP = Night Defensive Position, temporary defensive area usually of the smallest practical size for the force involved and in a circular shape surrounded by guard holes and mines. Used to create a secure area where infantry units spent single nights while maneuvering in the field.

Number One = English phrase commonly used by Vietnamese people to mean the best, very good, good, or just okay.

Number Ten = English phrase commonly used by Vietnamese people to mean the worst, very bad, bad, or not okay.

Nước Mắm = Pronounced by GI's as 'nook mom' or 'nook bomb.' Traditional Vietnamese fish sauce made from fermented dried fish and salt.

NVA = North Vietnamese Army.

OD = Olive Drab, dark olive-green color used by the Army for nearly everything.

OJT = On the Job Training.

P38 = A folding can opener about the size of a pull tab on a soda can operated with a thumb and forefinger.

Perimeter = The outer edge of a defended area, often circular. For an NDP it was where guard holes were placed. For firebases and other more permanent locations, it was defined by berms made of compacted earth, sandbags or a combination of both, with fixed bunkers dug into them. For both NDPs and more permanent bases, the area just outside the perimeter was laced with mines, the larger bases also had flares and other types of defensive items as well as coils of concertina wire. In all cases, guard positions had interlacing fields of fire.

Piss Tube = Empty Artillery round cases; open-ended four-to-six-inch diameter plastic tubes, stuck into the inside lower slopes of earthen berms surrounding firebases. They were planted at least two feet deep at about a 60-degree angle. You urinated in the top and it gradually soaked into the ground at the bottom.

Point and Point Man = The farthest forward tip of a military formation as it moves. The Point Man is the first man in a moving formation during combat operations, with the job of locating danger points and locations of the enemy before the main unit reaches them; also keeps an accurate pace count and assures that the unit moves along predesignated azimuths throughout each day. Works in cooperation with the cover man to assure that the location of the unit in relation to its starting point is known at all times.

Police = Aside from its usual meaning, 'police' is a term used in the military for clean-ups, usually of a minor nature, such as the morning police calls to pick up cigarette butts and bits of trash and debris on bases.

PRC25 = The "Prick Twenty-five" was the field radio used by the infantry. A very robust piece of equipment, but one that could deplete its batteries within a few hours if used constantly. With its battery, it weighed almost twenty-four pounds and when its long antenna was used it had the same effective range as the artillery, 18 miles.

PSP = Perforated Steel Plank, interlocking panels of varying lengths and widths used to construct air strips, bunkers and other structures; a variation that was not perforated was used for roof construction and other purposes.

QRF = Quick Reaction Force; force held in reserve to respond quickly to wherever needed.

Recon by Fire = Reconnaissance by firing weapons into suspicious areas before entering them; used only in designated free fire zones.

REMF = Rear Echelon Mother Fucker, U.S. military personnel in Vietnam who were not and had never been in combat.

Re-Up = Re-enlistment in the military.

Rifle Company = Each infantry battalion had four rifle companies, Alpha, Bravo, Charlie, and Delta and one reconnaissance company (Echo). Each "straight leg" infantry company had three straight leg platoons and one mortar platoon. Rifle companies normally operated within the reach of artillery located on firebases (a distance of eighteen miles in flat terrain), but occasionally ventured beyond partly because the mortar platoon could provide substantial support on its own.

Rome Plow = Huge, sharp-bladed dozers that cut down and broke-up trees and vegetation, ripped the ground, and then roughly smoothed areas to create fields of fire along roads and around bases.

RPG = Rocket Propelled Grenade. A shoulder-fired weapon used by the NVA and VC mostly against armored vehicles. The warhead has a shaped charge that uses kinetic energy to penetrate armor before exploding. It was very effective against the types of armor used by the United States and its allies during the Vietnam War.

R&R = Rest and Recuperation; week-long leave granted by the military during Vietnam tours.

RSL = Returned Servicemen's League. An Australian veteran's organization similar to the VFW (Veterans of Foreign Wars) in the United States. The RSL Club in Sydney was the author's favorite watering hole when on R&R.

S-1, S-2, S-3, S-4, S-5, S-6, S-7, S-8, S-9 = In the U.S. Army, S-1=Personnel, S-2=Intelligence & Security, S-3= Operations & Training, S-4=Supply, S-5=Plans (not in all units), S-6=Communications & IT Support, S-7=Information Operations (not in all units), S-8=Finance & Contracts, S-9=Civil Affairs (not in all units).

Saddle Up = A term held over from horse cavalry days meaning, "Get your gear and weapons ready and prepare to move out."

Section 8 = Military discharge for being mentally unfit for service; this designation ceased to exist at some point after the Vietnam War.

Shake 'n Bake = Term used for graduates of NCO School at Fort Benning, Georgia, between 1967 and 1972; "Instant NCO" was another.

Shithook = CH47 Chinook heavy-lift helicopter. These familiar two overhead rotor helicopters could carry up to 55 fully equipped combat troops or a little over 20,000 pounds of cargo. (See also Chinook.)

Slick = Bell UH-1H "Iroquois" Huey helicopter, the iconic air workhorse of the Vietnam War; it was designed to carry two pilots a door gunner or two, and seven troops, but, in a pinch, more could be crammed onboard. It was used for troop, equipment, and water transport, medevacs and sometimes in support of ground troops.

SOP = Standard Operating Procedure.

STRAC = Originally an acronym for a former Army command from the 1950s, the Strategic Army Corps. Its colloquial meaning applies to any military unit or person perceived to be "Skilled, Tough, Ready, Around the Clock," in short, a very squared away unit or soldier.

TDY = Temporary Duty. Assigned duties to a unit or place other than the unit or location of a soldier's permanent assignment.

The Gun = The M60, 7.62mm, .30 caliber machine gun. Each infantry squad had one. The gun team (a gunner and assistant gunner) carried the gun, an extra barrel and tripod and approximately 1,000 rounds of ammo. Every infantryman in the field carried 200 rounds of M60 ammo in linked loops crossed over his chest and back that could be quickly tossed to the gun team in combat.

The World = For U.S. service people in Vietnam this was a synonym for the United States.

Three-two beer = Beer with an alcohol content of 3.2% or less. Many states had laws regulating consumption of three-two beer differently from stronger beer, often allowing people between 18 and 21 to purchase and consume three-two but not stronger beer.

USARV = U.S. Army Vietnam.

VC = Viet Cong; guerrilla fighters indigenous to South Vietnam.

Ville = Any small settlement or town in SE Asia.

WIA = Wounded in Action.

Willie Pete = White Phosphorus. Used in M34 hand grenades and other weapons, it burns at 5,000 degrees Fahrenheit for sixty seconds. It was almost never issued to ground troops because its blast radius of thirty-four meters (112 feet) was greater than the thirty-meter (98 feet) average distance a man could throw it. However, it was issued atop Nui Ba Ra because the steepness of the terrain allowed it to be thrown safely downslope from the perimeter.

Wire or The Wire = Generic term used to describe the areas just outside the berms surrounding firebases and other large defended areas. The name derives from the presence of concertina wire in these stretches, which are also laced with mines, flares and fougasse.

Appendix 2 – NCO School Statistics (1967-1972)

Used with permission from the N.C.O.C. Locator web site at https://www.ncoclocator.org/index.htm.
Modified by author to include WIA estimate based upon ratio of WIA to KIA for all casualties during the same period.

Graduates	=	26,078
Killed in Action	=	1,100
Wounded in Action (est)	=	3,556
(Total casualties of ca. 18%)		
Congressional Medal of Honor Recipients	=	4

Appendix 3 – Men Killed in 5/7 Bn 4/1970-1/1971

Men in the author's battalion, the 5/7, 1st Cavalry Division (Air Mobile), killed in Vietnam and Cambodia April 1970-January 1971. Used with permission from the 1st Cavalry Division Association. Derived from the 1st Cavalry Division Book of Honor located on the 1st Cavalry Division Association web site at https://1cda.org/history/book-of-honor/vietnam-war-book-of-honor/#1495552700152-25d3b8ff-d607.

A Co, 5th/7th – 11 KIAs (6 in Cambodia)

HALL CHESTER GENE SGT	1970-05-09
COX LEWIS EARL CPL	1970-05-19
RIGNEY LARRY JAMES PFC	1970-05-19
FORD JACKIE LEWIS CPL	1970-05-20
HAZARD JAMES JOSEPH CPL	1970-05-20
HELD KEITH ARTHUR CPL	1970-06-01
THOMPSON DOUGLAS SGT	1970-08-14
HAMILTON MARCUS JAMES SP4	1970-08-27
CRAIG JAMES LARRY SGT	1971-01-07
FISH GORDON ALIDEAN PFC	1971-01-07
PRICE CHARLES MITCHELL SSG	1971-01-07

B Co, 5th/7th – 9 KIAs (6 in Cambodia)

SCHULZ RONALD DOUGLAS SP4	1970-04-14
MULLINEAUX BARRY THOMAS CPT	1970-05-12
WAINWRIGHT MICHAEL ALBERT SGT	1970-05-17
COONS ROBERT WAYNE SGT	1970-05-19
KEFFALOS CHRIS ALBERT SGT	1970-05-21
SANCHEZ JOSEPH SEBASTIAN SFC	1970-06-06
BURNS DARRELL EDWARD SGT	1970-06-23
BURGESS JOHN HARLIE JR CPL	1970-08-04
SENGSTOCK GARY DAVID SSG	1970-08-08

C Co, 5th/7th – 6 KIAs (4 in Cambodia)

BELON MARC BRADLEY CPL	1970-05-14
KETHE HENRY JAMES SGT	1970-05-17
MANIERE MICHAEL JOHN SSG	1970-05-20
BERNING ROBERT RAYMOND CPL	1970-05-28
MC LEAN WILLIAM EDWARD PFC	1970-12-24
HARRIS TERRENCE L SSG	1970-12-24

D Co, 5th/7th – 10 KIAs (4 in Cambodia)

BOBANICH JOSEPH A JR SGT	1970-04-19
HOWELL WILLIAM ERAY SGT	1970-05-07
LUNDY GERALD VERNON SGT	1970-05-07
NEELEY MARVIN EUGENE CPL	1970-06-07
MC KENNA KENNETH R JR PFC	1970-06-11
BELARSKI RONALD DALE SGT	1970-08-25
DICKSON RONALD GEORGE PFC	1970-08-25
HEARSCH JOHN PATRICK JR CPL	1970-08-25
WHITE MICHAEL EUGENE PFC	1970-08-25
BELTRAN ROBERT JOSEPH CPL	1970-10-12

E Co, 5th/7th – 0 KIAs

HHC 5th/7th – 0 KIAs

36 Total KIAs (20 in Cambodia), including 1 Officer (Captain) and 27 NCOs (17 Sergeants, and 10 Corporals)

Appendix 4 – U.S. Casualties 4/1970-1/1971

US Casualties April 1970 through January 1971[1]

Month	APR '70	MAY '70	JUN '70	JUL '70	AUG '70	SEP '70	OCT '70	NOV '70	DEC '70	JAN '71	TOTALS
Killed	661	920	547	503	448	365	325	300	298	243	4610[2]
Wounded	3832	4291	2972	2685	2505	822	1130	946	1044	972	21199

[1] Data derived from "Casualty Statistics on Southeast Asia, by Month" Source: Comptroller, U.S. Secretary of Defense, posted by The American War Library at http://www.americanwarlibrary.com/vietnam/vwc24.htm.

[2] 1427 deaths or 31% are classified as Non-Combat. I am not comfortable categorizing these deaths separately from the 3183 or 69% that were directly caused by Combat.

Appendix 5 – Place Names

Bien Hoa = Pronounced bin-wah. The large U.S. base northeast of Saigon where the HQ of the 1st Cavalry Division (Air Mobile) was located.

Long Binh = The large U.S. base northeast of Saigon where MACV, the overall Headquarters for U.S. and Allied Forces in Vietnam, was located.

Mondolkiri = Province in Cambodia where Charlie Company operated during the Cambodian Incursion.

Nui Ba Den = Black Virgin Mountain. A Lone mountain (monadnock) near Tay Ninh, Vietnam, rising ca. 3,000' above the jungle floor.

Nui Ba Ra = White Virgin Mountain. A Lone mountain (monadnock) near the village of Song Be, Vietnam, rising ca. 2,000' above the jungle floor.

Phuoc Long = Province in Vietnam where Charlie Company operated after the Cambodian Incursion, though some patrols may also have extended into neighboring Quang Duc Province as well.

Prek Kampong Spean = Navigable river forming part of the boundary between Cambodia and South Vietnam to the west-northwest of Tay Ninh. In Vietnam, the river is called the Sông Vàm Cỏ Đông. It flows into the South China Sea directly south of Ho Chi Minh City (formerly Saigon).

Song Be = Song Be (pronounced song-bay) was a small village on the northeast outskirts of Phuoc Binh (pronounced fook-bin) where FSB Buttons was located. It was situated just west of Nui Ba Ra and south of the Song Be River. This had already been the forward headquarters of the 2nd Brigade, 1st

Cavalry Division (Airmobile), but also became the forward HQ for the 5th Battalion, 7th Regiment of that brigade during and after the Cambodian Incursion. Grunts usually referred to it as Song Be rather than Buttons.

The Song Be is an important river that has now been dammed in several places creating large reservoirs that generate significant electricity. It flows from northeast of Nui Ba Ra and Song Be/FSB Buttons westerly and then to the south, eventually joining the Song Dang Nai to pass through Saigon and on to the South China Sea.

Song Dak Huyt = The Song Dak Huyt (pronounced "soong doc wheat") is a meandering river that begins at an elevation of 3,000 feet in the highlands of western Vietnam, flows west and then southwest where it forms part of the boundary between Cambodia and Vietnam, then more southerly back into Vietnam, eventually flowing into the Song Be River fifteen miles northwest and downstream of Nui Ba Ra and Song Be/FSB Buttons.

Tay Ninh = Capital of Tay Ninh Province located about 55 miles northwest of Saigon. The forward headquarters of the 5th Battalion, 7th Regiment, 2nd Brigade, 1st Cavalry Division (Airmobile) before the Cambodian Incursion. The firebase there was officially named FSB Garry Owen, but grunts always just called it Tay Ninh.

Tay Ninh Province = Province in Vietnam where Charlie Company operated before the Cambodian Incursion.

Map – Areas of Operation and Other Signif
5/7 Bn, 1st Cavalry

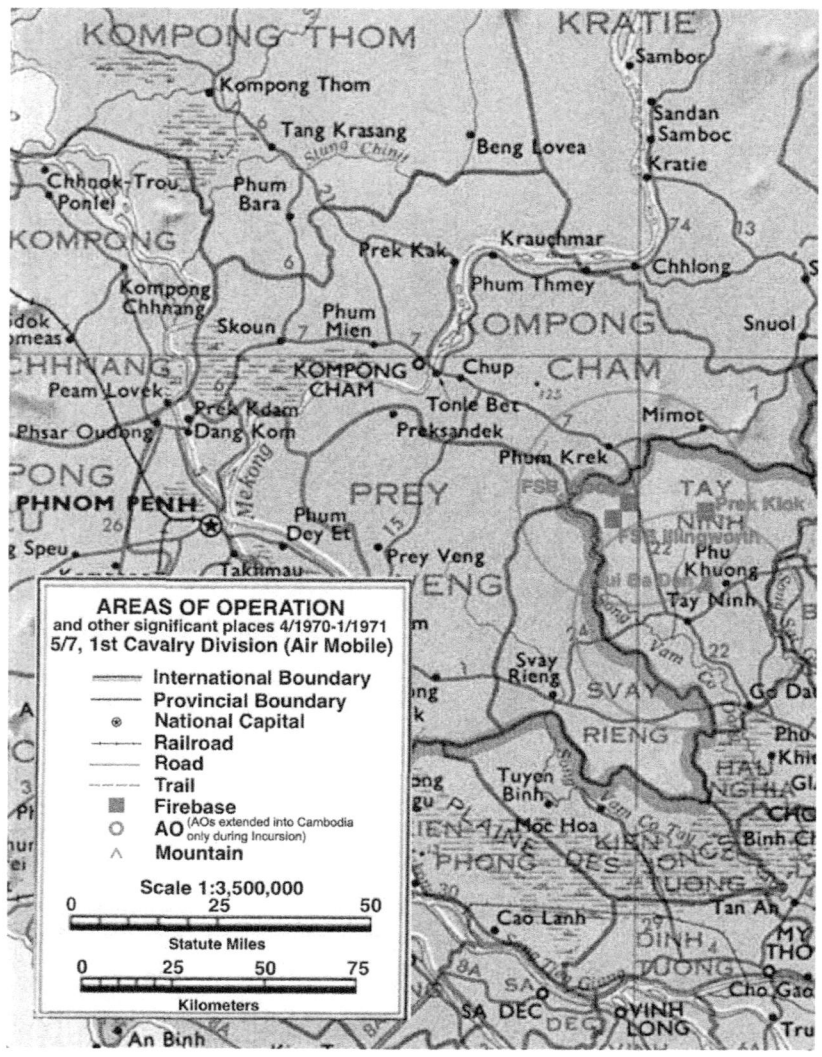

icant Places April 1970 through January 1971
Division (Air Mobile)

About the Author

Jamie Thompson was raised in the Chicago suburbs, graduating from Barrington High School in 1962. After attending college off and on at the University of Arizona in Tucson, Morningside College in Sioux City, Iowa, and Northwestern University in Evanston, Illinois, he was drafted into the U.S. Army in April 1969. In  December of that year he graduated from Infantry Operations and Intelligence NCO School at Fort Benning, Georgia, and arrived in Vietnam in April 1970, as a newly minted sergeant E-5. In his first month in-country, he became the straight-leg infantry squad leader of 1st Squad, 1st Platoon, Charlie Company, 5th of the 7th, 1st Cavalry Division (Air Mobile), serving in that capacity until he was wounded in Cambodia during the Incursion two months later.

 Following a three-month recuperation, he rejoined his squad in the boonies. When he was in the field, except during his first few weeks, he walked point whenever his squad had the duty. Upon discharge in 1971, he was awarded the Combat Infantryman Badge, Bronze Star, Purple Heart, Air Medal, and other ribbons and medals from both the U.S. and South Vietnamese governments.

After his military service, while attending college intermittently, he worked in the Tucson area, perhaps most memorably as a bartender and night manager for Gentle Ben's, a popular college bar/restaurant then and now. After this he worked in the printing business near Chicago and in Tucson for several years, where he met Nancy Wolff whom he married in 1979. In the early 1980s, Jamie worked as a department manager for a Kmart store in Tucson, until moving to Rapid City, South Dakota, in 1984. In the Black Hills he worked for the U.S. Forest Service where among other things he wrote environmental assessments for timber sales, then as a civilian federal purchasing agent for the South Dakota National Guard, and finally for the Forest Service again where he wrote numerous documents and administered permits relating to mining, recreation and other land uses. In 1997 he resigned from the Forest Service to attend the University of South Dakota School of Law, graduating with a J.D. degree in 2000 and passing the bar the same year. Jamie chose not to practice law, but maintains his membership in the bar. Also in 2000, he accepted a position with the U.S. Bureau of Land Management in Nevada as a Writer-Editor/Public Affairs Officer and later NEPA Planner, during which time he wrote most and edited all of the environmental assessment and management plan for the Black Rock Desert High Rock Canyon-Emigrant Trails National Conservation Area; in 2004 this plan won the BLM Director's "Four C's Award" and the "Federal Plan of the Year Award" from The American Planning Association. He retired in 2007 and now lives in the Reno area near his daughter and her family. In 2015, after a twelve-year battle, his wife Nancy died of breast cancer.

Between 1967 and 1986 he had seven freelance articles published in Chicago suburban newspapers, VFW Magazine and the Chicago Tribune. In 2000, he published an article on mining law in the Great Plains Natural Resources Journal, a law review of the USD School of Law. In 2019 he published *Point: Wilderness War in Vietnam and Cambodia – A Memoir* describing his military service from draft notice to discharge, but focusing on the daily existence, as he experienced it in 1970-71, of young American infantrymen in the field during the Vietnam War. Supported by other military branches and elements, grunts as they were called (and as they proudly referred to themselves) bore the brunt of the actual fighting on the ground. But the experience was more than combat; it was a daily struggle with the jungle wilderness, its terrain, its weather, its vegetation, and its warm and cold-blooded critters. He hopes *Point* adds to the factual record of that extraordinary time, and helps to assure that the truth of it is not lost to future generations.

* * *

If you enjoyed *Point*, please consider posting a review at
https://www.amazon.com/dp/b07y5q4jjs

Printed in Great Britain
by Amazon